Occupied Hearts II

Japan as the Occupier
&
The Occupied

**Based on True Stories
By**

Alice Parker

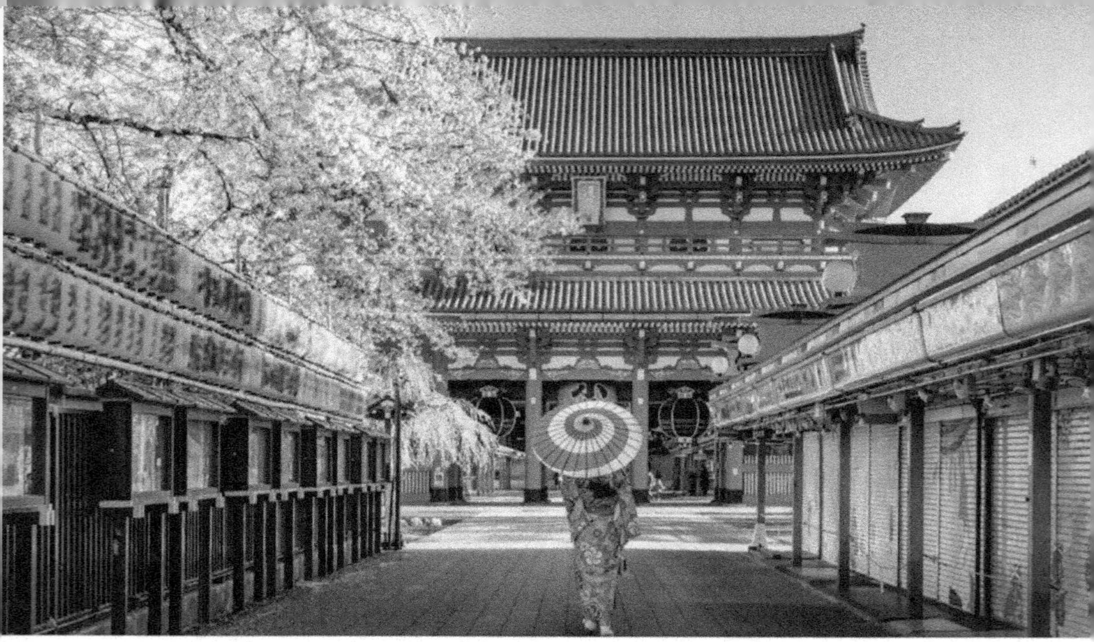

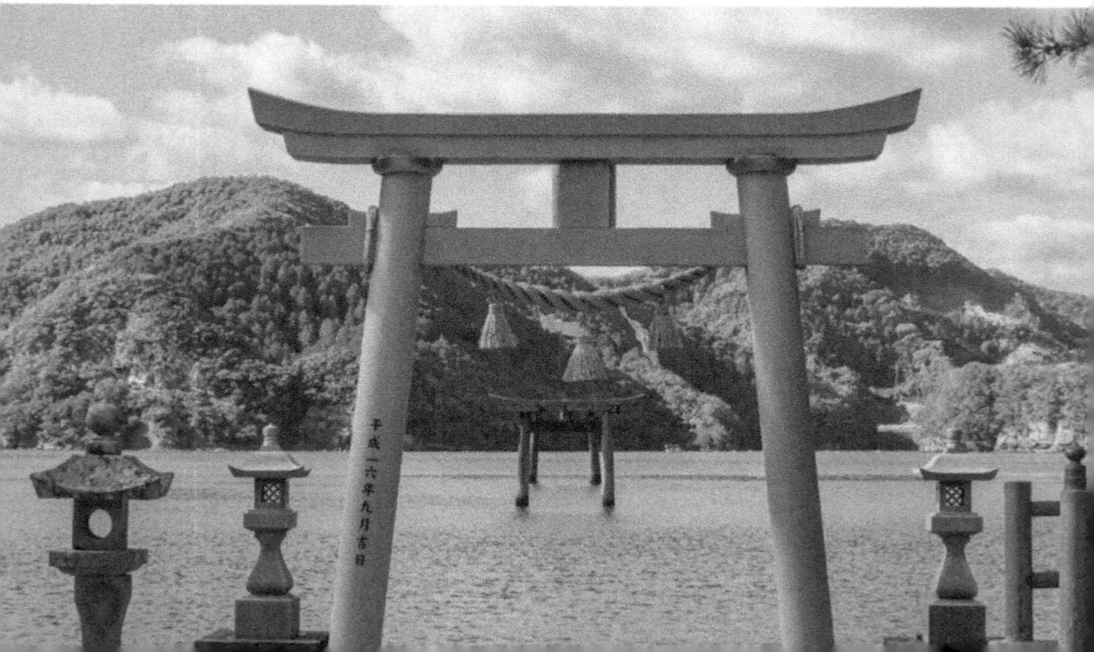
平成一六年九月吉日

EXPLORA BOOKS
700 – 838 West Hastings St. Vancouver, BC V6C 0A6
www.explorabooks.com
Phone: (604) 330 6795

ISBN: 978-1-998394-19-7

Table of Contents

Part 1: Japan as the Occupiers

"He never talked about the past four years; there might not have been any war at all, or it may have been on another planet and no stake of his risked on it, no flesh or blood of his suffered by it. There is a natural period during which bitter, though un-maimed defeat might have exhausted itself to something like peace, like quiet in the raging and incredulous recounting which enables man to bear with the living of that feather's balance between victory and disaster, which makes that defeat unbearable to live with the death of hope and love, the death of pride and principle."

William Faulkner
Absalom, Absalom!

Introduction

The history and personal stories you are about to read are true and factual - names have been changed or dropped for requested privacy, though recordings made. Some sections of the historical material are taken directly from period books, authoritative on the specific topic, with only deletion of non- essential information, which would be of no interest today. I have likewise added or condensed other details, simply to give more continuity and flow to the story. Since this was not written as a historical document, per se, these sections are not footnoted, so as not to distract the reader. Full credit and references are given at the back of the book. An extensive bibliography is also listed, along with a suggested, though dated reading list. The first use of a Japanese word will be *italicized* with a definition, or brief explanation following. A full list of the Japanese words and historic terms is also referenced at the back of this book.

No specific military texts were used, as these stories are of a personal-citizen nature, taken from individual experiences. I have no intention of rewriting history, but much of what was written about this period of time, did not relate to those people who actually survived it. The information I have used is from people who were there, and still I cross-checked my sources for as much accuracy as possible. If your experiences were similar to mine, growing up in American public schools, very little was ever mentioned or taught about this prior time of our participation in someone else's history. Yet, there is no way the total story can be told, because millions of lives were quite affected/effected, and they each had their own personal significance.

The definition of 'Occupiers,' which I used, includes the invading military - Japan, who had taken control of the foreign country. It also refers to the 'colony' of settlers who followed, either voluntarily for the financial opportunity, or were instructed to go by the government, to live in the conquered-foreign country. My definition of 'Occupied,' is the citizen-population in their own land, whose possessions and control was taken-over by the conquering-military government - Japan or the United States.

The last two Parts of this book has to do with the experiences of growing up as a *gaijin* - foreigner, in Japan. It covers from the end of the Allied Occupation, 1952 until after 1991, or the "Bubble Burst" of Japan's economy. It involves the younger and older generations of bilingual/bicultural living in Japan. Hopefully, it will give some insight into the difficulties of their daily life and culture adjustment. As well, removing some mystery of the Far East-Orient, and replacing it with some acceptance and understanding.

In some ways, it's not so different from others coming to the United States, or Western Europe following World War

II. There are advantages and disadvantages, of not growing up in one's own native country. We never miss what we've never had, yet we always miss what we *think* we could have had. Those lost experiences, whatever they might have been, can never be recovered; but some people learn to make the best of what they did have. All we ever really know is what we have personally experienced. Life is a journey, as they say, and the roads we choose to travel are not only ours alone, but unique to us, no matter how many other people we may passed along the way.

Prologue

To clarify, why I am sharing these stories I've recorded and written. I lived in Japan as a Corporate Trainer for seven years, exploring it and its culture extensively. Honestly, I loved the people, but despised the government, as well its atavistic-culture which controlled them so stridently. I became fascinated by the American Occupation of Japan, as very little was ever written about it from the people/personal side. As I began researching and sharing what I learned with other gaijin, especially those who had been in Japan for a much longer time, they referred me to others they knew for their stories.

I'd also become close friends to several of the missionary children, who had grown up in Japan. Surface friendships were a common-malady among the English teachers, as so many were quite transient. Yet some, when probed opened up with a wealth of information they considered general knowledge. It however, mesmerized me, who had traveled and felt I knew so much about many places. But, from my own homeland history, and its Occupation of my current home, Nagoya, I knew so very little.

With my first trip to Nagoya castle, supposedly rebuilt because of a bombing-error - mistaking it for the Prefectural Building - while not quite Disney's fairy-castle, it was fascinating to me. Adding to it, all of the sidewalks lined with blossoming, cherry trees, the national emblem of beauty and cultural. A few weeks later, I spent time in the Nagoya City Museum. And, while sometimes chuckling at their Jap-lish translations, also taken aback a bit, at their misinformation regarding some war history, I *was* knowledgeable about.

I knew I needed to do more real research, and decided from the pivotal moment, I had to put into writing, in some justifiable form, these fascinating narratives. My pandora's box began to explode with such emotional tales, I was not really prepared to hear. There was this driving need, in most of the Japanese I interviewed, for the world to know what harrowing experiences, their lives had been almost randomly- tossed into. Their involvement, in conjunction with the enigmatic Occupation itself, made it even more challenging and compelling to chronicle. Fitting it into my busy, work schedule, research for me became a new driven-passion, as it produced so many amazing stories.

I did not expect this all to be so shocking and heart-felt, but how not, when a devastating war was involved. Three wars, actually, as the Korean War was a major player, and then surprisingly, so was the Vietnam war. I felt honored at some of the very-special individuals who shared their lives with me. It touched and changed my life so profoundly, like nothing else ever had. After seven years, Japan truly never bored me, and though as I said a love/despised relationship, it became the most compelling relationship in my life. All of these stories were recorded and transcribed by me. I still have the tapes. Those which had to be done in Japanese, my good friend and translator Kazuyo Mizutani, helped me with them, usually joining me and the individual in shedding tears. She became as enthralled as I did, as she'd never known any of this history either. They were willing to tell me, a gaijin, under anonymity, what they never could have told another Japanese, because the taboo of talking about a lost-war.

Chapter 1: Background History & Korea Mentor & Scapegoat

"Our Imperial Ancestors have founded Our Empire on a basis broad and everlasting and have deeply and firmly implanted virtue; … should emergency arise, offer yourselves courageously to the State; and thus guard and maintain the prosperity of our Imperial Throne coeval with heaven and earth. The Way here set forth is indeed the teaching bequeathed by Our Imperial Ancestors, to be observed alike by Their Descendants and the subjects, infallible for all ages and true in all places …"

Emperor Meiji - in the 23rd year of Meiji (1890)

Perhaps it would be easier to understand the Japanese with some background of their indoctrinated belief on being descended from the Sun Goddess Amarterasu. They thus believed they were a special, unique race whose destiny was to *guide, or bring* other peoples under their perfect realm. Every Emperor, from the first, Jimmu in 660 BC, to Hirohito, who renounced his deity-ship in 1945, were considered gods and omniscient in all thoughts/deeds. The Shinto religion perpetuated these teachings, and also the law; so one's power supported the other.

Shintoism centered on the worship of gods (8 million) from nature, and were considered mythological ancestors, with the line between man and nature obscure or indistinctive. So, not unusual for men, who had accomplished something exceptional, to be made into deities. The leaders were both high priests and temporal rulers - in fact the same words were used for 'religious worship' and 'government' as for 'shrine' or 'palace.'

There were no *exact* ethical concerns associated with these religious ideas, except for the required sense of awe and reverence before nature and the Emperor. The concept of ritual purity was believed to have contributed to the Japanese insistence on cleanliness and one of bathing, to the point of literally boiling out any internal or external impurities.

The name for themselves at this time was Yamato, taken from the area of their concentrated strength of wealth and military power, in the Nara Plain. They ruled western Japan with a tightly-restricted caste system inherited through kinship, and controlled by intermarriage. Following their adapted version of the Chinese concept of monarchy, the sacred Emperor never was involved in battles, or originated from a military background, for he was above all of it, being a god. They may fight in his name, and he would be the puppet-leader of whomever was the winner, to maintain the symbol of State and unity of the people.

The Japanese islands' isolation permitted them to hold onto the transfer of actual power, at court, without a change in the Imperial line. Since they were relatively free from outside pressures, they could hold onto this outmoded institution, even when reality passed them by. They regarded change, especially from an outside force, as disruptive to the perfect order of things. A cultural conservation was created with exact rules - regulations for every aspect of life.

Until the sixth century, there had been large influxes into Japan by people from Korea. They, even more so than China, were the basic contributors to the building and development of Japan - its dynasty/ bureaucratic system, language, Buddhism/Confucian, culture and most customs. In fact, one of the few, truly unique Japanese rites was the 'soaking-hot bath.' For the next thousand years, their geographical isolation, and their personal choice to keep it so, helped create in the Japanese a defiant-pride to the point of arrogant-superiority, and even resentment towards their former contributors.

Korean knowledge flourished for more than two millenniums *before* the Japanese learned to read and write, as they *scorned* intellectual pursuits. The man of learning was discounted, while the soldier ranked first. Even after the importation of the art of writing from Korea, it was *unmanly* for the samurai to be caught with a writing brush in his hand. While in Korea, war was considered an *evil,* which interfered with the true purpose of man, the advancement of civilization. Whereas in Korea, learning, far from being scorned, was a badge of honor, for to win a government post, it was necessary to pass a literary examination.

Korea learned writing from China, but only a scholar had the time to master the involved Chinese ideographs - kanji. Yet, the common Korean people *wanted to* read and write. The Korean King heard their appeals and commanded his scholars to devise a simple alphabet. The scholars showed a creative ability amounting to genius, when they invented an alphabet so simple, any Korean of average ability could read almost any book, within a few weeks. Reading became so widespread, when the American missionaries arrived, they saw at once the value of the easy alphabet and used it for imprinting their Bible.

~ ~ ~ ~ ~ ~ ~ ~ ~

Hideyoshi, one of the great generals of the 16th century, helped to centralize Japan's feudalism, and build the military into professional samurai. He then embarked on the conquest of Korea in 1592. He figured it would be a stepping-stone to conquering the world, which to him meant China. They were stopped by the Korean and Chinese armies in northern Korea, and though Hideyoshi continued to throw wave after wave of men and ships - 500,000 over six years of battles, the campaign stalemated. Finally, he ordered a withdrawal from his death-bed in 1598. The troops brought with them the ears of forty thousand of their victims. These were placed in a mound near the statue of Buddha at Kyoto. The 'Ear Mound' stood for years, and teachers would bring their children to it, so they would have clear evidence, Japan was *really victorious* over Korea. Definitely, a loss the Japanese never wanted to admit, as failure was unacceptable.

Still, the invasion began the downfall of Korea, a successful civilization since the seventh century. Cities had been ruined, monasteries burned, libraries destroyed, many scholars put to death - a bitter struggle for existence consumed every moment. Thus, no longer time for the arts and refinements of life. Though they had repelled the Japanese, it weakened the Korean dynasty, with its highly evolved culture and military. The Manchu/Chinese moved in, and turned Korea into a vassal-state of China, cut-off from the rest of the world for the next several hundred years.

The bitter feelings have never ended between the Japanese and the Koreans, with their roots in this failed attempt. Possibly, the only bounty Japan received was from Hideyoshi's war efforts, was his appreciation of the Korean ceramics. He had the most famous Korean pottery-clan absconded, and installed them in Fukuoka, on Kyushu island. Even today, they are considered *traditional Japanese potters,* though their roots and technique came from Korea.

By 1635, Japan lay dormant and almost hermetically-sealed, except for little more than the port of Nagasaki. Ieyasu Tokugawa, Hideyoshi's chosen successor, put the final, iron-clad touches on the political reunification of Japan. In order to stabilize the regime from outside influence and retain total loyalty, all Christians were eliminated. Sometimes, the missionaries and their followers had the opportunity and choice of leaving on their own, but usually just tortured or slaughtered. In order not to be tainted by foreign ideas, most of the strictly-supervised trade was performed by a controlled group of Chinese merchants, through a small Dutch trading post, or with Koreans via Okinawa. News and knowledge of the outside world continued to trickle into Japan, via the same grapevine, in an attempt by Japanese scholars to study European advances. Even limited information of a place called 'Amerika' was known by some. Eventually, they opened three more ports covering the various islands - Kobe for central, Yokohama for northern and Sapporo for Hokkaido.

~~~~~~~~~

Into this cloaked state of affairs, the determined Commodore Matthew C. Perry, came sailing in to pry it all open in 1853, with the help of about a quarter of the United States Navy. With his cannons directed at Edo, (Tokyo), he waited out the Japanese, until they finally sent out an envoy, who agreed to receive President Fillmore's request for a diplomatic and trade treaty. Rather than chance having their city destroyed, or their essential food supplies blockaded, the Japanese eventually relinquished, for even then they could drag-out trade agreements. Little did Commodore Perry know, for the rest of Asia and most of the Pacific region, it truly was the opening of Pandora's

Box, and would take almost a century to contain it once again.

Since most of Asia, including China, had already been carved up by the European Colonial powers, had not the Americans arrived, it is likely other, less friendly powers would have gobbled Japan up entirely. Or, they may have doled out pieces to various interested countries, particularly, Russia, Portugal and Spain. Not that the United States stayed innocent of the same, for the Philippines fell under its rule, at the end of the Spanish-American War in 1898.

But, Japan retained its basic sovereignty, while shoguns - the military warlords, went the way of history, though not bloodless, or willingly. The Imperial Emperor system was reinstated, with a somewhat-Democratic political ruling by 1868. Thus, began Japan's leapfrogging into the modern industrial world, doing and gathering everything *Western* from Europe and the United States. In their haste and addiction, it became a mix-mash of something from each country - the Navy from England, the Army from Germany, the courts and legal system based on France, a myriad of medical, technical and communications from the U.S. Almost no Western country was ignored, as Japan rushed to learn, *imitate or copy* everyone. Creating their own ideas was not a basic idea, as individual creativity had always been so frowned upon. The tried and true was better.

Likewise, they wanted to flex their economic and military strength by going to war to capture more land, as the Europeans and American had done. Hence, they returned to the scene of their last embarrassment, to make up with great fervor their loses, and prove their true superiority, they believed they had. In 1894-95, they clashed with China over the control of Korea, and to everyone's surprise, they won. As long as they were in the area, and on a victorious course, they also took over the Chinese island of Taiwan. But, when they grabbed the southern tip of Manchuria, Russia, covetous of this strategic piece of terrain, persuaded Germany and France to join it, enforcing Japan to withdraw. A loss of face was once again made indelible upon them, and filed away in their vindictive-memory.

Japan then studied the secretive and tedious path of negotiated- pacts, and by 1902 had lined up Great Britain and other rivals of Russia, to not interfere in their future. So, back to the drawing board, and round two with the 'Great Bear.' This time when Japan became victorious in the 1904-05 Russo-Japanese War, every country took note. They assumed the spoils had been worth waiting for - the previous southern tip of Manchuria and the southern half of the Russian railways there in Manchuria, the southern-half of the island of Sakhalin in the north, and *unquestioned* control of Korea. Japan had won the race and now *the only Asian colonial power*. In less than fifty-years, it was moving among the 'big boys,' and it liked the feeling.

The impact of their success had some resounding reactions, as it bounced around the world to different populations. Never before had an Asian nation defeated an European 'white' country. The victory gave a stimulus to the national movements of other countries under European control saying, "They are not invincible … we can win; we don't need to feel we are inferior." Surprisingly, for many lower-level Russian peasants, it created feelings of excitement and almost gratitude, because it signaled the possible end of the *Tsarist-colossus* which had kept them all so trampled down.

Japan now made it clear, it didn't want any Western power meddling in its 'foreign affairs,' as it was the paramount-power in the Far East. When it quietly annexed

Korea in 1910, Western powers simply acquiesced, as if it was no great loss, or matter to them. To some extent, Japan was getting even for the unequal trade treaties it had been forced to sign with the U.S. and other European countries upon its opening. In reality, Japan was financially and materially near exhaustion from the fiscal and people cost of the wars. Korea provided it with the needed space to expand and to grow crops, for its burgeoning population. Most importantly, raw materials were accessible, with *almost free* labor for its expanding industrial base.

"Social Darwinism," - only the 'strong nations should survive - used so freely by the European and U.S. powers to justify their colonial acquisitions, was stretched even farther by Japan. It proceeded to politically-repress and economically-manipulate the Koreans under its power. Japan used the same racial-hierarchies and superiority-claims, they had heard from the Western Caucasians, as if it was their responsibility to *civilize and transform* the decaying Korean peninsula. Their 'double talk' had an additional denigration, in they were also giving their distant - meaning low - Korean 'brothers' *protection* from the Western powers.

Japan, finally master of the long-coveted peninsula, began to work miracles. Roads and railroads were built, mines dug, new land put under cultivation and natural resources of all kinds, unknown in Japan, developed. Barren hills were reforested, harbors were deepened, fisheries and whaling operation were financed, and plumbing made cities *livable,* for the incoming Japanese colonists. It looked like a new and better day for Korea, - but not for the Koreans.

Trade grew by leaps and bounds, but it was trade by Japanese, with Japanese, for Japanese. The Koreans had no part in it, except as a serf. The Japanese of Korea, numbering less than a million, used the twenty-three million Koreans as their *tools* in the exploitation of the rich land. The transformation began with Japanese settlers being sent to Korea to train them in their successful way of doing everything - farming, retailing, education and manufacturing. It was common for many of these settlers to be the second or third sons of a family, because they knew they would not inherit their father's property, and had to make their own fortunes.

A Japanese could order any Korean to work for him, and punish him if he didn't comply. Japanese foremen, without vestige of government authority, compelled villagers, at the point of a revolver, to work on the railroads at one-third the standard wage. Any effort of small store-keepers to compete on their own, without a Japanese partner was quickly checked. The Korean standard of living was reduced by at least half during the Japanese regime, and all of their basic rights to their ancient culture destroyed, along with their books and lives.

It did not take long for the subsistence-farmers, who barely eked-out a living under the Chinese, to become tenant farmers to the Japanese. Eighty-five percent of the people depended upon farming for their living, and their farms were systematically taken away from them, on one pretext or another, until eighty percent of the farmers became tenants of Japanese landlords. Many of those Koreans, collaborated with the latter for their own survival. They were heavily taxed for their 'training,' and poverty fell hand in hand with near starvation, as up to forty percent of the annual rice production was sent to Japan. Formerly, the rice yield in Korea was so bountiful, frequently older rice had to be thrown out of the storehouses, to make room for the new crop. Now, those who stayed, were soon subsisting on tree bark, roots and meal made from nuts. Hundreds of thousands of Korean peasants, with the blessings of the Japanese government, fled to work in Japan's flourishing, industrial economy until just after World War I.

By this time, Japan had again expanded its landholdings, by forcing concessions from China with its 'Twenty-One Demands.' It seized Germany's holdings in the Shantung Province in China, and acquired control over the German islands of the North Pacific, in the form of mandated territory. At the Versailles Peace Conference, Japan sat down as one of the five major victors - the first non-Western nation to have made it into *the club* of the great Western powers.

Though the Koreans had been forced to learn Japanese, as it was the only language taught in the schools, the racial prejudice again them in Japan was formidable from the beginning. Physically, one could only detect minor-differences between them and the Japanese. The Koreans did tend to be stockier, and their faces a bit more square, but it was their personalities which usually gave them away. They were more outspoken and jovial, than the stoic Japanese. Not only did the conquerors treat them as temporary-workers in Japan, they were paid far less than Japanese for similar work, and were housed in appalling conditions. This kept them in the continuous cycle of increasing and inescapable poverty, from which they had little recourse. Whenever they changed jobs, in search of better wages, or working and living conditions, the Japanese stereotyped-conception of the Koreans as 'delinquent, untrustworthy and lacking in loyalty' was confirmed. Thus, even poorer treatment was then justified for them.

A small resistance movement was eventually born, through the support of the socialist students, but there was little they could do to help the penniless, factory workers suffering under the police-backed management. Propagandists, who saw it as an opportunity to take advantage of both the situation and the prejudice, magnified any slight misdemeanor into claims the Koreans were all hooligans, irresponsible and even revolutionaries. This came to a culmination during the aftermath of the Great Kanto Earthquake of 1923. The police and local Tokyo militia rounded-up and slaughtered several thousand Koreans, blaming them for the resulting fires and destruction.

With the onset of the Depression, immigration policies were temporarily restricted. Then, by the late 1930s and early 1940s, several million Koreans were being forcibly-recruited into war-related industries in the dockyards, mining, construction and clothing manufacturers. If they had thought their factory bosses had been hard, they were nothing compared to the military ones.

By Mid-1937, Japan began full-scale aggression in China, and the eventual deployment of millions of Japanese military troops in almost every corner of Asia. Into this foray were brought the *ian-fu* - the 'comfort women.' To those military men, commanded to set-up the supply of sexual, female companions for the troops, any question of morals was not felt. Basically, the Japanese felt sex was a *bodily- function*, not really connected to feelings or emotions per se. They also believed they were actually doing a community service, in preventing indiscriminate acts of rape. Previously, there had been numerous anti-Japanese riots, as a result of the particular practice. Although, prostitution was legal at the time under Japanese laws, it was easier to use the Korean, Taiwanese or Chinese women, who were already there, and basically *available* for the 'procuring.' About eighty percent of the women used were from Korea, and recruited out of school, under various guises by their Japanese teachers.

In their typical, systematic way, the Japanese set-up, and even built hundreds of brothels all across East Asia, following the flow of troops from the late 1930s into China. The facilities were owned by civilians, but managed and regulated by the local occupation forces. A payment scale with detailed records, was organized for both the officers and regular troops, as sometimes the women also were separated into a hierarchy. In this way, when the men stayed in one area a long time, they would get attached to one woman, and bring her little gifts, or send out letters for her to her family. Most of the troops had no idea, the women, some as young as fourteen, more often sixteen, had been forced or coerced into their position. Others developed a sense of solidarity with the women, for they were mere, foot-soldiers - front-line cannon-fodder themselves, peasants fresh off the farm, escaping from their own poverty and starvation. The reality was, the soldiers only pastime was to go out on off-duty days to eat, drink and 'use' the comfort women.

This cruel treatment of many of the 200,000 women, often included them being raped repeatedly, beaten and suffering from sex, twenty to sixty times a day. They were like human toilets, as some soldiers used to queue, with their flies-unbuttoned for their few minutes of sex. Untold numbers of the women died either from mistreatment, venereal disease, or quite commonly suicide and insanity. Sometimes the colonized-women, who had been working in factories, were put into prostitution, if they had tried to escape, or angered their bosses in some way. To some women it made little difference, as they felt they would probably die of starvation and overwork on the twelve-hour, seven-day a week shifts, on machinery both dangerous and heavy to use.

As the Allieds were advancing, many of the women were machine-gunned, and others just left locked in their rooms with no food or water. With insult following injury, after the war they were left desolate, without money and rejected by most of those around them, no matter what country they may have ended up in. There was no way they could go home to shame their families, and they truly had no chance for a future of a normal life, with a husband and children. The few, whose time as comfort women was shorter, often kept their secret and married, yet they lived in fear of exposure. When they were found out, the conservative Koreans also turned their backs on wives and mothers. Only in their twilight years, with nothing to lose any more, would they break their silence and come forward to demand retribution. Their meager support came only from religious groups, as many of the prominent, Korean politicians were also collaborators or senior officers, in the Japanese Occupation forces. When a similar case was brought up by a group of Dutch women in Indonesia, the War Crimes Tribunal imprisoned or executed ten officers, but when the the victims were Asian women, they were generally ignored.

Organized prostitution in Japan was historically a war measure. The swashbuckling, General Hideyoshi, who as mentioned, began Japan's career of aggression in the sixteenth century by invading Korea, sought a way to keep his soldiers happy, while away from their wives. Thus, began the first 'comfort women,' who were then both Korean and Japanese. Since it proved a source of great satisfaction to all concerned, except perhaps the slave-women, the following Shogun Ieyasu Tokugawa, established the first *Yoshiwara* - a government run house of prostitution - on the outskirts of Tokyo. The buildings were erected and surrounded by a canal - the area had previously been a swamp - and a high wall with gates, guarded night and day, so none of the women-inmates might escape. (American Civil War General Hooker, is said to have 'encouraged' women to follow his troops giving 'comfort,' and said to be where the term 'hooker' came from.)

Repeatedly, the original Yoshiwara was destroyed by fire, with thousands of trapped women perishing in the flames, and every time it was rebuilt, on a still greater scale of magnificence. By the 1990s, the inmates were displayed in show-windows behind bars, as the prospective client strolled down the street, studying the comparative charms of the posing beauties, until he had made his choice. According to the official Japan Year Book, by the 1930s Japan had over 225,000 licensed prostitutes, and the great majority of them were owned by the four, great family-monopolies - Mitsui, Mitsubishi, Sumitomo, and Yasuda, or their group name - the *Zaibatsu.*

Each year in Tokyo alone, five million patrons spent twenty million yen in these licensed quarters, so the sale and rental of women contributed handsomely to Japan's war budget. The municipal governments were still involved in keeping the records, as a policeman with a book shared the lobby with a ticket seller. The applicant made his selection from a picture on the wall, chose a desired time, and was submitted to an inquisition by the policeman, as to his name, age, parentage and residence, to be entered in the book. Since accepted as a common practice, there was, of course, no loss of face for any man - single or married - participating in using these women. In this way, even the usual Japanese wife's second-class rating was higher than how these women were treated.

Personal Story 1: Japanese male, lived in Occupied Korea with his parents.

I was born in 1930, you know just one year after the Great Depression. At that time, my grandfather ran a clothes shop in Mie Prefecture, Kuwana, near Nagoya, and when I was born they were quite rich. But with the economic crisis (Great Depression), the shop went bankrupt, so then we couldn't live in Kuwana, because my grandfather got a stroke and couldn't move. So, my father who had worked for the shop, of course, lost his job and he went to Tokyo to find work. Then, when he went to Tokyo, I was in the first grade and we lived there for three years. Then, when I was a third-grader I went to Korea, because my relatives of my mother's side ran a big department store, which had its headquarters in Tsu, Mie, Japan. They ran that department store in Seoul, so our whole family moved to Seoul in 1939.

My father worked for that department store, and my mother for a while ran a dormitory for the workers of that store. After that, the store opened a small shop, and then my mother ran that shop. In Seoul there were three department stores, two were run by the Japanese and one was run by the Koreans. Though I don't know who the customers were at the stores - Koreans and Japanese or just Japanese, but at that time the richest people were Japanese. Of course, some were Koreans, but most Koreans were very poor. The employees of the Japanese department stores were both Koreans and Japanese, with the chief positions being Japanese. My father was chief of the restaurant department, until the end of war.

I studied three more years at elementary school which was Japanese only, of course, and then in 1942, went on to five years at middle school, what is not called junior high and high school, in our residential area. There were only a few very, rich Korean students who went to our school. They were the exception because, I don't know, special relationships or something with the Japanese. The teachers were also Japanese, and all the studies were in Japanese, so it was just like in Japan.

Most of our neighbors were Japanese and the area, I guess you could say was the 'uptown,' I guess affluent, especially in comparison to 'downtown' where most of the Koreans lived. At that time, they were very poor so they lived together, very closely. Ours was a nice place, almost no differences between what my grandfather had back before he lost it all, and other wealthy people in Japan. In the wintertime, it was very cold and the heating was different because the Korean houses had floor heating - the smoke from the kitchen fire goes under the floor which is made off stone. A very unique system, because the stone keeps warm almost all night, which is better than a Japanese house that doesn't have any heating after you go to bed.

Of course, Seoul is the capital and a very big city like Nagoya, so almost no difference in city life. Since that was the age of Japanese territories, everything goes by Japanese way and system. If you take a train or buses or even go to doctors, everyone speaks Japanese. Sometimes there would be a combination of kanji, the Chinese characters like in Japan, and katakana or kanji and some Korean language, especially in areas that had mostly Koreans. So we could read the newspapers and everything. But almost never, I would say, would you see just Korean language, because before Japan they were controlled by China, and I don't think they had a real clear (written) language of their own. They knew the kanji from before, but Japan did make them speak only Japanese, at least in public and their schools.

Some Japanese schools were in mixed residential areas, so those schools had more Koreans. But where it was just Koreans, they had their own schools, yet they still were forced to speak Japanese. They would even have to '*Japan-ize*' their names, for more acceptance, like today in Japan. If they learned any Korean, it had to be at home.

There were few incidences with the Koreans, and since I was just a little kid and kids like to play with other kids and sometimes those other kids were a Korean, but my mother said don't play with the Korean boy. So sometimes, I heard things that my mother said, but since the neighborhood was almost all Japanese, I had almost no opportunity to play with them anyway. At that time, the Koreans were very poor and once when I ice skated in a near pond, a group of older Koreans boys came and attacked me because they wanted to steal my shoes. Sometimes they say there was a conflict, I saw them, but I was not ever involved with it. I saw many older kids fighting with each others, because Koreans were always discriminated against at that time. I think the main cause of the fights was because of money. In the Korean school, I didn't see it, but I heard that the teachers were very strict, more strict than ours, so the teachers would hit them.

After the war, the situation completely changed with our surrender, and then the soldiers put down their weapons and they had to return to Japan. Everything then became Korean, was in Korean, so I tried to ride on the trains and the conductor was Korean, and the announcement, everything was in Korean, and of course, I didn't understand. I felt that it was now dangerous for me. The Korean people had quickly organized themselves and armed themselves with the Japanese weapons and put stickers on things and wouldn't let the Japanese use them. The Japanese were bad and had treated them very bad, so they wanted us to go back, to walk to Pusan, a very long distance, and go back to Japan. Many times I was afraid if I was identified as a Japanese, I felt I would be killed.

After American Occupation forces landed, and the Koreans self-organized army searched every house looking for weapons. My elder sister worked for the information center at the military base and she had a friend, and he was in the military police. One day he came to our house and he told us that he killed two Koreans with his pistol. Then he told me that he felt he was in danger, so he left his sword and the pistol in our house and he left. So they started searching in our area, and I was alone in the house and I was so afraid that I would be killed if they found that weapon. Then fortunately, my neighbor who worked for the post office, and he spoke a little English, so when the American military came to his house without taking off their shoes, he yells "Take off your shoes!" in English, and then they stopped searching. So, I was lucky with that incident.

We were able to ride a train to Pusan, but we were not in the section for humans, but the section for animals, goose, etc. It was a covered one. Sometimes, I saw the drivers of the trains, Koreans, stop the trains, and they made the Japanese pay them again and then we moved again. We, of course, lost everything and our only belongings were what we could carry on our backs. The money systems were changed, and though we had some money saved, it was gone or we had to leave it. It was a very difficult time.

My father was forced to stay, be an advisor or something about the department store because he was chief of the restaurant section, so he had to teach the Koreans everything to take over the store. Other top staff had to stay also, but I never asked my father what all happened, as that was not for me to know. So, my mother and two sisters had to go back without him, and we thought that we would never see him again, but he stayed around two years and finally found us in Japan.

We had heard in Korea, during the war, that there had been a lot of bombardments in Japan, but in Korea the American airplane came, but no bombs. We saw airplanes fighting in the air, but I saw no bombs. There was almost no damage in Seoul, except to the Japanese airfields. Most of the food was rationed, so it was very short. Fortunately, my mother ran the shop that is a ration shop, so we sold the rice and sugar to the residential people. We are not hungry. I really didn't have any hard times during the war. My father was safe working in the department store and mother too, my younger sister and I went to school and my older sister worked safe, too.

When I was a second grade in middle school, we had to stop studying and work in some factories. The Japanese and Koreans had to do this, I heard that some of the schools in the countryside didn't, they studied, but most of the schools in the city had to go out and work. I had applied for the military school for the navy airplane pilots school, but my eyes were too weak and color-blind, so I failed. But I think I have to fight, so I worked in the military airfields. When the American air raid sirens came, not too often though, we pushed Japanese airplanes out to hide in the caves. I didn't really feel so much danger at that time, but if the war continued I might not have been so lucky. So, sometimes we made area shelters and the senior high school students worked in the factories. On August 15th, the day that the war was over, my teacher said to me that today there would be no work because there would be an important announcement at noon, so then we heard the Emperor. Then I came back to my home and told my mother that the Japanese had surrendered and my mother was very, very angry and she said, "Japan never surrenders!" She believed this, and so did I believe this.

I saw the Koreans' resistance movement, and when the American planes came they would be wearing white clothes, and climbed on the top of a small hill to wave to the Americans. I never forgot that scene. I was told a lot of war stories at that time, so I have to fight the enemy and I felt I was a soldier, so I should not feel afraid of the danger. After the war, my militarism was gone, so I felt the danger was real and I was carrying with me all the time a knife and some poison. And, if some Koreans fight me, I will fight, and then take the poison at the end. I did this for myself, but nothing happened before we left.

It was a special ship that was taking us back to Japan, and we had to wait in Pusan just a short time, everything went kind of smooth for us to come back. The trip was very long, because we had to go a long way around the north, because there were still so many mines in the water. It was quite dangerous and some ships had been sunk. The ship was not very nice, and very crowded and cold, because it was November. We then returned to my mother's hometown area by train, which is now Suzuka, and I saw her parents, my grandparents. The trains were so packed with people that we couldn't even see out the windows.

Once I got to my grandparents house I went back to school, and this was the countryside and it feels very different. Also, now we are very poor, we have no house, as we have to live with my grandparents, and we have almost no money, but the other kids are from farmers and they have food, which makes them rich, and they have no damage from the bombardments. They are eating rice, but we are eating sweet potatoes only, so I hate to study with them, so I study at that school only one year, and then I went to school in Osaka. It was a radio operator's school, so I would like to work as a radio operator. It is a national school, so the school fees are free, nothing, and I get text books free and allowance, pocket money and food.

My mother had to move us to a very small house nearby after about four or five months, because my mother's elder brother came back from the war to join his wife and children, who had been living there with my grandparents. It wasn't so comfortable or a good feeling, so we moved out. I had my hard time after the war, as I was the only boy, I had to work and help support my mother, as well as go to school. Then the radio school was closed after one year because the American GHQ Occupation Forces, said that the radio operator sounded like a military kind of job. So I had to return to Suzuka and try again to find a school.

Fortunately, when I went to Nagoya to look for a school, I met a wonderful Catholic priest, he was from Boston, at Nanzan University (private Catholic school) and he helped me with a scholarship and even pocket money for me to go there. I never forgot that kindness even unto today, that is why my wife and I like to have home-stays to help foreigners when they come here, because it was a foreigner who helped me to get my education and speak English so well. So the times were not so difficult then, except for the commuting from Suzuka, as it was very far away from Nagoya and then I moved there, but it still was difficult to get to school. There was a streetcar then, so it took a lot of time between taking the trains and the streetcars, maybe two hours, oneway and, of course, they were very crowded.

Slowly, I could see how Nagoya was starting to be rebuilt, it had been quite destroyed by bombing (89%) and sometimes the houses didn't look so good, old wood or metals that they had probably found somewhere. Around Nagoya station, almost everything was gone, and it built back up selling vegetables, different kinds of food and drinks. That area was really dirty and black from all the burning with lots of left over stuff, because most of the buildings were gone. It looked very strange to me, and the smell stayed for a long time. But around Nanzan, it was not so destroyed and I felt more safe. After the war, most people were very eager to keep themselves, to live in the hardest sense, so we have no time to look around and 'admire' the scenery. We just worked for food, so I didn't look too much after I first saw it.

There were American military in the Nagoya area and Shirokawa Park was the American Village and the soldiers were stationed in that area. But not so many as compared with Tokyo or Kobe because they didn't use Nagoya Port as a Navy base. Some of the buildings, like Nagoya Hotel was used as the headquarters, were used by them. When I was a student, in daily life, we didn't see so many Americans, because they were mainly in that one area. But after I started working in the high school as an English teacher, I wanted to converse in English, so I would go over to the American Village. I had a friend there at that time, so I could meet many more Americans.

The American military CID (Civilian Intelligence Division), I think it was, came to Nanzan and told us that we should start a student body and then after we did, another CID came and said not to do that, so we had to stop. Sometimes I think maybe they weren't too organized. At Nanzan we had American teachers, and they were very friendly and nice, so I talked to the soldiers and they are also very friendly. My wife taught the abacus, so I taught some of the Americans the abacus, so we could talk in English. By this time though, it was only six or seven months and then they returned, some of them to North Carolina, but I forgot their names, I'm sorry. I think it was the 5th Army.

There was maybe one Korean student at Nanzan

when I was a student there, I couldn't be sure because many of them change their names to Japanese names (because of extreme prejudice). It seemed to me that he was Korean. Later I taught some Korean students (born in Japan) in my high school, and one of them told me after he graduated, that the Korean position in Japan is very complicated. Mostly they speak Japanese, and their ideas also gradually change like the Japanese people, but they are not Japanese, they are Koreans. But when he reads Korean, he is not Korean with the language or ideas, he is just like the Japanese. So he complained, that he was Korean, but not Korean. He runs a pachinko (pinball games) shop, so he make a lot of money, but his mind is very complicated. Most of the Korean residents think the same, I think. I know there is some discrimination, because they can't vote and they do pay taxes. My experience tells me that if they had lived a long time here, even if they had been treated bad, or they had been forced to come here, they had no relations in Korea, and after the war it was not so good for them to go back. Some Japanese still don't like them.

I came to Nagoya almost three years after the war, so by that time nothing was really happening with the Americans. Before that, I heard that there was a lot of war crimes by the soldiers, but that mostly soon after the war. There were almost no Americans in Suzuka right after the war, so I didn't see anything.

When I was first exposed to the Americans, my Japanese teacher during the war told me that they were demons because they ate people, and I thought they would eat me. I was very frightened, we were scared, and especially when we saw American soldiers in Seoul who were wearing some Japanese dress, a hat or carrying a kimono, or a Japanese sword, and they're walking around or riding in a jeep. We thought they had eaten people and would eat us. When I returned to Japan on board the ship, one or two Americans held my sister suddenly, jokingly, and laughing, but my sister, she was about eighteen at the time, she was so frightened, and we thought he was going to eat her. Now it's very funny, but at that time, that was what the people believed.

Once I was working in Nagoya and my family here started, I called my parents to come here to live, and my father started selling and delivering newspapers. Once he had gotten back from Korea, he had been selling coal, so not such a good job and their economic situation was not so good. They had been very rejected because they were very poor, because some Japanese people don't like poor people. (Culturally they believe you're being punished for ancestor misdeed, so you deserve it.) Things had not been good for them there. I know my mother was happier when we had more money in Korea because we were rich, but she was very close to her parents. I'm sure it was very complicated feelings between relations and money.

My uncle had come back from New Guinea, the jungle, which had very serious battles, and he had a nervous breakdown, and one year later he killed himself, … maybe he became crazy. I had an experience with my teacher when I was in Korea at the military school, he had returned from New Guinea and he was so strict with us. When I entered the staff room, I had to bow and say his name, and once I forgot and said the nickname we had for him. He hit and spanked me with a baseball bat, and I thought he would kill me. This was not just to me, but the other students too, sometimes. So, he was really crazy. I remembered that with my uncle and I thought that he must have been crazy too, because that battle was so bad, they killed each other so much, so close up. So, they are all very crazy. So, that was my worse experience of war, and I know war makes people crazy. During the Korean War our labor unions did some strange incidents, and killed some people, and a lot of it had to do with the communists. But personally I didn't think anything about the Korean War, because I didn't have any friends left in Korea, so I didn't feel anything particular. I think any war is bad. When I was a kid I wanted to be soldier, as I was taught that was my purpose to live, to fight the enemy, and I believed that, but after my experience during the war, I think that any war that kills humans is bad. Nowadays, the young people don't have any experience with war, and they just watch the war pictures, or the comic books about war. They don't know what it means, it's just on the screen or on the paper, there's no blood or suffering, just pictures. But reality, even in the victory side, … my teacher was not killed, he was safe, but his mind was crazy. That's the reality of war. So, now we have a peaceful constitution and when you have no weapons, then to keep peace, you talk.

SIDE-NOTE: The first gentleman remembers and added his father telling him after returning from Korea to study English, because the Americans would make everyone speak English, as the Japanese had made the Koreans speak Japanese. Also, Japan should always remember how much help they received from America, and that they did not treat the Japanese, as the Japanese had treated the Koreans, or others that they had 'annexed.'

Personal Story 2: Japanese male, lived in Korea with his parents as Colonists.

I'm now sixty-five years old and I was born in Korea, which was one of the colonies of Japan before the war. My grandfather and grandmother went over to Korea about seventy or eighty years ago in Meiji era. Their purpose was to make some fortune, they aimed at making money, about ten thousand yen, which about that time can be calculated at one-hundred million yen. My grandmother was a very skillful hairdresser and they went over to Korea, and several years later they built a very large house operating some kind of restaurant. What should I say, not a restaurant, but like the present cabaret or entertainment bar, but with a tatami mat room. There are many large rooms there, and many people entertained a drinking party, and seeing the geisha girls dancing. *Kiesan* - means Korean geisha girl. They operated it in Seoul, and lived in it until the end of World War II, for about sixty years.

I was born in 1928 and was brought up there for about nineteen years and came back to Japan in November, 1945, and entered college. I didn't have to go into the military because I was under the age, the fixed age to enter the army was just twenty. If the war was prolonged a little more, I should have entered the army. I went to a Japanese school with a few Koreans. The people who came to the club were just Japanese, half-business and half-military. My grandfather died before the war end and my father, my brother and I came back to Japan together, but my mother stayed there in Korea to look after her mother.

They handed over the house and business to some Koreans for nothing.

After the war, the Japanese army was disarmed, and it was expected that American forces, or Soviet forces would come to occupy Korea. We didn't know which country or army would come, so the situation for social order was very delicate and dangerous. We Japanese are very scared and hiding ourselves in our own houses. The Japanese army was disarmed, but still it existed in part of Seoul, and the Japanese bureaucratic governmental system and police system, where still existing, so Korean people couldn't make a riot so suddenly. The Japanese people, they were observing each other, but just the next day after the war ended, that is August 16th, the Korean people demonstrated and celebrated, and roared in multitude in the street. We Japanese were more and more scared. On that night, one leaflet was scattered near my house and we read it, "We tell you all Japanese, to go back to Japan by swimming, because we have no ship to lend for you."

I found a dead (Japanese) body lying in a dark alley. We were rather fortunate compared with a lot of Japanese living in North Korea and North China. For about a month Seoul was a vacuum city concerning any authority or controlling power, partly Japanese army still existed, but Korean government was not yet established. Unfortunately, the Korean statesmen were fighting inside of their party. I remember about one or one and half months later the American Army came to Seoul, and controlled them and the social order was restored. The American Forces and each soldier were friendly with us Japanese, so I didn't feel any uneasiness. I got friendly with some of the American soldiers and could talk with them.

We Japanese were arranged to go back to Japan by some repatriation plan. My family came to Pusan by train and to Japan by ship, but we could only take what we could carry. The train was arranged by groups and supported by the American Army, but it was not a normal train, it was one for cargo with no roof. We sat down sometimes and had to stand most of the time. In Pusan we had to sleep for two or three nights on that platform, and the ship was an old Japanese Navy ship. We all were on the outside deck, as the ship was very crowded, and it was very cold over night. But fortunately the ship was using steam, and it was comfortable for us.

We arrived north of Kyushu and there was no job or business for a very long time. We had no money and we had to rely on our relatives who were farmers in Mie Prefecture, near Osaka. I had been to Japan for sight-seeing when I was school boy with my mother. I was very astonished to see the sight of what had been Hiroshima. Just at the dawn, I watched the sight of Hiroshima from the box car. I could see nothing, and the whole land was filled with a reddish color. We couldn't see anything. But at that time most of the Japanese didn't know about the atomic power, the bomb. (The government never told the people what happened.)

My father had a small amount of saved money, so it helped our living to some degree, and when my mother returned, she went to work for daily wage in a nearby town in Mie. My mother was not so strong, but she could help only by laboring for a daily wage. Myself, I experienced many different kinds of part-time jobs, until I was able to enter college in Osaka. Everyday I went and returned between Osaka and Mie, it took about four and half hours one way. I got up three- thirty in the morning and hurried to the electric train station in Mie Prefecture, and four and a half hours on the train, I arrived at Osaka at about nine o'clock in the morning to go to college. At about three-thirty or four in the afternoon, I went back to Mie from

Osaka. Everyday I took about nine hours for travel. I was very young and energetic.

The part-time jobs in those days were very hard and laborious. Sometimes I was selling or vending small goods in the rural part. And sometimes I stayed in a fisherman's house and helped them labor early in the morning on the ship, and pull up the fish, and to boil the fish, and later dry them in the sun. Sometimes I engaged in physical labor in the construction site, very hard and very small wage. My father still had not been able to get a fixed job or business, but he finally established a small company dealing with agricultural products, and bringing them to Nagoya or Osaka and had a small income. It was an occasional job during the planting season.

After coming back to Japan, a building of my college was occupied by the American force in Osaka. My college building was very splendid and beautiful, but I couldn't use it, as it could only be used by the American Army. So, my college had to borrow this or that primary schoolhouse here or there, and our library was in that schoolhouse, and our lecture hall was in this schoolhouse. I didn't have any relations with the America Army, or any soldier after the war here. I saw many American soldiers in the street, but I never talked with them.

I was very young, and hadn't saw or studied about various things, as most Japanese were very somewhat friendly or naive, without no prejudice or hostility against Americans. Fortunately, I didn't have any bombing or propaganda experiences. During my college life, I studied economics and sociology, so I came to know a more accurate aspect of the U.S. Occupation policy and about the international situation. I came to criticize, more or less the right turn of the American policy. I thought, and was taught, that the American policy on first stage of the Occupation comparatively democratic, and it could promote the democratization of our country. But, I know that it was a period of, the existence of Far East Committee in Washington, and in 1947 or 1948, the American policy to Japan dramatically turned right (conservative).

Japan became a barrier to Communism, and a few years later the Korean War broke out and Japan became more and more a subordinate country to America, and America forced Japan to be this barrier against Communism. Most part of Japanese power were friendly with America, and they didn't like Russia (Soviet), more or less, so maybe they didn't feel such a strong contradiction about this. But on the other hand, a certain number of Japanese intellectual people were put under the influence of socialism. I was one of them, and saw they feel intimacy or approval of socialism and socialist countries. Many Japanese intelligent people were, in those days, under the influence of Marxism, so criticized Japan becoming this barber against Communism. In those days, labor unions and Japan's Socialist Party were all involved with Communism.

When I finished school, after six years of study. In the Japanese old educational system, university students need six years study - three years for preparatory courses and three years more for professional training, main courses. I didn't focus my study on a certain category or subject, but I studied as widely as possible, so I read as many books as I could - history, literature, English, economics, etc. Then I entered a trading company in Osaka, and that company went bankrupt, so I came back to Mie Prefecture and then found a job in Nagoya.

First I worked for an American movie company - RKO - Radio Pictures, the Nagoya branch. In the early days, there were many *Tarzans* and *Going My Way*, starring Bing Crosby and *It's a Wonderful Life*. We were only working for distributing of these movies. I was a booker, booking the movies, distributing the movies in different theaters in different towns. I didn't need to speak English there, only Japanese. RKO-Radio Pictures, also closed, and it was changed to Disney Pictures distributing company.

Just at the same time, I took the examination for teachers, and fortunately I succeeded in it and I became a teacher. At first, I worked for a night school, for five years and then I moved to day time school, and then for about thirty odd-years I was working for that school.

It's my great regret that I didn't learn to speak the Korean language. I cannot understand almost all of the words in Korean. To them, the Japanese language was the obligatory language. They can speak Japanese, but we Japanese cannot speak Korean, because we did not have to use it. I worked a while for a Japanese language school, and there were some Korean students who came to Japan to learn the Japanese language, and they were very hard working. We made friends with each other and they always said to me, "Please come with us to Korea! Do you know Korea? Korea is a very beautiful land and country, I want you to see Korea." They always said to me.

I had a delicate and complicated psychology, and I didn't dare to say that I was born and brought up in Korea, because I cannot speak Korean at all, while I was born and brought up there. If once they hear that their teacher was born and brought up in Korea, and couldn't speak any word of Korean, then they must have complicated feeling, because such a kind of person was product for colonization. But, my fellow teachers in younger generations said to me, 'You mustn't hesitate so much, because you, yourself didn't do any bad thing.' And adding, 'The time changed, you are old, out of date, or your sense of feeling is out of date.' But, I don't think so.

Koreans, their psychology is not so simple, still at

present. In my childhood, while I was living in Korea, to be sure my family, or most of (regular) Japanese did not do any bad things, directly. In my house, many Korean maids and workers were living and working for us, and we had a very friendly relation with them. But, especially in the rural district in Korea, many Japanese exercised violence, and did many bad things.

Economically, there were many changes during the Korean War. There was a lot more business for Japan, and the Japanese superficial, economic prosperity maybe originated from the Korean War. Before the Korean War, Japan was still very poor country, but during and after the war, Japan became gradually prosperous. I didn't always approve of the Security Treaty, I criticized the existence of many war, military bases chiefly in Japan, but comparatively, many Japanese are not so conscious of our social situation, or our social problems, so perhaps they don't feel so strong objection or criticism, I suppose. I was afraid that the U.S. might pull Japan into one of its wars. I can't accept of any establishment under the American hegemony. I think it's bad to be controlled, it's bad for the world to be controlled by some super-power, or all-mighty country, such as the U.S. or the former Soviet Russia.

Of course, I had some experience with the blackmarket. I feel now it was a symbol of war's destruction, and I remember only feeling miserable. First of all, the general economy in the country was destroyed. Common people were very hungry, and hovering or loitering in the blackmarket wishing to have some meal, any kind of meal they desperately needed. The blackmarket was controlled by some rich Chinese, Korean, Japanese and Yakuza (Mafia). Such kinds of people managed the blackmarket selling various foods at an extraordinary high price to common people. It was very miserable. I was only a student, but sometimes I brought a small amount of rice in my bag, and sold it to the merchants there for my school expenses. I bought some rice at a lower price and brought it there, and sold it at a little higher price. It was very occasional.

I have never been back to Korea and to be sure, Korea is my home land, and I want to see and meet some Korean friends, but I don't want to go there only sight-seeing tour. I want to see my old school house and my old dwelling, maybe it's disappeared, and my familiar road and street and alley, with my camera, but for that purpose the situation in Korea is not good. With my camera, though in the narrow street or alley, people may think that I was a former Japanese colonist, and there may be problems. I have had no contact with them (Korean friends), but our alumni association of my primary school and middle school in Korea are now in Tokyo and Osaka, planning the 50th Anniversary of the alumni association. It will be held in Seoul, so I'm going to join them, maybe in August or September next year. But it's still only a plan.

My childhood was surely an unforgettable memory, whether it was happy or not so, (compared to those who lived in Japan) I could not say so simply. It was not a bad experience, I don't think that I say that it was good experience, as I never have thought about it, as it just was my experience. During my college life, I was very moved to see the Occupation Forces promote the democratization of Japan, but the first occasion I was shocked to find that the Occupation Forces were not always that democratic a power. I don't remember exactly now, but we Japanese experienced the so-called Toho strike, and Toshiba strike and Yomiuri press strike. The laborers gathered together, picketed, and in a sense, occupied a factory in order to resist the nationalization of members, or the decreasing of the number of laborers. We students not only, but many intelligent people had some sympathy or support for those laborers. But on that occasion, the Occupied Forces dispatched the tanks and cannons, military guns to the factory, and forced them to stop. We are quite astonished, because we had been believing that the Occupation Forces were the symbol of democracy, but they didn't practice it. So, it was my first shock.

Another strong impression was that Tokyo International Military Court, the daily proceedings of the trials were broadcast on the radio every day. We listened to it, and finally the chief judge sentenced Tojo and other former generals saying, 'death by hanging.' At the time, I was for that trial, and war criminals such as Tojo and others should be punished by death, because of their crime, I thought so. But the voice of the chief judge of the court, was very impressive to me 'Death by hanging.' (He smiled with satisfaction, as he said these last words slowly in conclusion.)

SIDE-NOTE: Many Japanese lost their children when the Soviets came into North Korea. The parents either gave them away, or had to kill them for the protection and good of the group. Koreans in Japan during the Occupation made a moonshine called *Kasutori,* which had a strong after-affect. It had a terrible taste, but charmed the people who had little money to buy it. The fact that it could also be dangerous, even killing some, did not matter either. It gave a short respite from the pitiful life they had. Thieves and bank robbers were seen as almost Robin Hoods, since they usually stole from the wealthy or foreigners. Once a bank robber even persuaded eleven bank clerks to drink some 'medicine' which was poison, and he walked out with ten thousand yen. With the social chaos, which gave birth to many opportunists, and tremendous shifts in people's fortunes, it was still a society of polite impositions. This was the extent of impingement when brought about by one of higher status or power, even one who only implied as to having that status or power. Many Koreans were quick to take advantage of the reversal of their position.

Part 1 - Japan as the Occupiers
Chapter 2 - *Manchuria* - Millions Dead & Denied

"The newly founded Nationalist government of Chiang Kai-shek was attempting to gain back some control over Manchuria, which the Japanese by now had firmly in their economic grip. Rising Chinese nationalism made it clear that time was fast running out for any further cutting up of the Chinese melon. It was, in a sense, now or never."

Edwin O. Reischauer,
The Japanese Today

Manchuria was the plum of the Orient, as it was twice as large as Japan and Korea combined, and fabulously rich in minerals. Those minerals, totally lacking in Japan, abounded in Manchuria with the Fushun bed of bituminous coal, being the thickest in the world at 417 feet. Oil shales in use had a capacity of a million tons of fuel a year, as well as iron ore being plentiful. The soil of Manchuri a was the most fertile in all of China, due to the cover of grass, so its yield per person was the largest. Therefore, their living standards were higher, and their status more recognized. No other section of China had so many roads, or so many vehicles, and railways which spanned 6,600 miles, more than the rest of China together.

Having been in Manchuria since 1905, the relative independence of the Japanese armed forces made it possible for them to transform a sense of national crises into an actual change in foreign policy, and a shift in political structure. By 1928, certain elements of the Japanese army in Manchuria had engineered the assassination of the Chinese warlord of the area, and protected by the army as a whole, had escaped censure by the civil government. "Compared with the poverty-stricken conditions in Japan," wrote General Honjo, before the Japanese seized Manchuria in 1931, "these regions appear indeed to be the happy-land of Heaven. If they are brought under our administration, our Empire will in less than ten years acquire a wealth exceeding that of the United States of America."

Following these footsteps, in September 1931, a group of army officers in Manchuria, with the tacit-approval of their superiors there and in Tokyo, staged an incident on the railway near Mukden, the Manchurian capital. This then gave them an excuse for the Japanese army to overrun the whole of Manchuria during the next few months, and set up the puppet-state of *Manchukuo* the next February.

The civil government in Japan, unable to control the situation for fear of provoking an army coup d'etat, was *forced* to accept the abrupt return to empire-building, and thus attempted to justify it before the rest of the world. It also found itself swept along by a huge outpouring of popular patriotic-fervor. When the League of Nations condemned Japan's actions in Manchuria, the Japanese simply walked out, sealing the fate of the League.

National euphoria over the seizure of Manchuria, strengthened the hand of the military leaders immensely. Pressures by rightist- zealots, particularly among the younger officers, gave them arguments for *tilting national policies* in the directions these men advocated. The ultra-rightists tended to champion the impoverished peasants, who provided the bulk of the soldiers, and to exorcise the privileged classes of rich businessmen, and powerful politicians. They saw their own function to be the assassination of 'evil leaders' around the throne. This then cleared the way for a military seizure of power, and an undefined 'Showa-Restoration,' named of the year-period of the new Emperor, which had started in 1926.

Young army officers almost brought off the coup d'etat on February 26, 1936, when they killed a number of government leaders and seized part of downtown Tokyo. After indecision, the army and navel commands eventually suppressed the movement, and executed its officers. They hoped to put an end to the factionalism among those of their commands, which had become severe in recent years. The decline in the actual power of the Diet (Congress) continued, until in 1937, all party participation in the cabinet was eliminated under a new prime minister, who was an army general. In essence, Japan had become a Military-ruled nation.

In the same time frame, the army had been extending its control over parts of Inner Mongolia and North China. On the night of July 7, 1937, unplanned-fighting broke out between Japanese and Chinese forces near Peking. Chiang Kai-shek's government demanded an overall settlement of Japan's creeping aggression, while the Japanese military dug in its heels in response. In all effect, the Pacific front of World War II had started.

The puppet-Emperor Pu Yi, who had been deposed by the Chinese Nationalist during their revolution in 1911, was installed by the Japanese over Manchukuo in 1934. Even before either event, life had not been easy in Manchuria, for it had been tossed between China, Russia and Japan. One problem was the extensive class of clever, intelligent warrior-bandits. They could number into the thousands, and commonly took the law easily into their own hands under Japan's Occupation. Their destructive fires burned more hotly than ever, as each strike took on a patriotic color, for they were also fighting for freedom from the Japanese.

Here was an area of half-million square miles, to add to the quarter million of the Japanese Empire. Down the center of the country swept a flat plain, deplorable from a cynic standpoint, but providing rich, virgin soil to the Chinese peasants, who were willing to work it. Japan had pleaded she needed space for her crowded farmers, but when she got the space, her farmers refused to take advantage of it. They would rather be squeezed and pinched on one-acre farms in lovely Japan, than have any number of acres in a flat, dusty no-man's- land. In bleak Manchuria, a winter was forty degrees below zero, and then leaped abruptly without pausing for spring, into a blazing hot summer, and then back, with no autumn, into another freezing winter.

Japan organized a colonization program, offered free passage to Manchuria, free land, and government loans of from one thousand to five thousand yen - a considerable amount of money then - per family! Each village of colonists was guaranteed free schools, a physician, a veterinarian, hospitals and free seed. In spite of all this government-largesse, Japanese peasants preferred to stay home. They knew in Manchuria under Japanese rule, they would sooner or later be subject to the same exorbitant taxes they had suffered in Japan, and they would have to compete with native farmers whose standard of living was lower. The Chinese farmer could raise and sell more, because he was content to work harder than the Japanese, yet live on less. For these reasons, the Japanese colonization-policies largely failed. Only 750,000 Japanese civilians went to Manchuria, and 89% of them were government and business people, not farmers.

Most of the Japanese residents in Manchuria were there as overloads and exploiters. When they owned land, they employed Chinese to work it. The typical Japanese refused to emigrate unless they needed to badly enough. If their business had failed, or the family inheritance had gone to the first son, as was tradition, or perhaps if their wealthier wife's family was giving them a chance for their own success. Few went for the challenge, or the spirit of adventure, for it was not an ideal of the Japanese society or belief. One stayed close to home, property, and those who could help support them, if needed.

The Japanese did produce some scientific advancements with their endless hours of painstaking-experiments, as they adjusted and changed the soy bean, American apples, pears, and plums to grow well in the Manchurian climate. Knowing war would some day cut-off Japan's supply of American cotton, the laboratory adapted cotton to Manchuria, which was no small feat! Japan also prepared to grow her own wool on the backs of Mongolian sheep. They succeeded after numerous cross-breeding attempt, with French-merino wool to get the production needed, and the quality they desired. Unfortunately, once again these great achievements had little financial benefit for the Manchurians, as the advantages were reaped only by the Japanese.

There were other biological experiments not so agreeable, and definitely not beneficial to the Chinese. They - Chinese political prisoners, or simply peasants chosen at random - were usually the subject of such experiments in what was called Unit 731. Japan was not alone with its biological and chemical warfare laboratory, but it was more secretive. The detailed accounts of their killing-research would first be a blessing of freedom, then much later a haunting, death- quell of retribution.

In the cities, as well as on the farms, there was much physical evidence of 'progress,' while the emotional and physical condition of the people became worse. A visitor would be immediately impressed upon arriving at Dairen, Manchuria's most southern port, for from ship to shore there was a pier much larger, longer and finer than any which fringed Manhattan Island. Following were broad streets lined with new, handsome stone buildings, built to last, as there was nothing 'extempore,' for the Japanese believed they were there to stay. The city fairly boiled with activity, while the statistics of imports and exports handled through the port were imposing.

But behind the scenes, if revealed, a somewhat different picture existed. The City of Bachelors, as it was called, held ten thousand men - Chinese immigrants from Shantung. They were employed as basic, slave-labor by the South Manchuria Railway to work on the piers, and were paid much less than a Japanese. There was no way for them to quit and go home, as they were likely to be in debt to the company for food and lodging, if their long barracks could be called such. To additionally keep the men under control, their recreation center was an opium den, and they were rarely fed meat. Thus, a more listless lot could hardly be imagined; muscles were stout enough for work, but spirits seemed long-dead.

In Harbin, it was a different story entirely. One could truly feel Russia there, for it teemed with 'White' Russian exiles from the old Tsarist regime, who had fled the country when it turned Soviet. They equally scorned the old Chinese or new Japanese ways. They were the largest white population under Asian rule, but too proud to work for either master. They lived in dismal poverty, begged on the streets, and told any stranger who listened, the highly-colored stories of their supposedly, aristocratic past. Indeed, some of them had once belonged to noble families of St. Petersburg and Moscow, yet to most unknowing-Asians, this was meaningless.

Soon throughout Manchuria, the housing, a greater proportion of food, especially meat, was confiscated for the Japanese military and colonist population. Much of the rice and wheat produced was also forcibly requisitioned and sent to Japan. This left the local Manchu to survive mainly on a corn meal, which was said to taste only slightly less revolting than it smelled. They occasionally could get some maize or sorghum, but they had to have contacts either in the black-market, or on the farms. This limited diet was quickly depleted by the work force, having to put in seven days a week. Only government offices, schools and factories, working directly for the Japanese had a day off.

Though all children were educated in Japanese, by Japanese teachers, with textbooks following Japanese indoctrination and ideology, yet most Japanese children attended separate schools. These were well equipped and well heated, with shining floors and clean windows. Meanwhile, the local children had school in dilapidated temples, and crumbling houses, donated by private patrons, but still heatless. In some areas in winter, the whole class often had to run around the block in the middle of a lesson, or collective foot-stamping to ward off the cold.

Discipline was also Japanese style, which included hitting the children as a matter of course, for the slightest mistake. Also punishment for failure to observe the prescribed rules of bowing to the teacher at all times, strict etiquette of dress and presentation. Both girls and boys were slapped hard on the face, and the latter were also struck on the head with a wooden club. Another punishment was to be made to kneel for hours in the snow. Outside the classroom, a definite *deferment to all Japanese* - children, as well as adults - was required. One had to bow and make way on the streets for even the youngest Japanese, while the Japanese children were allowed to slap local children for no apparent reason at all.

But those families were the lucky ones. Over five million people, about a sixth of the population, lost their homes, and tens of thousands died. Laborers were worked to death in mines, under Japanese guards to produce exports for Japan's industries. Many of these laborers were deprived of salt, and did not have the energy to run away. By the mid-1940, with the war running badly in the Pacific, the Japanese ran short of labor, so local and Japanese children were then conscripted to work in textile factories. Again, a natural matter of course, a difference was seen in the jobs they did, number of hours worked, food served and general care provided. Also, the Japanese children were rarely beaten. Those were the companies of the Zaibatsu, which concentrated on the military-related industries, made great fortunes from the exploitation of Manchuria, its natural resources, and cheap labor.

Torture, even death by garroting, was not unusual for such minor infractions, as not bowing to portraits of Pu Yi, insufficient acknowledgment of a Japanese official, or speaking-out against the Occupying government. The psychological torture, for some, was more devastating to bear, especially what was put upon the local children. Its purpose was mainly threat or fear, through the showing of actual, practiced power and control. Part of this was the forced- watching of newsreels of Japan's 'progress' in the war. They were far from being ashamed of their brutality, and even vaunted it as a way to inculcate fear. Some of the usual fare included Japanese soldiers cutting Chinese people in half, and prisoners tied to stakes being torn to pieces by dogs.

These films included lingering-close-ups of the victim's terror- stricken eyes, as their attackers came at them. While viewing all this, the local children were closely-watched by their teachers and Japanese officials, to make sure they did not shut their eyes, or stick a handkerchief in their mouths to stifle their screams. Needless to say, the local children had nightmares for years, and closely obeyed the prescribed rules. More often than not, they committed suicide, if they thought they had committed an infringement. Over the fourteen years of close scrutiny, hundreds died.

Even when education was allowed, it was the Japanese culture totally set upon them. The girls, from junior high on, were only instructed in 'the way of a woman' - meaning the running of a household - cooking and sewing, tea ceremony, flower arrangement, embroidery, drawing, and the appreciation of art. The single most important idea imparted, was how to always please one's husband. This included how to dress, how to do one's hair, how to bow, and above all, how to obey, without question.

The crucial rigors of this detailed training was the point, which Japanese officials often plucked their fiancees from among the locals, in addition to the Japanese girls. Intermarriage was encouraged, because it assumed Japan's presence in China would continue, and even prosper. Some of the young ladies were chosen to go to Japan to be married to men they had not met. Many of the local families were accepting of all this, for in trading off their daughters, they received a greater rationing of food, and preferential treatment. Since similar practices had been part of China's history for thousands of years in dealing with warlords, it was not such a matter of morals, and no one considered the teenage girls having any feelings.

The Japanese did encourage more active sports than their Mandarin predecessors, but the unspoken-rule-of-thumb always, only be the Japanese children could triumphed at the games or contests. The Japanese would not accept humiliation from their captive subjects, even from those naive locals, who did not comprehend their arrogance. The offenders suffered severely under the pretense of having broken some regulation, or violated a rule.

As the war was winding down again the Japanese, they became even more paranoid somehow the Chinese were contributing to their downfall. They searched-out for collaborators, traitors, or other conspirators. Toward the end, the Japanese turned on each other, accusing whomever may have been too soft, or weak with the locals. Within days of the surrender, locals took their revenge, sweeping down on all Japanese with an unleashed ferociousness. Few escaped via suicide, while any remaining majority of the ruling-authorities died mercilessly, at the hands of the entering Soviet Red Army. Many of the Soviets remembered how Japan had previously beaten them in the Japan-Russo War, so their revenge was dealt out excruciatingly. Still, "We'll be back," a surrendering-Japanese general told the Manchurians, for the Japanese had long memories, and *bushido* (warrior-way) required revenge.

The Soviets foresaw the mushroom-cloud could lead to the easy picking of the Manchurian plum, so they acted swiftly at dawn on August 9, three days after Hiroshima. Apart from the surprise and speed however, Soviet success was enhanced significantly by the collapse of Japan itself. Hit by the second atomic bomb strike on the 9th in Nagasaki, the Japanese Generals had already ordered their troops to lay down their arms. The Soviets maintained their advance, but against units whose officers had committed suicide or fled, leaving demoralized soldiers to surrender en masse. Manchuria was once again in Soviet hands by August 20th, and the Japanese were marched off on their fateful, long-walk to the Siberian labor camps.

For those non-military Japanese, few choices were left to them. If their nationalism was strong, they had but one choice, suicide. If the husband loved his wife, they ceremoniously plan their departure, dressing themselves and children in their finest kimonos, etc. Then, on the tatami mat in their home, the father would kill the son and daughter, then his wife and finally himself. If he did not care for his wife, he would simply do himself in, with a gun. If he wasn't nationalistic, he'd leave the wife and children to their own death, or survival, whatever all it may entail. The women and young girls were all but promised rape, as the Soviet soldiers ran rampant.

A few Japanese who had befriended some of their Chinese neighbors were taken in, or mothers, being more concerned about their small children, would beg Chinese friends to take them. Many of those who tried to escape with their children, killed them for the safety of the group, when their crying endangered it. Others left their children along the way for their own protection, or believing they might be found and saved. A large group of widowed-

Japanese, military wives, or those whose husbands had been taken prisoner, were stranded in Antung, on the border of Korea, trying to escape the marauding, incoming Soviets. There were many stories of these stragglers, who wandered the hills of Korea for months foraging, and sometimes were helped or taken in by the locals. Eventually, most reached Pusan for repatriation.

Short Personal Story: The small, older Japanese-custodian smiled, as he finished telling his story. "I must have been a good baby, because I'm here now. My mother told me that out of thirty babies, women were trying to escape with, only six of us survived it all."

For the Manchurians, expectations of liberation were soon squelched by the realization of the new Occupation. It did not take long for some to look back on the Japanese, as bad as they were, they had been less a menace, as they had shared a similar Asian culture, whereas these hoards of 'Caucasians' seemed barbarous - even when they weren't mistreating them. There was a most definite, expressed-feeling the Soviets felt the Chinese were similar to the Japanese, and both extremely-inferior to themselves.

Though conflicting statistics still emerge, it is generally acknowledged since the 1990s, over *six hundred thousand* Japanese soldiers were held in the Soviet Union detention-work camps, mostly in Siberia. Of the number, approximately ten percent, or over sixty thousand, died. Also, almost a thousand Japanese civilians and non-Japanese collaborators held, of whom an even greater percentage died. Most of the prisoners of war were not released until the late 1940s, or early 1950s. These Japanese came home to be rejected and punished still further, for the humiliation they brought upon their country and families. In the eyes of their countrymen, there was *no acceptable* POW. One must die with pride, rather than suffer the indignations of being captured. There were many also, who had become indoctrinated with

Communism, either out of choice, or it was easier to accept it to be released. When they were repatriated to Occupied Japan, they then became the problem of the Allied Occupation.

~~~~~~

Bushido - What it really was:

In exploring the extensive indoctrinations of the Japanese mind, it is well to look into the *hoax* called Bushido. *Bushi* - means knight, *do* - way. Bushido, therefore is 'the knightly way' or 'the way of the Samurai.' Curiously enough, the real Samurai never heard of *bushido*.

It would be hard to find in history, a more amazing-deception practiced by the rulers of a nation upon its people. The Japanese, ultra- conservative power-brokers - the Zaibatsu, and the military leaders (many times one in the same), bent upon enslaving the masses to their will, totally fabricated bushido in the 1890s. They then had it put into the schoolbooks, knowing well to deceive the people, it is necessary to start with the young. These military-nationalists, also knew to impress the Japanese with any doctrine, it must *seem to have been a tradition*. So, the ultra-rightists made bushido *retroactive*, built to order like a fake-antique, and put forward as the ancient, sacred philosophy of the race, thus connected to loyalty to one's Shogun, or the Emperor. The Japanese believed it, for who would doubt a textbook?

Foreign scholars were also duped, as British and American historians and encyclopedias refer to 'bushido' as Japans age-old code of chivalry. But, the real test would be *if* there had been such a thing as bushido in the time of the Samurai, then the writers of the period would have mentioned it. Yet, the great, early historians of Japan, Kaempfer, Siebold, Satow and Rein, never once used it. *Bushido was not in any English or Japanese dictionary published before 1900!*

Not only the word, but the custom it describes was synthetic. The 'ancient chivalry' of Japan was a modern invention. Japan had none too noble a past - but when a past had been deliberately glorified by the Imperial Army, one must ask, Why? To hold the Japanese people in subjection. During the 1880s, the flood of European and American ideas were endangering the authority of the oligarchy - the Zaibatsu. They felt it necessary the eyes of the nation be pried away from seeing free, democratic-style in foreign lands, and go back to the *master-and-slave* psychology of old Japan. So, Bushido was invented.

The people, particularly the children in the schools, were told *bushido was as old as the Japanese race*. And, it was 'the way of the Samurai.' But what was the way of the Samurai? It was complete obedience to their masters. Therefore modern Japanese, if they wished to emulate the Samurai, must be *obedient*. They must forget the foreign ideas of free will and individualism. They must, like the Samurai, live only to do the will of their military lords. From what had been seen of the actions of many of the Japanese soldiers, one might ask what does bushido add up to? The total looks very much like barbarism, what the Japanese often accused foreigners of being.

In postwar Japan, and even in modern times, the bushido-myth was still being jealously guarded. If the cult of obedience to master and lord could be kept alive, it would serve as the basis of a new oligarchy - the Zaibatsu. So, even after the control of the Allied Occupation was withdrawn, it continued. The Company, the job, the boss, whatever the new master - lord, and the Japanese people still were slaves. A cult of slavish-obedience had no function or place, in the self-reliant democracy the Occupation thought, they could and did develop into Japan.

* * * * * *

The Hundred-Year War:

The Emperor's rescript of surrender - without the word 'surrender - explained the Emperor was *concluding* the war, because of his benevolent regard for the *human* race. The war, if continued would "... lead to the total extinction of human civilization ... This is the reason why we have ordered the acceptance of the provisions of the joint declaration of the powers."

Imperial rescripts were immortal. Whatever was *supposedly* issued by the Emperor Jimmu, twenty-six centuries ago was still quoted. Emperor Meiji's rescript on education was a *holy text* in the schools, and his rescript to soldiers was committed to their memory. Insofar as Japan having a Bible, it would be made up of the Imperial statements. Those who composed the surrender-rescript with the Emperor, knew well the time-bomb they were laying, when they had him say: "We cannot but express the deepest sense of regret to our allied nations of East Asia, who have consistently cooperated with our Empire, towards the emancipation for East Asia ... Having been able to save ... and maintain the structure of the Imperial State, we are always with you ..." This will go down through the years as a clarion- call from the Emperor to his people, to rise-anew for "the emancipation of East Asia."

The day the Occupation forces began to land in Japan, a Japanese policeman was seen tearing down a poster. An American officer snatched it from his hand and called an interpreter. "A Hundred-Year War" was the caption in large kanji characters, sprawled down the right side of the poster. Then, in vertical columns, reading leftward: "Never has Great Nippon known defeat. The present difficulty is but *a stepping-stone* to the future. Rallying around the Imperial Throne, fight on, for this is a Hundred-Year War."

For two years before surrender, according to Swiss-observers, who remained in Japan during the war, the nationalistic government had been building up the hundred-year war psychology. The posters, and others like them, had been displayed everywhere. Also, there were huge, painted-signs using billboards, some contributed by the weapons manufacturers - the Zaibatsu. The newspapers carried hundred-year war announcements in display advertising space, in news stories and editorials. There were hundred-year war films, and even popular songs were written on the theme, with radio commentators continually speaking of it.

Envisaging defeat, Japan's militarists were planning for the long future. Japan was being conditioned to lose one conflict, but to prepare for another - and another and another - for a hundred years if necessary, until Japan's program of conquest was fulfilled. At the end of it, the Emperor would rule the world, of course. The idea was put forth, based on a century was a short period of time, in a nation with a history of 2,600 years, and they only had to be patient to win. Considering the dozens of troops, over the next decades, which had continued to hide-out in obscure islands and fight on, this belief was taken as fact by many.

Personal Story: Japanese Male born in Manchuria

This interview was done in Japanese and translated by Kazuyo Mizutani

My father had a grocery store business in Shizuoka (near Mt. Fuji) and because of the recession, the business went down and he eventually lost his job. So, he went to Manchuria to find a new business there, as it was promised. In Manchuria he had a futon - bedding shop - in the Japanese community in Hoten City (near Mukden) and was very successful. At first it was just my parents and my elder sister, and then I was born the following year in 1939, and following were two more younger sisters. These good times only lasted three years, because my father had to go to the war in Northern China in early 1942.

Then my mother had the responsibility to raise us four children by herself. She was not able to run the futon business by herself, so at first she just sold out all the inventory. Then we raised chickens and sold eggs to our neighbors, or bartered the eggs for other things. There were only about one hundred Japanese families, so she also did business with the Chinese. She was always very fair and honest with them, because she was alone and didn't want any problems. The Chinese in that area were mainly farmers and a few shopkeepers, and as it turned out when things got very bad - only a little food and coal to keep us warm - these Chinese were very good to us, and shared their food and coal.

I was too young to go to school when the war first started, but my elder sister went to Japanese school. I don't remember playing with any of the Chinese children at the time, but then most of our neighbors were Japanese. I cannot speak Chinese now, but I think I could then, because I can remember going into the local shops and getting sweets, or my mother buying other things from the Chinese. My mother told me it was important to be nice to the Chinese, and she was right because some of the Japanese weren't so nice to them and after the war was over they took revenge on these Japanese. It was a reverse situation, and most of them really deserved it. Some of these other Japanese did not have enough coal and it was a very cold country, so things were even more difficult for them.

I remember very clearly, and my mother told me too, many Japanese were crying when the announcement came about the end of the war, Japan surrendering. There were some announcements from the airplane, paper-flyers and loud speakers, everybody so sad and crying. Things became very confused, and people began to panic about what to do and how to get money. One day a Japanese man came to our house and he told my mother he knew where my father was, "He's in a prisoner of war camp," he said. So, my mother was very happy to know he was alive, and she took some food and stuff for the man to give to my father. But this man was a fake, and he was just trying to rip-off my mother, and take what little money and stuff we had.

Then later he came to me and he said, "Do you want to see your father again?" And, of course, I did, so I went with him. I never even said anything to my mother, because I was so excited. I didn't know it at that time, but he was kidnapping me. He was going to sell me to a wealthy Chinese family, because in those days, the Chinese believed the Japanese were a very good race, and it would be very lucky for them to have Japanese blood in their family. So, sometimes kidnaping happened. Anyway, I followed him to the train station, but the train didn't come for a long time. So the man took me to the next station, we had to walk there, too. I was then very tired, and this was no longer exciting, I guess. So I started crying, and the man didn't know what to do, so he abandoned me. Finally, my mother and sisters noticed I was gone and this man had also taken things from our house. In the community, we had a kind of neighborhood protection, or defense group, so they all got together and went looking for me. At last, after searching for several hours, they found me at that next station.

My father did not return to Japan until 1948, as he was in an American prisoner of war camp. He was very lucky because, of course, if he had been taken by the Soviets he may have been killed, as so many were. The Soviets were very, very bad when they came to Manchuria. They raped and killed many people, Japanese and Chinese, and almost everyday they came to our houses and took things, threatened us and stole even old pots and broken things that really had no value. They just seemed to want anything that was ours.

It was about a month or so after the war ended, the American Forces came. They came before the Soviets. For a while though, we had both of them there, in and out of our town, but neither of them ever helped us with food or anything. Before that, there were many Japanese military who had escaped from the military, and they had taken a lot of supplies, guns, food and things, and they tried to sell these things to the Japanese and Chinese people. Then, the regular Japanese military came and were looking for these run-away men and the things they had stolen. They went from house to house searching for them, and if they found any of these men or those military things, the people who had helped them, or bought those things were then killed.

This was only the beginning, as from then on our little town was invaded almost every day by the Chinese, Japanese military, Americans, and Soviets. They would come to loot, rape, and shoot any people who fought back, or resisted in any way. Many of the Soviet soldiers had watches up and down their sleeves, which they had stolen from the people. It didn't matter if they were broken or not, they just wanted to display how many they had collected. The violence toward the women was the worst though, because many of the rapes were right out in the public square, and then if the husbands saw, they went crazy with rage. This was also the American soldiers doing this, because I saw it once. The women were told to wear old, dirty, floppy clothes, and they even put coal dust on their faces and tied down their hair, so they would not be attractive in any way. But sometimes this didn't help, they were still raped.

My mother was once held up by some drunken American soldiers, and they wanted some valuables, but we didn't have anything left. Still they pushed for something, so my mother gave them a broken record player and they finally left. In our community, we had a lookout tower, and the man looking out could see for a long distance, so when they saw some soldiers, or a jeep coming they shouted and sound the alarm - "The Russians are coming!" or "The Americans are coming!" All of the people would then run to the community hall.

We would gather together, because in big numbers the soldiers would not come in there to bother us so much. But somet-times, some people would be slow getting to the safety of the center, and then they would be the ones preyed-upon by the soldiers. They would be the victims, because they had not gotten to safety in time. The soldiers would also then go from house to house looking for people who might be hiding.

Once my family didn't get to the center in time. There were a lot of drunk American soldiers who were trying to come into the house, but my mother had blocked the door, so they started to machine-gun the front of the house. Behind our house was a cornfield and my mother told us to escape into it. The corn was very tall and thick, so we went to hide very deeply in the corn. But the Americans had seen us escaping, so they followed and kept machine-gunning into the cornfield. My mother put her hand over my smallest sister's mouth and told her if she made any noise, she would have to kill her, for the soldiers would hear, and kill all of us and take her away. Finally, the soldiers gave up and went away, maybe to look for other people.

This all went on for over a year, so our lives were

very tormented every few days by one group or another of soldiers. Amazingly, my mother was able to keep us all together, and even keep her chickens and sell some eggs, so we were able to keep living. We really didn't do much at all, there was no regular school or anything, because we never knew when we might be invaded. Of course, we never went out at night, although they usually didn't come at night. During this time my mother started to feed us this special medicine- mixture, she made from some herbs and eggs. It tasted terrible, but she made us take one spoonful every day. There was a lot of disease the soldiers had brought in with them, because they were not clean, and many, many people got sick and died.

Everyone had to wait to leave for Japan, because there were so few boats, and the American military controlled who cold leave, and when. It was done mostly by towns, and the American military had left the previous Japanese officials still in charge of the people for everyday things. Since there was still very little food, and the trip itself would be very difficult, the Japanese community officials made a rule each adult could only take two children, and they would only be giving out that amount of food. My mother though, refused to leave any of the four of us. The officials, and everyone else, were very very angry with her, because she broke the rule, and they would not help her (she was ostracized). So, we had to share the little bit of food for the whole trip, which was several weeks time. I remember when we left, our next door neighbor's son, who was my age, was not with his family. I did not see him anymore, so he was left behind, or sold to the Chinese. As a matter of fact, even some women who had only two children, they left them behind. But my mother, she would not leave even one of us.

At last the American military ordered us to leave, and first we took a train from Manchuria to what is now North Korea. It was a shipping-kind of train car (freight-boxcar), so we sat on the floor, or stood up about four or five days. The train would stop often, and sometimes the

Chinese people would come when we had stopped for several hours, and try to take our things, or threaten us to give them something. So, we all put our belongings in the middle of the car, and then we all sat around them to protect them. Along the way, there wasn't much food, so many Japanese began to abandon their children.

Sometimes they would just give them to the Chinese, and other times they would simply leave them by the side of the railroad tracks. Some grown people, and children too, were still dying from hunger and disease. Then after this time, we had to walk for another two days or so, to get to the (North) Korean port where the ship was leaving from. My mother was carrying my youngest sister, and she had me tied by a string to her, and then my elder sister tied to her other side, with my younger sister tied to her. This was the only way she knew she wouldn't lose us, as no one would help us. Then, we were all carrying the few belongings we had left.

The ship we went on was an old oil tanker, and it was just empty space inside, no seats or beds, or anything. All we could do was to put down a blanket, or cloth and try to lay, or sit down on the bottom of it. If we had to go to the bathroom, we had to climb the ladder up to the deck and go-off of the railing. There really wasn't any toilet facilities. My elder sister then got some stomach illness. Then all the people forced us to get off the boat, because they thought it was contagious.

The ship stopped at Cheju Island, just south of the Korean mainland, because there was an American prisoner war camp there. But they didn't have any real medicine, and they didn't give her any treatment, except twice a day they would come and spray us with chemical powder (like DDT), to kill bugs or something. We all had to take off our clothes and then they would spray us, but they did feed us, so it wasn't so bad. Amazingly, she survived, and I believe it was the herbal-egg medicine my mother had made us take, which saved her. We stayed at the camp for almost a month while we waited for another ship to come and take us to Japan. At last we arrived in a small city north of Kyoto, on the Japan Sea side.

We then had the long train ride of several days to Shizuoka, my mother's home town. We stayed there for six months and then we went to Nagoya, my fathers family, and we lived with them. My mother worked as a nurse's aid at the hospital, and she had other jobs too, sometimes. Suddenly, with no notice, although almost a year had passed (in Nagoya), my father showed-up. Then it was 1949, and I was ten years old. My mother had two more children, but things were not good between them, so my mother divorced my father (Divorce, still rare today, at that time it was unheard of). Of course, my mother had to move out of his parent's house and she took all six of us to live with her. It was very difficult for her, but she supported us with many jobs. (*I could not believe she would do this at such a desperate time as the Occupation, so, breaching all Japanese decorum and politeness, I asked if he could tell me why she divorced him?*)

(*Hesitation and controlled resentment*) In Manchuria, my father had been very successful, even rich, and he had spent much money on running around with many women, and treated my mother badly. When he came back from Manchuria, he expected special treatment because he had been a prisoner, and of course, his parents, especially his mother did so. He was never concerned for how my mother, and us children, had suffered and all the terrible things she had gone through to protect us, and help us to survive. He always was only concerned about himself.

(*This man is very angry, the veins in his neck are sticking out.*) Now, he is dying and only my younger brother will spend time with him, and take care of him. I have never seen him, and I do not want to see him, since my mother divorced him. (*As we continue the interview, it is as if he is now relieved in telling us something, he could not tell any other Japanese people.*)

The Occupation troops were still in Nagoya, and in

56

fact a large number were stationed in Tsunami Park, which was their GHQ and it was near our house. What I remember most is that was the first time I ever had chocolate. It was given to me by a soldier, as I walked down the street (*He is smiling now*). One problem was we could not go into the park, or use it any way until after the Occupation was over. Shirokawa Park area was where all the American residences were. There weren't too many bad things which happened, but my friend's father was run over and killed by a jeep, and they never even got compensated from the military for it. There were only a few hundred of them, and other than seeing them with pan-pan girls, most people didn't pay any attention after a while. Around Komaki (the military airfield), there were many of the ordinary houses turned into brothels, but I didn't see anything like that in our neighborhood, just the Japanese women going with them (*pan-pan girls*). It's a nice residential area, and my mother never talked about those things.

We were so poor, I mean everyone was, it was an ordinary thing, we were all the same. My mother was so good with money, and even when she went to the black-market, she managed to buy things we needed. Actually, from China we had brought three watches, my mother had really hidden them very well. Still, two of the three were taken, or she had to give them-up, so now she only had one left, which was actually my watch. So my mother took that watch out to a farmer and exchanged it for rice and vegetables for us. We had no one helping us, and we all had to work together to survive.

My mother often talked about the hardships and experiences in China. After she died, twelve years ago, I wrote all of it down, so I would remember everything about her, and all she did and suffered for us. My mother was a very strong woman, and I think she could be a good symbol to other Japanese woman. My mother's policy always was, though we are poor, be a good, honest person, and not someone people can criticize. She said life in

China was incredibly bad, and the American snd Soviet soldiers did terrible things to us, because the Japanese were the intruders. For the children, the situation was just like hell, because death was right there waiting for them. Even the revenge from the Chinese cannot be blamed on them, because we Japanese did it first to them.

When the Korean War started, the Japanese economy was boosted and many people were happy about the economic recovery, and publicly they were speaking 'the Korean War is good.' But, my mother felt it was not true, because people forgot what happened in China. Then, there were other Japanese people who were against the war and those people who supported them, and these people were Communists. My mother told me when the election took place, Japan had to be reborn again, but we need new politicians, we need the Communist party for Japan. She said then she was gong to vote for the Communist party, although she had a very emotional feeling toward the Communists, because they raped and stole from many in China. In her mind though, Japan Communist was not the same, so it was a difficult decision.

I believed her decision since being in China, she was always right, so I believed her decision (to vote for them) was right, too. Later she joined the Communist Party, I never really understood what it all meant (*Many Japanese were quite naive about politics, the promises of the "Lovable Communist Party" - their Japanese name, sounded like the answer to all their problems and prevent any further suffering.*).

Short Personal Story:

We used poison in China from the very beginning. It wasn't employed openly, since the Geneva Convention forbad it. We took special care to pick-up the expended canisters, and remove all traces of its use from the battle fields. Four times I went in (called back to service), if you include my initial active duty.

No body fights a war because they like it. "Nation's orders," "Emperor's orders" - that's what they said. What could you do, but o? If an order was issued and you didn't go, you were a traitor. There's not one soldier who ever died saying, *"Tenno Heika Banzai"* (Long Live the Emperor!) I was with hundreds of men when they died. The dead lay with grimaces on their face.

Nohara Teishin,
Japan At War

Side Note:

As recently as May, 1994, the Japanese Justice Minster Shinto Nagano, speaking for the government, denied the 1937 Nanking Massacre. Rather than the 200,000 - 300,000 Chinese that are believed to have been killed, they say the battle only involved *a few thousand*, and those were solely military, not the civilians claimed. Most right- winged nationalists also, still insist the Pacific war was not an act of aggression by Japan, but *the liberation of the colonies* held by the white-imperialists.

After numerous international complaints and demonstrations in China and South Korea, Prime Minster Hata later dismissed Nagano, but no formal acknowledgment about Nanking was ever made. Although sporadically, former military have come forward confessing their own participation in the atrocities of Nanking, and other areas. They have also urged the government to cleanse itself, and clear the record of its war crimes by apologizing, as West Germany did in the 1960s. These men have been scorned, their lives threatened, and the mayor of Nagasaki was nearly killed, when he spoke out about Japan's war of aggression.

The "Greater East Asia Co-Prosperity Sphere" was first used in August, 1940. It's crucial importance was propaganda why the Japanese were in Asia, to 'help our backward-brothers' fight the white- imperialistic invaders. Of course, easily believed, when there was an abundance of signs, such as those in Shanghai which said: "No dogs or Yellow People" allowed."

* * * * * *

"Life was not a valuable gift, but death was. Life was a fever-dream made up of joys embittered by sorrows, pleasure poisoned by pain; a dream that was a nightmare-confusion of spasmodic and fleeting delights, ecstasies, exultations, happinesses, interspersed with long-drawn miseries, griefs, perils, horrors, defeats, disappointments, humiliations, and despairs. - the heaviest curse devisable by divine ingenuity; but death was sweet, death was gentle, death was kind; death healed the bruised spirt and the broken heart, and gave them rest and forgetfulness; death was man's best friend; when man could endure life no longer, death came and set him free."

Mark Twain
Letters From The Earth

Part 1 - Japan as the Occupiers

Chapter 3 - Vietnam and Southeast Asia - How it all changed history

"We hate the Japanese," a prominent Hanko Chinese said after the Japanese had been expelled. "But we have to recognize that they rid us of extra-territoriality and foreign concessions. They have given Asia an entirely new perspective on the relationship between Asiatic and European powers."

Willard Price,
Key To Japan

The Vietnamese were established as a distinct people by the 2nd Century BC, occupying the historic regions of Tonkin, to the North; Annam, in the Center; and Cochin China, to the South. Tonkin and Annam were conquered by China in 111 BC. In the 2nd Century AD, the *Champas* kingdom emerged in central Vietnam. The Chinese were driven out in 939, and the Annam empire grew, defeating the Champas in 1471, and expanding south into Cochin China. European traders and missionaries began to arrive in the 1500s. The French captured Saigon in 1859, and in 1862 they annexed Cochin China, which was later merged into French Indochina.

Following the fall of France to Germany, Japan seized North Vietnam in the summer of 1940, in order to strengthen its stranglehold on South China, and the U.S. reacted with economic sanctions. This acquisition was one of the few benefits for Japan in joining the Axis Tripartite Pact, as they had received no prior help from Hitler or Mussolini. When Japan occupied South Vietnam the next summer, in order to gain bases for a possible push southward, the U.S. took the further step of banning oil shipments. Faced with the prospect for a dwindling oil supply, with which to further its war in China and meet possible attack by the U.S., the Japanese *were forced* to make a quick choice among three courses: backing down in China, negotiating a compromise settlement with the United States, or waging war to seize the oil of Indonesia - then called the Dutch East Indies.

The government was unwilling to do the first, unable to achieve the second, and therefore settled on the third choice. Striking aggressively, and decisively at Pearl Harbor on December 7th. (*This was actually a repeat of a tactic used against Russia in 1904.*) In order to neutralize the American Navy, while Japan pushed south. Before starting the war, the military consolidated its policy-position at home. The Army Minister, General Hideki Tojo, also became the Prime Minister, thus putting the civilian government fully under the military.

The Japanese knew the U.S. had far greater economic and military capacities than Japan. But, they thought if they struck rapidly and seized the whole of the Western Pacific, Americans would find the road back to victory too long and arduous to be worth fighting for. Especially, if the Nazis had won in Europe, in the meantime, which they had said they could do. Within a few months the Japanese overran all of Southeast Asia, and a vast region stretching from the borders of India to New Guinea and Guadalcanal. Guerrilla forces, who had been fighting sporadically against France's almost hundred years of domination for more than a decade, organized under Ho Chi Minh in 1941, to then fight the Japanese.

In the British withdrawal, down from the Malaysian peninsula towards Singapore, during December, 1941 - January, 1942, the British forces suffered 25,000 casualties, as they had lacked any significant air cover. These were largely Indian divisions, of whom Prime Mister Winston Churchill had a low opinion of, as he thought them not as good as 'white troops.' Churchill also believed the Malay peninsula itself was strategically unimportant, and weeks after the Japanese landed, he admitted the Malayan campaign was doomed. He felt England could not defend the area, once the Japanese had command of the sea, while they still fought for their real homeland (*England*) against Germany and Italy. In effect, Churchill and others had prejudicially referred to Australians, as having come from '*poor stock*' and '*an inferior people*' with poor nerves. Their true priority was clearly Great Britain, especially England.

The only allowed significant British troop reinforcements to arrive in Malaya, landed only seventeen days before their capitulation in Singapore. Their other real problem, the British military leadership, or lack thereof, (*many officers were Lords, etc. wanting to be in the war, but had virtually no military training*) as the general in charge was known to be weak and indecisive. He had never responded to the first Japanese infiltration tactic - except to retreat - and never proposed any counter-offensive action. His failure as a general, and an uninspiring man, totally out of his depth, was reflected in the British soldiers he commanded. The only major resistance shown down the peninsula came from the forthright Australian troops, who were very successful. Had similarly aggressive tactics been used against the

Japanese earlier, they might not have reached Singapore as quickly as they did.

As it happened, the Japanese were basically exhausted and out of supplies, when they captured Singapore - *which they did on bicycles* *coming across the bridge from the peninsula!* Another week or so of resistant fighting, could have seen a very different result. The British plan of withdrawing to Singapore was fatally flawed. The Australians thought they were only fighting until the British fleet of reinforcement troops arrived, as they were deemed sufficiently powerful to defeat the Japanese fleet. Instead, the ill-prepared British government diverted them to Rangoon, to be used in Burma in time to prevent its loss. The Australians were still geared up and prepared for more fighting, when the British chose to simply surrender.

Unfortunately, the British-trained Burma troops, just as the Australians and British in Singapore (7,000 in all), ended up in Prison of War camps. Within three months 2,500 were dead, mostly British, as they had not led as 'hardy a life-style,' as the Aussies or Burmese. So, the Australian hatred of the Japanese remained quite strong for over many decades, because of their cruel treatment. Yet, many Australians still felt Britain really totally responsible, for they had left them at the mercy of the invading enemy. Only a few weeks later, February 19, 1942, the Japanese bombed Darwin, subsequently killing 243 people. The city was attacked sixty more times, including the day General MacArthur arrived, following his escape from the Philippines.

Japan's original justification for going into Asia was to rescue the continent from 'its colonial status.' Although this was not essentially true for China or Korea, it sounded good to the Japanese military, as they had been indoctrinated to believe every country would be better under Japanese rule. Interestingly, years later as Japan was losing the war, it kept its promise to these Asian countries to make them free. For if Japan could not have them, then neither would their former colonial powers. The Southeast Asians may not have loved Japan, or how it treated them during Occupation, but Japan made them politically-conscious.

These millions of Southeast Asians had never before heard such ideas as independence from '*white-supremacy*,' and '*Asia for Asiatics.*' Many who had been numb, and unresisting under British, French or Dutch rule, were later stirred to demand rights formerly undreamed of. Japan, knowing for the last three years of the war, it was likely to lose Southeast Asia, had deliberately driven in the stakes of freedom so deeply, they would remain solid beliefs after the Japanese departure.

Forty-five radio stations had broadcast in eighteen languages the crimes, real and imaginary, of the 'white-man.' If there were formerly-Chinese who did not know of the Opium War, they were told, as Indians were told again and again of the Amritsar massacre. French oppression in Indo-China, and Dutch exploitation of the East Indies, were portrayed in their blackest aspects. Filipinos were repeatedly reminded of America's first act in their land, to crush the Philippine Republic. Then Americans' own treatment of the '*Negro*' in the 1930s and 40s was then taught from one end of Asia to the other. Countless millions of Asiatics learned from these broadcasts, how the United States opposed independence for *colonel-peoples*. Japan made full and diabolical use of America's unwillingness at the San Francisco Conference, to endorse complete freedom for dependent peoples.

Film, press, and radio constantly reiterated the story of the precipitate-flight of the white-overlords from their Asiatic possessions in 1942. To most Asians, a miracle, but they were now beginning to believe if it could be accomplished once, it could be again. All this telling propaganda, was backed-up with deeds as the Japanese went further, knowing they would soon be out. They could afford to make extensive concessions to the Southeast Asians - concessions which would seriously embarrass the returning white-overloads.

Remission of all land taxes was delightedly received by the Burmese, and independence was granted to them August 1, 1943, while the Philippines celebrated independence October 14, 1943. Self- government was promised to Malaya, while provincial and municipal councils entirely made up of Malayans, were established. Although the Japanese did not get into India, they psychologically invaded it by establishing a "Provisional Government of Free India," under the leadership of Subhas Chandra Bose, whose prestige was well known. Dutch East Indies was promised freedom, and Java, for the first time, partially governed itself through a newly-formed Javanese Central Council made up of native leaders.

Siam - Thailand profited materially from the Japanese Occupation, as it was presented with 26,770 square miles of territory sheered off from Burma and Malaya, and 21,750 from Indo-China. The British and French would have a fight on their hands, trying to get it back. Even as the Japanese troops were being repatriated back to Japan, they secretly left agents to infiltrate, and assist in the coming wars of independence. Some of these were Japanese who had gone native, others had been natives who had gone 'Japanese.' Their purpose was to sabotage the colonial governments, organize revolts and propagandize the people for their ultimate struggle. Considering what happened, they were all successful, though some took longer than others.

The Japanese-controlled air waves and newspapers of Asia gleefully related the *New York Times* story of May 11, 1945, which stated the United States, Britain and France had all 'hesitated to list independence as an ultimate objective for dependent people, in case this promise should eventually jeopardize their plan to create strategic- bases in these areas.' And, the same paper's headlines of May 7th, were put before the eye, or drummed into the ear of Asia's millions: "U.S. Will Oppose Colonial Liberty ... Americans Indicate Line Up with Britain and France Against an Independence Pledge."

After the fall of France in 1940, there was never any real possibility the British Fleet would be used for the defense of Singapore. Churchill's over-riding aim was to win the war in Europe, essentially by involving the Americans. Britain and most of the European colony-holders felt they could always re-capture their colonies, in the future, if actually needed. They had barely recovered from destroying the Nazis, when they realized things would never be the same again for them in Southeast Asia. Once the Japanese were ousted, it was the opportunity for the Southeast Asians to dispose of the ruling, colonial administration, and prepare to gain their ultimate goal - independence.

In Indonesia, the occupying Japanese forces had helped to organize the nationalists, at first in the hope they would make Indonesia a loyal agent of Japanese interest. Then, when Japanese defeat loomed, as a way of frustrating any attempt by the colonial Dutch forces to resume power. However, with Japanese strength waning, and the economic climate in the Dutch colonial islands becoming harsher, in 1944, there was a series of popular revolts against Japanese rule. The Occupiers were forced to concede to the nationalists demands.

On June 1st, 1944, Dr. Achmad Sukarno demanded

immediate recognition of Indonesian independence, based on the principles of nationalism, humanitarianism, democratic government, freedom of religion and prosperity for all. Eventually, the Japanese promised it, but before it could be ratified, the Japanese surrender was announced. Sukarno, in turn declared independence, announcing on the radio he was now the first President of the Republic, and established his power base in Java. The new Republic was armed with weapons, mostly given to them by the Japanese.

The Dutch administration, refusing to recognize the new Republic, was also not able to immediately return to reclaim Indonesia, as they were still rebuilding their homeland. The British were put in charge of the archipelago, disarming and repatriating the Japanese and maintaining order, until the Dutch could return. They were not prepared for the formidable, organized and armed-guerrilla fighting units, and the war was on again. Once the Dutch took over their own battle, the situation turned quite bloody, with their unmitigated slaughter of 160,000 Indonesians. The wanton destruction and killing came to such a point, they were accused of atrocities similar to those of the Japanese and Nazis. The Dutch finally capitulated, and Indonesia gained its independence in 1949.

On September 27, 1945, an American colonel was killed, and an American captain seriously wounded by a nationalistic group of Annamites, called the Vietminh. They had, with Japanese approval, announced the independence of Annam a few months before. The Vietminh, armed with Japanese machine guns, resisted the return of French rule, and resented the coming of British and Americans, in the interests of restoring Annam to France. Japan and the Japanese were forced back into their homeland, but some seeds of independence were left behind for others to sow, and perhaps become more successful than they had been.

Interesting Side Notes:
(1)   Some escaped Nazis had joined the French Foreign Legion, only to be sent to fight the Vietminh in Indochina.

(2)   The Japanese soldiers were widely scattered on the uncounted islands of Southeast Asia, and many of them had sought-out the companionship of the native women. Many of these were mutual liaisons, as the troops in the early years had extra food and valuable goods. Also, estimated 30,000 children were produced from these unions in the five years. Many Japanese preferred to 'stay native,' and remained on the islands with the families they had created. Others, who returned to Japan, later received 'brown-paper packages' from these forlorn and scorned women of Southeast Asia. The commonality of these packages became infamous, as they contained letters, photos, and other mementos establishing their extensive family relationships. Though some Japanese families survived the shocking, public-embarrassment and undeniable evidence, suicide was again a regrettable-escape for the guilty husband, and/or his wife, for their *loss of face* in their society. So, these Japanese soldiers may have survived the war, only to die at their own hand in their homeland.

Personal History: Japanese male posted in Vietnam in 1944

This interview was done in Japanese and translated by Kazuyo Mizutani.

I had a really miserable time during this period of my life, and I will never forget it. In fact, I have been reading a lot lately, now I'm retired, about the difference between how the British Military and the Russian Military treated their Japanese hostages. We weren't prisoners of war, because the war was over. It was very different how they treated them, how each country treated them. I was an administrative officer at the airplane-parts plant. So, I handled all the invoices and also personnel, because we had to hire local people to work in the plant in Saigon. I was there November, 1944 until the end of the war.

I joined the Army in September, 1943, and was in training until July. We had left from Kyushu, Japan, in July 1944, and from that time until the end of August, I was on a ship traveling to Taiwan, the Philippines, Singapore, Guam and all around the Pacific, trying to avoid the American Navy while stopping at our ports. We were twenty, smaller ships, surrounding a large ship, with troops, supplies and so forth. We were going very slowly, so we were an easy target for the American submarines, especially at night. Three boats were sunk. From Manila to Borneo, again American submarines came, but this time the Japanese air force was watching, so they were OK. From Borneo to Singapore, the Japanese destroyer took care of these boats, so they were OK again, and we had no damage between those points.

It was a thirty-five day trip from Kyushu to Singapore and we had no bath, no chance to shave, and many men got lice. The troop ship had three levels, which were each divided again into three levels with a space of maybe one meter per man, and there were almost two thousand men on board. We also had an airplane, trucks and other supplies filling every bit of space.

My actual time in Vietnam working was not bad at all, as the Vietnamese people are very nice and were very kind to us. We didn't have problems with them, and they still had the French controlling them, until they kind of surrendered. We put the French in prison in March of 1945. It was only a short time until August, when the war was over. It wasn't really a prison, just their barracks and they weren't allowed to leave them. It was only for soldiers, not their families.

The French had been helping us before, so we were on friendly terms. North Vietnam had fought against the Japanese Army, but South Vietnam helped us. Their French general, he had a good relationship with the Nazis. I think the British came from Burma, as the officers were British, the lower-rank soldiers were Indian, Gurkhas, I think they were called. They were very fierce-some in the way they acted, very good soldiers. During the war, Japan had built the railroad from Burma to Thailand. They had used the British forces to do this work, so some of these same former prisoners came to watch us this time. So they did not treat us very nice. We had abused them badly I know, so now they could abuse us. They were pretty hard on us Japanese.

The British kept the Japanese military-hierarchy in a special prison, and then they would tell our officers to instruct the rest of us, as to what kind of work they wanted us to do. We really weren't treated too bad, because I had heard in Russia, and some other countries, the Japanese were really treated very badly. Before when we were at the plane factory, we were in the city, but then the British made a camp out from the city, suburbs maybe. We had enough food, but still not as much as we would have liked, as I was hungry often.

Actually, my worse experience was when we had the surrender ceremony. All of the British officers were lined-up under the Union Jack, and we were lined-up across from them in rows, with our officers in front. One person at a time, we had to surrender our sword and knife. It was so difficult and I was so embarrassed, because then we didn't have anything anymore, and we were no longer Japanese soldiers. Five days before this, we had given the British our guns and rifles, but because the swords are so important to us, we asked for a full, formal ceremony for us to give them-up. At this time too, was all the old British soldiers watching and standing around. They kept their guns pointed at us the whole time.

Every day everyone, but the wounded, had to work at the Saigon harbor. The British supplies had to be brought to the camp, so the Japanese had to do the manual labor. The British had a warehouse at the harbor, so we had to take our leftover supplies to there, too. We were working side-by-side with the Indian soldiers, and soon they became very friendly to us, and sometimes they even gave their clothes to us, when we did a very good job. The local Vietnamese tried to steal some of the supplies from the warehouse, so the British put booby-traps with small bombs around the warehouse. Many Vietnamese got killed or hurt very badly. I could understand they wanted these things, because they had very little food. But, we Japanese soldiers were very loyal to the British Military, because they were now in charge of us. We never did anything bad, and they treated us very good, then.

We commuted to the harbor everyday by trucks, driven by the Indian soldiers. There was a high tower for communications in the camp, so they could talk to the harbor and around the camp was barbed-wire, about three meters high. Outside the camp was the special prison for very, high-level Japanese officers, who were recognized as war criminals. They were not treated so well, and much of the time they were starving, so sometimes we felt we should give them our leftovers, since they had been our officers. We only got three-hundred grams of food a day, so sometimes we didn't have much ourselves. It was mainly rice and dried fish.

There was a market for local people and the French, and also the British bought a cow from the French at the market. The French killed and butchered the cow, and cut it up into very large pieces. We Japanese had to carry the heavy, bloody hunks of carcass, from the market to the storage warehouse. This was the other terrible time I had, because as I was carrying the cow, the beef, the blood was dripping and running down on my skin and clothes. It was a most terrible feeling and it made me feel so very dirty, unclean. (*It is very taboo in the Buddhist religion to deal with animal blood.*)

We did get to eat some of the beef, but I remember only a few times. The French and British got the good parts of the cow, and since they didn't like to eat the internal organs, liver etc., that is what we had to eat. There were about five hundred Japanese in the camp, and it would take thirty men everyday to carry the cow pieces, so I only had to do this dirty thing once. We usually had canned beef to eat, and we had a lot of canned fish, but it was three or four years old, so it usually wasn't any good.

When we carried the cow, the local people and the French could see us, and it made us even more ashamed to be hostages, and have to do such a dirty thing. So, that was the second of my terrible experiences - the first would always be surrendering my sword, and then this carrying the bloody cow. Japanese high-level officers were just supposed to watch the men do this work, but some of them felt sorry for us, and helped to carry it, also. Another bad thing about this was, when the cow was chopped up, sometimes a bone comes out of the meat, and it is very sharp. It can easily cut the skin, and quickly we would get infected in the cut. Since such a hot country, many men would get pus in these cuts, and it would give them a lot of problems.

Although these were bad experiences, the camp was not so bad. Every night they would do theatre plays, music like shamisen and people volunteered to help entertain each other. We organized a marathon for recreation, and some different exercises. Sometimes the local Vietnamese offered food, and we would exchange some of our things for it. We could swim in the river, and sometimes we had a good time. We finished all of our labor work the end of December. Then we were sent to an area south of Saigon that was like islands, kind of a resort area. It used to be called Saint Jacques, or San Jack, we called it. We took a boat from Saigon to there and we got to stay at the nice, French cottages, while we were waiting for a boat to take us back to Japan. It was very convenient, and easy for the British to take care of us, watch us.

We had nothing to do at the cottages and we were very relieved. But for some people, now all the tension was over, they got sick and many of them had to go to the hospital, because they didn't know how to relax. Almost every day, we had to take some soldiers to the doctor. There was a rumor also, which may have made some of them sick, that we were going to be sent to South America, the Amazon forest to work. It wasn't true, but because we had treated the British prisoners so badly, we thought they would do this to us, you know revenge. Because we believed there would be revenge, so that's why the rumor came up, but it wasn't true.

Everyday we had time to kill just fishing, and sometimes we went to some Vietnamese houses to exchange our personal things - watches, pens or so, for fruit. So we sat around waiting for five months from January to May before a ship could finally come to get us. We could catch oysters and lots of different fish. We were basically free, except the British really didn't want us to have contact with the local people, because they were afraid we would get diseases from them. Malaria and cholera was avery common, and other types of diseases from the water and things being dirty.

Since the Vietnamese were now so friendly with us Japanese, many of the soldiers ran away from the camps to be with them and become civilians. Some of them too, joined the Vietnam military. The Vietnamese women were so nice to Japanese men, so many of them ran away to be with them. The people who escaped from the camp, many of them were from the Hiroshima or Nagasaki areas and they knew, they had heard about their cities being bombed with the atom bombs. They felt the atomic bomb had destroyed their city, so they didn't want to go back to their own cities.

This Vietnam army was planning to fight against the French, and they wanted to have the help of us Japanese. On the other hand, the French asked the British to give them some of the Japanese prisoners to fight against the Vietnamese, and the British cooperated with them, but the Japanese refused. Since the British and the French worked together, when the French were shipping supplies from the harbor, the Vietnamese military would try to hijack these supplies, many times it was guns. The trucks were guarded by British and French, and many of them got killed protecting these weapons. So, after so many of them got killed, they ordered the Japanese military prisoners to guard the trucks with them. The Vietnamese Army needed these weapons for their independence, but after the Japanese were put on the trucks, they didn't try to hijack them, because they didn't want to hurt the Japanese. During the five months, maybe just two or three Japanese got killed.

Americans dropped a lot of bombs, so all of the railroads were destroyed, and first of all the French had to repair all the bridges and railroads. Again, the Vietnamese attacked the French workers, while they were repairing them, so again they made the Japanese soldiers do the repair. Many of the Japanese were better skilled workers, because they were the ones who had built the bridges and railroads. Each group of fifty Japanese had to send ten men, or one hundred men total, to repair these bridges and railroads everyday. So, not everyone had to work everyday. I had been in administration, and I didn't know how to do that kind of work. But it didn't matter, because they said the professionals would tell us what to do. I had never done real, manual labor work like that before. It was very difficult. Sometimes the higher-level Japanese officers would come to the work sites to cheer us up, but few of them actually worked.

An American ship came to pick us up, because there were no longer any large Japanese ships. Some of the group had to wait another three months, because there wasn't enough room. Those who had to stay longer, had to do more guard duty to protect the British and French from the Vietnamese. There were a few dozen who decided not to return to Japan at all, as they had married Vietnamese women, or had joined to fight with the Vietnamese. They needed higher-level Japanese soldiers, who could teach them how to fight the French. Many of them were offered a big promotion if they would join, or even a woman if they wanted one. The Vietnamese needed our knowledge of military things, so they were trying to offer everything they could to us to stay and help. But honestly, they didn't have very much, and most of us just wanted to go home.

Before we had turned in our guns to the British, the Vietnamese had also asked for our guns and bullets. Any man who would give them a gun and one hundred bullets, you would be made an officer right way. Because my section had hired a lot of local people, we could speak some of each other's language. They would come to our camp at night, and ask us to please help them get some guns. Many of these same workers later became officers in the Vietnamese Army, because they could speak some Japanese and recruited Japanese to help with their cause. Some of the Japanese changed their mind at the last minute, when they heard the ship was coming and then they came back to the camp. The senior Japanese officers beat them up, because they had left their fellows to do their work for them, and that is not the Japanese was. They did get to leave, but the officers told them they should be ashamed for not doing their part of helping.

Now everyone was busy and excited getting ready to go back. There was one officer I heard of, who married a local Vietnamese and he became rather famous. He joined the French Foreign Legion and then came back to Vietnam, when there were many Japanese trading companies coming to Vietnam to do business, he contacted them. After the Vietnamese Communist came into power, he and other Japanese there, were told to leave, go back to Japan. He finally escaped from Vietnam to Bangkok, Thailand with his wife and then to Osaka.

We left May 1, 1946, and we came into Hiroshima on May 17th. I was still in uniform and the Australian military was taking care of the port. When I got off the ship, they made us take all of the insignia off of our shirts and caps. I was very shocked to see Hiroshima, because it was just nothing, everything gone, just flat, empty. We were there for two days and it was so terrible, and I was very disappointed. From there I went home to Nagoya, and again it was almost like nothing at the center of Nagoya, where the train station used to be. It was all gone. My family was in like the suburbs, and when I got to my hometown station I was crying, because everything was OK. I was so happy to see everything just as I had left it, and everyone came to see me and they were so nice and accepted me. (*Many soldiers who had surrendered were rejected by their families*) I kept crying, I was so happy.

Then I went to work for Mitsubishi Heavy Industries - what used to be airplanes, but now we were making farm equipment. Also, I did repair for American military cars, and fixed other things for the American Occupation forces. The people from the American company, North American - or Northrop, came to my company to teach the people at my company how to make new airplanes. I got to go climb Mt. Fuji with some of those engineers, and I took them around to see Nagoya, even though I worked in the car manufacturers division.

Slowly things got better, but it was almost four years for my family before they had enough food. We could eat rice just once a day, and the rest of the time we had to eat sweet potatoes. Sometimes the Americans gave us powdered milk, and we were very appreciative. My family was just all salarymen, (*office workers on a monthly salary*) my father and brothers and me. Our salary was maybe five hundred yen a month. We all had some savings in the bank, but the government had frozen the money. We couldn't get it, so we had to live on just five hundred yen. We had to sell many things - my mother's kimono, jewelry, other things of value, to the farmers, so we could get rice and other things to eat.

After the Korean War started, the business started mushrooming and everyone started having a good life. I worked overtime everyday and weekends, too. I made jeeps and tanks for American fighters, and the machine guns on the airplanes. We made so many things for the American military. We were so busy, and it was so good for us Japanese. Of course, it was good for the Zaibatsu, and they were able to grow strong again. Before the Korean War, we couldn't make any of these military things, we had to make farm machinery, but then MacArthur said he wanted us to make the military things again for them. *Though we had only been making farming equipment, still we kept those military machines in good shape, polishing and oiling them, so they were ready right away to make the military goods again.* I worked very hard, because of Japan, and to help build it back up again. I did not work for the Americans, I worked for Japan.

I read this article by this Japanese soldier who was also in Vietnam. I want to tell you about it, because it is very important to me. He had refused to join the Vietnamese military, even though he was from Hiroshima. One day in May he was riding in a jeep (*in Vietnam*) and he saw an American plane coming down very low. He quickly took off his uniform and hid in the bushes, - he actually saw the smiling face of the American pilot. When he returned the jeep, his clothes were full of bullet holes. His mother had given him a good luck, sacred charm, and he believed it was the charm which saved his life. He wrote a letter to his mother, to let her know the charm had save his life, but after he got back to Hiroshima, his mother, his father and all of his family had died in the atomic bomb. He didn't know if his mother ever go this letter, but he believed his mother and father died instead of him.

These things are very important to know, because there should never be any more war. I am studying Vietnamese now, because I want to go back to Vietnam, so I can maybe see some of those people who were so kind to me.

Personal Story:

Japanese man stationed in Singapore, then Prisoner of War under the British in Southeast Asia. He was an administrator in Singapore during the war and one of the few who spoke English. He became a prisoner of war under the British for four months in Singapore, three in Thailand and four in India - where he learned to love Indian food very much. Since his English was so good, the British used him the most, also because of his own diligence and interest, his English greatly improved. When he speaks, there are certain nuances, and a slight British accent with certain terminology. He felt he owed a great deal to the British for his 'English Education,' as he referred to it, with no bitterness or remorse whatsoever. During the Occupation, he became the interpreter to the Governor General of Aichi Prefecture. When Queen Elizabeth had a short stopover in Nagoya, on her way to Ise Shrine with the Emperor, because of his government position, he had an opportunity to express to the Queen his 'appreciation' for his British-English training from the British troops.

My English is self-taught. I picked-up the art of conversation when I was captured and a prisoner of war by the British. In Singapore, I was liaison officer between Lord Mountbatton's HQ and Japanese HQ. Once I had an audience with him (*as a POW*), and then later on, I had the honor of meeting Queen Elizabeth in Nagoya (*as the Governor's interpreter*). My salary was very low, scratching at the bottom, however, I had an unexpected honor given to my duty. I used to work for a company that was in China and when it was lost, I was fired. I was discharged with 800 yen, so I had no job when I returned to Nagoya. I had no means to live on, so I took the examination to be qualified as an interpreter for the Occupation Forces, but the employee who gave me the test was an employee of the Prefectural government. He said, "We want good people like you, and you should have a good mind to work for the Prefectural government, instead of the Occupation Forces." So, I changed my mind. I would have to wait a week before going to work for the Occupation Forces and I had no money. Whereas, if I went to work for the Prefectural government, they would have me start working on that day. I was again, the Liaison Officer, now between the Occupation Forces and the Prefectural government - July of 1946.

I worked with many different departments. First, the city of Nagoya was placed under the military 1st Division, and I acted as a Liaison between the military government. They set-up an office on the third floor or the Prefectural building, and the Governor often met with the chief office of the military, and I very often was the interpreter. I was a local government employee, so I didn't have much influence in the industrial business area. Most of the large industries were bombed- out, and only some of the medium and small ones were still in existence. Like, the ceramics and such, in Seto City, and so forth.

The most important economy of Japan was to obtain the foreign currency, you see. In order to import the materials, they encouraged the ceramics of Seto to make the cheap, ceramic-wares to be exported to the U.S., which the Occupation Forces encouraged. The marking on them was "Made in Occupied Japan." They also tried to attract the foreigners to the scenic spots and historical sports of Japan.

Moreover, so far as my duties were concerned, they (*Occupational government*) wanted me to report all activities of every department of the Prefectural government including hygienic, engineering, the police and so forth, which I did. Along with these duties, I had to accompany them for the first time viewing of these buildings. I didn't have any large aspect of the picture. Though the Occupation had wanted them to stop all the military production, when the Korean War started, it was like *please*, start military production. They called it

"Official Purchases.' They made Toyota produce military vehicles, so they can save the expense of transportation from U.S. to Korean War.

Special contracts with Toyota, Nissan, Mitsubishi and so forth. So in reality, they had them producing a variety of things for the Korean War, this was, of course, against the new Constitution and Article 9 (*'no war involvement.'*) The Toyota factories were almost totally ruined during the war, so this was quite hectic, but a great opportunity for them to rebuild. They had made these same military vehicles for the war, but this time the American military was helping them with blueprints, metal and everything else.

A great boost to Japan, but still a very terrible situation, as I became acquainted with many military people, and nearly one third of them died (*in the Korean War*). The main hospital was there right next to the Prefectural building, and I actually saw them being carried in there. Of course, Komaki (*airfield*) was also the drop-point for all of the bodies before they were shipped back to America. I visited the hospital on sympathy-calls several times. The government was rebuilding everything very fast. The people were so depressed because of the war, and it was the mood of heavy feelings, yet the Korean War brought hope of change.

And everywhere, so many English conversation schools were popping up. Most of the American military had nothing to do, so many liked helping with teaching the English to me, and even at some of the schools. When I approached them and asked them to help, they were all happy to help at the school (*YMCA)*, where I also was doing some teaching. There were about 25 in the class, and sometimes I would have almost as many teachers (*the U.S. servicemen*) who came with me to teach.

There were many Japanese military men in Nagoya, and some military equipment still intact, if not excellent condition. Most only had needed fuel to be used in the war, but of course, gone. But as time progressed, after a few difficult years of Occupation, the Americans really had very little to do, and enjoyed their leisure time well. The Japanese were very peaceful, and were happy to have the Americans there, as they spread their money around well. Most of the soldiers were entertained with tourist-style tours, like cormorant fishing.

After the Occupation Troops left, though housing was till short, the government tore down whatever (*Western-style)* houses that were not old or moved to another location. They simply felt the houses weren't of the design and style most Japanese would want. They also used a lot more electric and fuel oil, and still the Japanese could not have been able to afford such luxuries at that time.

Fuel, particularly gasoline for cars, became such a premium on the black-market. Much of it came from the American soldiers themselves, selling it out of the U.S. supplies, so the MPs put a red dye in all the GI barrels. They would then do periodic checks of the cars and trucks to see if there was even a pink-tint to the gas. Just as quickly, the Japanese learned how to filter the dye out with charcoal, so the black-marketing of gas continued almost totally unabated.

Much of the land, where the buildings had been bombed and burned out, nothing was rebuilt because of the lack of money. These numerous patches of high weeds were more than an eyesore, as they were more reminders of Nagoya's massive destruction. The greatest success came from the rewards of the Korean War. There was still a rice-ration card into the early 1960s. Though rice could be bought on the open market then, it was cheaper when the ration card was used. A real big problem was controlling the Koreans, because they wouldn't pay attention to the Japanese police. Only the Americans could control them, because the Koreans had guns. They were quite active in the black-market and prostitution.

Those Koreans who didn't want to leave Japan, were allowed to stay, but many of those who did stay caused problems. It would have been better for Japan if the American military would have made them leave. Yet, it was understandable, as bad as things were in Japan, it was better than in Korea, especially once the War started. Japanese made the rule themselves that all guns for average citizen would be banned. Many of the veterans who were handicapped from the war, with loss of limbs or other disabilities, were often seen at the train stations, or other common, public areas begging for money, food, etc. The government did have a small relief program for them. The begging became rather lucrative in the later years, especially during the Korean War, and even into the late 1950s. So the numbers remained large, or even increased wth others not injured from the war also trying to collect money from a passerby. They wore old uniforms or grayish white ones, representing their having been in the hospital.

I was wounded four times, yet I never did this. It was a pretty good business, because the American military did feel sorry for them. The real returning soldiers, had many problems being accepted into the society, and most never talked about their experience, some even changed their name, if they had been well known. If I talked about my military experience, then, I would have been tagged as a militarist. Most Japanese didn't want to have anything to do with the veterans. Suicide was not uncommon for many reasons, though a percentage was probably those rejected military men. The Americans were much more understanding, so kind and generous. They never treated us like the British did to their POWs.

When I was a prisoner of them for the first three months, they were quite cruel. I don't like to say that, but it was true. Later on, when I began acting as the liaison-officer, they treated me much nicer. I guess because I was useful to them. They bore a great grudge against the Japanese, so much was revenge. I revisited Singapore some years after the war, the place where I had been stationed for five years. I came in a week or ten days after Japanese first invaded.

In Nagoya, (*the first years*) we were very busy with the tax reform, and the land reform SCAP brought in. I often went with the Americans to the schools, where they checked on what was being taught. We spent many months going around the several prefectures checking the soil, and testing it. I think it was to see how it was, and what fertilizers could be used. (*Japan at that time was still using 'night soil' or human excrement as their fertilizer. This was a common cause of disease, if the vegetables weren't thoroughly washed.*) I was often questioned by them about our culture, they were most curious with Shintoism.

For recreation, I often took them to Toba to watch the pearl divers, and much too often I took them to the cormorant fishing up in Inuyama. Once in a while, I would take them to the hot springs. One Colonel didn't know the custom of the Japanese bath, so pulled out the plug of bath when he was finished. He didn't know we all would be using the same hot water to soak in. It was very inconvenient, but I don't think anyone ever said anything to him. The officers' wives formed a kind of club, and the Japanese ladies who were good at speaking English attended to entertaining them. They sometimes demonstrated the different creative hobbies to them - flower arrangement, tea ceremony, etc.

When I was young, I was a regular attendant of the Bible class given by the Dr. Smyth, a great scholar. Mrs. Smyth held me in her favor, and even after going back to the U.S., she kept on writing me. She came back to Nagoya again later and taught at Kinjo College, English Literature. She invited me to her house several times. She donated much of her property to the church. I also knew the McAlpines, the third generation of missionaries. You see, m*y mother was one of the first three students taught by Mrs. Anne Randolph, who started Kinjo.* My mother, when she was 62 years old, when the old Mr. McAlpine was back in Nagoya, he came to see her. He was 93 years old, and he was very happy for the reunion.

My mother was the eighth daughter of a famous, but poor Samurai. They couldn't afford to give her any higher education, but old Mr. McAlpine approached her father and persuaded him to send her to the school. When they started out the school, no people came because the Japanese at that time didn't like the Christianity at all. I had the pleasure of knowing the famous musical family also, who came in the mid 1950s, who were also at Kinjo. The handbell concerts made Nagoya very famous.

Because I came to the Occupation almost one year after it started, I have no knowledge about whether or not there were any American POWS held in Nagoya. Only a few of the B-29s were shot down. My wife had many bad experiences with the bombing of Nagoya, because of the incendiary bombs and the fighter planes coming down low, and strafing them with bullets. Her home was burned, and she was injured several times. She was only twelve years old and saw the city completely laid to waste. In Singapore, it was only the B-17s that bombed us, no B-29s.

Until the Peace Treaty was complete, it was only the Americans, but after, they were called Security Forces and stayed in Moriyama, which is now used by the SDF (*Japanese Self Defense Forces*). I visited them (*the Americans*) once a month for the governor, and we had regular dinner parties, to which the officers were invited. It was important to keep friendly relations. Many Japanese still worked for them, on the base and in their homes.

The Nagoya mayor, though very polite to the Forces, would still jokingly say, "Please move out of here." But it was good they were here in 1959, when we had the Ise Bay Typhoon come into the area, and destroy many things. The American aircraft carrier *Kersage was on its way to Vietnam,* and it stopped to help with many helicopters rescuing people who were stuck on their roofs. They saved many people from being drown. Sixty percent of Nagoya area was inundated with the flooding at the time. Nagoya was very involved in a sense with the American forces in Vietnam, also. In the early period of the Vietnam War, Nagoya area built a lot of the guns and military equipment. Toyota produced many different kinds of vehicles, and there were some joint projects too, *where the Americans shared much information with us to make these things, especially technical ones.*

Side Notes:

(1)   The British General Gracey could not imagine turning Vietnam over to a bunch of *upstart-natives*, who might even be Communist. If the Potsdam Conference had recognized Ho Chi Minh and his newly- formed government, Ho would not have needed to turn to the Chinese communists for help. Ho had been educated in Western schools, and a great believer in equal rights. But, he turned to Marxism because the Democratic governments he had seen, did not practice what the preached. Still, until the day he died, the man he admired, and who had influenced him the most, was Abraham Lincoln.

There were about three thousand Japanese soldiers in Vietnam at the end of World War II, and those who were in the middle of the country - Danang and Hue, or in the North - Hanoi, did not have as much choice as to what they could do. Where the French were in charge, the Japanese were forced to fright for them. The Communists also kidnapped Japanese and made them fight for their side. So, the Japanese soldiers sometimes ended-up fighting each other, when it wasn't even their battle anymore. Finally, when the Communist beat the French at Dien Bien Phu in 1954, the Japanese were allowed leave, as did the French. Some of thee Japanese military had been in Vietnam since the beginning in 1940, or fourteen years.

Many of those Japanese had married Vietnamese women, had children, and even taken Vietnamese names. This did to matter to the Communists, as all Japanese were forced to leave immediately, and by themselves. Finally, after 1975, when the Vietnam War was over, the Japanese were able to return to search for their families, few succeeded since the war had scattered and killed so many. Most of these Japanese had married again, or had returned to wives and families in Japan. Still, when they were able to find their Vietnamese families, they supported them, and even brought them back to Japan to visit or live with their families there. They started an organization to help the Vietnamese, built a school, and set up a scholarship program. It is perhaps the happiest story from all of the Japanese Occupations.

(2)   Authorized by the Shogunate, Japanese vermillion-seal trading ships, called at a port in Holan (Vietnam) during the late 16th century, and the Japanese community of *Nihonmachi* was established. The 450 wooden houses (circa 18th c.) remaining are considered to be one of the world's outstanding collections, and designated a National Historic City by the Vietnamese government in 1984.

(3)   Japan paid reparations included $100 in 1956 to 1.2 million Dutch, affected by the Japanese Occupation of their colony. As many as 300 Dutch women were forced into brothels under the guise of working in restaurants or shops. A total of $3.9 billion was paid to the Philippines, Vietnam, Burma, and Indonesia. But sadly, the un- repenting Japanese government never officially paid China or Korea one yen in reparations, or even gave any official recognition of their crimes and atrocities in those countries.

Part I / II Japanese As the Occupied – Segue Chapter 4 The Nisei - Caught In- Between

When children of other immigrants spoke of ancestry, they would proudly say, "I'm Irish," "I'm Italian," "I'm English," the Nisei would say, "I am an American." They wanted their rights as an American clearly understood, since their 'Japanese' parents had few.

Bill Hosokawa,
NISEI, The Quiet Americans

Quite difficult for most democratic people, but particularly Americans, to believe or even understand what was done to the Nisei, who were born and raised as American citizens. They were victims of occupation just as the Koreans, Manchurians, or the Japanese under the Allied Occupation. They also were put behind barbed wire fences, with machine guns pointing their way for every restricted and controlled movement. The following history may give insight to what the term 'clash of cultures' can mean, especially when it is within the same racial heritage. 'White' Americans are only now looking at what they did in the not so distant past to various American minority groups. Time and again, individuals in those groups have risen above the racial prejudice, and still ultimately had faith in America. A country which they proved they loved more dearly than life itself, and for the freedom which was once denied to them.

Historical Background:

The first Japanese colonists, Issei, came to California in 1869, trying to establish a tea and silk farm colony, but many physical and weather problems abounded, precluding any long term success. Not until the 1890s did any significant number, over a thousand, begin to immigrate. Prior to this, some Japanese sailors had been kidnapped, off the streets of Yokohama and Tokyo, to work in the Hawaiian sugar and pineapple fields, but the majority who came on their own were farmers from the Southern Honshu and Kyushu areas. Another large group also went into the Seattle area, and these young males were looking for work, or going to school to learn English. Through arranged marriages by their families and picture-bride services, soon the first *Nisei,* or second generation came into existence and by law, had U.S. citizenship.

If the Japanese had thought it difficult keeping their culture intact before, via their small clustered groups and neighborhoods, it was nothing compared to what they now faced. Their children were involved in public schools with other children of mixed races and nationalities. A considerable number of Japanese had become involved with Christian religions, originally because they had often offered free English lessons, as well as assistance with housing, food and jobs. Their tightly-knit social order, which had reigned so totally in Japan, was having its values, customs, and culture disintegrated almost before their eyes. Added to these problems, were the racial prejudice and legal limitations put upon the parents.

By 1930, there were 138,836 Japanese in the U.S., mainly on the West Coast, representing just a fraction more than 0.1% of the total population. Less than half - 68,357 - were American born. Now firmly into the twentieth century, these Nisei, like any other young Americans, were trying to find their way, understand their identity, and fit into the modern culture surrounding them. Like most second generations, they wanted to be more like their friends, than their parents. But their search for who they were, and what their place was in the country of their birth, was not a simple or welcome journey. First of all, they knew they did not physically look like children of other immigrants from Europe. In addition, as they looked inward, they had to acknowledge most were painfully shy. This may have been the result of youth, the influence of their culture not to speak-out to strangers, the effect of the times in which they lived ladened with prejudiced, or perhaps a combination of other factors.

They were inclined not to speak-up - in class, in social gatherings, or even in their meetings when others were discussing their own shortcomings. The bulk of the Nisei sat in despair quietly, as their own discussion leaders simply sat on their hands, and were not outgoing. Most were inclined to be clannish, and some outsiders said they were too earnest and serious. They did not know how to relax and have fun, it was as if they had been born old! Others said they were overly self-centered; they lacked aggressiveness, and their interests were too narrow. On top of that, most suffered from an inferiority complex, yet did well in school. A few even demanded the Nisei break-out from the influence and protection of their communities, or tear away from the domination of their parents, to make their own way in the 'white' community.

While many of these criticisms had a certain basis of fact, their individual short-comings were really no greater than those to be found in any group of adolescents and young adults. Their doubts and their persistent self-analysis were largely a reflection of the pressures to which they were subjected - 'be American' / 'be Japanese.' The fact they lived under unusual cultural, social, and economic pressures was undeniable. Their Japanese cultural heritage demanded respect of elders, filial piety even to the point of sacrificing one's personal desires and ambition. As well, unquestioning respect of authority, a deep sensitivity to the opinions of one's peers, and a sense of group, rather than individual responsibility or choice.

Yet, in public school, the Nisei were taught to question and challenge, encouraged to make their own decisions, be aggressive and to assert their individuality. To make matters even more confusing, their parents, how one was taught at home to honor, respect and obey, in turn urged the Nisei to honor, respect, and obey the teachers who, unconsciously and unintentionally, were indoctrinating youngsters with a conflicting philosophy. Their only 'public' statement may have been their academic excellence, which in essence satisfied both group of family and school.

Many were sent on subsequent visits to Japan, sometimes even a period of employment in Tokyo with the Society of International Cultural Relations. Unfortunately, they found most of the mediocre educators and leaders in Japan looked down upon the Nisei. Mostly because of their American ways, their ignorance of the Japanese language or its proper use, and because they were the offspring of socially-inferior peasant-emigrants. Thus, the Nisei were stymied in their native America, and scorned in ancestral Japan.

Somewhat more acrimonious were the Issei-Nisei arguments over Japanese foreign policy. The 1930s, as previously mentioned, were the years of fascist-aggression in Japan which led it to World War

II. Japan was slipping out of the hands of it civilian leaders, the civilian premier was assassinated, and within a year the Japanese Kwangtung Army had seized Manchuria. A few months after the January, 1932 attack on Shanghai, another Premier was slain by military reactionaries, marking the effective end of party-government. The Issei read about these developments in dispatches from Tokyo in the Japanese language press, which was often in contradiction to what was published in American newspapers, the Nisei read. The reports of inspiring-Japanese military victories over 'Chinese bandits,' violating Japanese troops sweeping over the Chinese mainland, defeating the 'corrupt, pillaging mercenaries' of Chiang Kai-shek, made heady reading for the Issei.

A powerful Japan was a source of pride, and in their experience had shown an aggressive Japan meant great security for the Issei. Japan's military victories were triumphs they could identify with, since their lives in their adopted-country were marked by many defeats and frustrations. They could not understand why there was so much American hostility toward Japan, or why China was winning so much sympathy, or why there was growing boycotts against Japanese goods, and an embargo against shipment of steel and oil to Japan?

But most of all, when the Nisei took the popular American stand against Japanese aggression at dinner table discussions, many Issei complained bitterly. They felt their sons and daughters were being misled by the biased and inaccurate accounts inspired by Chinese propagandists, and published in the American press. Yet, while arguments raged at home, few Nisei spoke out in public again Japanese militarism, when they themselves were Japanese. Perhaps, they felt the need for a united community front against an unsympathetic world. Or, perhaps they did not want to seem to be defying their parents in public. Or more so perhaps, they failed to understand the significance of their failure to take a position.

These Japanese communities were sometimes extremely static, made up of some people who had changed very little from the time they left Japan. This may have been from choice, because of their lack of English, or more often it was the racial prejudice and discrimination. This had pushed them back into their segregated communities, where they fed and supported each other, socially and mentally. Though the Japan they had known had changed considerably, in their memories it would always be the idyll, they had been forced to leave behind, usually for economic reasons. In reality most, if not all, would have not been able to, or even have wanted to, fit back into the contemporary Japan. These Isseis had actually become anachronistic-beings, not really comfortable in either the country of birth or residency.

The Issei had tried to carry on the time honored practice of *enryo,* reserved, restraint, deference or diffidence, meek and mild action or behavior. It had both a positive and negative effect on Japanese acculturation. One could observe it in situations, as diverse as their hesitancy to speak out at meetings; their polite refusals: of any invitation, especially the first time being asked; of a second offering or helping of food outside the home; to ask questions, even when confused or expected to do so; or their acceptance of a less desired object, when given a free choice; their lack of verbal participation, especially in an integrated group; and their hesitancy in asking for a raise in salary. These were all stemmed from *enryo*, the stoic, revered cultural base.

The inscrutable face, the ambiguity of a noncommittal answer, the behavior reserve can often be traced to this norm, so the stereotype of the shy, reserved Japanese in social situations was often an accurate one. It helped the Japanese 'look' good in Caucasian-eyes, because of their lack of aggression and high conformity, knowing 'their place.' But for the Nisei, the cost of the goodness and humbleness was quite high. A full development of an individual's potentials would surely be hindered under such a norm, and most Nisei were trying desperately to break-away from some of these embedded cultural traits.

This cloistered-insularity resulted in not only out-of-date memories, but fostered no new ideas to emerge. To the Issei, their essence of being, was only the cold business of making a living, and raising the family, within the ingrown-confines of fellow countrymen with like-beliefs. These people had borne together the affronts and injustices of America stoically, as by law, they had not been allowed to become naturalized citizens because of the Oriental Exclusion Ace of 1924. Yet, these same Japanese vowed for their Nisei children, it would be different because they were native-citizens and this gave a positive meaning to their lackluster-life.

Unfortunately, most of this dream was not to be for the Nisei either. They were too restricted from choosing a place of residence, and in California were not allowed inter-racial marriages. The state also locked them out of many of the jobs, they had been educated so well to do, strictly because of race. In many instances they were not much better off than their Issei parents. For many Nisei, this did create a basic resentment for all things American, or in other words, 'white' was the privileged race. Yet, for many it manifested the opposite, making them want to be the ultimate American, no matter what their physical appearance was. They wanted to fully use everyone of those rights their parents had been denied.

Into this long stance of discovering who they were, came the badly timed and unprepared for - at least mentally by the Japanese- Americans - Wold War II. Shortly after the German armies had invaded Russia, along a two-thousand mile front in late June, 1941, the French-Vichy government acceded to Japan's demand for military control of all French-IndoChina. Alarmed by an escalation in Japanese aggression on the Asian mainland, the U.S. on July 26th, abrogated its treaty of friendship and commerce with Japan. Then freezing all Japanese credits in the U.S., and halting all shipping between the two countries. For many Issei businessmen, doing commercial import-export, their income and assets came to a screeching halt, and closed- government-ears would not accept their complaints or pleads.

The news of Pearl Harbor, for most Nisei, ran the gamut of shock, bewilderment, anger, shame and sorrow. Their's was deep anguish and despair, because the land they had been taught to honor by their parents, had committed an act of war against the country they loved. Within twenty-four hours the FBI had picked-up and detained almost one thousand Issei and Nisei. Some were held ten days or more, without explanation or reason, other than their being Japanese. Those Nisei of age, were listed 4-C, not subject to military service.

As the Nisei had pledged support for the U.S. through JACL - Japanese American Citizens League - many governors of Western states had given reassurance and understanding of their beliefs and loyalty. Weeks later when their evacuation was invoked, only the governor of Colorado, Ralph Carr, stood by to defend the rights of the Nisei and welcomed them to Colorado.

Germany had Hitler and Italy had Mussolini, as both figures had been prominent on the movie newsreels, and were easy to hate and caricature. But there were no handy targets in Japan for patriotic-ire, as General Tojo and Emperor Hirohito were unknown, or also virtually unrecognizable to the American public. Old stereotypes were dusted off, and the Japanese enemy was pictured as buck-toothed and bespectacled, with the hiding or sneaking portrayal added because of Pearl Harbor. The racial-canard was quickly applied to the Issei and Nisei, though they were not the enemy, and had nothing to do with Pearl Harbor.

Just like the basic American prejudice against the 'Negroes' of the time, the physical characteristics of the Japanese made it simple to segregate them. All became '*Japs,*' no matter how many generations they had been in America. Admittedly, there was some basic resentment toward Japan for the humiliation, as the U.S. military had been caught napping at Pearl Harbor. It was certainly easy to point the finger of righteous-anger at the Japanese treachery, in an effort to lighten the weight of the government's own culpability.

Could white people really believe they were helping to win the war by throwing a brick through the window of a Japanese grocery store? Or, by firing a shot from a speeding car into the home of a Japanese farmer? Their mentality was little different from the *'sheeted and hooded,'* ignorant KKK night-riders in the South, allowed to torment and kill the 'Negroes.' The true dichotomy came though, when Californians wanted to *make sure* the Army would work the Japanese truck-farms, once the Japanese owners had been put in the concentration camps. Because, of course, they did not want their supply of food cut, from the Los Angeles markets.

JACL continued to demonstrate, especially the Nisei's loyalty, with telegrams and other public statements. But the Japanese community had been too-segregated for too-long, accepting the prejudice and discrimination put upon it. Many excuses were made by the government, as it was too vastly overwhelming, to separate the dangerous-sympathizers from the loyal Americans. The Japanese, as a group, did not speak-out strongly about their rights, as they were swept along with the rising clamor for evacuation. Even staged, publicity-showing Nisei donating to various war funds and loyalty pledges did not help, as they were only temporary measures to slow down their unwarranted exodus.

In one fell-swoop, the Treasury Department effectively put all Issei and Nisei out of business, as bank accounts and assets were frozen. Individuals could not even get money to buy food. The general public went into a frenzy, after one or another false report of sabotage, or collaboration was reported. Even when cleared by the Attorney General of any wrong doing, it was more exciting to talk about the 'might-have-beens.' Issei and Nisei were fired from jobs, where they had no prior problems. For others, business licenses were cancelled and even some hospitals refused them service. As if overnight, they became persona-non-grata.

As the Japanese military began to mark-up some pretty spectacular successes, scattered thousands of miles across the Pacific, the fear of them invading the West Coast created suspicion toward the American Issei and Nisei. Though there were more Italian-born aliens (51,923) and

German-born aliens (17,528) than Japanese-born aliens (8,726) in California, the idea of placing *these enemy-nation aliens* in internment camps was ignored. It was simpler to recognize, thus concentrate on the Japanese alone. Bigotry was fed by the *white-racist groups*, like the Native Sons of the West, who influenced Lt. Gen. John DeWitt to make the decision, and stand by it years later. So, he put all Japanese Issei and Nisei, born in America and Citizens - in camps.

Few people or groups stood-up to speak-out against the idea of putting the Japanese far away in camps, but the most active were the Quakers. Others supported the idea of mass-internment of aliens, and their citizen-children as a *humanitarian-thing*, so it would not separate or break up the families. Truly, it was believed, only the disloyal people would oppose evacuation for their country's safety.

President Roosevelt never made a personal decision or commitment, as to the Japanese being interned, but left the handling of it to his Secretary of War, Henry Stimson. Though it was a military order, it was as much a civilian request by the politicians, racist groups and businesses which influenced Stimson to make the order. This was the same man who turned away ship-loads of Jewish refugees escaping from Europe. So, he did not hesitate to evacuate and intern, over 110,000 people of Japanese-origin from the West Coast.

The Supreme Court approved it as a 'legitimate exercise of the war powers of the President.' - Executive Order 9066 - February 19, 1942. Most military and political leaders *expected* the Japanese to be disloyal, because of the discriminatory way they had been treated by America. So, it was this curiously, distorted-logic which influenced their belief. There was absolutely no justification, yet it was necessary to relocate and evacuate the Japanese, though no acts of sabotage had occurred since Pearl Harbor.

It later became obvious, money had been as great a motive as prejudice, regarding the internment. Numerous groups, who had voiced their opinions, especially the Native Sons of the West, would profit by eliminating the competition of the Japanese farmers and shopkeepers. Those who had justified this action, were saying it was for *the Japanese's own protection,* and cited *they would be massacred.* They never bothered to check, as only severn Japanese had been killed, and only twenty-nine cases of vigilante-violence had occurred. And most of that, the first month after Pearl Harbor. These were not the kind of numbers necessary to 'proactively-evacuate' 110,000 people. But, if it was for their own protection, then why were *all the guns pointing at them, and not at the public,* who supposedly wanted to hurt them?

In most cases, a six-day notice was given to the Japanese evacuees, which meant tremendous personal loss, as profiteers descended upon them purchasing household goods for a fraction of their value. Any lack of cooperation in the evacuation, which was called a military order, would be an act of disloyalty and treated as thus, with necessary violence control, fine or imprisonment. None happened, except one strawberry-farmer plowed under his crop when the government refused to give him two extra days to pick them. *He was then fined for destroying government property,* as they had seized it. But the government had not made reparations either.

Temporary shelter for thousands of Japanese were the fairgrounds and race tracks - horses were moved out and one Japanese family was moved into each stall, with the manure barely cleaned-out. They were under armed-guard at all times, though there was never a violent or resistant act perpetuated. They had always been law-abiding residents and citizens, productive, and proud of their communities. Now, they were inmates of cramped, crowded American-style concentration camps. They were treated like prisoners, while being deprived of privacy, dignity and their rights. Years later, it would be compared by many, to what had happened half-way around the world in Europe to the Jews and others, with only a different ending.

Yet, these evacuees pitched in at their temporary centers and later at the permanent camps. They made life for themselves as livable and serviceable as possible, since the military had no experience in handling families under such dire conditions. Without the Japanese support and cooperation, it would have been pure chaos, as there had been no real plan as to what to do with them, once they had been moved out. In spite of any resentment, the evacuees realized they had to organize, or simply do without.

Evacuees were also called upon to help maintain and perform the daily work at their permanent camps, and be available for temporary outside agricultural work. Suddenly, those who had rejected them, saw a use and need for able-bodied workers doing cheap labor, as the war drew off their other men. Once the camps were turned over to the new government agency - WRA - War Relocation Authority - necessities like school, medical treatment, religious services, and other human problems, the Army had not concerned itself with, were put into effect. A program of employment and college education, with resettlement in the Eastern part of the country, also began. A curious side-note, the government had hired anthropologists to work in the camps, as if the Japanese-Americans were so exotic, they needed specialists to handle them.

Many employers were willing to accept the Japanese, since they were so highly qualified, but their co-workers and the unions rejected them. Some of the worst reactions came from other minority groups, because the Japanese *were* better educated and more willing to do any job for any amount of money. Their eagerness to work overtime, even when not asked to, and do extra little things, constantly caused friction with the other established employees, who had built up a status quo of implicit job duties.

On the other hand, some Japanese had been badly influenced against other minorities, especially the Jews and the Blacks - as both lacking greatly in numbers on the West Coast at the time. They would often refuse to work for them, though they had been offered excellent jobs with good pay. Many times some Japanese would refuse to work with other taboo-Japanese, or to share accommodations. These prejudices existed from the old Japan, especially against the '*Burakumin*' - village people. They were the pariah or untouchables, because traditionally they had been the tanners, animal killers, shoemakers, etc., as Buddhism forbade the touching or dealing with blood and animal flesh.

The Project Director of each of the ten centers had a staff of Caucasians, and also evacuees as aides, working side by side. Many times these 'aides' were just as good, or even better qualified, as many were professionals and university graduates, but they could not be paid more than nineteen dollars per month. Though it was a caste system of sorts, friendships and trusts were built between them, which in some ways made up for their previous treatment back home on the Coast. Surrounding them all was the barbed wire and armed soldiers.

By the time the last of the evacuees had been settled into their camps, it was November, 1942, and the tide had turned in the Pacific to America, with the Battle of the Coral Sea and Midway. In reality, the setup of this fiasco of military security and sabotage prevention, cost the taxpayers $88 million-plus in 1944 dollars, and then could no longer be called a military necessity. Interestingly, the rash of racism against the Japanese was maintained by many groups, organizations and media, citing their peace and safety. Particularly in California, those who had taken over Japanese businesses and land, did not want to see them returned. Of course, with any government project, even when it is realized to be unnecessary or a mistake, it can not be stopped, as then the waste of money would have to be justified.

The Nisei knew the only way they could convince other Americans in general they were loyal, was to fight and bravely die in the war defending the American freedom, which had been denied them in peace. Finally, the War Department accepted their proposal in January, 1943, and the 442 Regimental Combat Team was organized to fight in Europe. Like the black soldiers and fighter pilots, they had to die to prove their ability and loyalty.

One might say luckier Nisei, those with a fluency in Japanese, were recruited for Japanese language school. Only one in ten Nisei, understood any useful amount of his ancestral tongue to be trained in the use of it. The U.S. Army and Navy both had Japanese language schools, and though the Army had a tradition of less discrimination than the Navy, the Nisei interpreters had an enlisted status, regardless of education, while the Caucasians had an officer status. The Army language school was in Ann Arbor, Michigan, and the Navy was at Berkeley, California, but had to move to the University of Colorado in 1942. The Navy did not accept Nisei in the service, *but* they used them as instructors.

Being the *Sensei*, instructor, to so many Caucasians gave many Nisei the feeling of superiority they had never received before in the U.S. In Michigan, the Army had more than fifty Japanese-Americas as faculty members. Prior to military language training, perhaps less than a hundred non-Japanese could speak the language to any degree of usefulness. Always, of course, necessary to learn the language of the enemy. Codes had to be broken, signals analyzed, propaganda countered, military operations diagnosed, economic and political trends monitored. And eventually, with supreme American confidence, prisoners would have to be handled, troops called upon to surrender, and negotiations conducted for the surrender.

All Nisei loyalty was regarded as doubtful because of Pearl Harbor, so many non-Japanese were trained to detect if any Nisei were misinterpreting or deceiving them. The Navy, Army, military intelligence, signal corps, civil affairs and miscellaneous government agencies trained almost fifteen thousand people to speak Japanese, of this, over six thousand were Nisei.

Ironically, while the Americans were learning Japanese, in Japan they were trying to abolish all existence and usage of English, in their purge to purify the Japanese language. This was not easy, for since the Meiji Restoration in the 1880s, thousands of English words had been put into use in science, medicine, technology and modern living. The Japanese military had a false-sense of security in their beliefs no Americans, not even Nisei, could fathom the complexities of their language, so they were extremely lax about its use.

One set after another of war plans fell into American hands, and the Nisei quickly translated them, often helping to turn the tide of battle. These Nisei were also on the front of every battle of the island- hopping campaigns, up until the surrender ceremonies in Tokyo Bay. In the flush of victory, their valiant accomplishments went unheralded, as their audacious efforts unfortunately, were never revealed back in the U.S. Because of the secret-nature of their work and, of course, not wanting the Japanese military to know the U.S. had an upper hand, few knew of their contributions. Perhaps, if Americans had known, their prejudices would not have been so easily fanned against the Nisei. In the end, seven Niseis did receive officer's commission, yet few who risked their lives received any recognition or medals, even after the war.

For many Nisei who were *Kibei,* - had schooling in Japan - there was a strong chance of running into school friends, or distant relatives on the battle fields. Some even had brothers who had been caught in Japan when the war broke out, and had not been able to return to the U.S. The translation/interpreter job was not finished for the Nisei, with the end of the war. For unlike Nisei combat troops, they had to continue into the Occupation aftermath, and its difficulties.

The Nisei combat forces - 442nd, 522nd, and the 232nd - were made-up of both previous Japanese military members from the 100th, who had been put on standby, and new volunteers from the internment camps. Their motto was 'Go for Broke,' and their valor as crack troops in Italy and France was legendary, as more than eighteen thousand individual decorations were won - *more than any other Regiment/ Battalion*. They knew they were fighting prejudice along with the enemy, and thirty-three thousand Nisei proudly served in World War

II. The 442nd and 522nd were among the liberators of Dachau concentration camp, near Munich, in 1945. The Jewish people freed from the camp, found it hard to accept the diminutive-Asian men as

U.S. soldiers at first, and the veterans themselves adopted the name of 'Unlikely Liberators.'

Years later, photographs of the liberation were put in a juxtaposition with ones showing the same Niseis, visiting their parents and families behind the barbed wire of the U.S. detention camps. In 1943, long before his eminent fame, Ansel Adams was requested by Manzanar (in the Eastern Sierra) camp Director Ralph Merritt, to photograph the people and harsh circumstances. Both men were criticized for doing so, but Adams published his photo-book in 1944 - *Born Free and Equal*. A full, story-book called *Manzanar,* with photos was published in 1988, and was one of a few done. Obviously, the government did not want any of the details of the internment camps to be photographed, or stories published.

Finally, on December 18, 1944, the Supreme Court ruled the indiscriminate evacuation of all Japanese - Issei and Nisei had been unconstitutional, as 'guilt of endangerment to the country,' as well as their loyalty had never been investigated. If life's foibles are looked at with the belief 'something good always comes out of something bad,' then of the internment camps, it can also be said. By the time they were ordered closed by the Supreme Court, almost half of the internees had been dispersed out through the job-relocation program, to a university, or to the Army. This brought them freedom in more ways than one.

Separated from the protective environment of the clustered- Japanese cultural-community, they began to blossom with their new found independence, as they spread out to many new states. They could assimilate into various communities more than ever before, and put their scarred-past behind them. Much like what happened with Japan itself, through the extensive American Occupation. Eventually, the younger generations learned to let go of the restrictive, cultural- bind and to be more open, or at least not so xenophobic of all who were not Japanese.

For those who had not relocated, particularly the older Isseis, they had little else but to return to what they thought they had left behind on the West Coast. Accustomed to a previous life of hard work and long hours, for many the internment camps had almost been an escape. Yet, one which gave them much trepidation on what they might expect when they returned home. In some ways, the war had only made things worse - acts of violence, farm property deserted by the tenants, and businesses ruined. Even their old ghettos had been taken over by new minority peoples, with plights of their own. Much of their stored goods had been ransacked, pirated, or confiscated by the military. Along with this, suppliers and municipal offices made it difficult for them to do business again. But, it was not all bad, as many found the open-arms of friends and old neighbors waiting to help them launch a new life.

Once all of the WRA centers were closed, the total tab to the taxpayers came to almost $250 million (1944 $). On the other hand, the Federal Reserve Bank estimated the Japanese evacuees lost over $400 million, and this amount only on the things they could measure. But the Nisei had changed, for they had learned to fight for their rights in WRA, and now they fought for them in the courts. It took years, but the last of the legal entrapments of discrimination and racial prejudice were set aside, and the Issei were allowed to become naturalized- citizens in 1952.

Several other issues to be noted: The hundred thousand residents and citizens of Japanese descent in Hawaii were left alone, as they were both needed for the military effort, and the materials needed to build internment camps just were not available for them. More than anything, their military governor, Lt. General Emmons, defended and spoke up for them, while making it difficult for the 'military' to move them out of their homes. Eventually, less than two thousand Hawaiian-Japanese were shipped to the mainland for internment, and these were a combination of those 'potentially dangerous,' or not of an asset to the economy.

With hindsight, particularly with the highly decorated Nisei soldiers, apologies - from the President on down, were finally extended by all previous accusers of their disloyalty. The distinct, *sole exception was Earl Warren*, who had been a very, vocal Attorney General of California, and later a still, anti-Japanese governor. Although, he perhaps redeemed himself before becoming Supreme Court Justice, by appointing the first Nisei judge on the mainland. Some historians later believed, as Chief Justice, Warren's monumental decision of reversing, 'Separate, but Equal' was *influenced by his silent-guilt* about the internment of the Japanese.

Interesting Side Notes:

(1)   Following the extensive bombing of Japan, started in early 1945, the Japanese sent aloft six-thousand, unmanned 'balloon- bombers.' Each balloon carried five incendiaries and one anti- personnel bomb. On May 5, 1945, one such balloon killed a minister's pregnant wife and five children on a church outing at Bly, Oregon. Some federal officials hoped it would remain a military secret,

but it did not.

(2)   The only time the Rose Bowl was played outside of Pasadena, California, was in January, 1942 - for fear of Japanese bombing. It was played in Durham, North Carolina.

(3)   Chiune Sugihara, at the Japanese Consulate in Lithuania, in 1940, saved the lives of an estimated eight-thousand Jewish refugees by issuing them transit-visas through Japan. This was done under great duress, and against explicit instructions from Tokyo, over a period of about three weeks, working almost twenty-four hours a day with the help of his wife. He was still writing visas and passing them through the train window, on the day he was forced to leave the country. Upon his return to Japan, Sugihara was dismissed from his position, his pension revoked, and lived in disgrace, yet said he never regretted it. He was then honored by Lithuania and Israel in the early 1990s. Typically, *Japan made no comment.*

(4)   Approximately two-thirds of the Nisei soldiers came from Hawaii, and most were straight off the sugar plantations with Caucasian owners. They spoke pidgin-English, having seldom left the farm confines, and were considered by those from the internment camps to be crude and rude in their actions. They had no realization of the oppressive situation, the others had lived under in the internment camps, *until their commanding officer had them visit one* in Arkansas. This shocking experience, built them all into the cohesive, fighting-group whose valor distinguished itself later.

Personal History: Japanese male Nisei interned in a camp.

I'm a true Nisei, my parents immigrated from Wakayama, Japan and I was born and grew up on the west Coast. The term Nisei, just technically means second generation, but socially it really means a person who grew up in a particular period of history - 1920s & 30s. So, that's when we're talking about most Niseis. A specific group of people, who are pretty old these days, and the ones who suffered during the war, got put into the camps, etc. So, I grew up in Seattle and went through the public school system in Seattle, up to the war. I had never been to Japan, until after the war.

I was born in 1928, and I have a brother who was a *Kibe*, a Nisei who was born in America, but educated in Japan. Kibes themselves have different kinds of histories, because they were sent back for a whole variety of reasons. Some were sent back because parents wanted them to be educated in Japan and some like my brother, who's really my half-brother. My father's wife died, and he sent their two children back to Japan to be raised by my grandparents. My older half-sister lives in Okayama, Japan, was also born in America, but she's only visited lately. I have another older sister, who is a Nisei like me.

So, for the beginning part of life, it was just my sister and I, until my brother came and joined us a little latter. I went to Japanese school and participated in a lot of the events in the Japanese community before the war, and it was a very tight community. I went to a grade school, and I guess you'd call it a ghetto-school, because there were six hundred kids, of which five hundred were Japanese. So you could say I grew up in a very ethnic community. As a matter of fact, I think I had one white friend who I grew up with. He was an oddity, a minority in our area, as most of us were either Niseis or Chinese, there were some Filipinos and a few Blacks.

My family spoke Japanese, and I started speaking Japanese first when I was a kid, and that's what gets me into trouble now as an adult (in Japan), since most of the Japanese I do remember are very, childhood expressions, and when they come out, people laugh at me in Japan, you know. Once I started grade school, then I started speaking English, to this day I've had students here (in Japan) ask me how did you communicate with your parents? Because my mother didn't speak a word of English, and my father spoke very poor English. He was a gardener, and he had to have some English to deal with the customers. But my mother didn't speak any English at all. Somehow all those years, then it dawned on me, I never spoke sentences with her, I knew certain words and I used those, - 'eat, where are you going, out to play, etc.' I just used words, never complete sentences, that's the way we communicated. (laugh)

They didn't push us, but all of us, had to go to Japanese school. I remember one of the nicest things about what happened after the war started, they closed down the Japanese school, and we didn't have to go any more. It was a real problem with a lot of young Niseis in high school, because they had to go to high school, and then go to the Japanese school. They ran into all kinds of conflicts - football games, dances, and that sort of thing. A lot of the Niseis were starting to rebel on the eve of WW II, all my friends and me, too, played a lot of hooky from Japanese school.

I remember, the first thing with the war experience came just about a year before, you could see the hostilities, the tension between the U.S. and Japan, even at my age you could sense it. For example, there was talk about the last boat to Japan leaving on a certain date, there was all kinds of things about embargoes, I could sense there was something. I kept asking my parents, "Hey, something's wrong here. Are we going to go to war or something?" My father says, "Don't worry, Don't worry. Japan and United States are good friends … nothing is going to happen."

I remember the summer evening of 1941, somehow it's vivid, a bunch of us sitting in the park one day and we talked about this. "What's going to happen if a war broke out between Japan and the United States?" Some of the guys said, "Well, our parents are Japanese citizens, so they're going to be treated like aliens, so they're probably going to be put away." Then somebody else said, "What about us?" "What?!? We're Americans?" But one guy said, "I don't think that war's going to happen, but I think they're going to herd all of us to somewhere." HE was right, that's exactly what happened. I will always remember how we were just sitting around that warm, pleasant summer evening. Then of course, that December 7th, war broke out.

I'll always remember, because we went to a movie. We had been sitting around, there was a gang of us, and we wanted something to do that afternoon and somebody says, "Hey there's some news on the radio that there's an attack at Pearl Harbor in Hawaii!' You know it's funny, I really didn't worry or get shocked, I just let go. "Oh, yeah." I was more worried about what movie we were going to, I was thirteen then. Actually we split up, because certain of us wanted to see one, and the rest of us another. So, there was just us two who went to one movie, and then during the movie they kept flashing on the screen - "All Servicemen, report to your post, Immediately." It was just a handwritten sign projected onto the screen and you could see people getting up and leaving, and you could hear newsmen yelling out in the streets, as the doors opened, "War!" "Pearl Harbor!" and that sort of thing. I came home from the movie, and my father was very intensely listening to the radio, and my mother was sitting there. They were very calm, but very worried though.

Then the next day, it was Monday and it was a funny day, because we all went to school wondering what was going to happen now. By this time I was in Junior High School, which was less segregated, there was still a sizable Asian group, but there were some Jewish and other whites.

We had an assembly, and I remember the principal saying be calm and all, about this whole thing. I was talking with some of my friends, and already the FBI was picking up some of my friends' parents, and fathers. One of them was just having a party, these *Isseis*, for someone who had just come back from Japan, anyway the party got misinterpreted to mean it was a celebration of the attack on Pearl Harbor.

The thing was so interesting, as out of our whole class, there must have been thirty of us, of which twenty-five were Niseis. We all got on a bus to go downtown to a rock exhibit, and we were all kind of embarrassed because now, well everyone knew about the war, and all. Nothing happened, but I remember being so embarrassed on that bus, since we were Japanese. As a matter of fact, nothing really bad happened to us all during that period, although there was a lot of panicky things going on. A number of Nisei, I mean their parents, got into trouble because the FBI picked them up and their businesses got frozen and they couldn't open up their shops. In one case I remember, her father got picked up the night of December 7th, and they didn't have any money, because everything got tied up and they actually had to borrow money, from some kind of a welfare agency, because it got pretty bad for them.

You could tell how they (FBI) were operating, because some of the kids were telling me their father's belonged to like veterans of the Russo-Japan war, or several of the Japanese organizations. So then, there was a pretty good chance you were going to be picked up. Also, not a Japanese-American associate, but if you had some kind of even remote business dealing with Japan. The principal of the Japanese school got picked up, I think for no other reason than he was the principal. Any kind of teacher of any Japanese things, … a guy who taught a Japanese dance group, he got picked up, and his wife ran the school. Then a very close friend of my father's got picked up, I really don't know why. His wife almost went psychotic, because she just didn't know what was going on, and she just fell apart. She had two young kids, she would come and leave them with my mother, and then just wander off.

There was the blackout and a few panicky nights, but then there was a couple of riots, because a couple of the stores had left some back lights on. Then there was a rumor about the Japanese going to attack the West Coast. But surprisingly, when you look back, there wasn't much violence. I mean we didn't get our windows broken, or very few incidents of people yelling at us, but we heard about other things. And then, little by little, you began to see what was going to happen, you could see it unfolding, the concern on people's faces. "What's going to happen to the Japanese? You can't trust them." And that sort of thing. We began to feel like not going out. Then, you got the feeling things started settling down again, with the holidays and all, like people got used to the fact we were at war.

Then starting around January, there was more and more agitation, all of a sudden you could see the American Legion was moving very quickly to, "Let's get rid of the Japs!" They were one of the big ones pushing, and the Native Sons of the Golden West. Then, about February after I had graduated from Junior High School, I started right into High School in 1942. And, in looking back, I think it was pretty clear something was going to happen to us. We had a Japanese -American athletic league, with some Chinese in it, but they dropped out.

One of the things you began to see were these red, white and blue buttons saying, "I'm Chinese-American" or "I'm a Filipino- American," just to make sure people didn't confuse them with any of us. Then, there was a couple of murders (of Japanese) and *Time* magazine had this article, very famous one or maybe it was *Life*, anyway one of those two, on how you can tell the difference between a Chinese and a Japanese It's one of the most classic-racial, they haven't lived that one down. I mean it's still being used in all the sociology books for its racism. I mean it was almost hilarious, yet it was frightening, too. (laugh).

So, you could say this all escalated from the American Legion to the Native Sons of the Golden West, with Kiwanis Club, the Chamber of Commerce, and all started rolling in and sure enough. Looking back, I can now see it was just as *economic as racial*. The main area that was economic was in the agriculture. This was where it all started, … where the agitation was, in the rural areas, where the Japanese had been running into a lot of antagonism, had been up until the war, because of their farming. Native Sons was basically a rural organization, and *Governor Earl Warren was one of the worst in this whole mess*. I didn't realize at the time, until I went back and started looking at it, the evidence was overwhelmingly, "Get the Japs Out!" (laugh)

There was very little support coming from any white organization outside of the Quakers, and they were consistent all the way through trying to help. We had a white minister tell us it was '*our own damn fault for* being evacuated, because we had our own churches, and all this and we should have mixed with the whites.' Gordon Hirabayashi became kind of my role model, as he refused to evacuate and his case went all the way up to the Supreme Court, he was a Quaker, and it was the Quakers who put him up to it. The *ACLU wouldn't touch him*, you know they were very timid then during the war, they didn't want to stick their necks out. But, the Quakers, the American Friends, they stepped in, they encouraged him, gave him the lawyers, everything. But, they were the only group. As a matter of fact, you just got this sense you didn't have a friend in the world.

Only one politician I can remember really, … interesting because he was a very conservative guy. He was the Mayor of Tacoma, Washington, who became a senator from the state, but he was the *only one who said, "This is wrong."* And, all the liberals said, "Kick the Japs out!' I always remember, because after the war when I was a student at the University of Washington, I started to participate in the campaign for the reelection of a Congressman, who later became a very famous Senator, Scoop Jackson. He was running for Congress in those days, and we were supposed to be going-out ringing door bells. I was right in there, until I read his record, he was right in there with the rest of of them trying to kick the Japs out. Of course, he wasn't the only one, later on a lot of them came back, and now we're friends of the Japanese.

You could see it back then, just a tremendous force. The funny thing was at that point we were't angry. Well, let me put it this way, we didn't express any anger; like my parents believed - *"Shikata-ganai!"*

- "What can we do about it?" Resigning themselves to the inevitable, just like everyone in Japan. So, they were trying at first to get us to move out on our own, to the East of the West Coast States. If you went into Eastern Washington, in Spokane, you would've been out of it. They built up what they called a 'Defense Zone' which was right on the West Coast, and if you moved out of that line, then they wouldn't remove you, because they were going to close this area off.

The trouble was, they kept making the Zone bigger and bigger, so some people who moved out, found out they were still in the Zone limit and they then had to move again. (They were supposed to do this on their own, at their own expense.) Very few did, but some people had relatives in Idaho, or something like that. I had a friend who left during this period. I met another person after the war, who said they moved to Stockton, only to find out later, it wasn't far enough, they were still in the Zone. So, they gave up and went into the camps from Stockton, and they were actually from San Mateo.

There was very little public expression of outrage of what was happening to us, most of us just accepted it. Of course, at my age I didn't have any choice. I think it's one thing when you got a bunch of liberal-whites telling you, 'go ahead, don't let them push you around, fight for your rights.' But, when you don't have any kind of support like that, and everybody says, 'you know, I think the best thing for your own protection, you ought to go.' Really, in the whole atmosphere, there wasn't any, any sense of what you would see now, any kind of confrontational type of reaction. No one thought of it in those days, no one except Gordon Hirabayashi.

There was kind of humor, of trying to make the best of it. My gut feeling, at the time, was there was so much anger at Japan for the attack on Pearl Harbor, and I don't think I'm underestimating it, any opposition or even support might have made it worse. I know a lot of my Nisei friends now, don't agree with me, but when I'm looking at the climate of the times, it just seemed inevitable something like it all was going to come up. I thought for a while we were going to be separated from our parents, and then I realized they couldn't do that, either the family goes or we don't go at all.

The orders started to come out in April and even up until then, outside of certain governmental actions, I don't think I really ran across very much personal hostility at all from the whites. You sort of had the feeling, Seattle or whenever, was drifting back to a normal routine and the war hysteria was sort of dying down. There was an article in the paper almost every day, 'Something is going to happen to the Japanese.' 'They're going to be kicked out' or 'One group favors it and goes on record.' So then, by May was the order, it went by stages, we had to go register, and you really got the sense of it.

There was an island off the coast of Seattle, Bainbridge Island, and there was a whole community of Japanese strawberry farmers, we used to go there a lot, we had some friends there. They were the first to get removed, and there were pictures of them being ferried from the island to Seattle. Then they were put on trains and sent to Manzanar, the main camp in southern California. It housed most of the people from the Los Angeles area, it was in the Eastern Sierras. It became the most famous of the ten camps, as some books were written about it.

But, at the beginning they removed us so fast, none of these camps were ready, so they had to put us into the fairgrounds. We got put into one about thirty miles south of Seattle, where they used to have a regional fair. They converted the fairground into four areas - the inside and each of the three big parking lots. They made each of the parking lots into a camp, built barracks with the barbed wire, the towers and the machine guns on it and everyone. Then inside the fairgrounds they made rooms out of the horse stalls, and the displays were for the animals, they didn't smell too bad (laugh). But you know, they were for animals, not humans. And then, under the stadium and this, or that empty space.

There must have been nine thousand of us. We were broken into these four areas and we couldn't even visit each other. Though they did after a while, let us make periodic visits to those other areas, so we were literally separated (fences around each area also). There were some houses in between and some farm land. There was a berry patch, I'll always remember, right next to our camp. This was when I first started to feel the hostility. These berry-pickers (white) would make fun of us, "You Japs," "You yellow-bellied Japs," and all kinds of stuff. I threw a rock at a girl and I hit her, I was so mad. Then the MPs, most of them were real hostile. This one guy, he just wanted one of us to try to make it through the fence, so he could have the joy of letting us have it, which *they were allowed to shoot us.*

It seemed the more they did to us, the stronger the hostility. The beginning, let's remove them, then let's put them in the camps, then once you got them into the camps. Then there was a strong movement to deport them - everybody, citizens and non-citizens, just send them all back. It just seems to get worse with each step. Most of the white friends we had, there wasn't one I know of who said, "Don't take this shit." Everyone said, "Why don't you cooperate." In other words, "Be a good little Jap." See the whole idea of confrontation was never really done. Gordon Hirabayashi was considered a trouble- maker by most of the Niseis, he was rocking the boat - so very un- Japanese. Maybe he had gotten just too-American.

So, we went in and we lived in this fairground-camp from May all the way until September, it was my *Summer of '42* (laugh). They put these temporary barracks up, with these wooden boards, and the summer got warmer and warmer, and the wood got drier and drier, and the cracks got bigger and bigger (laugh). I mean there were seven families to a barrack with only a partition between families, and you could hear a guy snoring at the other end of the barracks (laugh). We had to be in by nine, they put a curfew on us. We already had a curfew on us a few months before they moved us, we couldn't go more than five miles from our house, and had to be in our home by eight o'clock. They had removed each part of Seattle at a time, and so depending on what part of the city you lived in, was the same as the part of the camp. I lived in an area called Area A, it was a parking lot and just a squared-off thing. So, we still had all of our same neighbors, in fact our next store neighbor lived in the barracks right across from us, and most of our close family and friends were right down the line from us. It even remained the same way when we were put into the permanent camps, because they did it again (one section at a time).

During the day quite a few of the older people could work - dishwashers in the mess halls and they got paid a set wage, I think sixteen dollars a month or something. But at my age, we couldn't do anything, we just played and did a lot of athletics or just sitting around chewing the fat. There was a lot of little things like carving little statues, it caught on for a while, especially when they would knock these knot-holes out and carve it, and make little hearts or something. There were a lot of dances, of course, I was a little young for that, but it came a little later in my life. A lot of dances were in the mess halls for the older Niseis, there was a lot of social life going on, as there was nothing else to do. I think generally, given the situation, young people do what generally young people do, try to have fun. In the camps, it was no different.

Sometimes, some of the younger Japanese-Americans, who were not in the camps (born after the war) used to ask us years later, 'what did you do, walk around kicking the dirt, spouting obscenities at the government?' No, most of us were out trying to have a good time, we might not tell white people that. (laugh) But, you tried to make the best of what you got. We went around in 'gangs,' if you want to call it that, the situation almost created it. The gangs were based on people who lived close together. They were all we had, so we stayed together. I remember even in the temporary camp, before I knew it, we became friends with some folks who were Alaskan. By the way, if you want to see some interesting twists of fate, you should see some of this life history of what happened to some of these Alaskans. There was a guy there, I'll always remember him, as he came from Wiseman, Alaska, north of the Arctic Circle. He didn't even know he was Japanese, until someone, he claims squealed on him. There were a number of Alaskans who were mixtures of Indian. In fact, there was a family of four brothers, big, husky, white Russian, they didn't look Japanese, I mean such a little bit.

If they (the government) could show you had some Japanese in you, they could come after you. They didn't check everyone systematically, but if someone said you were, then they checked on it. There was one blonde woman there, the step-daughter of a Japanese who married a white woman, and she went into the camp with this daughter. They left after a while, but the husband had to stay.

So, we spent the summer of '42 there, I always remember it was a warm summer. The feeling you got was everything against you, I think it was symbolized. We always used to listen to the radio, still in the camp. Bob Hope, you have to give him credit, he never really made fun of us, but Red Skelton, was something else.

He was my favorite comedian up until then. You know they always have this monologue at the beginning, so Skelton was saying, "You know one day I was working out in the sun all day, and I was squinting real badly, and I as I walked down the street, someone said, 'Hey, could you come over and mow my lawn before you go back to Santa Anita.'" Which was the race track, which housed the Japanese in the LA area. So, I thought, you son-of-a-bitch, he's making fun of my misery, and I never listened to him again. To this day, I don't even know what happened to him. Now, Hope, I don't think I ever heard him say anything against the Niseis, well the Japanese maybe, but then everybody did. I was hurt, I was really hurt by Skelton.

I remember too, the older Niseis, wondering what they were going to do, because they were going to have to decide, where is their future, particularly military-wise. But at the time, being in the army wasn't an alternative, because there were some Niseis in the camp were discharged, because they were considered enemy-aliens. One guy, he had the humiliation of having the FBI come into the camp and take his army uniform away from him. He had worn the cap during work, and some MP or somebody, spotted it, and complained.

In the fall, they put us on a train and it was an overnight trip to Idaho. The camp I was in was called *Minidoka,* near Twin Falls, Idaho. The trip, itself, had some interesting sidelines, one of them was the cars were very old and dusty. It was still hot, so we opened some windows, but cinders from the locomotive would come in, and you would have your face and hands get all black. In the evening, we're going along the Columbia River, and they made us close the curtains. Why? What were we going to do, spy on the dam? They had an MP on each end of the car, they just stood there. One time when the train stopped, my father stepped off the train to smoke, they grabbed him and said, "What's the matter with you?"

See again, I wasn't angry, I was embarrassed my father did that. I'm angry now, when I think about it, but I was more embarrassed he did such a thing to be scolded by this MP. In light of the very poor conditions of the car, they weren't cattle cars, they were coaches, but not the most comfortable things. But, they had a diner on the train. You went into the diner, to eat in turn. Anyway, beautiful dining cars - table cloths and black waiters, and they served us this beautiful roast beef dinner, we had a choice, fish or beef. We didn't have to pay, it was all part of this trip of being shipped to this camp, (laugh). But it was like the Last Supper, you know before we got put away (laugh).

Then we got to the camp, well we got off the train and the camp was still another maybe twenty miles away, so they put us on some buses. We could only have two suitcases each, and you had to be able to carry everything. Although, the second move to the permanent camp, we were able to pack a few things into cartons. They came and picked them up, and shipped them ahead to Idaho. Most of us had sold our stuff pretty cheap. We didn't have much, our furniture was very old. I think my father sold everything for like eight or nine dollars to get rid of it, and other people in the same way. There was a lot of bitterness and particularly aimed at Jews at that point, although I don't know how valid it was. But the idea they came in and 'jewed' us down, and that kind of notion. But there was a lot of people running around, trying to pick up deals, and somehow or other, the idea they were Jewish, broke out. It certainly wasn't true in our neighborhood.

My father, as I mentioned, was a gardener and had a truck. One of his customers had agreed to store all his stuff with them, most of his equipment including his car. They were very good to us, but did tell us to go to the camp, and 'be a good American.' The excitement for me at this time was we bought suitcases. I had my own suitcase. I never had one before in my whole life, so I packed all my stuff in the suitcase. All of us bought big boots, the word had gotten out we'd need them.

Anyway, going over to the camp on the bus, there was this Lieutenant, and he says, "There's your new home." You look out there, and there's this big cloud of dust. (laugh) Then when we got there, and he kind of looked at us, and he said, "You know, for whatever it's worth, Best of Luck." I think it was the warmest thing any official said to me at the time. (pause and sigh) I always remember it, and I think after, I can't remember anybody every saying anything kind like it.

I stayed in this camp for three years, and the first year was really bad. We got there in September and it was just dust, dust, nothing. There was nothing planted. In the winter, when the snow came, gees, the mud was up to here (ankle), we had no roads, nothing. I mean there were roads to there. The first winter, you just couldn't go anywhere, without being in ankle-deep mud. Then they started to put gravel in, so we sort of had sidewalks. After, it was pretty much just a social life, there was a dance somewhere almost every weekend. Later on, we started a big farm, we all cleared off a lot of land, because it was right out in the middle of sagebrush.

Our camp had a big, swift irrigation canal, which almost circled the camp, so first they had the barbed wired faced with the machine-gun towers, the whole bit. Then, they found out no one was going to run out, because there was this swift-canal. So, there was just this one area behind the camp, which was the only place the canal didn't run through, and it was just miles and miles of sagebrush. You could see way out there. So, finally the fences started to come down. I understand in other camps this wasn't true. So, all the MPs did was guard the open space, which became the entrance and had a big MP guard house.

In our camp there were forty-two blocks, and each block had twelve barracks, six on each side, with a mess hall, and a laundry room in the middle with a boiler room. Then each barrack housed six families, and the rooms varied by how big the families were. If you had more than eight, then you were allowed two rooms. So, the biggest rooms could house up to seven, there were five in my family, so we got a 'seven size.' Then there was a smaller room for just couples or three people. They were the regular military-type structures. We had about ten thousand, and the people were predominantly from Seattle and Portland.

Later on, they started to move people around to different camps after about one year or so. They came up with a loyalty oath, this is crazy, it was a famous questionnaire. I can't remember Question 27 or 28, but if you answered "no" to both of them, out. One you had to swear allegiance to the United States, and the other was you would be willing to serve your country, this was for Niseis.

The original loyalty-oath demanded you repudiate any allegiance to Japan, which the Issei, quickly objected to. If they had agreed to it, in effect, they wouldn't have any kind of citizenship, because they couldn't become American citizens, by law. So, then they turned the question around a little bit, and they finally asked, you wouldn't do anything to harm the U.S. government. But if you said 'No' to both of them, what they started to do was segregate you out.

They had started to use Tule Lake camp, in Northern California, almost on the Oregon border, to put what they considered the disloyal-elements into. So, anyone from all the other camps, who had said 'No, No,' were all put together. Which in effect made it worse, when they concentrated all the troublemakers, so then they did have a lot of trouble afterwards.

Later then, the whole idea was to close the camps eventually, by relocating all the people into the Midwest or the East Coast. Of course, a lot of people, particularly the older ones, once they got into the camps, they didn't want to leave anyway. You get kind of dependent, you don't have to cook any more. You could work for sixteen bucks a month. But for many Issei, like my father, a chance for them to relax a little bit. Yet, I don't think he enjoyed it very much.

His comment when we first got there was, "This is it, we're going to be in here for the rest of our lives." Just like Indians on a reservation, it was his motto. And in a way, you start to look at it, and you start to think, it makes sense. They're encouraging us to be farmers, be self-sufficient and eventually it would be kind of permanent, and then we just lived there for the rest of our lives. At that point, none of us had any idea what was going to happen to us, how long the war would go on, or where we would be? Would we be sent back to Japan? You know the possibility existed. These things, it was really strange, and you got these rumors going around first year, and then eventually you got some direction.

The first thing was this loyalty-oath and about the same time, they came around asked the men to volunteer for a new military unit, the 442nd. There was a lot of discussion. The lights were burning all night long, these Nisei guys would stay-up all night-long arguing. Really interesting, because it was a real 'should I' or 'shouldn't I.' Finally at the end, what happened was friends started becoming separated over the whole issue. So, the gangs in each block, started to split-up into pro-American and pro-Japanese factions.

Probably, the majority of the Niseis were moving in the direction (gung-ho, to show their loyalty to U.S.), but there was a substantial group who said, "I'm not happy to go out and volunteer for anything, considering what's happened to us, but if I have to go, I'll go, but I'm not happy about it." It was a lot of grumbling and lively discussion (laugh), and I think even today there's a lot of people who don't talk to each other because of this whole situation.

There was a whole group who wanted to go back to Japan, some of them I think were Kibeis, and there was one group who led a riot down in Manzanar. They were dismissed as pro-militarists - Japanese and others saw them as really objecting to the whole evacuation, but they were predominantly Kibeis. There was quite a few a them who went to Tule Lake, and some even wanted to go back to Japan to fight with the Japanese. Some of them got deported, like ones the FBI picked-up, and others were held for a long time, even after the war out at Tule Lake.

One interesting twist, of a girl I grew up with, her father got picked-up on the night of Pearl Harbor, for whatever reason. Anyway, they weren't put in the same camps as us. They were sent to a camp in Montana, and there was a big one in Crystal City, Texas. They weren't run by the Interior Department as us, they were run by the Department of Justice, as they were considered enemy-aliens. So this friend, Marion, and her family were going to be deported and we had a big party for them in the camp, she was in my school class. A few months later, we got a letter from her and she was on the Swedish ship. They used it in the Indian Ocean to exchange Japanese prisoners and Americans - Diplomats and whoever from Japan, it was some agreement. So, she's on this ship being sent back to Japan and the letter is so sad, 'Here I am going back to Japan, and I don't know what's going to happen to me, I know so little about Japan.'

I always wondered all these years whatever happened to Marion. So, in 1985 I went to our camp reunion in Seattle, there were four hundred of us, and we had this big dinner. I don't know who thought of this crazy idea, but they said, "Would all the men at one table go and hug all the women at the next table." So, I get up and go to this next table, and hug this woman, and its' Marion! I talked with her and asked what happened, as the last we heard was this letter we got. She said, 'We got to Japan and because I could speak English, after the war, I got a job in an American military hospital.' Somehow through all that, she managed to get back to the States, get her citizenship cleared, got herself a nursing degree and she's a nurse. She got married and was living in Sacramento, not too far from where I was living actually. It was such a surprise!

I have another good friend who was part of this gang I went around with - actually, he was part of it at the temporary camp. Then his family got split away from us at the far end of the camp. Yet, every day he would come down to our end, and play with us, bring a change of clothes, eat with us. The only time he would go back was to sleep at night. We rarely ate with our families, we always ate together as a gang. I probably ate with my family five times in three and half years, at over the holidays - Thanksgiving and Christmas, etc.

One day at school, somebody said to him, "Hey, I hear your family's going to be deported to Crystal City, Texas.' His father had been picked-up by the FBI. He didn't know about it, so he ran all the way to the other end of the camp and his mother told him, 'Yeah,' they were going to leave the next day. In fact, when he got back to his room, the MPs were there helping them pack, so he came running back and he was almost in tears. I remember two of us sat up with him all night. Then the next day, we went down to the gate, it was early morning, and they got into a car and were driven off. I didn't see him again until this reunion. I thought they were going to be sent back to Japan, and then there was a delay, a delay, and then the war was over.

Anyone could work, as I said, as a laborer for sixteen dollars a month, … well doctors got nineteen dollars, and so did school teachers. There was a regular school, pretty good, white teachers, most of them. There was a group of people, who were basically missionaries, who came into the camps. I fell behind in a lot of areas in high school, but not math because of the math teacher I had, and she was a missionary-type teacher. There was one teacher, my sister and I are still very close to. To this day, I don't know why she came into this camp, she was not a missionary. She was a very liberal, kind of Peace Corps-type, and after the war was over, she went back and got her Ph.D. in sociology. Two of the Nisei students were her classmates at Chicago, and they sort of finished up together.

My problem was a lot of distractions, and I didn't want to go to school. We could work part-time if we wanted to, and one of the things I started to do very early, after the first year, some friends and I joined the coal-crew. We delivered the coal to the camp and in order to do it, which is very dirty work, you come out with your face black. They give you special meals, you got pork chops or a little piece of steak every night, so food's the way they get you to do this kind of dirty work, and you eat in a special mess hall. But for me, it wasn't so much, as the fact we got to drive the trucks.

I was only fourteen or fifteen and I wanted to learn how to drive a truck. So, as the older Nisei started to leave because of military, or other job opportunities in other states, us younger guys took over. I did it for three years, part-time and a lot of the time, I just worked full time and didn't go to school. We got a clothing allowance, which was about five or six dollars. They issued some kind of clothes, like old military-type of clothing, not anything you'd want to wear. During the harvest season, they let you out of the camps to go work around the farms in Idaho picking potatoes. But that's also where you really started to run into the hostility, where I really realized it.

You do it enough times, I think I went out and picked potatoes three different times and worked in the fields. I was not regarded as a very good worker, I was just not a farmer's son, like a lot of other Niseis were. But, you learned very quickly, on a Saturday after picking potatoes all week, and you come into these rural towns, there's always a place - pool hall or a bar, where all the local rednecks congregate. You learn to stay away from those places, but quite often you can't avoid it and you run into them. Then you get pushed off the streets, one of the worse things, you go to a movie, and it was really bad. As long as it was dark it was OK, but these movies, there's an intermission and all of a sudden there's popcorn boxes, peanut bags and everything comes flying at you.

When we went to help with the harvest, we would live with the Mexican migrant-laborers in their camps, and the farmers came and picked you up and you went to work on the farm. In some cases, you lived with the farmer. I remember one season we lived on the farm, we lived in a little shack. We were free all the time we were't working, we could go to town and it was in October. They close the schools for harvest, so we left the camp and at the end of the month, you come back to the camps. Whatever money you earn was yours, they didn't take it from you.

It was a chance to be free (laugh), but I really realized there's a lot of white-folks who don't like me. Just about every town had a place if you went in they won't serve you, they kick you out. Fortunately, there usually was one or two places who served you in a civil way (laugh), so you'll tend to go there. But we had been in places where they'd come up to you and say, "We don't serve Japs in here, get your yellow-ass out of here." And, to be honest with you, that's the first I ran into, those kind of things, up until later then in Seattle, I rarely ran into any situation.

I always thought once the war was over people would know we were all right and everything would be OK. I didn't finish high school at the camp and when we came back to Seattle, I returned to the high school there. As I listened to some of the older Niseis talk about high school, it was a very mixed group, socially snd economically. Some of the richest families in Seattle, their kids went to my school, and there were a lot of blacks and other minorities, so it was really diversified. These older Niseis were always telling me they treated the Niseis real nice, and how these white-folks were real good, and I had this image of this high school. So, I spent my last year at this high school they had talked about, and I suddenly realized all the impact of racism, and the feeling of it was not an aberration - these people hated me! This high school, for all they had told me, it certainly didn't have any good feeling for me at all. Probably the most unhappy one year I ever spent.

In some ways, I felt worse that year than I did in all the time I was in the camp. Just the feeling of not being wanted. I found out for example, unlike what my Nisei friends had told me, the graduation dance was segregated. The white kids had their graduation commencement dance at a country club, while the Japanese/Nisei and Chinese had their own little graduation dance, and then the blacks had their own. The year I came back, was the first year they integrated the school, so there was a lot of flack.

I mean these girls were saying, 'my parents won't let me go to the dance, because it's going to be mixed,' and all this kind of stuff, which made me feel even worse. I didn't go to the dance, I didn't even go to the commencement (laugh), I was so alienated. I hated the teachers, I think the teachers hated me (laugh) and I hated the clerk. I went one day after the commencement to pick up my diploma and she says, "You weren't at the commencement, well here's your diploma!" Then she throws it at me (laugh). I think what got me into sociology was *that* specific experience of *that* year, and it wasn't so much of the camp or maybe it was (laugh). But that one year in that high school, really seemed to hit me. This is not just the situation, these people really looked down on us.

Then, over the years since, just little by little I began to see the way my thinking was then, very much oriented into pursuing the American Dream, and becoming part of the white-middle-class. And, I suddenly realized, 'Hey, that's out your league, it's not the way it's going to go,' you know. I think it began to sink in specifically then, as it was a very bad year, since my father was dying of cancer, which made it even worse. My grades were so bad from high school, I couldn't get into the university. I had to take some special classes.

Fortunately, during my miserable year I met a white fellow who lived in our camp, who was an anthropologist. They called him a 'community analyst.' His job was to live among us, and just sort of study us, to try to find out what's troubling us, then write these reports to the government. He was a very nice guy, and somehow he managed to steer me toward more intellectual study. In a way he saved me, because he made me realize 'I got to get out of this' somehow. I need to get more educated, and I need to develop a different way of looking at this. Really, very troubled then, I wanted to quit high school, the year I was so miserable. Interestingly enough, the principal said, if you want to drop out now, I can probably scrape up enough credits for you, so you can get a diploma. My idea was just drop-out to go in the army. By the way, my best friend, in fact we were in the same block, we went to school together, we took showers together, we ate together, we did everything together in the camp, except he went to sleep with his family at night. So, he and I were very close. He went back to the same high school, and he decided to go into the army in February. So, in this class we all had to write a paper about what we wanted to be, and he wrote a paper on why he wanted to be a detective.

The day he went to say good-bye to the class, before going into the army, the teacher said, "You wrote a very good paper and I want to commend you for it." So, he was happy when he left. No sooner did he go out the door and she said, "I don't know why he writes a paper like that, he's a Japanese, he knows he's not going to get a job as a detective. Why does he want to waste his time writing a paper like that?" She says this to the whole class, as he would've never known it, except one of his white friends told him (laugh), so shows the kind of situation we had.

Anyway, this anthropologist-friend sort of guided me in a direction and eventually, I decided I wanted to get a university degree, even though my grades were terrible. He introduced me to some students at the University of Washington, white students, very liberal and it was the first time I met whites who sort of accepted me. It really impressed me, as all the ones up until then were very hostile. Actually, I never had a close white friend, who I could say was a friend outside of the classroom. Until, I was in my senior year at the university, all my friends were Niseis. So, in my junior year, I made friends with this fellow, and we became very good friends. He just passed away last year, but he was my first white friend.

So, as I went along, I got more and more involved in sociology and interestingly enough, the more I got involved in sociology, the less I got involved with race-relations. Then, once I started teaching sociology, the last area I wanted to get into was race-relations. I taught statistics, population problems, and now I find myself sort of going back to it. It took me a long time, I never in all the times I taught, particularly in my first fifteen or twenty years, I never even mentioned my camp experience to anybody. Among my friends, of course, we talk about it all the time, but never to any of the students, never to anybody outside my ethnic group did I mention it.

One of the things I remember, when I was a student at the university, in my junior year there was a professor who was very much involved in the whole evacuation. He thought it was such an injustice and made a bid deal of it in this class, what was happening and all. So he would periodically stop and say, "Isn't it true, ...?" I'd kind of duck under the seat, because I was so embarrassed. If this had been said by other Nisei, like we felt we had done some horrible thing, and as if it's why we were put in. So, once we're out, we'd vow to be one hundred and ten percent true-blooded American.

It took me a long time to start talking about it, and I think in a sense the whole civil rights movement did one thing, it was to think about how we did nothing. Which I think was truly important - I think you shouldn't be afraid to holler, when there is an injustice. Somehow, when people are screwing you, you shouldn't feel there's something wrong with you, other than there's something wrong with the system. It took me a long time to understand it all. I think it's not only the Japanese, I think the blacks felt the same way, kind of self-hatred.

Now you look back on it and you say "Oh, my God!" I could understand even the passiveness we did, and I'm not ashamed of it. See, the civil rights movement in the South, had a lot of middle-class support in the North, … we had nothing! (Upset)

We had our reunion in 1985, and it was real nice. I think most of us came out of it pretty good. However, there were a lot people who weren't there, and I don't know what happened to them. The people who were there, were certainly the ones who were able to turn things around for themselves. The other thing too, I think as you look back, you get a little more emotional about it. One of the things which happened during the compensation hearings, I had friends who I know testified, and they just broke down, these had been tough guys. I was kind of surprised. So, as people are still talking about it, I think they're more open about it. There are however, even with the compensation thing, there's a large group of Niseis who don't want money. They think they're too proud to accept it, quite a few are from the 442nd Military Regiment.

People who were real close in camp, but went their own ways. I don't think I could say I saw careers broken. I know a lot of people changed their views and did a lot of different things, I know I did. Before the war, of course, I was very young, but I thought I was going to end up being an engineer, which is what most of my Nisei friends are now. But because of my last year in high school, some how or another it really got to me. I had Nisei friends who went the same year, and they didn't feel the same way I did. In fact, they alway thought I was being overly sensitive, but some how it really got to me. Up until then, I had this feeling, we as Niseis would be acceptable in American society. This was sort for an aberration since of the war, but it wasn't. I had to come to grips with it all, and now what am I going to do?

They always thought I was a little too sensitive, and most of them are engineers, in business and pharmacists - and they're making a lot money right now (laugh). They thought I was crazy for going into sociology, but they could understand why I went into it. I think if it hadn't been for this camp experience, I wouldn't have been any different than them. I probably would have gone on to something like them, and been a good, little Nisei boy with my degree, but this experience really switched me around.

They did give us a train ticket to wherever we wanted to go. They also had a hard time closing the camp up, with some of the older people who didn't want to leave, because they didn't have anywhere to go. But eventually, they closed the camps, except the Tule Lake camp they kept open. That Camp got divided into two groups there, one which was the pro-Japanese and those who weren't. They left, but the hard core, kept their hair cut short like the Japanese military. They wore sweatshirts with the *Hinomaru* - Rising Sun, and ran calisthenics around the camp every morning. They marched around singing these Japanese war songs.

They were training for the Japanese army, I mean what they thought they were doing. A lot of them did not go back to Japan, however they just eventually left. Then some of them came back from Japan after the war, as then they suddenly realized it wasn't what they wanted. Many of them had never even been to Japan, and then they went there, denounced their American citizenship and finally wanted to come back. This was when the ACLU finally became a little more active, and started to help these people. In San Francisco, there was an attorney who was really trying to help them, and he defended Tokyo Rose, she really got railroaded. She got absolutely no support from the Japanese groups - and some others who wanted to get their citizenships back.

Most of our friends and neighbors went back to the old neighborhood, and some of the Isseis got their businesses back, but most of them were too old to start over. They worked as janitors, dishwashers in the hotel, and such. The feeling in some areas wasn't good. I went into a shoe store, and had a shoe salesman throw a shoe at me, so we had some bad experiences. We went back to an apartment, about three blocks away from where we had lived, and it had become predominately a black area then. Discrimination was pretty bad.

My first year at the university, when they asked me what I wanted to major in, and the advisor said, 'I better make an appointment for you with the teacher placement bureau.' And in effect,

'What do you want to major in education for, because you'll never get a job?' It was true, before the war the grade school and junior high school I went to, the clerks were both Nisei women who had teaching degrees, but it was the best they could do to get next to education. Surprisingly, in 1948 when they told me all this, by 1952, everything just switched around, I couldn't believe it. The 1950s were a good time with the U.S., and in fact they were asking for Nisei teachers by the time I graduated. Niseis were getting into jobs you never would have dreamed of before the war.

One of my friends I grew up with, he was a chemist and he got a job as an analyzer of the urine of horses at the race track every summer, to see if they were doped up or not. But it led to a job in the criminology lab in the Seattle Police department. Here's a Nisei, and you would have never thought anything like it would have been possible, and now he's the head of it. I think, what happened was when the opportunities opened up, there were a lot of educated people willing to take-up these jobs, which they couldn't get before.

There's really two groups of Japanese now, there's this group I'm part of, who goes back to our parents immigrating before the war. And then, there's another group of Japanese, Shin-Niseis (New Niseis) and they basically came after the war. One of things I find interesting, and maybe I might want to research it out, is 'What is the Japanese- American ethnic sub-culture now?' When you say Nisei Week in Los Angeles, or Nisei Festival in San Franciscan during Cherry Blossom, you look at who's participating in it. Outside of a few drum majorettes, some dancers and a queen, the rest are not really Nisei, or even people from Japan. So, you wonder what happened to the Japanese culture? They finally got assimilated (laugh)!

You know the interracial marriage rate is very high. It's like you've got a bunch of cultural entrepreneurs or something. (laugh) There'll always be something called Japanese-American, but it will never be what it was during my time, when we truly were the Niseis. Like my friend said, "We didn't do too badly."

With his Ph.D. in Sociology, and being a retired Professor-Emeritus from San Francisco State University, he was just finishing his year, as an honored, visiting-professor at the prestigious, Nanzan University in Nagoya. Certainly, so very grateful for having him referred to me by a teach-friend, and giving me his extensive time, as well personal story.

Side Note on Tokyo Rose:

Iva Toguri was bon in Los Angeles, and had gone to Japan to visit relatives while going to school. She was not able to return to America, and through trying to support herself, she ended up at a radio station editing the English news. With little choice, she became one of some-thirty women, mostly Niseis, who were called *Tokyo Rose.* Her nickname was Orphan Ann, as she was incredibly naive and ignorant of being used. She never broadcasted misinformation, and only joked about the propaganda, believing she was giving the 'American boys' music and a kind voice. After the war, she let herself be referred as Tokyo Rose, thinking she was a celebrity to the military. Walter Winchell (not known as a kind man) touted on his radio show - though he had been informed from media-sources she was not guilty - and called her out as a 'war criminal.' President Truman, not wanting to look weak on the Japanese, had her charged in 1948. She was in prison until 1956, and later given a pardon in 1977.

Part II - Japan & the Japanese As the Occupied: Chapter 5 - Tokyo: MAC, SCAP & GHQ

"In the world of the blind, the one-eyed man is King." An old proverb Japan, since the Shogun-Samuri days, has always feared and revered power, as well money. If someone should have both, they could control everything, without question.

The Japanese women changed into their formal kimonos and the men into their *harui* - kimono-type jackets. They then sat bowed, on the tatami mats to listen to the voice of the Emperor give his rescript of how they should act during the upcoming Occupation. "… bear the unbearable and endure the unendurable." Following this, all kinds of rumors about the Americans had begun to spread, including those which said it was an American trick and not the Emperor who had spoken. There was a general belief, the occupying troops were filled with hatred of the Japanese, and would be unrestricted in their behavior toward Japanese life and property, as Japan had been to those they had occupied.

Many people, especially women, thought it prudent to leave the cities. Factories issued poison capsules to women workers, girls were instructed to wear their bulkiest *mompei* - country-style, baggy pants and blouse - and to cut their hair, so they would look more like boys. They were told *not to* bear grudges, believe rumors and gossip, yet, they were also told they should stay indoors and not go out alone. If they did go out, they must not respond in any way to any American soldier, even if he spoke Japanese to them. No makeup or colorful clothes were to be worn, as if the average woman still had such things. On the pitted-strip, of Atsugi Naval Air Base, August 28, 1945, starting at about eight-thirty in the morning, sixteen American planes landed. Appropriately enough, Mt. Fuji, the one image almost all Americans knew of Japan, loomed impassively purple in the distance. Clouds of American fighter aircraft hovered-protectively above the rapidly-descending C-54 'Skymaster' transports, as if some fanatics of the nationalistic-military had escaped with several planes. One hundred and fifty Signal Corps men - engineers, radio specialists, interpreters - were in the initial party. Within forty-five minutes of touchdown, the men established radio communication with Okinawa, a bee had already been set-up.

To watching Japanese, it seemed *each American* knew exactly what he had to do, and the efficiency with which the unit went about its work was impressive. So very, un-Japanese, as no group-controller/ officer was seen spelling-out what they should do. Japanese officers, in full-dress uniform with swords, clustered nervously about the landing strip, not knowing who they should salute, since all the Americans were in work uniforms. If someone was in charge, again he certainly wasn't dressed any differently - very un-Japanese. Battered hangars surrounded the field with wrecked aircraft, while the other few working-aircraft had their propellers removed, in accordance with American orders. Anyway, no aircraft fuel for them to do anything.

Atsugi was strategically located about twenty-miles west of Tokyo, just on the edge of the great Kanto plain, yet near enough to the coast, to be within-range of naval gunfire. Four hundred warships and aircraft carriers were assembled offshore, carrying enough planes to darken the sky. The first night, those few men on shore, knew they were the only occupying-force in a nation where three to four-million men were still under-arms. It would be a week or more, before a large number of America troops would be brought in. Practically self- sustaining, the Atsugi force had brought along food, gasoline, and other necessities, but were dependent upon the Japanese for ground transportation. Though there were a few American-made automobiles and some trucks, 1938 and 1939 vintage models, but to use them the GIs had to wrestle with the smelly, complexities of charcoal-powered engines, wartime-Japan's gas-savers.

A Japanese bus, was the only available transportation to Yokohama, for an Allied group who arrived August 30, and it broke down after only two miles. One of the officers, set-out on foot in search of alternate-transportation, using sign language and relying on the fact he was in uniform, as well armed. He eventually commandeered a fire engine. At two in the afternoon the same day, General Douglas MacArthur flew in, and for the Japanese the Second Coming could not have caused more commotion.

Considering, of course, pre-arranged by MacArthur's vast personal Press Corp of *fifty*, there were over a hundred press- correspondents waiting. He descended from his plane with all the pomp and ceremony of a conquering-hero, though dressed, by Japanese-standards, more like an inexperienced private. Of course, he was puffing on his corncob pipe, wearing his sunglasses, battered, sweat-stained cap, and outfitted in his plain, open-necked khakis. As usual, with no decoration or insignia except the five-star circle on each collar-tab, and jacket-shoulder strap.

Always being the epitome of affectation, MacArthur was *not* unaware of *his place* in history. It was *Him alone* changing history, by setting his foot down on the sacred soil of Japan, for *his occupation* of it. Nothing, *absolutely nothing* he did or would do, went without being totally choreographed. And, his casual-dress was on purpose to fully, but subtilely, disrespect the formalness of Japanese military and their loss. He would not even 'dress' to meet with the Emperor. His distaste for Japan and the Japanese people was clearly displayed and spoken of, as often as he could do so, without Washington reprimands. Because of them, he felt, he had to leave his 'cushy,' adored-post in the Philippines.

Meanwhile, over at Yokosuka Naval Base near Yokohama, the bulk of the battle-scarred GIs and Marines were arriving without a show, and were neither threatening, nor fearsome. In fact, they had an empathy for the gaunt, skinny Japanese on-lookers. They had *both* been through so much in the past four years, as the Japanese sad eyes reflected mutual pain and sorrow. At every intersection, stood a young, fresh Japanese soldier, rifle and bayonet at the ready, with his back to the convoy. This was precaution against any possible attack or demonstration, but on the whole it was a dismal scene, with little triumph for the victors. Most of the troops smiled and waved from the trucks, as they threw pieces of gum and candy to the children. (No one had told them, no children or adults had ever seen gum, and had no idea how to just chew-it.)

To the older Japanese men, these were not the acts of a military person. Though the GIs were mostly, big and looked alike, they seemed much too casual with their caps tilted this way and that. Perhaps, the Japanese thought, the Americans had not had the same respectful, strict training as the Japanese. Their sacred military caps were always worn at exactly the *same tilt,* and their uniforms had identical creases, down to even *all* their penises being worn to the left. Any deviation in appearance would have been severely punished. The only uniformity these strange, gawky Americas had was their quick smile (*NEVER* acceptable for a Japanese soldier), and friendliness.

Later in the streets of Tokyo and Yokohama, the people would stop and stare to watch how casually these troops strolled, more like civilians. They were so much *unlike* any Japanese soldiers, who had strutted down the street, clattering their swords and stamping their boots. The GIs had been portrayed as being brutal and uncouth. One old woman watched horrified, fearing the worst, as three, huge- Marines lumbered up to a Buddhist temple.

The men then plopped down on the steps, and removed their cumbersome, combat boots before proceeding, caps in hand, up and into the house of worship.

The universal-Japanese controlled-docility came not only from the Emperor's rescript, but also from the old proverb: "Whichever side wins is the Emperor's army. Whichever side loses is the rebel army," During the many shifts of power in Japan, the victorious Shogun had always issued his commands in the name of the Emperor, the constant source of stability. So, the Americans were no longer the enemy, and MacArthur was the 'conquering Shogun.' Most people had no idea how they should conduct themselves, other than with their *obeisance* of constantly bowing, even to the lowliest private. The expansive Asian war had gone on so long for the Japanese, then the end had come so quickly. Most Japanese were confused, dazed, weary, but most of all, hungry, for another typhoon had wiped out a goodly portion of their meager rice crop. Then, so much of it had continually been sent to the army, even with the end coming.

Some Japanese had actually believed they would be taken to America to become slaves, like the known-Africans of the past. Most servicemen, on the other hand, were briefed on their mission by lecture and the film - *Your Job in Japan*, produced by the Intelligence and education Department, yet lacking greatly in the numerous minute-details of the daily culture. It showed a physical-brain, presumably Japanese, being molded and hammered by Occupation technicians, and finished by being 'jam-packed with *Democracy*.'

A popular misconception was there were no liberals among the Japanese. There were many liberals, but nothing much was heard from them during the war, as they were in prison early on. Japan held some twenty-thousand political prisoners, who were not just Communists, and those liberals not in jail, were under close surveillance. This was the fate of many Nisei, who were stuck in Japan, and then later made to work for the Japanese military government.

Most of the Japanese were too-relieved, to harbor much resentment against those who had defeated them. They soon turned what little energy they had into hatred against *their* national leaders - military and political, who had lead them into the hopeless-war for domination and power. This was soon the growing-basis, for a new Japan-nation built on pacifism. Not only the loss of millions of lives, but destruction of property, life-style, and culture. MacArthur, as Supreme Commander, filled a vacuum in leadership, his pompous- arrogance and aloof-way was accepted, as they put him on par with the Emperor. They were used to being told what to do, so someone to direct them out of the rubble, organize cleanup and rebuild the cities.

~ ~ ~ ~ ~ ~

The Facts:

The Japanese fire-bombing statistics were horrendous: 1.8 million killed, 8.7 million homeless; over 90% nationally of city dwellings destroyed - Tokyo, over 1 million of the 1.6 million residential buildings; Nagoya 89%; Hiroshima 60%; Nagasaki 36%. Basically, people slept in dugouts, shacks, the remaining portion of their bombed-out, burned homes, hallways, remaining subway/train platforms, sidewalks or their offices or class rooms. Visually, the impact was much more than any photograph could reveal, as most of the homes had been wood, unlike the brick or concrete-built European counterparts. Thus, a thick, black ash and soot was virtually everywhere, with the lone, metal poles, or chimneys of the more modern houses or bath houses, standing like sentinels, left to guard over nothing.

Occasionally, there would be a lonely *godown*, a kind of large safe, built from brick or other heavy material, in which wealthier families had kept their valuables. Some of these godowns had been built large enough, people were now living in them. Scraps of tin or metal, along with charred-pieces of wood, had sprouted-shelter sufficing for families, or leftovers of families gathering to support each other. Added to the war debris, garbage was strewn everywhere, as the usually tidy-Japanese had neither a working, collection system, nor motivation for doing so.

Deep holes pocked streets and broken-up sidewalks lead to what once had been beautiful, landscaped-gardens. Seen currently clogged with rubbish, overgrown trees, blackened bushes and stagnant pools, where fat gold fish - *koi* - had merrily swam. Various stone sidewalks and steps lead to nowhere, as the burned, rock-remnants of rambling, gracious wooden houses only remained. One advantage of a burned-out house, the land could be used to grow vegetables, but one guarded them day and night, as crime had invaded, from the poverty.

But most noticeable, and un-photographable was the odor. Pungent in its ripeness of a mildewing stench, or perhaps *brew* would be a better description. Most ingredients had been 'cooked' by the humid, summer sun, drenched, but not cleaned by the rain. As one came upon different areas the smell might change slightly, yet usually included unlimited, incinerated objects, including those which might have had life; urine and feces; molding and rotting items left, where they had previously belonged. Added to this was the repetitive-buzz of the quivering masses of flies, millions of well-fed flies. Hard to ignore the evidence of what had made them so abundant, as the flies wrapped around things, like a draped, black cloth. One had to suppress a shudder, realizing how fruitless life was for so many.

Definitely desolate, and repugnant at the same time, as it spoke of lost souls, along with lost hope. Everywhere, sometimes wandering, as if in a strange land, were these homogeneous-scarecrows, hungry, shoeless, and ragged. Many wore, literally bits and pieces of what could be called a clothing collection. They seemed to continue on, one step in front of another, as if they had become quite accustomed to the hardship and deprivation.

The mind, if not the body, would still remember the old, soft feel of soap, the hot soaking bath, a warm, clean futon - *mattress bedding* - and something separating the sole of the foot from the filthy, scorched earth. Even the youngest looked old, with unkempt hair, gaunt-drawn faces, and weathered-skin, the color of dead leaves. Most were set-off by eyes too sad to die. The desolation was more profound than ruin, as these people were long-past the weeping stage, and simply existed in the survival-mode.

Most ex-military Japanese swallowed their pride, and took whatever jobs they could to support themselves, or their families. For others, they used the 'spoils' of war to set up a business of building *new* homes to replace the bombed-out ones. Others drifted to the 'twilight societies' of vice, corruption, or the black market, to play on the habits and weaknesses of mankind. Only handfuls, still clung to threads of hope, thinking they would get their retribution against the Americans, who had brought them shame. Those not so physically- blessed, were considered pariahs to society, the visible war-cripples, who were painful reminders of loss. They used the term '*apres guerre*' - rather than combat-fatigue or battle-fatigue, when referring to those men. And blamed it as the basis for a rise in irrational crime, where before even petty-thievery had been rare. They were in such a derelict- state, almost lifeless, whereas before, by nature, the rudiments of everyday courtesy, had been more sensitive to them.

Everything seemed so much more wide-open and even expansive, since the houses removed by the bombing. Could this have really been a previous tightly-knit culture, teeming with active people hurrying to jobs, shopping and school classes? Now, there were only scattered stones, bricks, tiles, pieces of corrugated tin, broken crockery, as if in a surrealistic landscape. It was decorated, too, by the occasional water spigot, stone garden-lantern jutting out of the ground, which had previously been of some use. The black, burned-swaths across tree trunks looked painted for some special event, and contrasted to the embarrassing, yet humorous free-standing, resilient porcelain bathtubs and toilets. They appeared to be waiting to be used. The stillness resounded as a reflection of the devastation. Then, only broken by the clinking of the distant, infrequent trolley, which would never have been heard, so far from the street. How many personal stories could be told from the trinkets, mementos, and keepsakes poking out amidst the heaps, glinting-off the glaring-sun? How many lives had disintegrated along with the wreckage, and utter hopelessness and sorrow had been left on the ground, to drown in the tears shed? For the lonely scavengers searching, these may have been the only fragments left of their happy lives, before they had known the results of an expansionist's war.

Even with the conditions of over half of Tokyo in ruin, and literally hundreds of thousands of people living in the streets, SCAP (Supreme Commander of the Allied Powers) requisitioned quarters for *three-hundred-thousand* troops and hotel accommodations for over *nine-thousand male and fifteen-hundred female*, American civilians. They commandeered *housing for seven-hundred staff families*, and appropriated *almost five-hundred of the best houses for its officers*.

These were all put into first class, *Western-style* condition, and equipped at Japanese expense and labor, using scarce-materials for every conceivable modern comfort. By December, 1949, *Japan had built for the Occupation* over twenty-five hundred new houses, reconditioned almost six-hundred apartment buildings and turned-over another six-hundred more dwellings. With each house, apartment, etc. came Japanese care-takers of every sort, maids and houseboys, at the rate of five per General, four per Colonel, etc. This was the *only benefit* to the Japanese, and the economy, which barely existed.

To make daily life *easier* for the "*Occupationers*," over six- hundred railway cars and one-hundred-twenty urban-trolleys were *taken over* - the fact these were in short supply for the Japanese did not matter. This drained Japanese resources and delayed their own rehabilitation/rebuilding, but it didn't matter, the needs of SCAP- MacArthur came first, though they were supposed to be there to help. Perhaps, this is where the preverbal, ironic-phrase: *"We're from the Government, and we're here to help..."* came from, and the sad joke it implied, as to doing anything but. Actually, MacArthur's SCAP had *no intentions* of rebuilding anything they had blown up. The Japanese government had assumed they would, since SCAP was Westernizing everything else, why not the city of Tokyo? Of course, unfortunately what SCAP did under MacArthur's rule, and what Washington had planned to do, varied considerably.

Once the Reconstruction Board was set up, labor and material was to be rationed out on 'greatest need' basis. Black marketers and racketeers paying off the lower-level, American Occupation workers in charge, diverted much of this to the construction of brothels, 'romance' cafes/hotels, movie houses, and gambling joints, to keep the American military entertained and spending their money. This was all done under the diverted-eyes of SCAP, as MacArthur's distain for the everyday-Japanese trickled-down to all levels, and well-accepted as the way things were done. Needless to say, the program limped along badly in the large cities under government control. In the rural areas, the people were totally ignored, so rebuilt their homes on their own. By 1948, only half of the houses needed had been built. At least three-million more were needed, and as late as 1952 - when the Occupation Forces formally pulled out, over one million Japanese were still living in makeshift-housing.

Even when zoning and building laws were established in Tokyo, Osaka and Nagoya, both public and private contractors violated these laws with impunity. Again, with the usual business side- payments to both Japanese and American officials. In this way, the *Yakuza*, organized crime, grew to control the building construction industry. The Japanese government contented itself with grandiose- plans, which sounded and looked beautiful, but were totally unrealistic or impractical, as well as un-financeable. They kept their heads in the clouds, allowing Japan to be rebuilt helter-skelter and haphazardly, without regard to codes, congestion, or convenience. Just as in 1923, after the Great Kanto earthquake, the chance to start over from practically, cleared-land had been wasted.

* * * * * *

MacArthur was unprepared, as he did not expect the end to come so soon, and no plan had been detailed. Early in the war, the U.S. began planning the "Occupation," as they had expected their success. But, constant dissent between various groups made any final planning hopeless. The joke was the whole Occupation Plan was dreamed-up on the plane over from Manila, and considering some of the results, probably not far off. Technically, the Departments of State, War, and the Navy, made up the Coordination Committee, as well the JCS-10 (Far Eastern Commission of all the victorious nations) was to give the official orders.

But MacArthur drew distinctions, as to which *he would obey*, as implementation for an order was totally under his control. The Japanese politicians would appeal to MacArthur, tongue in cheek, against certain directives to win public favor, as all JCS-10 directives were published in the newspapers. The politicians cared almost as little for the common Japanese as MacArthur. They were, and always had been, only for Japanese Business, no matter what harm or danger came to the general Japanese population.

At least, MacArthur did one positive thing by not letting Japan be quadrated off like Berlin. The Soviets, who were rarely consulted or kept informed, wanted full control of a set area, and pulled-out altogether when MacArthur refused. Except for their participation in sitting in on the War Crimes Trial, they had little power with governing. The Soviets then concentrated their influence into the newly-freed Japanese Communist Party, which was renamed the "Lovable Communist Party," seriously. They knew how to do propaganda in the very best way, and had a great following from the naive, burned-out Japanese. They willingly followed *any* political group who promised them food, jobs, and equality - even one which had absolutely no track record of previously doing any of those things.

Miscommunications, along with egos - even where they had no reason to exist, put inept people in charge of whatever area with some value, and reigned from the beginning, as everyone scrambled for a position of influence. Ad hoc meetings in Manila for the installation of the Occupation directors on September 6, were then changed again to a military administration by September 10, and this did not make the Japanese happy. They had just come out from under one bad military rule, and did not want to go under another. MacArthur reverted again October 2, with ten staff sections to deal with non-military and civil affairs. Still, most of the heads of these department went to *friends and associates as rewards*, with no concern about their ability or training, or how much they would be looking to gain for themselves.

Research records show, numerous Americans scooped-up control of a variety of Japanese property and businesses. Few of the Washington selected and trained staff filled posts of any stature, and always had to report to a military head, who reported to MacArthur. They were soon relegated to the back, as their knowledge threatened the military chiefs. So, all the time and money Washington had spent training people to run the Occupation, turned into another, fruitless- government program. These Washington people were also restricted from any direct communication to Washington, so *king*-MacArthur could continue to *run his team* the way *he wanted*.

Many of the staff workers came from closing-offices in the military sections, and for adventure, curiosity, study, or just the higher pay allowances, with exceptional benefits for overseas work. Most would not only *not* have qualified for civilian-American jobs, they would never have been paid even half as much, with all the extras they received, including cheap servants. The quality and efficiency varied, as did the expectations based on other misleading promises of participating in a history-making time period. The civilians and military clashed as always, and the animosity was accentuated even more, with the former being on higher salaries and a forty-hour week. For the military, MacArthur's own stance of the superiority of a military mind, fed egos like in no other instance in recent history, except for the German military. Red tape was abundantly used by both, with so much in-fighting, it was amazing they got anything done. Just as the Japanese had been guinea-pigs for the atomic bombs, they were again being used for the SCAP-Occupation experimentation.

SCAP had total censorship of all military action by everyone, and it created a malaise of exceptional proportions. Ineptness was only a small portion of the problems they created, to be endured by others. The paranoid, morbid suspicions of the extensively-layered circle around Mac Arthur tried to protect him against belittlement, and his tendency for aggrandizement multiplied almost daily. By the time he was expunged by President Truman, the reality showed for such a long period of time, more should have actually been accomplished.

Clearly, no one in Washington had ever gone back to even check, if any of his claims had become fact, or just figments of his delusional-mind. The sole fact, MacArthur had NEVER ventured forth from Tokyo, and his section chiefs were under orders *not to leave* the capital without permission. Only those in the provinces knew the truth, and they begged for inspection tours, or at least to have their reports read - all was in vain. To question SCAP-MacArthur, was disloyalty, and devoted section leaders 'spared' MacArthur the pain of contradictory-details from the field. Subordinates deleted any *unpleasant* news, so a fifty-page report got whittled down to perhaps five pages.

Much was disregarded out of ignorance, but more was intentional, as MacArthur's contempt for any opinions outside his circle, or for anyone who questioned *his* trumped-up expertise, was not easy for him to bear. MacArthur knew basically nothing about Japan, nor the Japanese, as he had lived mainly in the Philippines. He resented greatly when the Japanese had marched in so easily, and taken it over. It must have also been quite embarrassing, to make his hasty retreat to Australia. Though not quite so hasty, as he and his wife refused to leave behind any of their extensive furniture and belongings - taking up space on the ship, which could have carried more people to safety. Also embarrassing, the *verified fact* MacArthur had accepted half a million (US 1942) dollars from the Philippine government.

One might call it 'gift' money, in the typical Asian pay-off- term, to guarantee *he and his* American troops would *ably defend, protect and otherwise keep* the Japanese out of the Philippines. So, MacArthur did not want to follow anyone's plan but his own, even though he did not have one. Most of all, he did not want any '*Japanophiles,*' or sympathizers. Any serious criticism was called *Communist-inspired*, as how could the instilling of Democracy be wrong? Of course, it was his rather skewed-version of Democracy, he was talking about.

Interesting Side Note: MacArthur had not felt the Japanese had done much improvement on their own the first year of Occupation, so he had been quite critical of them. When invited to return to celebrate Philippine

Independence in July, 1946, he was profoundly-depressed by what he saw, as it looked almost exactly as it had when he left. The Filipinos seemed primarily more interested in what they could extract from the Americans, for their separation/independence. Whereas, the Japanese had been seriously trying to get things going again for themselves, since MacArthur had refused for them to receive so little from the Americans.

* * * * * *

The first reforms, long planned by Washington, were instituted under the so-called "Bill of Rights." These SCAP directives guaranteed freedom of speech, assembly, religion, and political activity. This provided for the release of the thousands of political prisoners. The election law was amended to lower the voting age from twenty-five, and to guarantee the right of suffrage to women. Land reform was ordered, the education system restructured, and government financial support of State Shinto religion was abolished. In fact, one could say every phase of Japanese society was changed according to these directives written in Washington, or perhaps as re-written by MacArthur. They were carried out by zealous SCAP personnel, imbued with the missionary-zeal of creating a new nation.

Japan would be Democratized, though no one ever took the time to explain exactly what it was, or how it was better, or even different from what they had before the war. Considering how MacArthur was running it all, one could not say he was leading by example. So, for the Japanese, these new concepts could only be learned by demonstration of how the American put their own 'rights' into practice. The treatment of their own 'Negro' or black troops was not a good example of Democracy to be shown, yet visible to all.

Yet, one of the best examples was the War Crimes trial, which MacArthur had little control over - much to his disappointment. This was where the Japanese saw some of the American trial lawyers defend, as well as prosecute, the former military and civilian leaders. For many Allies, especially Americans, they were rather shocked at the amount of information being revealed, as to how they- the US had *contributed* to Japan's attack on Pearl Harbor.

To the Japanese, it had never been an act of aggression, but desperation as their economic preservation had been controlled and jeopardized by the "ABCD" - Americans, British, Chinese and Dutch." Over and over again, it was proven *misinterpretation* of telegrams and communications, with the difficult innuendos of the ambiguity of the Japanese language, had been at fault. Truly, not so much by inept, American interpreters, just those tending to report more what their military superiors *wanted to believe*, rather than what actually stated.

Even Roosevelt, up to the end, had wanted to send his drafted compromise, stipulating the Japanese withdrawal in China. But, the political and military pressures from Britain and *particularly the Soviets,* made him succumb, and ignore the last changes for peace. Even with an extremely-prejudiced Chief Justice, most of the International Tribunal wrote dissenting statements. Yet, most Japanese knew there could be only one outcome of these trials. They wanted scapegoats, as much as the Allies. Over the two years, the court battles were quite impressive and revealing to all.

After the expunging of all top politicians, much was expected of the few lower-level Japanese ones, who had only done what they were told. Now, new decisions, suggestions, and creation of ideas were expected from these novices, who had never even been allowed to make decisions, (Only top Japanese hierarchy EVER made the decisions) much less know *how to* go about doing so. And, this was all to be carried-out under national, bankrupt conditions, as well with people-dropping in the streets like flies, from starvation.

MacArthur would not accept *the fact* of the lack of food, from crop failure and the typhoon. He felt it was a ploy for American aid, though Washington waited for his approval to send it. He insisted the Japanese army had squirreled-away tons of food in the mountains, and he was simply going to wait them out, in producing it for their dying people. So, not until mid-1946, MacArthur finally accepted the reports of more than ten-thousand had died, he reluctantly requested food rations be released from Washington. Then only a third was sent, as to the way his staff had ordered it.

Though corruption among the new Japanese politicians was just as prevalent, as it had been in pre-war Japan, still it remained unchecked by SCAP. Again, MacArthur felt the Japanese people deserved who they had voted into office. In many instances, this actually fed and encouraged the untold numbers of U.S. military, who participated in the black market, with the fortunes they made off the desperate Japanese.

Many spoke or wrote of Democracy, while the ruling was by military-autocracy. Even the laws of the Japanese Supreme Court, had to follow the rules of the Occupation-SCAP. And, those rules were definitely-different for any American military, than for the Japanese citizens. Not surprising the Japanese questioned the hypocrisy of this *so-called* Democracy being demonstrated before them, which they were expected to embrace wholeheartedly. Unfortunately, most of the military were only looking for a promotion, Legion of Merit, or other commendation, which would come with overseas duty, as well the other side-monetary benefits of being there.

With all of these contradictions, the Occupation was still considered to have been successful by Washington. Even though after its end, much was repealed, modified, or simply ignored, as most programs failed. Japanese chose which points to ensconce, and endeavored not to try to mirror American-methods, where they went against their basic culture - the *Wa* - or the Japanese Way of doing all things. Still, the real problem had been the vagueness of the concepts of liberty, freedom, and Democracy itself, had never been even closely-realized in all of Japan's history.

Those American basics every U.S. citizen was supposed to take for granted, even if not received, but practiced, as if they did have them. In reality, to most Americans, it would be difficult for even the more eloquent to note simply and clearly what Democracy etc. was in one's daily life. The constant contradiction of the military made most ludicrous, much less misleading, as when directives were issued with no intent of follow through. The Japanese understood they were for the record only, and everyone went through the motions, with no one doing much of anything for real changes.

Many of the Americans there felt because of Japan's war record of atrocities, fanaticism, and cruelty even to their own troops, they would be incapable of becoming a Democratic nation. How short their memories were of what other countries had done in the name of Democracy, including the U.S. to the Native Americans, or the 'freed' black slaves, less than a hundred years before.

Historical-amnesia was a disease most countries conveniently developed, when speaking ill of others. The fact no hostile, foreign- solider had ever set foot on Japan's ground in its *two thousand plus- year history*, did not seem to temper this mixed-judgement of the Japanese. Rarely did an Occupation worker consider, how Americans would have responded, had the tables been turned, and they the occupied-ones, controlled by foreign-speakers with a strange culture.

The previous Western revolution, - Meiji Restoration, 1868, - had come in hunks and pieces digested by society, before more was taken on. It had too, been somewhat *by choice* to participate in and with the rest of the world, not forced by a face-to-face Occupation. Most naively, they believed what worked for Americans, would surely work, and be welcomed, by the Japanese. So, following MacArthur's negative beliefs, why bother to check on their history, social strata, customs, or anything else. Did not *everyone in the world* want to be just like the Americans, and have a country just like America? Simply put, but shocking to some, No.

Even before the Occupation forces had arrived, government and administration reforms were introduced by the Japanese - new rights, freedoms, etc. These were flatly rejected as being insincere and insufficient, yet shortly after MacArthur's arrival, SCAP produced a set which almost paralleled them. This slight was considered to be exactly what it was - MacArthur's SCAP wanted *any and all* credit for whatever reform was put into place. There would be no working together, no compromising, much less collaboration, no sharing of ideas or suggestions, … merely the imposition of the conqueror's prescriptions. Again, hypocritical came up, as some Japanese even feared being made a colony of America, as part of their punishment.

A basic characteristic of the Japanese culture - to follow what a leader had told them to do, good or bad - demonstrated so well in war - made SCAP think the Japanese were happy with what they were doing for them. This cooperation was a veneer - granted, one which extended six years, yet, when SCAP did realize some of the discontent, they merely blamed it on their favorite scapegoat - the Communist Party propaganda, which SCAP had once supported. When stricter rules were put in, to supposedly control the Communist, the Japanese felt it irrational, as all were being restrained in their thoughts and actions.

The mere issuance of an order or directive, was to make it accepted and palatable to the Japanese, no matter how contrary to their culture or custom. Many U.S. military felt it was part of their job to change these centuries-old customs. Though there were many within SCAP, who were said to have had great understanding of Japanese psychology and affairs, little of this was obviously shared, or trickled down to any layer of the staff.

There was no cultural guide, and most of these Japanese experts on the staff were silenced, so as not to clog up the 'efficiency' of the SCAP work. The inner-circle, and especially the inner-sanctum, of the Supreme Commander rarely gave an audience, but stayed aloof and unapproachable. Many said, as the Japanese Emperor gave up his deity-ship, MacArthur assumed it - and quite comfortably, too.

The pattern within the levels of the SCAP staff was separate concentric circles - no crossing over into or out of their respective circles. And, control was tightly held with strict reprimands, transfers or demotions. All the more, a helping-hand to a newcomer must be avoided, and speaking to a Japanese official, except briefly for specific business, was *reprehensible*. There was great scorn shown toward anyone studying non-military aspects of Japan. Need, had they wanted to investigate, *allowed* research materials were slim to none.

Personal collections were kept private, disregarding if they had originally belonged to the military or the government. Most rejected any information written after 1937, as tainted by the Japanese Military government. SCAP distrusted all dates, especially statistics which they did not produce themselves, favoring themselves. The proposal of efficient 'fact' finding services to be established was rejected three different times. SCAP did not want to know what the Japanese felt, or how their programs were being received. Not so much as any newspapers, carried any wanted feedback information. Military, and civilian workers, lived in their limited foreign world. Except for the occasional Kabuki, they were oblivious to the Japanese world … surrealistic, a faux and self-created Utopia, and of course, rarely questioned to keep your job.

For most though, the peacefulness was disquieting. The docile Japanese response gave false hope the Occupation would end quickly - no demonstrations and no obvious bitterness. When the Japanese did complain, such as about Soviet brutality in Manchuria to Japanese POWs, they called it typical insolence, on the Japanese's part. On the other hand, the Yokuska Liaison Commission publicized minor incidents of SCAP personnel against the Japanese. But these numbers were quickly brought under control, from over three-hundred in the first few months, to only thirty, by the end of the year.

The 'Public Relations' of MacArthur (a full staff of 50, personally-chosen men, *paid by the Occupation*, only answering to Mac) were at a constant battle with the press, and accused it of tying to sabotage the Occupation. The continuous conflict of statements coming from SCAP was part of the problems, as they were full of contradictions on almost a daily basis. Yet, when questioned, the usual accusations of Communist-intent were hurdled at whomever for whatever reason.

They were true victims of their own Public Relations, as most SCAP believed they could do no wrong, and were paranoid about hearing anything which might suggest differently. Perhaps, they too, had taken to heart MacArthur's title of Supreme Commander, as meaning he was infallible in judgement, and *naturally* understood all things. One resulting factor was the use of spies to watch each other, or 'those' who questioned what was being done. They rarely hesitated to call in the MPs, or even the secret service, once they felt they had sought out a 'Red' leaner. Staff were deported regularly on simply the basis of asking too many times what something meant. Blackmail regularly resulted, and the personal escapades of even upper-level personnel, became highly entertaining to SCAP and the Japanese alike. If suspicion had not been the basis of MacArthur's press relations, many reputations could have been saved.

If the Japanese press did not print the official, verbose- statements, no matter how redundant, they were labeled as reactionaries, and dangerous. At the same time, the press questioned the validity of MacArthur's press corps, as they were caught sensationalizing, or creating *entire false stories* for their or his own benefit. Such as the *invented-plot* to assassinate MacArthur on the eve of the May Day demonstration in 1946. Still, the biggest problem was SCAP *never* set-up a board of central planning for the rebuilding. There were no priorities as to what should be done first, based on needs, resources or implementation, for over-all effect. Each Occupation section remained sovereign in itself, and going in its own direction, wherever it was.

Consequently, the government section ended-up endorsing, or appearing to endorse, several different political parties. On the surface this was good, but these parties were mostly backed by racketeers, Communists, and various past politicians. The SCAP people were easily duped by each party using some form of 'Democracy' in their intent. The controlled and restricted interaction with Japanese, made SCAP vulnerable to anyone who simply reiterated their own words. After embarrassing stories hit the press, the underlings tried to suppress this information. This 'support,' unbeknownst to them, had a great influence in the elections, as the Japanese people wanted to please MacArthur, just as they had pleased their Emperor. Then SCAP turned around and blamed the people, who had voted crooks and Communists into office.

Added to this was the lack of thoroughly, competent interpreters. Many were not officers and could not allow their ignorance to show, or indeed ask the chief to slow down, repeat or stop. Both sides stayed vague on most topics, as the language's own ambiguity protected them, from any loss of face in saying too much, or committing too far. Many of the Nisei from Hawaii or California, descended from Okinawa or Kyushu, so had problems with understanding the many different dialects, even idioms, as well their varied-use of honorifics.

On the other hand, some Department Chiefs felt English was the best language, and let the Japanese worry about their own translation. SCAP had no idea how many Japanese had graduated from western universities, and some of the Japanese who were quite proficient, yet never volunteered the information. They learned so much more by *not* speaking English, and only listening to what was being said around and about them in English.

Feminine-Japanese companionship, especially of the English- speaking variety, was generously offered to the high-ranking officials as they arrived. Most of their families did not join them until later, if at all, and many enthusiastically accepted. To call them 'spies' may not have been an exaggeration, as they worked for the Japanese government, and informed them of everything which took place in the officials' residences. The service was not limited to women, or just for men. The oldest trick was still working, and soon was extended to the awarding of the contracts for the rebuilding process.

One could say, MacArthur was notwithstanding being above receiving *'presentos,'* as he accepted a suit of medieval, *gold armor* as a personal gift. Until turning the yen into dollars was declared illegal, the armed forces remitted back to America eight-million dollars *more than* their total pay. Someone, and not just the Yakuza, was making money from the black market. To say this undermined confidence in the integrity of the SCAP Occupation was obvious. Scandal after scandal, minor and major, continued into 1952. It had been proven Americans could be 'bought,' whether by women or bribes, so even the innocent were suspect on both sides.

Though his orders came from JCS-10, MacArthur tacitly- insinuated they were his own creation. When he did stray-obviously from the directive, rarely was he questioned by JCS-10, as they felt they might discredit the whole Occupation program. MacArthur ignored most other commissions, or agencies who in some way were to control, question or limit his decisions. The main focus was MacArthur wanted to draft the new Japanese constitution all on his own, without interference from anyone of any authority. This was not in the original Washington or Potsdam Treaty Plan, as the previous constitution only needed to have some of the military government restrictions lifted from the people.

Actually, a Japanese idea to make Japan a non-military sort of 'Oriental Switzerland.' Soon many cabinet members and political parties were issuing their outlines for a new constitution to MacArthur. None were acceptable to him, as if he even read them, as he wanted the destiny of the deed to be only his. The Emperor totally accepted the loss of his previous prerogatives, and spoke to the people in March about a new constitution. He never mentioned, of course, SCAP had already written it, and the Diet had been coerced to accept it. In spite of the fact, all legislations were "Passed" by the Diet, it first had to 'pass' MacArthur.

Much of this was done verbally, as no written record could exist of this secret control. MacArthur, through SCAP, could override any law passed without his approval, if the Diet had not passed a MacArthur legislation, he would have it put through as a Cabinet directive. This was, of course, totally illegal, and against the very constitution MacArthur had written. MacArthur's escape was always the same - "the by-passing of the Diet had been essential to the Democratic results, and was a justifiable emergency device." The courts were ruled in a similar fashion, using whatever methods MacArthur felt necessary. Justice was blind and definitely prejudiced, as their rulings concerning SCAP and its associates, were quite different from those ruling the Japanese.

The continual, serious, Communist-inspired riots made MacArthur regret the anti-war clause of the Constitution. In July, 1950, a special security organization for national internal defense was established. The term National Police Reserve was used for the seventy-five thousand men. This obvious circumvention of the Constitution's Article 9 was, and still is, an embarrassment to the Diet, as it should have amended the 'non-military/no war clause."

* * * * * *

Through the original Potsdam Treaty statement, a purge of all those Japanese who had 'mislead or deceived' were supposed to rid Japan of its past problems. President Truman and his Joint Chiefs of Staff listed top military officers, chief ultra-nationals, and other advocates of aggression. They were 'to be arrested and then barred from all future posts of public and substantial private responsibility. As well, direct Japan's economic efforts 'solely for peaceful ends.' The vague directives gave MacArthur more unchecked, destructive power than any one person, supposedly-sponsoring a Democratic process ever had. Most were removed strictly because of the positions they had, rather than for any deeds they may have done. Again, many cronies befitting from their removal.

On the other hand, MacArthur personally protected a number of high-ranking officers, who had been closely *attached to Nazi- Germany in military or diplomatic* ways. Some of these were even placed on Occupation payrolls, and given special privileges, while maintaining full acknowledgment of their rank. Various explanations were given, one being they were working on a Japanese history of the war, or they were coordinating Japanese and American intelligence concerning Soviet activities. Neither was ever verified, nor answer why MacArthur had taken such a personal interest in them to begin with. Again, simply his personal and secret prerogative to do so, because he could, and then got away with it.

This purge was also supposed to break up the *Zaibatsu* - the monolithic, Japanese business-combines who controlled nearly every phase of Japanese trade and industry. Surprisingly, a greater task than SCAP ever realized. They were not seen as the historic, great builders and employers of Japan, but as the sinister-monopolies, who had fed the tyrannical and sadistic military. Totally, lacking any international business acumen, SCAP did not consider these conglomerates, dated back to the Meiji Restoration or earlier.

Their vast roots had been extended into the U.S. economy, as well as Europe, for several generations. Those American and European international business partners deplored this short-sighted program of systematic dismemberment, as it did not support *their own* long term growth, with the new potential Japanese customers. The continued increase of war taxation, had also severely eaten into profits, which limited Japanese business expansion, and the protection of their employees. This did not mean the Zaibatsu had not participated in producing parts or equipment for the military. They did not usually have much choice, the military was the only customer with money.

The four big holding companies - Mitsui, Mitsubishi, Yasuda, and Sumitomo, were singled out among the eighty-three destroyed, as their founding families were not allowed to retain, or so much as acquire, any of the securities of the dissolved companies. The fifty-three top individuals members, of the leading Zaibatsu families were instructed by the Occupation authorities to divest themselves of their personal securities. Then, pay a ninety-percent tax on any remaining assets, such as real estate and personal property. For a representative group whose main thrust was to be Democratization of Japan, one might question this infringement of rights to personal and private property. SCAP-style Democracy in action again, unquestioned.

One cannot also say Japan, itself did not have anything to do with the procedure, called "democratization of the economy." The Cabinet in the government, submitted the dissolution plan to SCAP. This included the names of all of the people - from owners, directors and auditors - who were required to resign their offices. Then a question, which has no direct answer: Who benefited from the Holding Company Liquidation Commission, which took over all securities owned by the previous held companies of the Zaibatsu? And, who designated to 'dispose' of these securities? A layered-maze holds the secret, but quite *a few Western names* have been researched, as *still receiving monies* from Japanese connected trust funds.

Could such sweeping statements be said: "All Japanese in high-company positions were selfish, brutal and supportive of the military" or "Many of their subordinates were good men, capable of taking over to run these multi-dimensional corporations," efficiently, or even sufficiently? Again, in Japanese business culture, ONLY the top-titled people made decisions. How were these subordinates suppose to do this without having ever done so before, or even been trained to do so?

Following, the Occupation forces also instituted a political- purge, which swept almost every civil servant from office in Japan. This all-inclusive dragnet scooped up millions of Japanese, whose positions placed them far below the decision-making level. They were though, generously given the opportunity to prove their innocence, by filling out detailed questionnaires *in English,* which were screened by the Japanese government (?!?!) under SCAP supervision. Those who did not pass approval by their peers were blacklisted, and forbidden to hold any government post at all. So, those few who had stayed in their official posts to help keep whatever balance they could in the military- controlled days, were tossed to the wind without any reward or acknowledgement. Of course, in the usual Japanese way, pay-offs were extensive as to who stayed and who was forced to go.

Into the turbulent future, trying to build something from destruction, Japan was deprived of all of its leadership class - business and political. Ironically, one could say they were totally back to square one, where they had been almost one hundred years prior. Yet, actually worse, as the stocks of raw materials were depleted, and all major cities, except Kyoto, were destroyed. Add to this, the constant shortages of food, due to decreased crop production with lack of manpower each successive war year. The Japanese people were exhausted from years of deprivation, and the humiliation of facing the former-enemy on a daily basis.

A slow recovery to say the least, with benign GIs contributing generously by giving children candy instead of rice, or civilians sugar instead of meat. SCAP said the Japanese government was responsible for feeding its people, and taking care of them medically, when the only ones with abundant food and medicines were the Occupation forces. To this there was no response, as the same weak-kneed Japanese politicians and businessmen, who had stayed in the background during the war, never saying or doing anything. As they had once fawned on their own military, they sang hymns of praise of the Army of the Occupation, calling themselves 'moderates and lovers of peace' only. If SCAP thought the former industrialists were self- serving, they had nothing on these new ones, who brought new depth to practicing-toadying.

After the harness of the war-crimes trials, Zaibatsu busting, and purges of all leadership, the Occupation forces felt the Japanese had now experienced the justice of free enterprise. As well, the political reform through the great, democratic system, with leveling of the class structure. Theses sudden changes, especially for the uneducated-peasants, who were the majority of people, brought on more shocks than the war itself had. They had lived most of their lives, from generation to generation, in a benevolent feudal system, which some may have violated and others resented, yet it had direction. Now, those they had depended on, were as poverty-stricken as themselves, and those who had been second, as best, were only leading in circles by telling SCAP what it wanted to hear. Recovery was an unknown goal, which would take years just to find the right path to follow.

In a fairer extent, SCAP did break-up the secret police rather quickly, considering it affected five-thousand members. In no time though, the purge turned into a disastrous three-ring circus, which a later-day Senator Joseph McCarthy would have been proud. Since SCAP really did not know which individuals should be purged, they naively asked for recommendations from the Japanese government. So, this meant any members of any groups, which had existed prior to and during the war. Of course, opportunists took the chance to rid whomever they wanted, as SCAP rarely questioned any accusations, even anonymous ones, or names issued to them. The accused were denied a fair trial, or an opportunity to prove their innocence. Once again the knowing-Japanese questioned the integrity of this American Democracy, which was supposed to protect individual human rights. MacArthur reminded them, the former-military government had violated these civil rights, too, as if excused of doing the same.

The political-machinery was put into motion for justice and democracy, as it crunched away the careers and lives of tens-of- thousand of Japanese. Many believed MacArthur was trying to *at least* reach the three-hundred thousand number, equal to the Nazis who had been purged from German life. The fact Japan, and the Japanese, had been so tightly controlled by such s relatively small militaristic- expansionistic group was unacceptable to SCAP's thinking.

Most branch chiefs jumped with zeal, to be given credit to cleanse Japan of all of its previous reactionaries. To make the purge a more bitter pill to swallow, it proceeded under the guise the the Japanese government did the removal, of the cancerous people from its tainted society. Interestingly enough, the Communists were the least affected, at first. The purge collected virtually the entire managerial and administrative staffs of the largest organizations and corporations. Who was to take over to rebuild and lead Japan into the economic future, of course, was not planned? And, whether the new leaders would be more honest or democratic, also had not come into the facts. Just, purge and let the consequences take care of themselves.

Once again the leftist-Communists, who had gained so much favor with SCAP and MacArthur, were able to have purged any and all politicians who in the past had spoken against them. The fact these victims had also spoken against the military government did not matter. Japan was also now lacking government leadership. This was extended to include all mayors of the smallest villages, who may have been appointed, but also had probably acted under duress. The extensiveness of some purging included relatives to the third degree, which the Japanese government protested violently again this unfairness. It fell upon deaf ears.

Eventually in 1949, the purge hit the Communists, all in the educational area, interestingly enough. By 1950, a reverse process was happening as Prime Minister Yoshida's office had reviewed numerous extensive complaints and some ten-thousand were cleared. Finally, when General Ridgeway took over in May, 1951, after Truman removed MacArthur, all but convicted war criminals were released from jail or all restrictions. For many who committed suicide, or lost every possession, it was a little too late to have justice. Not surprisingly, the acquiescent Japanese never created any aftermath, despite their lives having been left in ruin.

* * * * * *

With the Emperor being relegated to a human standing, rather than his previous deity-ship, MacArthur wanted him brought closer to the people, so the most stringent nationalist would accept his fall. For some, simply hearing about the Emperor's daily habits were sufficient to humanize him. Yet, for the dyed-in-the-wool

164

worshipper, nothing short of revealing the Emperor was not Japanese, would have changed their belief. For all of his life being swathed in tradition, put upon by the Imperial Household for a millennium plus, the Emperor was quite an aficionado of all things Western, from clothes to food. He did not so much as own a kimono, nor a single pair of *getas* - wooden clogs - and he rarely ate miso soup, rice and fish for breakfast, as the majority of his subjects did everyday.

In the first photographs published of the Imperial Family in the Palace in *Life Magazine,* Japanese and Westerners alike were shocked to see the prominent bust of Lincoln, which had always been in Hirohito's personal study. Much had been falsely written about the Emperor and the Imperial Household, as his and their main function are notoriously misconstrued by SCAP. The Western media was trying to create stories where there were none, or at least not very exciting ones. Categorically, the Throne was the symbol of power, always venerated, esteemed-sanctification, as the man sitting on it changed.

Hirohito was not the tyrant or malcontent of a Hitler or Mussolini. Just a man of very limited power, especially when wanting to deal with the militaristic government and their diehards in the Diet. The Emperor never really had governed the people, and the details of his deity-ship had been manipulated, to be used as the spearhead of the fanaticism. Hirohito was a quiet man, who seemed to yield to his emotion only reluctantly. He was more naive and gullible than the pasty-monster created for the purpose of expansion, and a reason to die for. The layers which surrounded him, also isolated him from much of the real truth, just as MacArthur's staff did for him.

But the Emperor had the excuse, he rarely left the Palace and spent most of his time with spiritual duties, his garden and his extensive fish research (Some of it was recognized and registered at the Scripts Oceanic Institute in San Diego, CA). MacArthur, on the other hand, had total-freewill to go anywhere, to inspect anything, but then facts and reality could be harsh findings, he had no interest in.

Even Hirohito, like his predecessors, did what he was told and signed what he was instructed to. As in the past, no Japanese Emperor had dared take any other action. Yet, he did speak out after Hiroshima, and *tried to surrender,* but again the little known Japanese honorifics of the Imperial Household language could not be appropriately translated. As the American military pressured the interpreters, they had no clue his honorific Japanese had surrendered, so indicated he said, "No." Then, after Nagasaki, Hirohito tried again, and finally they accepted his honorific-convoluted words.

Hirohito then went back to his reticent, stoicism when the Occupation and its puppet-government took over. The Occupation- SCAP, felt it was to their advantage to keep Hirohito as a useful tool, as the people still obeyed 'his' orders. All this was done under formal- courtesy and protection of his rights. The surrender of the Imperial Sovereignty had never been agreed to in the Potsdam Treaty, and SCAP had no concept of this implication, although it was very real to the Japanese people.

Hirohito had offered to abdicate to show his deep sense of responsibility, for the resulting calamities the war had brought upon his country. Many Japanese of high, political level favored his abdication, for in the direct Japanese tradition, *it would have quickly and completely absolved all of their responsibility.* To point, in the past, a police official felt it incumbent to resign, if not kill himself, for having carelessly led an Imperial procession astray, and school principals resigned for mispronouncing the difficult, rarely-used words of an Imperial Rescript. So, even the more educated Japanese were often lost, in what the Emperor was saying to his people. This deep-set tradition was totally accepted, as it reenforced the Emperor-deity- difference from them.

SCAP, in their ignorance of *any* Japanese customs though, did not want him to become a martyr, and in many ways treated him no differently than any other Japanese. MacArthur felt all the more the Emperor must 'come to him,' so questions were never asked of him, and reforms were countenanced implicitly. When they finally did meet, MacArthur did not wear a full-dress uniform - he wore his usual open shirt khakis. Of course, so shocking, the Japanese considered him totally ignorant of etiquette, never thinking of it as simply *disrespect* of their Emperor.

Colonel Whitney, one of the most suspicious of all SCAP leaders, trusted no one and felt everyone was trying to undermine MacArthur and himself. He had the greatest influence on MacArthur, as their offices had connecting doors, so he could enter anytime. The Imperial family became the focal point of his distrust, so he created a series of embarrassments for them. He had stripped away any power Hirohito would never have dreamed of using. Whitney insisted all Japanese nobility resign their titles and become commoners. These titles had only existed since the Meiji period anyway, so it was not a situation of numerous generations. As commoners, they had to register at city offices to get their ration card, then stood in line for personal and home necessities. Though they received financial settlements, they had to pay taxes and much was later lost through bad investments, as they had little business experience.

Seventy-five percent of the staff of the Palace were dismissed, but more than twenty-five thousand Japanese people per year signed up - a year ahead - to clean the sixteen hundred acre grounds. In January, 1946, a public poll showed ninety-percent favored Hirohito, which continued through 1951, the last poll done. All but four of the eighty-nine political parties supported him, and in 1951, only the Communists opposed him. Whitney encourage Hirohito to make inspection tours around the country.

He deviously hoped, when the people saw him as an 'unimposing-bespectacled-figure' with a weak chin, round shoulders, nervous tic at the corner of his mouth, and a high-pitched voice, they would no longer pay homage to him. Much to his chagrin, Whitney could not have been more totally wrong, as thousands of Japanese people poured out to still worship their Emperor. Obviously, more to their hero-worship than looks.

Hirohito made more personal appearance in more parts of Japan in two years than he had for the entire preceding twenty-five. Though he did cut a poor figure by American standards at first, his visits encouraged towns, villages and cities to quickly clean-up the war rubble, rebuild the roads and bridges, as well as paint and repair. Soon his visits were considered a boon to the area, his popularity soared and he was nominated the most popular man in Japan.

Again, SCAP was shocked and angered at the *ignorance* of the Japanese people. Of course, since MacArthur himself had never visited outside his headquarters, they had only 'heard' of his existence. Also, quite a Western misconception was the Emperor ever really feeling himself Divine. And, he had no problem denying this or calling it a myth.

Although, at the close of the Occupation, Hirohito duly returned once again to the sacred, Grand Shrine of Ise. At the tombs of his ancestors - Emperor Jimmu and others - he profoundly reported Japan was once again a free nation. By July, 1952, Hirohito sent out photographs to schools who requested them. Then, all Imperial household regulations abolished by the Occupation were re-installed, under the auspices of the Diet and constituents numerous requests.

* * * * * *

Though the Occupation had promised to reduce the civil services, they were actually increased by eighty-four percent in three years. Many of the new decentralized prefectural and city governments grew larger each year, as most had previously been volunteer, and now they were on salary. They took over countless jobs which had been controlled before by industrial and commercial councils. The purging of so many industrial leaders gave them more access to power. Those who may have collaborated with the Japanese military government, burned records or moved to other localities, or even exchanged jobs with some on a lower level. Unquestioning-loyalty to a superior allowed this to happen, and still does in modern Japan, as a lower level employee will stoically 'volunteer' guilt to protect a superior.

Much of Tokyo's 'reform' was carried out with the skillful help of former Foreign Office attaches who spoke English, so knew what to do or say to make MacArthur and SCAP happy. Somehow, the glorified ability of speaking English made these people unquestionable, as to their intentions or honesty. Things went from bad to worse when MacArthur called in specialist Blaine Hoover, and he declared no public servants be allowed to join unions, strike, etc.

He *thought* they were all Communists since they had been protesting. The upcoming demonstrations and elections in early 1947 reflected the people's feelings of going against SCAP, as well by supporting bureaucracies. If they had to choose, they chose who they knew. The Government division of SCAP became obsessed with a Communist take over, and wanted all strikes banned. So much for the newly-installed civil rights and liberties. Again, in SCAP's total ignorance, they were the ones feeding right into the Communist- influences of the Japanese people.

There was no understanding of Japanese politics, for they did not relate to those of the U.S., or any other Western country. The glorious names, slogans and promises meant nothing, as the elected need not rely on the locals for financial support. Therefore, once elected and secure in his funding, he may wholly disregard his constituency. Numerous candidates ran on an independent ticket, then once elected sold their position to the highest bidder, changing parties frequently, as the money or his position changed. Most of the time, the real manipulators with the influential connections to the wealthy corporations never ran, but stayed behind the scenes funneling the money, while dolling out the government contracts. Not that this was truly any different than politics in America. Though Americans were planted behind a two-party system, the heavy money stayed in the background, pulling strings in the infamous 'backroom' deals.

In Japan tainted contributions from rice lords, racketeers, etc. were discretely channeled into the party treasuries. People continued to elect them, since the choices were usually limited, and still 'reform' politicians must have the support, backing and consensus of the Diet. Not understanding the total camouflage of the system, and despotic, political parties could not possibly create Democracy, SCAP tried to get involved. Of course, the few Japanese politicians who were available and not totally incompetent, were not consulted by SCAP - just too time consuming to bother with facts and details, which might result in SCAP losing total control. The Japanese press burst out in chorus, as the Diet thwarted any SCAP changes in their political process. So, it resulted with each bill of any Diet changes being amended, delayed and finally dying a slow death, usually years later.

Any improvement would have to come from within, so the Japanese politicians were clever enough to give SCAP token- accommodations, or convoluted explanations of supposed reforms. Simply saying they desperately were seeking Democracy, immensely satisfied SCAP. Interestingly enough, once SCAP withdrew its interference, a lot of the hypocrisy drifted away, too. Since they no longer had to mouth alien-slogans to win MacArthur's favor, they could concentrate on real issues. Enough syndicates were dragged into the open to clean up their acts.

Most difficult for SCAP to insist on integrity and honesty, when such a blatant and extensive black market was being run in every corridor, except perhaps MacArthur's, and only because he never left his office. SCAP, on the other hand, claimed any real or imaginary rejuvenation or democratization of Japanese politics, as having come from them, since they felt Japan incapable of making any progressive changes on its own. The fact any improvement was made, after all of SCAP's discordant, antagonistic involvement, was miraculous.

As the purge was still fresh in the minds of government people, at the bottom of much of the SCAP-Diet problem was cultural miscommunications. SCSAP's idea of a truly Democratic Diet would be one in which free discussion and debate took place, with questioning each other's intentions, rather than the usual Japanese heckling. They wanted the Diet to be like the U.S. Congress, and few Japanese could comprehend it. Too, there seemed to be no breaking of the political contributions by the large corporations, who expected proper 'appreciation' from the party or individual. Though scandal after scandal of bribery was revealed, the process merely slowed temporarily. All of this was basically for naught, for in reality few laws were passed by the Diet - usually it was private bills passed through the Cabinets. This was not new, for since the Diet's existence, it had passed few bills every year. All was just a grand facade, rather immature in its decision-making, based on the need for group- consensus, rather than letting an individual see a bill all the way to law. (To be clear, decision-making, deductive reasoning, etc. to come to a logical decision, was not taught in any kind of political or business classes in Japan.)

On paper, no country had ever been more revolutionized in politics, social, education, health, labor, etc. The laws were enacted under pressure from SCAP, but they were rarely, if ever, enforced. Despite the newspapers clamoring scandal and violation, the culprits would be

171

dutifully brought in, with resulting fines or jail terms reduced to almost nothing, or dropped completely. Disregarding safety regulations, courts logged in penalizing offenders, but little follow through of punishment.

The continuance of child-exploitation had rare violations reported, considering small and medium-sized industries worked children more than nine hours a day, no one was was punished. Their obvious excuse continued to be the lack of men available to do the job, blaming the war. Obviously, lawmakers and judges gave only lip- service to Occupation sponsored reforms, and applied the new legislation with great reluctance. Drug abuse also soared unchecked until November, 1953, as it was estimated over one-hundred thousand Japanese were using heroin and morphine. Almost magically, once the Occupation, and most of the military was gone, so was the abuse problem. Remove the source - you remove the problem.

Time after time, once SCAP got a certain law passed through the Diet, they lost interest in seeing its enforcement, despite the fact flagrant-violations were obviously noted in the newspapers. This type of precedence did not go unnoticed by the Japanese. MacArthur simply continued to hail each as a triumph of Democracy, never wanting to know how he was surrounded by failure. For his prize Corrupt Practices Act - following sworn confessions in court and before the Diet, unequaled sums of money were spent to buy votes, so corrupt candidates were used to swing elections.

And, in spite of open admissions of wrong-doing, no action was taken to enforce the law. Yet, MacArthur and SCAP, still sent only glowing reports back to Washington. In this way, Americans would know their hard-earned tax dollars were accounted for respectively. MacArthur himself had rescued the former-enemy from their 'feudalistic, war-mongering ways.' Money well-spent in preventing another World War, MacArthur 'humbly' told them, and they gullibly believed it. His staff of fifty personal press relations did their job well.

Often the court judges were not hostile, nor recalcitrant, but simply lacking the pragmatic philosophy of American jurisprudence. They often failed to understand the new laws based on American modes of thought and ideals of Justice. Circumstances, rather than the letter of the laws influenced them. Once MacArthur was out, General Ridgeway authorized the Japanese to review and revise legislation previously directed by SCAP. The atmosphere changed totally, as Japanese ideas emerged.

* * * * * *

As most Japanese did not understand the difference between liberalism and Communism, they assumed the latter was what they should have, since they did not know the former. This trend was increased by Soviet sympathizers, who realized every opportunity to tie SCAP and MacArthur to the Communists. Since censorship was restricted, many misconceptions went un-contradicted. In the early days of the Occupation, the Communists made no secret of their plan to 'Sovietize' Japan through labor unions. Because of SCAP's instance at first on free speech and open political organizations, the Japanese *thought* MacArthur was pro-Communist. When he insisted all political prisoners be released from prison, mostly Communists, and labor unions to be established, they were all *sure* he was pro-Communist.

MacArthur did not take this seriously at the beginning and saw no peril, thus he did not slow down the budding-Communism. Once again those in charge, who were supposed to have expertise, or at least experience and knowledge, did not handle the situation correctly. As it got out of hand, they hesitated to let their superiors know about the escalation. And, since they were all secluded in their own 'happy- bubble' SCAP and Mac had no clue as to what was truly happening.

The Communists had incited workers to seize control of key communications and productive enterprises. Disregarding numerous complaints, SCAP did nothing until fifty-thousand Tokyo municipal workers had attempted to take over the government. The Communists were not just another political party voicing to be heard, but a highly trained and militant international conspiracy.

SCAP did not have a good working relationship with the media, and attacked it for the disparagement of publishing any 'minor misconducts' by American soldiers. Though the press was usually friendly, supportive, and displayed mostly articles praising the Occupation, MacArthur wanted NO negatives whatsoever. SCAP therefore swallowed the pro-Allied material published in the Communist controlled papers, they created for themselves. This incredible propaganda, lead SCAP to naively believe the Japanese wanted this kind of leadership.

The extensive freedom of the press given to the Communist, increased the idea of SCAP being supportive of them. This freedom included increasing their paper-allotment for the Communist press, while regular newspapers had to reject subscribers and cut press runs. The only directive SCAP enforced was there may be no criticism of SCAP. When newspapers retorted SCAP had merely replaced the Japanese militarists in censorship, more freedom was given to Communists. U.S. correspondents were freer to write their criticism for U.S. papers. They heartily pronounced how MacArthur was showing leniency toward Communism, if not down-right support, while the Communists echoed anti-British and French sentiments.

The pro-Moscow line was reported to be strong even in the army-managed *STARS & STRIPS,* where Communist-minded soldier/ reporters consistently threw out the incoming agency news unfavorable to the Soviets, but ran daily commentaries frankly paralleling the Communist line. This definite leftist-tendency carried over into books, art, theatre, magazines and movies. The obvious opportunities to 'expose' Japanese to 'the Democratic way of life' were lost, as SCAP seemed more to support the Communists.

SCAP spent most of its energy clamoring for a united-front against a *non-existent,* reactionary enemy of pro-nationalists. MacArthur's blindness to what was going on right outside his door, with numerous SCAP staff supporting Communist heroes and their ideals, could only be construed as, he was a true friend of Communism. The Communist leaders were clever enough to work within the Occupation framework, of wanting only to help the Japanese to come out from under their previous suppression. In spite of it becoming obvious, the Communists were behind attacks on the Japanese Prime Minister, food distribution riots, a coal production slow-down, interruption of essential services, food delays for rationing, and paralyzing tax collection. MacArthur still failed to publicly condemn them.

By 1946, it seemed SCAP did not want the words Communism, Soviets, or much less Russians mentioned. They simply referred to the problems being with 'disorderly alien philosophies and foreign influences.' As late as 1954, MacArthur refused to comment on the reasons for his silence. Reports were issued sending home 'any SCAP who supported anti-Communists activity.' It could be said the Communists leaders were clever enough to dupe MacArthur and SCAP, as they managed to conceal their support came from the Soviet Liaison Mission, and its staff of several hundred, who actively guided and financed them. The fact they consistently used the word Democratic, and their only concern was for the general welfare of the Japanese people, was apparently enough to fool SCAP.

Though a variety of sources consistently tried to tell SCAP differently, their ears and eyes were sealed to any derision of the Communists. Truly, MacArthur and SCAP opposed Communism as an aggressive force elsewhere, they just benignly allowed this 'bird of another feather' to grow as an independent, reformist-group in Japan. As time went by, more SCAP officials began to question the unlimited freedom and pro-stance toward the Communists. Then most were quickly silenced by blackmail, as the Communists had the staff- resources to spy on their private and public life-styles. Some of these, actually later-leaked valuable information to discredit SCAP. In so many ways, SCAP was self-defeating in their desire to get Democracy across to the Japanese. No one, who had knowledge of the prior Soviet Generals on SCAP's staff, ever questioned what their involvement was in the whole Communist growth, and acceptance by MacArthur.

To another extent, no paper was to be used for anything which was printed in Japanese for the Japanese people. How were they then to learn, when they were only told the vague principles in English? The culture-wise Communists made sure every piece of propaganda from the Soviets was translated and printed in the simplest, yet most detailed Japanese. And, it always insinuated their total support for the common, working, struggling Japanese person. Since the registered Communist membership was listed at seventeen-thousand in 1947, SCAP and MacArthur felt they had no problems with the other seven- million unionists! Of course, the Japanese were *not required* to register their political-affiliations.

To the Japanese, who had never really tasted Western-style freedom or justice, the idea of individuality was selfish, and almost evil, as it could not have been more opposite of their cultural-group ideology and stoicism. So, to the typical Japanese, educated and uneducated from the countryside to the cities, could not realize the Communists imperiled all these privileges. You never miss what you never had. SCAP gave generalized American-style warnings against Communism, saying it disregarded private citizen rights, was atheistic and suppressed the press, free speech and representative government.

This was not shocking or scary, as compared to what the Japanese saw before them: men in military uniforms with rank and privileges, putting-up signs limiting Japanese access; while they, themselves, enjoyed unlimited food, more than adequate housing, and exercised extensive prejudice agains their own of a different color - the obvious discrimination against black-enlisted men - there were none of any rank. It all was extensive and easily seen. SCAP was a military government, and the Japanese did know the previous military government had also lied and controlled them. What they saw they believed, more than any words SCAP or MacArthur could say.

Amazingly, all Japanese did not instantly and enthusiastically join the Communist Party. Though many Japanese, held contempt for Chinese and Koreans, they took pride in their Asian brothers who stood up to the Americans, by running their black markets so openly. What the Japanese saw, always had a greater affect - the tawdriness, drunkenness and vice surrounding the Americans army camps. And with time, the lack of any effort from MacArthur on-down, to appreciate anything of the Japanese culture was well noted.

But most of all, the almost insulting-assumption in everything American being good, and all things Japanese were feudal. All this worked to the Communist' advantage. Though only a short time in Japan, Soviet troops had quickly earned reputations of more notorious and contemptuous nature. Yet, they were soon forgotten, once the local Japanese-Communist came in with their soft-pedal ethics.

The GIs, on the other hand, were visible everywhere, spreading their cigarettes and money around to buy whatever and whoever they wanted. They paraded with the 'pan-pan' - prostitutes - girls in one hand and a bottle in the other. They sprawled drunken in building doorsteps, train cars or even staggering down the sidewalks, until the MPS came swooping out of nowhere, to dump them into jeeps and hall them back to barracks. So, the examples of ideals, Democracy, and life-style, were not always well-exemplified to the Japanese.

Luckily, the Red propaganda became too sure of its success and grossly blundered. In 1950, hundred of Japanese-repatriates returned from Siberian interment, and many were die-hard Communist agents. If they had entered Japan quietly and fanned out over the country, victory could have possibly been theirs. But under strict orders from Moscow, they kidnaped ship captains, held sit-down strikes in railway stations, and rioted. Worst of all, they scorned their parents, families and visited local Communists Headquarters, as if they were Shrines. Many repatriates had not been allowed to be returned to Japan, unless they had sworn allegiance to the Communist Party. These multiple evidences, as well as truths coming out, about the Soviet treatment of the Japanese, made them begin to realize the Japanese-Communists were more loyal to the Soviets than to Japan.

They began to self-destruct without SCAP's help, as various departments continued to pay no attention to the gross propaganda. A good thing Moscow overlords were much more buried in dogma, working by the Marxist book, which lacked any elasticity, for they had faltered and erred at the very door of success in Japan. What in most countries had taken years for the Communists to foster and dominate, in Japan it had been practically handed over: hundreds of leaderless unions, key industries with millions of docile-workers believing their propaganda, and unlimited promotion, seemingly endorsed by SCAP. It would have been a 'sure thing' in the broadest of terms. In the end, their aggressiveness hung them, for the Japanese did not look at strikes or shut-downs as statements of power, but a nuisance. They wanted their electricity, trains, phones, etc. working, not periodically shut- down for purposeless statements of Communist power.

Eventually, MacArthur had to clamp down, restricting public servants the right to strike. In response, the Communists brought out SCAP's racial treatment of Japanese. These things were easily seen by the Japanese and resented, as American special privileges on the trains, buses, Japanese exclusion from the nicer restaurants, hotels, beaches and movie houses. And, not just the exclusive Frank Lloyd Wright Imperial Hotel, the Japanese could not enter or use any Western-style hotel. These were all the result of regulations drafted for the 'protection' of the servicemen, but they had become racial segregation. Though complaints followed in the papers, MacArthur did nothing, as usual. Because of the strict ban on all derogatory comments to the Occupation, he was once again led into false complacency. The American press abounded with criticism, while the Japanese again began to feel only the Communists were standing up for Japanese rights, as a free nation and not a colony of America. Especially with its extensive garrisoning of Okinawa, the Japanese felt they were losing the soil from beneath their feet. A few stoic Japanese did feel it was retribution, for what they had done in Korea, China and Southeast Asia. Yet, most Japanese had no idea what all the Japanese military *had done* anywhere in Asia.

The Communists never mentioned the Kuril Islands, and its own slow repatriation of Japanese 'war criminals,' who were actually only soldiers and civilians. One could definitely say MacArthur had become a victim of his own glorifying, Public Relations. Always believing he could never be wrong, he naturally accepted the exaggerated assurance Japan had become truly Democratic, and any action against the Communists was unnecessary. Servile flattery had him believe he alone created policy, which was carried out, followed, and addressed to the letter. A solid myth of infallibility, also built on the premise the Japanese worshiped him more than the Emperor, for he had fed them, - almost, finally - and had never disappointed them. Yet, for years following his departure, the Japanese would think of *MacArthur as controlled by the Communist.*

By 1949, the Communists carried thirty-five seats in the Diet. But, these successes were soon lost as propaganda swelled to demonstrations, and finally to violent rioting in the summer of 1949. The Communists seized a police station, wrecked a train, killing six passengers, overturned a locomotive, killing three, and the unsolved death of the President of National Railways was blamed on them. They quickly lost public sympathy and support. Everything boomeranged, as SCAP finally moved, and put the clamp down on the Communists.

By 1950, the purge on the Reds in government employ started - over two-hundred in schools alone were forced to resign, on twenty- four hour notice. Nearly elven-thousand in government were remove, some under the guise of cutting expenditures, while numerous 'voluntarily' retired to avoid their Communist connection being exposed. Two-hundred were dismissed from the media and nine- thousand from various other industries. The government-provided salaries for labor union bosses were curtailed, and all privileges for the Communist Party itself were suspended. In response, the riots were escalated, which was again exactly the wrong thing to do. Losing support again, the infighting among the Japanese-Communist leaders became more vicious. The peak anti-foreign violence occurred on Memorial Day, 1950, when demonstrators stoned American soldiers, eight officers were court-martialed and sentenced to ten years.

SCAP then went overboard against the Communist newspapers, and quickly militaristic control was echoed against them. The press then began to sensationalize about bloody riots. Police raids to 'uncover' Communist press and other groups were authorized by SCAP, and to all extent it was *de'ja vu* of pre-war times. Of course, any direct criticism of the SCAP directives was forbidden. SCAP then reassured the Japanese insurrection by the Communists was imminent. This was easily supported by boasting from heavily, indoctrinated- repatriates from Siberia, about liberation armies from Soviet-soil waiting to invade. The rioting continued sporadically around the country for various reasons. As courts were jammed, those Communists who had strongly oppressed the Constitution as a Fascist document, now clung to it, as the only guardian of their freedom.

Once the Peace Treaty was signed - in San Francisco in April, 1951, - formally ending the Occupation, all Japanese who had been court-martialed by SCAP were released. The Diet then got to pass their own anti-subversive bill, to protect themselves from further Communist rioters. The bill was greatly criticized for its vagueness of 'instigations' as being a crime. Before a vote could be taken, the violent and purposeless May Day riots of 1951 took place, convincing all of the bill's necessity.

The whole process left many Japanese confused about which form of government truly gave them peace. The Democracy of SCAP seemed too lenient, and the totalitarianism of the former militarists, while reducing crime, controlled everything, and everybody else at the same time. As the riots subsided, the Japanese Communists returned to 'a support of the people' doctrine, and many Japanese began to feel it best favored true Democracy.

If SCAP had not kept its head in the clouds, as the demigods they thought they were, many of the problems with the Communists would have been avoided. The Japanese would have then had a better portrayal of Democracy. But as military, SCAP used power, not persuasion or demonstration. Aloofness never sells, but it is especially hard to accept when differences, such as racial, are so great. For all their talk, SCAP never spoke to the Japanese people, or used words they could understand. Rarely did SCAP recognize what the Japanese, could or were capable of doing on their own, but what they should or must do, or not do. Considering the Japanese had been indoctrinated for so many years with their military's Fascist ideas, they were not in a position to choose a government which would be Democratic. One cannot expect a 'cripple' to run a race. No group of people, who have grown up in serfdom, should be asked to assume overnight all the Democratic responsibilities, and obligations of free men.

Perhaps, as controversial as MacArthur's firing was, it was the best thing President Truman could have done. The sincerity of the Americans had come into question more, as the Japanese began to stand on their own two feet. The Communist had instilled a lot of questions about the Occupation practices, which grated more and more on the Japanese. SCAP certainly preached Democracy, but rarely practiced any part of it. MacArthur was the greatest offender of them all, for he was in charge, and set the precedent. MacArthur spurted constantly militarism was dead, but all he stood for came from military, not civilian, power.

Finally, when President Truman, in his finest hour, relieved MacArthur on March 11,1951, then the Japanese *did believe* the military *could be* the servant of civilian power. In a sense, it was the greatest act of Democracy 'for the people' which had ever been demonstrated. For many in the Diet, they suddenly realized they could have also done the same to General Tojo, and the ultra-militarists, thus avoiding the whole war and expansionism. When Lt. General Matthew Ridgeway came in, the isolation-policy ended, as he inspected each and every division on a regular basis.

* * * * * *

Along with the immediate exiting of all of MacArthur's cohorts, was the closing down of the "Great MacArthur History" project. As previously mentioned, fifty men, with some women added later, receiving extraordinarily, high salaries, had solely concentrated for six years on writing the Occupation histories, 'according to SCAP,' of course. Housing, Japanese assistance, equipment, etc. for them had exceeded three-million dollars, which in 1951, was truly a lot of money. The entire staff knew their purpose was to glorify MacArthur - though unspoken, the U.S. Presidency was targeted.

Nothing, of course, went into any file without the personal approval of MacArthur, or directly written by himself. This meant other Allied participation in the Pacific war was omitted, as well as other branches of the U.S. service. The Marines' work was considered minuscule, the Navy relegated down to the simple role of ferrymen, and even the military accounts were changed. For example, *MacArthur eliminated the Battle of Midway* as being non-essential, since he had not participated in it. Yet, no final comprehensive report was published to justify the extreme cost and wastefulness.

The official title of the report to be "MacArthur in the Pacific," so it reeked of being a military autobiography for commercial publication, which had been done entirely at the taxpayers' expense. The basic rules of the writing were: all actions had to be successful, avoid controversial material, all policies and actions originated with MacArthur and most importantly, it did not criticize MacArthur in any way. Thus, no word appeared concerning the destruction of cyclotron accelerators, the changed policy toward big business, the political uses of the purge, the violent controversies over birth control, the thousands of unwanted American-Asian children, breaches of trust by some Allied officers, or simply the wholesale waste of funds by the SCAP- Occupation. All this caution of precise-input of MacArthur's history, and still never printed.

Not until the end, under Ridgeway did SCAP accurately report the true state of Japanese opinion. They did truly resent those foreigners, who complained of what they regarded as short-comings in the Japanese way of life. Foreigners were often objects of envy, because of their luxuries and special foods, when the Japanese had so little. One well known colonel even had soil shipped - at government expense, from his home state of Texas - so he might grow his own 'authentic' American vegetables for his personal enjoyment. Always, the language barrier had hampered the cultural differences, and any mingling on equal terms. Foreigners believed Japanese to be exclusive, yet the Japanese were sure Westerners were prejudiced. Most of the time, the foreigners made no pretense of so much, as if trying to understand the Japanese.

In general, the American cultural interest was limited to elementary language lessons, flower arrangement or tea ceremony training, and a few visits to Kabuki, at the Imperial theater across from the Palace. Not unusual, when they made these rare appearances it displaced the Japanese out of their coveted-seats or boxes. Though sometimes a Japanese, of some status trying to impress the foreigner, so cutting through the long queue, marching up to the theater manager to demand a box for the Americans. Without the slightest hesitation, he would remove the small Japanese party, them leaving without a word, then usually giving obeisance.

Few Americans rarely had enough knowledge to be dazzled by the great pine tree in the center of the stage, the costumes of extraordinary design and color. What they noticed, and complained about often, was the exacting-high pitch of the voices and the stinging, lyrically-strange, seemingly off-key music. They were often surprised, by the sudden cracking of wooden blocks, the jerky-strumming of the three-stringed shamisen, moving rapidly to great climaxes, both in speed and volume, while the chanting chorus filled in the pacing of music, words and action. It definitely was nothing like a New York Broadway Musical, or Opera if even knowledgable of them.

Little attention was paid to Japanese news, despite it being in the English newspaper, and Americans wholly ignored Japanese literary art, drama, native music, etc. The indifference of SCAP extended to cultural or sociological affairs, ignoring the human value, or whatsoever trying to understand the psychology or philosophy of the Japanese. So, as if they did not want to be confused by any details or facts. Most SCAP foreigners were given little, if any briefing. Japanese in turn, were to study the social and cultural life of the 'little Americas' of Tokyo - Washington Heights and Grant Heights.

A large amount of information filtered down from the servants to the general population. Most Japanese were surprised more Americans were not religious. Especially since it had been insinuated Christianity could be Japan's 'saving grace' to adapt. Japanese had also expected more Americans to be proficient in music or art, as social graces of the aristocracy, which they thought the Americans, as conquerors, would be.

Japanese were surprised too, Americans read less than they, and tended to read much trivial matter, especially imported women's magazines. The GIs particularly, read comics, - which would later dominate the Japanese reading habits - detective stories, and Westerns. The Armed Forces Radio offered less classical music, and the Americans rarely attended Japanese recitals, concerts, art exhibitions, or even English lectures. Their entertainment tended to be eating and drinking socially, rather than intellectual or discussion groups, with bingo being the largest attraction of all. The Americans were a cross- section of the country and population, but most were from a younger group, and not chosen to be ambassadors of culture. Still, these Americans did not seem desirable to copy, as the Japanese had been proposed to do.

The Occupation had been filled with wives, secretaries, office clerks and others who had no previous war experience. These foreigners became a kind of 'nouveau-riche,' with many flaunting their new-found finances and superiority, as if they had earned it. Some rowdy interlopers were on a par with the amateur carpetbaggers, looking for bargains or collectibles on every corner, in exchange for their PX food or trinkets.

Those who became protective of the nationals, were quickly reminded of Pearl Harbor, Bataan or even Nanking, but never a whisper about Hiroshima or Nagasaki.

The desecration of property, old cultural buildings, and other items were not unusual by them. To many older Japanese, these people - foreign men and women - fulfilled the ancient beliefs all foreigners were vulgar and inconsiderate barbarians. Since they were the only ones with guns, they often took sport in killing the tame ducks, quail, and other birds in the parks and ponds, which starving-Japanese had not touched out of respect for them.

The greatest shock came from the waste, as the Japanese had lived under restricted condition for more than a dozen years with the expansionistic-war. The extravagances may have begun with food, but it extended to overheating their homes, big motor cars, special trains and duplicating creature comforts they had left behind. Once Japan received its sovereignty, these luxuries were highly taxed, and the Japanese government set a system of higher prices for foreigners to pay for goods and services. For those on fixed, former-salaries like missionaries, it was quite difficult, or they simply had to give up buying any foreign goods.

The Japanese were also highly entertained by the pomp and ceremony of the MPs around GHQ - General Headquarters. The Japanese had certainly had their own, but they usually had dressed for a specific purpose, like making announcements or messengers to, or from the Emperor. With the Americans surrounded by rubble everywhere, and the dichotomy of how MacArthur dressed, as if just returning from the field, the formality was solemn for his 'comings and goings.' Encircling the Dai Ichi Insurance Building - SCAP and MacArthur's GHQ, were a few durable buildings which had withstood the bombings. They were a bit seedy, but had been cleaned-up, as they were within MacArthur's *view,* as if his eyes were not to set on anything unpleasant. The Dai

Ichi itself, had rectangular columns, rising five-floors and scrubbed to a respectable gray-white.

As usual at a certain time, the crowds lined the street across from the entrance, held back with no effort. The stunning MPs, tall, massive and even good looking, as chosen for this exulted position. Their perfect uniforms were trimmed off with white gloves, and bright shoulder epaulettes. A hush suddenly came over the crowd, as MacArthur stepped through the great portals to walk briskly, the few carefully-staged steps, to his waiting new, shiny-black Cadillac.

Murmurs rippled through the crowd, with some older people bowing their heads reverently, as they had for the Emperor. The younger Japanese people merely watched in frank-curiosity, as the American soldiers snapped salutes, and finally a few Japanese gave a modest cheer. The look on most faces was a set, almost half-smile, wanting to please, and ready to respond in whatever way. Though MacArthur never reacted or responded at all, as if there had been no one around but the MPs. This was all given to a man, who had publicly called them, 'a nation of twelve-year-olds."

The sideshows were not limited to MacArthur's passage, as wherever the gigantic MPs were directing traffic, alongside their half- sized Japanese counterparts, entertainment reigned. The exaggerated jerking-movements of the MPs almost out-did their costumes, as they could barely be called uniforms. They would goose-step on and off from the corners, replacing each other, and once in place, leap in the air, while madly swinging their arms around, as if on pivots. The Japanese would enthusiastically try to replace them, and the laughter would be an embarrassed-type from the Japanese, and hearty chuckles from Americans.

Japan had not become Utopia to the Japanese, for no nation can simply gain Democracy by proclamation, but much had been accomplished. Some would say the Occupation had become its own worst enemy. Committed to a Democracy which it believed, but did not practice very well, it copied Japan's prewar methods against which it had thundered condemnation. Secret police, censorship and inquisitorial methods, dictation to the Diet, orders to the courts, constant commandeering of goods, facilities and services, discrimination against the lower ranks, of it own, as well as Japanese - all these existed in the name of freedom, equality and Democracy. Yet, it was this continued denial that undemocratic practices were being followed, which was the greatest wrongs the Occupation did. This terrible pretense continued, until McArthur's exit.

There were fears where none were necessary, and ignorance of reality, when it stared them in the face. The Japanese heartily hated the memory of their own former leaders, who had brought them to destruction, and they had no intention of martyrizing them. Silencing all criticism made the Americans look totally hypocritical, as they fervently espoused free speech. But, by breaking open Japan, much had been released, as there was opportunity for growth out of the complacency of the past. As individuals, the GIs did more with handing out candy bars and cigarettes, than MacArthur did giving out rationing cards. Thousands more were helpful in uncounted anonymous ways, than those easily remembered as drunks.

Japan needed time to blend the old with the new, and make its own democracy, not an ill-fated American one. Japan truly wanted reform and change, but on its own terms and not force-fed. To the Japanese, it was more a Renaissance-Reconstruction than a revolution, as much as Meiji Restoration had been almost a hundred years before. Change had to come from within, not from above, like a smothering- blanket. The Japanese politicians may have ceremoniously received MacArthur's orders, but they just as carefully ignored them. In the end, the Japanese people made the changes, as they were ready and could see the benefit. Sometimes a little candy went a long way.

Personal History: Miki Sawada's Occupation children

This is not an interview, but taken from a biography of her life.

Less than a year after the official beginning of the Occupation, the first child of mixed Japanese and American parentage was born. The radio announcer, who made the *positive* comment about it being 'a symbol of love binding the two shores of the Pacific,' was fired. This view was not shared by most Japanese people. Though this child may have been wanted, it did not take long for reports of others tossed aside, as if part of the debris in Tokyo, still surrounding everything. Neither SCAP nor the Japanese government wanted involvement or responsibility.

To the unflinching rescue, was a most unexpected source. Miki was born into the Iwasaki family - founders of the powerful and wealthy Mitsubishi conglomerate. She married a diplomat, and became Miki Sawada. She had lived most of her adult life overseas, spoke English fluently, and was conversational in several languages. She was the toast of Paris, New York, or whatever city they were posted to in the 1920s and '30s. She had only know the good, beautiful life of a wealthy heiress, with international diplomatic privileges.

Returning to Japan in 1936, Miki found her country devastated by poverty from unemployment, crop failure, and heavy taxation due to the massive war effort. Gone was the freedom and democracy she had experienced growing up, for now she was under suspicion and her activities watched, simply because of her previous overseas life-style. Miki's three sons were eventually conscripted into the military, and she was left alone with her daughter to face the bombings of Tokyo, while her husband was shipped off to Burma, against his will. He was later charged with war crimes-conspiracy, though he had been forced into diplomatic administration by the military government, but eventually he was cleared.

Miki's strong Christian beliefs and determination to live, were the few things which helped her through it all. After the war, except for her immediate family, she was almost as much a foreigner in her own country, as the Allied Occupation people. She had more friends overseas than at home. Yet, Miki could no longer be the 'belle of the ball' with the Americans, for not only had all of her famous, family fortune been wiped out by the purging, they were massively in debt for special-imposed taxes. It didn't matter though, as entertaining was not her destiny anymore.

Fate fell into her lap as a wrapped bundle, with an unfortunate dead baby enclosed. Miki was riding on a crowded train, when as the train jerked suddenly, the small package tumbled from the shelf above her head into her arms. Because of the strange weight, feel and size, Miki unwrapped it, only to find a dead child of mixed heritage. At first the train conductor accused her of being the mother, and through her harassment by the authorities, she discovered what a mushrooming- problem the abandoned children had become. With prejudice on both sides, Miki knew neither Japan nor America would help support these mothers, or their children.

Having been inspired by the orphanages of Dr. Barnardo in England, so many years before, Miki felt she should do the same in Japan. Not too far from Yokohama, was her family's large summer estate, one of the few things they still owned, though in disrepair and closed by SCAP. Miki had only enough money to pay the taxes and get the estate back. She then called upon many of her foreign friends, such as Josephine Baker, the famous American singer living in Paris in the 1920s, to help her with this charitable endeavor. Soon, Miki established the Elizabeth Saunders Home, the namesake coming from the faithful, British-governess of the Mitsui family, who had remained in Japan during the war. Ms. Saunders had died shortly after, snd left a small legacy 'for those who cannot help themselves.' So, a fitting tribute for the dedicated governess, in name now, to be the savior of these abandoned children, no one wanted to help.

The children desperately needed medical care for basic health problems created by the war, such as lice, worms, natal- undernourishment, scabies and exposure from being left-out in the weather, as well the usual childhood diseases. SCAP regulations, of course, forbade dispensing American medicines to foreign nationals, despite them not being in short supply. Many of the foreign doctors who helped treat the babies and gave medicine, were reprimanded or transferred. Little medicine was available from the Japanese side, and most doctors or hospitals preferred to give it to 'real' Japanese. These babies were a stinging reminder of a defeated Japan, and what some young women felt they needed to do to help their families.

Likewise, they marred the impression of perfection and democracy the SCAP-Occupation authority was trying to present. Their existence, and therefore their assistance, was categorically denied by SCAP, who also implied the 'loose-style' of the Japanese women were responsible for making 'good American boys go wrong.' They made no effort to encourage men to assume the responsibility for their children, or to provide for the mothers. Abandonment then, became almost a creative endeavor for these mothers, who wanted their babies to be taken care of, as they left them bundled-up, with bottles included.

Babies with light brown hair and blue eyes, or dark skin and curly hair, were quickly spotted and stigmatized. Most Japanese who had lived overseas knew from their own experience of rejection, these children would not be accepted into its closed society. They also had to be schooled separately. The limited access to the community by the mixed-blood children, usually created painful experiences for them, from being taunted to physically abused. They then became political footballs, as red tape adoptions actually took an act of Congress to allow each and every child into the United States. This process could take months, or more than a year. Then some of the military families wanting children had to give up, because transferred out of Japan.

They may have had to face some prejudice in America too, but it was considerably more heterogenous than Japan, especially with the large number of war brides. Miki worked relentlessly, traveling back and forth between Japan and America, raising money for 'her babies,' finding them homes, and trying to influence the political restrictions. As American media promoted her work, laws were finally changed.

Though an accurate census of these children was never allowed by SCAP, the conservative estimate was placed between five and six thousand. Over sixteen-hundred of those children passed through the Elizabeth Saunders Home, and over a thousand were eventually adopted into loving families. Many others were relocated to farms, and other self-sufficient communities in South America, as several of its countries have large, prior Japanese populations.

Since the American military presence continued after the official end of the Occupation in 1952, the numbers continued, though a trickle in comparison. Also, as time went on, abortion became a more common solution to the age old problem. (*Madam Butterfly* never had a good ending, just a simpler one.) Being a basically Buddhist country, the Japanese believed with death, the soul is released for another life, so no religious conflict, as with most Christian-Western countries.

Comic Cultural Side Note:

This is a well-known, insiders-story about a typical-SCAP high echelon officer. He was given a large, magnificent painting of a horse and a deer by a Japanese businessman, who had managed to receive from him many lucrative contracts. The SCAP official took great pride in the painting because of its size, and the fact of who had given it to him. He often pridefully showed it off to all entering his office - Japanese and foreigners.

The Japanese in their indubitable, controlled, polite manner, never uttered an iota to him, only praise and acknowledgement for *his having received* such a fine, representative of the animals and nature. Eventually, the artwork had become the talk of all those in the know around Tokyo. Then, a visiting, foreign Japanese-speaking friend shrieked upon his first seeing it. Shocked at his response, the SCAP officer questioned his rudeness. The friend then informed him 'Horse,' uses the Japanese sound-syllable 'Ba,' and 'Deer' the same as 'Ka,' which together mean: 'BAKA' or 'immense fool' or even ruder common references. Knowing the language had its advantages, or not

Part II Japanese as the Occupied: Chapter 6 - *Kyushu* and Southern *Honshu* - Repatriation: The Ins and Outs

Struggling soldiers not all of them tramps, ruffians, but men who had risked and lost everything, suffered beyond endurance and had returned now to a ruined land, not the same men who had marched away but transformed - and this the worst, the ultimate degradation to which war brings, the spirit, the soul - into the likeness of that man who abuses from very despair and pity ... They came home to nothing with nothing after years of nothing, but war and deprivation.

William Faulkner,
Absalom, Absalom!

Most of the six and a half-million Japanese soldiers, several hundred- thousand civilians, and over five-thousand prisoners-of-war returned home through Kyushu and Southern Honshu, these being the closest ports to Korea and the Pacific Islands. (Okinawa Islands - five-hundred-miles south of Japan, after being captured in 1945, was strictly maintained as an American Military Base until 1972.) At the same time, over two-million native Koreans, Chinese and Taiwanese, who had been brought-forcibly, or came on their own to Japan to work, were being shipped back to their homes. Supervising all this naval traffic was mainly the BCOF - British Commonwealth Occupation Forces - made up of a majority of Australians, lesser numbers of New

Zealanders, the Indians and a few British, of course, who were mostly the officers.

Several different ports had to be used, but mainly they were Fukuoka, Nagasaki, Sasebo, Kure, Hiroshima, and Otake. Almost anything which could float was used, from old Japanese freighters to fishing boats. The trip could be quite dangerous also, because the area had been extensively mined, and the process for removing them went very slow. This perilous, deadly job had been turned over to the Japanese Navy, with supervision by the U.S. Marines. Naturally, none of this could be done without paperwork, so most transfer centers had holding camps where thousands of families, or individuals might have to stay three to six months, or more.

Many homeless-returnees would try to decide where to go, if they did not have a family to return to. Numerous prisoners-of-war *chose* not to return to their families, especially if they had been officers, as it would be too embarrassing for the relatives. As well, quite common of these prisoners, who felt immense humiliation for having surrendered, was to contact their wife and ask for a funeral to be done in their name. In Japanese tradition, *better to be dead*, than to lose face. Still, some lowly privates were rejected by their families, or sometimes a family would be willing to move, so they could start a new life together. Other soldiers changed their names and sought new identities. Not difficult. since so many families had been wiped out.

The Japanese government sent letters to all families of the military, saying the sons and husbands were killed heroically, despite when they knew many of them had been captured and were in POW camps. The government even went as far as sending the *supposed-* ashes in sealed, un-openable containers of those 'dead' soldiers to many families, in spite of no direct proof of their deaths. So implicitly, the government contributed to the non-acceptance of the returning prisoners. Avoiding disgrace and embarrassment, of having to welcome back someone who had already been given a funeral, was more important than the actual living person.

One could constantly hear the old comparison of the *true-* soldier - a Samurai death likened to the brief, beautiful life of the Cherry Blossom. It had been indemnified upon so many, as much more glorious than life could ever be - cluster, bloom, be glorified, fall and die. There was something about myths, the Japanese not only liked believing, but liked trying to live. To some, they were obviously more important than life itself. Many of the last-trained kamikaze pilots, regretted not having been able to receive the death-glory, while others were glad it had ended before they had been sacrificed. The large number of fighter planes, still intact and sitting on the airfields, had only lacked the precious fuel, which had run out months before the war did.

While some returnees were hanging-out waiting for a train ticket, they let destiny decide their destination, simply the first seat available to anywhere. The air was filled with their dispirited, defeated feelings, as every inch of the stations and platforms were covered by their tired bodies. Unfortunately, this mix of ethnic and racial groups was not a prequel to the United Nations. There were racial and prejudice problems more within the troops, rather than between those who had so recently been an adversary, if not enemy. Battles broke-out on a regular basis between the black and white soldiers in bars, night clubs, geisha and prostitution houses. There was definite repugnance displayed between the British officers and Indian troops, who for too long had given loyalty without receiving compassion or compensation. The Brits were the originators of 'white-supremacy-privilege' within the military ranks, it merely spread to all else.

The Aussie troops tended to carry a heavy-animus against the Japanese, with the extreme mistreatment and death of so many of their own soldiers as prisoners. They often displayed these feelings eagerly, in their newly reversed situation. Added to this, the U.S. Navy commander still maintained a distrust of the Niseis, for anything which was considered confidential or of a military importance. There were no real spies to catch, and only a few black-marketeers or possible war criminals to be tracked down, though paranoia and mistrust of all abounded.

Part of the continuing problem, most these in charge were new troops, not those battle-experienced, as the first had been. The fighting troops were rightfully shipped home in late 1945, and early 1946. Perhaps, because of their lack of first-hand fighting with their prior enemies, these young replacements felt the need to prove their combat knowledge, strength or courage. Sadly, the Japanese repatriates and homeless were not up to playing their supposed-part as opponents, for the inexperienced-Allies search for glory. Consequently, the soldiers who took over, became rather abusive and degrading toward those left- over Japanese.

On the other hand, the Koreans had lived under conditions resembling serfdom, and followed Korean gang-bosses, exacting their own personal-hatred against the Japanese. These newly, freed-Koreans carried fresh, extensive resentment and hostility toward just about anyone who crossed them. They moved around in gangs, stealing, raping and generally causing problems while waiting months to leave, or have their status clarified.

The extensive black market brought instant wealth and power to a few, who quickly spent the easy money on liquor and other vices. Problems ensued, with those Koreans who felt they were equal to the Allied Forces as conquering heroes, and demanded to be accepted as such by the Allies and the Japanese. They thought, since they had been the first victims of Japanese Imperialism since 1910, they should have more freedom and special treatment. In some areas, they joined forces with the

Burakumin - 'the Japanese-Untouchables' - who were rejected by their own society. Certainly a dangerous and complicated mix for the Military Police - MPs to deal with, as everyone was easily agitated. Most people had suffered so much, and no longer wanted to be pushed around by anyone.

* * * * * *

In the Otake Center, which was the fourth largest, and considered best for their reception service, eighteen-thousand people could be accommodated at one time for both sleeping and eating-facilities. It had been a former Marine training center, and the two-storied wooden buildings housed everyone: from the two-thousand Okinawans, who had been forced-out to come to mainland-Japan, to others whose homes were destroyed in the bombing-fighting, along with miscellaneous military, and civilians, Chinese and Koreans. Squalor and unhygienic over-crowding became the norm as men, women and children shared living spaces.

They all only had enough room to lay their in mats on the floor to sleep. The bedlam varied from undisciplined children racing around, to people playing musical instruments. People quickly learned to settle in, for sometimes it would be weeks or months before they were assigned to a ship-out, or a train up-country. For those who had just arrived by ship, they had already gotten used to the situation. For them it had been worse on-board the ship, as there had usually been standing-room only.

There was absolutely no privacy in the open areas, and one had to accept dressing or undressing in front of the whole group, or not at all. Once the summer heat and humidity swelled into 1946 and again in 1947, the rank-smell of such overcrowding could only be imagined. Since little ventilation existed, and in typical Asian-style, few people ever went out into the open-air to deal with the unfamiliar. Though hard to believe, but they did have better conditions than the local Japanese. The transients were fed, clothed and housed by the Allied Occupation, more than most others had been during war-time.

A reasonable standard of cleanliness was attempted, but water and space facilities were again limited. To many, such conditions were accepted without complaint or question, as the Japanese belief in fatalism, with the culturally built-in helplessness of what they could do about it - *Shikata-gani.* Beneath this also was their stoic, martyred- feelings they were to be punished, for what their military government had done for so long, to so many others, in so many places.

In a protective measure, the authorities were aware of the dangers of disease in such conditions, so everyone was vaccinated against cholera and typhus. After injections, all were dusted with DDT powder by the nurses - all openings, cracks and crevices of their bodies from their hair to their toes. These nurses were covered for their own protection, including masks over their mouths and noses, and hats on their heads. Before leaving for anywhere, everyone must have their certificates showing both inoculations and repeated dusting had been done. All of their clothing, as well any possessions, had to be checked and dusted before laying them in the sun for airing. Those leaving Japan were limited to one hundred kilos of luggage and two- thousand yen given for each person.

~ ~ ~ ~ ~ ~

The first signs for many of these BCOF troops were the looming mountains, as their ships followed the route from Guam to Kure, and entered the Inland Sea, between the islands of Kyushu and Shikoku. Most of the men hugged the railing of their ships, staring-hard into the distance, amazed by the extremely rugged and inhospitable appearance, while the symbolic first rays of the rising sun framed their view. The uninviting-coastline, rose steeply from the water's edge to high peaks, some snow-capped, and scarcely-offering a foothold to a goat. There were few signs of dwellings or cultivation in this section, only the scattered fishing boats gave evidence of some habitation.

In Kyushu, terraced-hillsides and small villages dotted the thick-layers of mountains stacked in progression, as if lined up behind each other, marching toward the sea. Especially to the Aussies, the coast would be regarded useless, yet they could see every piece of land, except for bare rock, had been pressed into use. The startling, contrasting-beauty was not lost on these tough men, as the ships, now under the guidance of a Japanese pilot, threaded their way among minute-islands and rocks.

Sometimes they came so close, the stunted-pine trees could be seen hanging precariously to the few patches of earth, on the precipitous sides of granite. Gliding here and there around them, on the glittering-water were the busy, fishing-fleets. Daily life, as much as it could, was proceeding as it had for centuries prior, without knowledge of the ravages of modern war.

One particularly barren-island contained two, tiny coves where a few acres had been laboriously put under cultivation, and supported several dozen cottages. Just offshore, a few men and a lot of boys were working very hard, rowing and fishing. As the ship passed close by, comments from the troops began: "Now, I know why the little devils were so tough!" "I don't blame the Japs for wanting some more land." "I know I'd never live in such a place." "They would have enough to live on, if it were flattened a bit." "There are too many vertical acres and not enough horizontal ones." Thus began a grudging-sense of pity for the Japanese, in their hard-fight against the natural difficulties of their native land.

For most of these troop ships, the first sights of 'real' civilization - concrete docks, piers and pilings - were a bit shocking and had nothing mystically-Oriental about them, after the rustic and pastoral views they had seen.

200

With so many, the romantic Far Eastern mental pictures, one could almost forget it was an industrial society which had fought the war, and been the enemy. To those knowledgable of Japan's history, the detailed images of renown-writer Lafcadio Hearn, had permeated expectations more than reality-wanted to accept. This misty picture was quickly broken by ill-clad, unkempt and unshaven Japanese dock workers, who were noisily begging for cigarettes in their new, broken-English. Perhaps the revulsion of a dream-dissolved by such a scene, which prompted so many to toss their butts at them, or even worse, fresh cigarettes just out of reach and into the water. The scramble became an amusing game to those who had not previous shown such cruelty, or apathy toward them.

The first lesson of the day was on venereal disease, which all the Japanese women supposedly carried like a plague. No one seemed to question the validity of this, or where the women might have gotten it. At the same time, the Japanese women on the base had little appeal in their mismatched, worn-clothing, as they did menial work and shuffled around not speaking, nor wanting to be spoken to.

This bizarre-sight was entertainment to some, as they pointed out, or counted, how many different discarded items an individual wore. They were intrigued by the various ways they tied together the pieces of cloth, or torn clothes to keep their skin or underwear from showing through the oversized jackets and balloon trousers - *mopei*. The covering of their toes, while managing their woven-straw sandals or wooden clogs, *getas* - was the greatest challenge, and brought guffaws from several of the soldiers. Easy to feel superior and also unnecessary, as these small, runty, sad-looking Japanese constantly- humbled themselves, bowing to all soldiers. Keeping their jobs for the Allies was more important than any taunts or jeers, for most had families depending on them, and work was scarce.

It only took a day or two for the reality of the food shortage to sink in. Untold numbers of children and women almost lived-out of the mess-hall trash cans, grubbing out the food or directly begging for the leftover food scraps. Though a few GIs brought out bread and food for them, it was only a drop in the bucket, as so many Japanese could not be fed by just the leftovers. A hopeless, pitiful sight, and the insult to their dignity was definitely overcome by the emptiness of their stomachs. They would scatter like startled-sheep, when the MPs came into sight, for their fear of the Japanese police was embedded, by years of mistreatment and absolute domination.

If you are going to preach democracy, you have to feed the people before they are going to listen. They were being denied the food which they knew was there, and readily available to the large numbers of soldiers and transient camp dwellers. To convert the Japanese to democracy, the Allied military was going to have to stop thinking of them as enemies. Though it would be difficult for the American people to accept sending food to their enemies, this was what had to be done. A common ground was needed. They had done the Food Air-Lift for the Germans without questioning the process.

For many of the Niseis, some working in the kitchen, it was a sight they could barely grasp. They had been told so many proud stories of successful ancestors, many having come from the surrounding areas, who were now holding-out tin cans, cups, buckets or other various containers at the kitchen door. One could glance over the crowd, and see how some had tried to dress in their best, yet obviously frayed, well-worn, color-faded kimonos. They'd done their hair as stylishly as possible, but no longer having any decorated hairpins. These women held their heads high, as they quietly waited their turns, alongside white-haired old people, and shoeless, probably orphaned, children.

Giving them the clean-leftovers had more pride attached to it, than the see then picking through dirty and greasy edibles. One had to be moved to watch, as an old woman took the bread, she had just received and put pinches of it into the mouths of the babies, strapped on their mother's backs, while they waited in line. There simply was no food, and these were the lucky ones, to have a military camp so close by, who could give them handouts.

Most stereotyped-attitudes against the Japanese dissolved after contact, and one could see their obvious abject-state. Indeed, those fresh-out of foxholes softened within a few days from the Japanese giving them special treatment, being more worshipped, than despised. These newly-enlightened men began to get into, and enthusiastically experience the cultural customs, as they fumbled their way with chopsticks, and hit their heads on the low-beams of typical Japanese houses or public buildings. They did not hesitate at having to awkwardly remove the clumsy combat boots, as they curious wandered into restaurants, temples and homes. They soon found to their liking the hot sake - rice wine - and the demure, shy Japanese girls irresistible in their fawning ways to the big GIs.

Unfortunately, not all military were taken by the ethnic, educational-adventure, and there were numerous men with little or no overseas experience, who held posts with tremendous power. Some had a strong sense of their responsibility to the job, and remembered who everyone was dealing with - *the former enemy*. They were apt to lump together the women, children and old people into the same category as General Tojo.

Many of these also believed, since their title spoke of authority, they must possess some, all the more where it obviously did not exist. They were all too ready to offer gratuitous and pompous advice, when unasked for, and sometimes under the guise of being protective of Japan. Their sincerity confused the Japanese, though they eventually learned many of those in charge were manipulative, and basking in their power. These, they quickly put into the same category as their own previous military rulers.

As daily life settled in for the BCOF and American troops, it was not just sake-drinking, geisha-romping, or Zen-enlightenment of life. They had to deal with the locals, and the more confined transients who were waiting for processing, and eventual transportation further into or out of the country. Several British officers came under chastisement for their conduct and feelings of superiority, not only toward the Japanese, but to others of the BCOF. Britain had perhaps lost more financially from the war than any of the other previous colonial powers, and they were then fighting again, to reclaim those lands. Their own harsh-mistreatment of captured Japanese soldiers, and occupation administrators on Galan and Renpan islands, south of Singapore, resulted in the unnecessary-deaths of hundreds of Japanese. In the Kure area, some British had been known to drive their vehicles directly at Japanese on the roadside, despite the fact there was plenty of room on the road. Obviously, it was done just for the fun of watching them jump out of the way, usually with their parcels or bags of produce for the market flying off in all directions. Before the war, private motor traffic in Japan was not large, and in some districts almost rare. Certainly, some Japanese sorely-tried a driver's patience by their lack of road sense, but this fact did not justify what amounted to terrorist-tactics on the civilians.

Several times, they had also endangered the occupants of their own vehicles. Japanese had been directed to give sway to all Allied vehicles, for both safety's sake and of setting the precedence of who was in control and had power. Added to this, the Japanese began to complain-strongly about the petty thievery, particularly by the naval forces. The Japanese had so little, and what they could sell was so cheap, for the Allies who wanted souvenirs. To steal it, might have meant nothing to those who pilfered, but was the livelihood of the Japanese shopkeeper or vendor.

One of the first things which impressed the Allied personnel, as they began to compare things to their own countries, was the relative abundance of rubber and the scarcity of leather. The Japanese seized the world's main rubber-producing areas early in the war. The full force of this fact was brought-home by the novelty of seeing many, lowly-horse carts with solid-rubber or pneumatic tires. Most boots and shoes were made of rubber, or rubber with canvas, while one rarely saw any of leather. The country-style Japanese clung to their wooden clogs, and only those more sophisticated in the larger, northern Japanese cities wore leather. When a citified Japanese appeared in leather, particularly a woman, she was stared at and shunned for violating the Buddhist precept of an animal skin being worn against one's human skin.

Hats were not worn by women in the city, with the nearest approach being a kind of handkerchief, or small towel wound around the head, but not usually tied under the chin. Women working in the fields sometimes wore broad-brimmed straw hats, as a protection against the sun and rain. School children wore uniforms, or substitute portions of former ones. The girls in navy-blue, sailor-types, and the boys more often in military-looking jackets. The color, style and design of each person's dress, delineated what their stature or rank was within the community, or their specific work category. Costumes for special occasions like weddings or funerals, were also strictly relegated to one's position in the family, and financial standing within their group.

The Japanese rigid custom of a constant semi-smile, or forced laughter, while speaking of misfortune, pain or embarrassment was one puzzlement most Allies were mystified with. To say it would be disconcerting to have someone laughing, while describing the death of members of their family, or their own personal injury, was obvious.

Some soldiers would react with anger, believing the Japanese were heartless, and exemplified the cruel characteristics of their torturing of POWs. To most, it was beyond their comprehension this cultural-habit was a device for the all-importance of saving-face and disgrace, as them having been the victim of the misfortunes of war. It did not matter to those who had escaped it, as they were such a minority.

The Allied Forces generally did not have to push people around, as they themselves were catered to, and received preferential treatment from the Japanese for everything. Adjustment was not so easy however, when the privileges were not available, and they faced the realistic problems of riding a long distance in a third-class car. Ordinarily, Allied soldiers had second class coaches provided for them. If no seats were available, the conductor cleared out enough Japanese occupants, so the servicemen had adequate room to sit down, and not be crowded. This kind of service and treatment was new to most soldiers and quite convenient, so many quickly came to accept it, and to expect it. But occasionally, because of the limited availability in certain regions, one might have to take a train which had no second class coaches, or board where no conductor was available to clear the conqueror's way.

Then travel for the Allies became exactly what it was for the Japanese in those days - a long, painful-struggle to keep on their feet, with others pressing against them from all sides. As the train lurched, Japanese of all ages careened into any open space. Sometimes their snot-filled noses were stuck under the foreigners. Malnutrition had brought colds to all, and handkerchiefs were almost unknown. It was a close-encounter with real life, which most soldiers preferred not to have. In the countryside, there were more of those too, who stared or even gaped at him, with their mouths open and blank eyes watching. To the foul odors of breath and body, were added the ubiquitous packs and bundles full of pungent-dirt - human excrement was used as fertilizer. Or the dirt-covered vegetables, which the Japanese carried from farm to city on passenger trains. The system of food distribution had broken down, and the black market prices were unaffordable to all common folk.

Sometimes, there was an advantage to having one's feet pinned to the floor, by a sack of sweet potatoes. If you lurched as crazily as before, at least it was within one's spot. There was no compensation though, for the radishes which scraped back and forth across exposed skin, as they caused quite a rash. An aggravated-soldier might wonder why these people could not make some other arrangement for their bulky household goods and packs, but they had no alternative means of transport. It brought to mind so clearly, how sluggish governments - Japanese and Allied, did nothing for the people, to alleviate their daily problems. To many, much the same as before the war, so for these local, country people, nothing had really changed.

In the meantime, innocent babies suffered on their mother's backs, and were buffeted mercilessly by the jolting crowd. Sometimes, these little bundles would be eagerly feed a small bowl of rice, within the jerky movements of the trains. Mother and child would persevere, as she shoved small fingers full of rice into its waiting, open-gapped mouth, much like a baby bird anticipating crumbs, or worms to be dropped in. The smeared face would be swiped clean of each grain, pushed into the tilting, groping lips. Many Allied men would save the sugar and candy from their K-rations, just for an opportunity to watch some baby suck blissfully on it.

Yet, in the overcrowded conditions, the babies were no longer cute, as they sucked in their mouths the mucus, draining continually out of their noses. One might get a double dose of a child-emitting out of their other ends, the smothering, acrid-smell of both old, stale urine and excrement. In spite of a toilet sometimes being available, there was no way to make even one step toward it, in the pressing crowds. A lucky mother, who had a seat, would not hesitate to stick her infant's bottom out the open window, as the train stopped. Then the excrement had been safely deposited on the platform, or on the shoes of the mobs pushing to get on. Afterwards, the baby was brought in, and matter-of- factly rearranged to nurse at the mother's breast.

Also common, on these crowded trains, was for the more energetic people who boarded through the windows, and many seated inside at windows, accommodated them. This was done in such a usual manner, obviously not a new situation, as the Japanese were used to having far more people than facilities to handle them. Few would ever get angry about the discomfort, but also few tried to minimize it by acting sensibly at each stop. The crowds trying to get abroad, would press into the entrance before letting the outgoing group exit, with the result being a long deadlock of opposing forces.

This usually resulted with only the old, women with infants or children given way to efficacy. There was an abundance of shoving, burrowing, charging and shouting, with no gallantry or wisdom being shown, or any kindness to those smaller and weaker. This affray was entertainingly-absurd to observe, until it was repeated stop after stop, as if they never learned from the previous disaster. It would be years before the trains could afford to have conductors at the stations, who controlled the people with their perfunctory, white-gloved hands.

These irrational sights lent themselves to the comparison of ants, or other insects in their tenacity of trying to accomplish something, which from a distance could be observed as being hopeless, or at least a wasting of great energy. Truly, the Japanese had become totally dependent on someone to direct them, in the most basic functions or daily routines. The Allies were supposed to help them in whatever way they could, and try not to criticize their customs or culture. Still, there was a great gap which separated Western morality from those of the

Far East. Many foreigners were easily devastated by the discovery of all sorts of personal Japanese habits. Obviously, the strained situation quickened human weakness to adapt to foreign attitudes, or elaborate new molds of morality suggested by the circumstances. How the Allies, in a typically Japanese situation would have reacted, as would a Japanese who had been used to a life of privilege. Thus, natural to want to spare oneself of seeing the suffering of the masses, though disregarding it meant more suffering for them.

As part of their job or just for recreation, many Occupation troops also traveled around the rural districts by jeep. The reactions of the Japanese men were certainly the most difficult to understand. Usually, these men took little notice of the troops passing through. Sometimes they merely continued their work, as if nothing had happened, but mostly they watched with expressionless faces. In some country towns, the older men frequently greeted the troops by smiling, raising their hats and bowing, or waving hoes or whatever they may happened to have in their hands. Many of the younger men were still wearing old military or naval uniforms, basically because of the lack of other clothing. These had been stripped of badges or insignias. Some would stand and leer at the Occupation forces, or get a noticeable degree of pleasure from seeing them in some sort of minor difficulty, like a stalled engine or being totally lost.

Yet, most Japanese did their best to be helpful - despite no one spoke their language - to give directions or information. There were others, too, who would fall over themselves to give assistance, and then bow profusely to apologize for whatever - their lack of English, ability to repair or help or, simply for their existence. Their innate-fear of the military, lead to rarely a trace of passive-resistance or hindrance. Perhaps they felt the more they cooperated, the quicker it would all be over with, and the Allies would leave.

The most striking thing of any part of Japan, was the natural beauty of the scenery. Some would say such people did not deserve such lovely surroundings. If even the peace and tranquility of nature should have brought contentment, it should have been brought to these Japanese. Yet, one cannot help wondering why a people, amid such beauty would ever nurse thoughts of world conquest and domination. Few Allies ever understood how duped the people were and believed, they were fulfilling their Emperor's request without question.

From many hotels near the beach, one could sit by the sliding windows sipping tea, and watch the fishermen drawing in their nets, to the cadence of a slow and strange chant. If one waited long enough, the sunset could be seen behind the pines along the beach, usually with a small craft, threading its way between the rocks in the bay. Added to this picturesque beauty, would be the gulls and hawks scavenging for their food. This enchantment could lull many into forgetting where they were, and what they were there for.

As would be expected, the attitude between most Japanese men and women about the Occupation troops was quite different. The men felt humility, as Japan had lost the war, in spite of them not having been in the military, or supportive of the late military government. Now, they were a poor people, what little glory they had experienced was long gone and useless, as they scrabbled-around for food in shabby, worn-out, dirty clothes. The Allied men were taller, well-fed, and had lots of money. They were wearing clothes made from fine material the Japanese had not seen for years. On top of this, most Allies were quite light-hearted, laughing frequently at what some may have felt nothing, *or at their expense.*

What they often resented most though, was not the attraction these men had for their Japanese women, but the attention so many of them paid to women in general, helping them carry bundles, or making-way for them in doorways and sidewalks. The women quickly took notice, for they rarely felt wanted, or treated as if they were worthy of any consideration by the Japanese men. These men, who had nothing to feel superior about anymore, *still* treated their women

like servants. So, what woman would not swoon after, and choose the Clark Gable-substitutes? The Japanese men resented they were not even able to compete romantically. Few would not have known how to go about it, as courting was not within their culture to do, with arranged marriages never requiring any *thing like romance* by the man. It did not take long for the soldiers to see the obvious separation of the sexes, and the inferior position of women. They not only followed silently along behind their men, but usually were carrying a heavier load than the men! The Japanese women were doing tasks which females in their own countries would never be *allowed to* do, much less expected to perform.

Constantly, women were seen carrying huge loads of firewood on their backs, along narrow, precariously steep mountain paths. A wooden frame would be strapped over the women's shoulders, and around their waist to support the weight, which was often more than their own. Construction work was done in a similar way, with wicker baskets attached to bamboo poles, filled with dirt, stones, and various, reusable-rubble. With their diminutive size, and overly, graceful gestures of the young, amazement at the capability of the older ones.

Quite easy to see the attitude of the Japanese men toward their women, as he was the absolute ruler, and hardly a moment a day went by, without him imposing his will over the weaker sex. Also, this was clearly evident among children, for at play the boys would not be equal with the girls, but drive them away from whatever spot the former chose for their activities. The women not only did all the domestic chores, but did them while waiting on their husbands at every beck and call. The strength shown by many of the smallest, frailest and oldest of women made one wonder how she could do it, except for the fact of precedence.

Japanese, who were used to the naturalness of mixed bathing in public baths and hot springs, or women going bare-breasted outside their home in humid summers, had no sexual concept or thoughts of being un-puritanical. The typical Japanese woman was quite modest and retiring, keeping herself totally covered from neck to toes. The daily kimono had several layers of mixed, multiple assorted prints, usually in dark, drab colors. Western dress was not common, except in the larger cities, and then the dress or skirts were longer than what the Western women were wearing. Once married, these women thought of themselves as only servants to their families, and sex as something of only a man's choosing, and she would never consider denying it. Women were of service and subject to men - first their father, then husband and finally son, whom had been indulged since birth. Depending on space, either she slept with the children, or the whole family slept in the same room.

When one was invited into a Japanese home, - though a rare occurrence - the husband acted as host, while the wife waited on all, not participating in any way, but only serving. Traditional Japanese women, no matter how well educated, did not join a men's discussion. So, not uncommon for those Allied personnel, curious and quite interested in learning more about Japanese culture and family life, to experience some bizarre situations. One such incident happened when two older, well-educated interpreters were invited to the house of a famous Japanese professor. The evening was almost half-over, when they found out the woman waiting on them was his wife, who also was a professor, as well.

Quickly, with apologies, they tried to engage her in the Japanese conversation. She then explained, custom did not allow her to be in the same room with them, so she spoke to them *from the other side* of the *shoji*, - paper screen - while kneeling. Especially even more disconcerting to the foreigners, was when they then learned she had been educated in the States, and also spoke excellent English. To the husband and wife though, there was nothing strange about the situation. In fact, the Japanese man had considered himself to be quite modern and open, in having *accepted* such an educated woman for his wife. Usually, well-educated Japanese women were not accepted for *omiai* - arranged marriage, simply because the Japanese men did not want someone smarter than them, or who would not wait on them. The Japanese woman's education was her choice, or implicit in choosing *not* to get married. In the coming decades, this did improve somewhat. The Japanese were sometimes too accommodating and servile,

to truly build any kind of equal friendship, when all things were in favor of the Americans. Unknowingly, those foreigners who were honest and eager to know the Japanese, exploited them through their ignorance of the host country's customs and culture. For example: frequently troops invited to their homes ate their ration-bound hosts down to bare cupboards. Custom maintained they must provide excessive amounts of food and drink, while most Westerners were taught not to refuse any food. Also, GIs who dated the daughters, then accepted to stay over night in houses, already badly overcrowded with bombed-out relatives, and usually caused great embarrassment. This was inevitable because of Japanese etiquette not allowing 'No' to be said to a guest. The gaijin didn't know refusal was *expected* to first offers, one must be asked three times before saying 'Yes.'

The Japanese were at a loss as to handling the Allies properly, and were not able to adapt themselves to the situation adequately, when traditional rules did not apply. Added to this difficulty was the people's prior fear of their own military, which was transferred to the Occupation forces. So, when an overly-sociable GI wanted to stay overnight, his host could not suggest he leave, and his language, or sign language, was not sufficient for him to indicate this. He was the military man, he was in charge, he had the power - he could not be said 'No' to. He was also bigger, which prevented the Japanese from resorting to any direct means of eviction.

The Allied personnel were slowly learning bits and pieces of the intricacies of the controlling Japanese culture, yet they still filtered everything through their own native experience, which would distort it quite frequently. Another great mistake was to take gestures and compliments at face value. Rather, these words and actions were only part of the formal politeness, etiquette, and protocol in the Japanese customs, required of them in a particular circumstance. Once they became cognizant it was all merely pleasantries, many would then accuse the Japanese of dishonesty and insincerity. The basis of the Japanese language was ambiguity, as their own American English and culture had a more straight-forwardness of speech, especially after one's initial meeting. A constant problem, in which most of the Allies expected the Japanese to act in Western ways, and if they did not, then there was something wrong with *them*. It rarely occurred to the Allies, not only would the Japanese *not know how* to 'act Western,' but why should they have to do so in their own country?

One could say, the Allied lived like the life of the European- colonials, since they did not intend to become a part of the society. They continued to be a foreign observer, living on the fringes of the Japanese society, in quite the same manner to which they were previously accustomed. The Americans, particularly, came to Japan, or to any country in the Far East after the war, with what they liked to think of as a *charitable-attitude* toward human beings. This was probably more true of the new tourists or businessmen, who lived there before the war, than the average GI whose kindness and generosity was given so much publicity. Not that the GI was less well-intentioned than pre-war visitors, but he thought of the Japanese as conquered-servants, if not the enemy. Therefore, any little act of charity toward them, seemed to be more or bigger than it was. Most Japanese, also expected to be treated like they would have, or did treat their enemies, so to many it all did seem like a great charity.

For those military who began to concede and adopt the new life-style, appreciation and enjoyment of the rhythms of Japan were opened up to them, temporarily at least, relieving the stress of their Occupation chores. Soon, they began to notice the staccato-clacking of the wooden clogs on the pavement, the early morning song of the vendors, wafting-up about different Japanese delicacies, the clatter of shop-front shutters, and the neighbors sweeping the street with rice- straw brooms in front of their homes or shops. Everything had a pattern, a ritual, a timing, which was followed religiously, as it always had been. Then, easy to see how foreigners who were drawn to it, could become quickly mesmerized by it all. At night, the stumbling- shuffle of drunks returning home, or to the military base, became quite similar, and accepted, too.

As the ears revealed new melodies, their eyes also, began to see the aesthetic-beauty of the unpainted wood, aged slowly and variegated in its richness of colors in the shrines, temples and homes. Topping them in most villages, were the roof-tiles made of the local earth color, which made a striking symmetry in their usual clustering. Only the family crest on the trim, designed one house from another.

Actually, there was usually one town man who would form the tiles on his knee, in the same fashion as his ancestors had. If something should happen to him before a particular roof was finished, they would have to start all over again, because the new tiles, on a different knee, would not look *exactly the same* to the discerning-eyes of the Japanese, and their need for perfect symmetry.

~ ~ ~ ~ ~ ~

For some, a curiosity and for a few others, the need to reinforce their belief in power and might. But whatever the reason, no-one left from a trip to nearby Hiroshima or Nagasaki, without having their moral-fiber totally changed. Somehow, the black and white morality of defeating Japan became a dingy-gray, once the bomb had been dropped. It seemed to taint all the hard-won battles of men face-to-face, following the premise of fighting a 'good, clean fight,' as the surrender had become an anticlimax.

When the train made the stop in Hiroshima, nothing could be seen, but the twisted carcass of a department store, which had been between the station and the cracked chimneys of the university on the hills. The only buildings which were still somewhat standing, had been of ferro-concrete construction. Everything had been burned down so completely, it was hard to believe what had happened, or indeed, what had existed before. Definitely, the war correspondents and curious military, got more than bargained for.

The Japanese here looked more indifferent and sullen, going about the ruins with vacant, expressionless faces. Yet, they showed no outward signs of resentment toward the Allied soldiers. When spoken to, in Japanese especially, they replied as readily as elsewhere. The majority of Japanese who prior gone to to Hawaii and the West Coast, were from the Hiroshima-Kyushu vicinity. For those who had not sent descendants, there was sometimes some resentment of Nisei, who came bearing great quantities of gifts for their relatives.

As hoarding had become a common practice in the difficult times, not sharing any of those gifts, added to the lack in their lives.

These actions did not live up to the politeness within a household, and extended to neighbors.

People shuffled around in the vast emptiness, trying to build shelters from gathered, charred pieces and crumpled metal, while others seemed to be trying to cultivate the ground for growing something. The desolation was perfectly concentric, so easy to see where the blast had started and spread. Sickeningly-ironic, to see the almost perfect ring of burned and blackened stumps of trees, on the further outskirts of the blast. Then interspersed, were the twisted metal poles, going-off in every direction, as if by futuristic design. Most, of course, had no clue remaining in the area increased their odds of developing cancer and dying from the radiation.

By the first anniversary, August 6, 1946, coming just before the Japanese holiday of *OBon*, - the Buddhist-ritual of recognizing dead ancestors - the idea of encouraging peace began to surge. It became all the more apparent by August 15, the first anniversary of the end of the war. By this time internationally, many had begun to question and also condemn the bombing. And when, John Hersey's book *Hiroshima* was published, some Americans were so shocked, they challenged the validity of the bomb at all.

Most had only previously known the bomb as a powerful, awesome, mushroom-cloud, which instantaneously made them the country with the greatest military might. Now, some guilt began to set in - had it been worth the lives of over three-hundred-thousand Japanese. Total of Hiroshima and Nagasaki combined, instantly-killed or died within the first few years of radiation poisoning - and those mostly civilians? Had a million or two million lives really been saved, by not having to invade Japan?

Recent research, and the release of documented files, had shown *neither bomb* was necessary. Nagasaki mainly happened with the slow response of the Japanese military parliament, again as well misinterpretation of Hirohito's statement of surrender. The so-called number of lives which were to be saved from not invading Japan, had been inflated from the actual planning document of each military level. They kept growing from the first estimated numbers of worst- case scenario of twenty to twenty-five-thousand deaths.

Numerous critics within the government circles began to speak out, Admiral William Leahy, who in 1945 held a position similar to todays's chairman of the Joint Chiefs of Staff, said "The use of this barbarous-weapon at Hiroshima and Nagasaki was of no material assistance in our war again Japan … In being the first to use it, we … adopted an ethical-standard common to the barbarians of the Dark Ages. I was not taught to make war in that fashion, and wars cannot be won by destroying women and children."

Other military experts, like General Dwight Eisenhower and General Henry Arnold, felt an invasion would never have happened, as they *ALL* knew Japan was on the verge of collapse, for lack of fuel. With the Soviets planned declaration of war, and assurances to Japan its Emperor would not be harmed, no deaths would have occurred in an invasion.

Some historians hold President Harry Truman feared he would be criticized as 'soft' on the Japanese, if he told them they could keep the Emperor, *before* using the bomb. Truman, after only eighty-two days in office, and virtually no national, political experience, was trying to fill the mighty, big shoes of the late President Franklin D. Roosevelt. Ironically, on the morning of his death, on FDR's night stand laid the unopened letter from Albert Einstein, again begging him *not to use the bomb.*

Roosevelt had not even informed Truman, of a single detail about the atom bomb, and he, himself had little comprehension of its meaning or power. Unfortunately, one of the few friends Truman had in Washington, was the South Carolina politician, James Byrnes. Realizing Truman innocence and inexperience, he *manipulated him* toward his own hawkish-beliefs, and the importance of political image. Yet, Truman never recanted the act years later.

Roosevelt had the power snd personal strength to stand up to Prime Minister Winston Churchill and Soviet General Secretary Joseph Stalin. Once Roosevelt was gone though, Truman was easily swayed, or better yet *bullied*, into using the bomb. Great Britain had lost more economically in Southeast Asia with the Japanese capture of her colonies. And, were then making rumbles of independence, stirred- up from the long, Japanese presence, to *stand-up against* their 'white' oppression. Stalin's Russia, had never gotten over *their loss of face*, at being beaten by the Japanese in the 1905 War. These were not people dealing with compassion, but revenge. Truman was unaware of the fact the bomb would be used more on civilians, rather than the fighting, military 'enemy.' The sting of Pearl Harbor was also easily brought up and inflamed, for more influence on Truman.

Truman, having come more from a business background than a political one, realized how the taxpayers may feel about the bomb's two-billion-dollar price tag - 1945 U.S. dollars! He may have felt the need to justify the expense by at least *testing it out,* though it could have been demonstrated on an uninhabited island first. Truly, Truman's inexperience did not give him credentials to question the figures on probable lost of lives the military had given him, or their reason for pushing for the use of the bomb.

Again, the justification of 'saving all those American lives,' made the decision to go ahead with the lesser of two evils - dropping the bomb and not invading. There was the additional fact of the national collective-unconsciousness of the time, conditioned by years of war. Many were thirsty for blood, clamoring for revenge, yet impatient to see the war end, by any means. Only by a heroic-act of will, running counter to the spirit of the times, could Truman have stopped the dropping of the bomb. In a certain sense, he was the pawn, the instrument, and the victim of the times and circumstances.

The ultimate answer by many though, Truman and others thought by using the might of the bomb, it would *scare* the Soviets away from their own Communist world aggression. Really? This, unfortunately, was the greatest wrong of them all. The Communist only strove-harder to develop or steal for their own, and eventually more powerful, atomic bomb.

So, exactly the escalation of nuclear arms, the group of sixty- three scientists, who sent a petition to Truman had predicted: "Unless an effective international control of nuclear explosive is instituted, a race for nuclear armaments is certain to ensue ... Within ten years other countries may have nuclear bombs ... We believe these considerations make the use of nuclear bombs, for an early unannounced attack against Japan inadvisable. If the United States were to be the first to release this new means of indiscriminate destruction upon mankind, she would sacrifice pubic support through the world, precipitate the race for armaments, and prejudice the possibility of reaching international agreement on the future control of such weapons." It took almost fifty years to halt the nuclear arms race for the major four countries, with all the smaller Asian countries then competing for their own.

There are many mocking-ironies which have come-out of the bombings. For instance, the largest Japanese-Christian Protestant population was in Hiroshima, and the largest Catholic population was in Nagasaki. The latter was famed for being the first city open to foreigners, and when closed, the twenty-six Christian martyrs killed consisted of seven foreigners and nineteen Japanese. The single largest group - over two-hundred - killed in Nagasaki were in the Urakami Cathedral praying for the war to end quickly.

The largest Prisoner of War facility in Japan outside of Tokyo, Camp 14 was in Nagasaki. Almost two-hundred Allied prisoners, mostly Dutch, British and Australian, though no Americans. Many were killed, - would the Allieds call this 'friendly fire?' While others were cited for heroic deeds of helping Japanese. The original bombs used on Pearl Harbor had been built at the Mitsubishi Shipyards, and Steel Works in Nagasaki. This was the only reason the people of Nagasaki could focus on, as to have been chosen to be destroyed.

Hiroshima had been a large military training base with tens of thousands of troops in training. But, by August 1945, Japan did *not* have an unlimited supply of men available to train for the war. Less than ten thousand in Hiroshima, and most were in barracks by the train station, more than a kilometer from the epicenter. A distance which determined life and death for many people. Yet, there were at least twenty-three American POWs killed, though more had met their same end in Tokyo. The greatest percentage of Nisei parents, and thus their ancestors, had come from Hiroshima.

SAD Side Note:
Tens of thousands of Korean forced-laborers were killed in Hiroshima by the bomb. Numerous statues and monuments were built in Hiroshima over the years, for any and all the dead, including a few for horses and other animals. Yet, Japan never *allowed* one dedicated to these Koreans. Recently, one was erected outside the 'official' Peace Park. Even in the experience of death, some Japanese did not want it shared with those, they were still most prejudice against.

Personal Story:
Arifin Bey, an Indonesian with a Ph.D. in International Political Science. He studied both in Japan and the U.S. This interview was taken from *Japan As We Lived It*, by Bernard Krisher.
I came to Japan in June, 1944, a year after Japan occupied Indonesia and after all of our schools had been closed down. I was then at the higher normal school and trying to find a way to complete my studies, when I read of an opportunity to do so in Japan. I passed an exam, went through six months of Japanese language courses, and left in April, 1944. It took us two months by ship from Singapore to Japan. I remember we were zigzagging all the way, trying to avoid submarines. A miracle we arrived at all, as almost all ships were sunk midway.

We were housed and taught at the *Hokusai* -International - *Gakuyukai* in Meouro, which used the building of the (former) American school. There we went through another ten months of Japanese language preparation, as well as preparatory courses for the university. In 1945, Tokyo was being bombed almost every day. But nobody thought the war would end so soon, nor would Japan surrender. Already twenty, so, when they asked me, where I wanted to go to study, I replied: 'I want to become a teacher.' There were only two schools of Science and Eduction then, in Tokyo and in Hiroshima. Because of the bombing, they suggested Hiroshima.

I got there in April. Four months later when the atomic bomb was dropped I was right there, at school at eight o'clock in the morning on the sixth of August. The reconnaissance planes passed over Hiroshima almost every day at the same exact time - eight o'clock. So, we didn't feel there was anything unusual: just reconnaissance, we didn't have to leave the building. In fact, at 8:16 AM, the all-clear signal was sounded, and our professor came to the classroom. Just as he took out his chalk to write down something on the blackboard, there was a flash, a big crash, and everything crumbled over us. Fortunately, we were in a wooden building. There were only four of us from Southeast Asia at the school, two in each classroom; all the Japanese students had left for the front.

So, after the big crash, everything crumbled down, everything went dark. We were rather surprised, at eight on a hot, clear mid- summer morning, it had suddenly become like evening. Under the debris we continued talking to each other, because none of us was badly hurt. One student said it must have been a big earthquake, so big we didn't feel it. Another said, perhaps it was a time bomb that had been set up earlier and now had exploded. Nobody thought of bombardment. Not until two days later, we read in the papers a special type of bomb had been dropped.

When we could see, we crawled out of the debris, and walked for about ten minutes back to the dormitory. On the way, we saw collapsed houses and smoke all around. The bomb was dropped at breakfast-time, with most people cooking their meals on their *shichirin* - charcoal grills outside. The impact of the bomb created a strong wind, which blew-over all the small cooking fires, and in two hours the whole city was burning (actually the impulsion caused most of the fires). Our dormitory also caught fire.

Luckily, Hiroshima is a city of rivers, and the government had already prepared rafts on the river for just such a calamity. We had just enough time to carry some forty girls, who had been felled by the flash and could not move, down to the rafts, to get-on ourselves to escape. We had put them side by side like sardines, but during the night most of them fell into the water and died (technically they were probably dead or almost, before falling in, if knocked over by the blast).

We survived only because we were still strong enough - we did not suffer immediate ill-effects of the radiation. The whole school had burned down, so we lived on the campus lawn for another week, until someone from Tokyo came to fetch us.

Initially, we thought we had escaped the radiation illness, but in fact we had been affected. On the way back to Tokyo, we stayed one night in Kyoto, where we were warmly welcomed by the foreign students there. We sang and played guitar all evening. We had a merry, merry time. But before morning, one of the Hiroshima students, a senior, began to vomit and an hour later died.

On our return to Tokyo, we were all taken to St. Luke's Hospital for a check-up. They discovered my white blood cells had been reduced to forty per cent, of the number usually found in a person. The doctor told me he had never treated such a case before, and didn't know how to cure me. He said if I signed a form absolving him of all blame should I die, he would try to do his best. What he did was to remove the blood from one part of my body and infuse fresh blood in another. So, in effect, I had a full-blood transfusion. This helped. I went through ten years of periodic checkups and I feel okay.

Personal History:
Of the many initiatives, which grew out of American efforts to 'democratize' Japan during the early stages of the Occupation, one of the most innovative is attributed to Winfield P. Niblo, the Chief Education Officer of the Nagasaki Military Government Team from September, 1946 to October, 1948. Niblo called upon his personal involvement in square dancing, and determined this American folk dance could serve as a popular vehicle for co- education *and democracy* in Japan. This interview was taken from an article by Lane R. Ears.

Prior to the war, Winfield Niblo served as a high school social studies teacher in Denver, Colorado. Upon entering the U.S. Army in 1942, at age thirty, he trained at first as a Field Artillery Officer, and later as a Special Agent in the Counter Intelligence. By the time he arrived in Yokohama, in December 1945, the war had ended. After serving less than a year with C.I.C. in Tokyo, Kanazawa and Saitama, Niblo became eligible for discharge. Instead, he accepted a civilian job with the Army, as Provincial Education Officer in Nagasaki.

The self-proclaimed, middle-class school teacher from Denver was extremely impressed by Japanese culture, and the country's high level of educational achievement. "I was young and energetic, so … the more I observed and experienced life in Nagasaki, the greater became my admiration and appreciation for its people."

Nibble's job was primarily to ensure the directives from SCAP regarding Japanese education were carried out, at the various local levels. The main concern of the directives was to eliminate 'militaristic and feudalistic' tendencies in the education system. According to Niblo, this was not a particularly difficult task, since most Japanese educational officials agreed with the ultimate objectives. Probably the most dedicated issue was the U.S. demand for co-education, (which was not common) but even in this area, Niblo found most educators to be cooperative.

In addition to being a high school teacher prior to the war, Niblo had been quite active in promoting recreational activities. He had been both a football coach and a trainer - caller of square dancing. His expertise in the latter, proved most helpful in Japan. Niblo not only appreciated square dancing's recreational worth, but also recognized its value in encouraging healthy, social relations between males and females. Quite by chance, however, how Niblo's square dancing skills were put into practical use in Japan.

"One evening, shortly after I arrived in Nagasaki, I was invited to a dinner party at the home of the Chief Physical Educational Section. Also in attendance, a group of physical education teachers of the city schools. Following dinner, the teachers performed a number of beautiful Japanese dances. When they were finished, I asked if they would like to learn some American folk dances. They said they would like this very much, so I arranged them in two lines with couples facing one another. I then taught them the oldest American dance, the Virginia Reel. They enjoyed it very much, and asked to learn more dances. So, I taught them several simple square dances. They learned the dances unbelievably fast. Thus, the American Square Dance was introduced to Japan. In a small sense, a little bit of history was made on that Autumn evening of 1946, in Nagasaki."

Square dancing caught on rapidly with the Nagasaki residents, spreading initially through the instruction of physical education teachers. They, themselves underwent folk dance training beginning December 1. The teachers, in turn, taught groups of adults and children. From Nagasaki, it spread to the outer islands and other prefectures in Kyushu. Funds were soon made available to send teams of four couples each, to neighboring prefectures to demonstrate and teach square dancing.

Niblo's secretary, years later recalled the introduction of square dancing in Nagasaki: "At first most people had some reluctance, as Japanese men and women were unaccustomed to dancing together. The whole idea alien to us. However, after one or two sessions, we became enthusiastic square dancers. The music was exciting and dancing became fun. As little other recreation available at the time, the number of dancers increased rapidly. Square dancing broke the barrier between the military and civilians, the Americans and the Japanese."

Both the domestic and international press quickly picked up on the story of square dancing. In late 1946, the *New York Herald Tribune, Time,* the *Daily News Foreign Service,* and *United Press* all ran stories on Niblo and square dancing in Nagasaki. They each examined Niblo's rationale for initiating the dance. "Niblo looks upon square dancing as a means of breaking down the traditional Japanese family taboo against social mixing between sexes. Overcoming the obstacle wasn't easy, for the average Japanese couple is mightily embarrassed, by any contact in public places. However, Niblo has dozens of enthusiastic endorsements of square dancing from Japanese. They consider it not only fun, but *democratic.*" Another press release noted how Niblo became so closely associated with the dance - 'in Nagasaki they don't call it square dancing ... It's Niblo dancing."

The local Japanese press also contained numerous accounts on the square dancing rage in Nagasaki, and its introduction into the regular school curriculum. Most pieces commented on the initial awkwardness of boys and girls performing the dance, but how they learned to enjoy it after a while. In July 1947, they reported: "For the people of Nagasaki, the worries of this fickle-world are nothing, since to the sweet music of American folk songs, they can dispel their worldly gloom and enjoy themselves in the interesting, graceful, and wholesome square dance. Practically the whole of Nagasaki is being swayed by this new form of community recreation. It is fast spreading among the people, both urban and rural, in direct proportion to the recognition of its educational, recreational and psychological value."

Also commenting on the initial impact of square dancing were the U.S. Occupational Authorities, in their monthly report from December, 1946. According to this report, not only teachers, but "Other groups, such as the Police Department and the Railway Employees, have also heard about this activity, and have asked for an opportunity to learn the dances." It is apparent from some of the comments, by lower ranking policemen and policewomen, the choice was not their own, but orders had come down from above. Although initially embarrassed by the dance experience, some did come to enjoy it, as evidenced by their testimonies of support.

The December 1946 Military Occupation Report, continued with the claim square dancing offered much more than healthy exercise: "This has proved to be a very interesting psychological and sociological experiment. It is very difficult for an American raised and educated, in close relationship with the opposite sex to understand the feelings that exist in the minds of Japanese individuals regarding the opposite sex. In the square dance, after the initial shock of close contact with the opposite sex is over, the participants were busy figuring out what to do next, so they don't have time to worry about how un-Japanese-like they are behaving.

In a short time, the inhibitions against social intercourse are completely relaxed, and the dancers are busily engaged in the dance with no regard for the violation of traditional segregation. The degree of appreciation and enjoyment with the *Nagasakians,* apparently derive from this activity, leads to the inclusion they have been starving for this type of inexpensive wholesome, community recreation, so much needed to enrich the cultural life of the average Japanese community." (No Comment, it speaks for itself and who said it.)

Niblo went on to help prepare a textbook and by 1947, it was estimated there were almost fifty-thousand, active square dancers in Nagasaki alone. It spread to the rest of Japan with the assistance of theMinistry of Education. A Folk Dance Training Course was set up and with Prince Mikasa, the Emperor's youngest brother, and his wife Princess Yurio participating and supporting it, the success of square dancing across Japan was assured.

Niblo was transferred to Hokkaido, as Regional Education Officer for twenty months, then sent to the newly established Youth Specialist Program within the Civil Affairs Section of SCAP in Tokyo. When the program was terminated in June, 1951, he briefly returned home to Denver before joining the U.S. Foreign Service, where he served in fifteen countries over the next twenty-five years. During this period, he also managed to complete work on his doctorate from Columbia University.

Following Niblo's retirement from the Foreign Service, he was invited back to Japan in late 1981 to participate in the twenty-fifth anniversary ceremony of the founding of the Japanese National Folk Dance Federation. On the Emperor's birthday, in 1982, Niblo received the Third Class Order of the Sacred Treasure, for his contributions to Japan. The following statement was made at the time of the award: "(It) took tremendous courage for Dr. Niblo to promote friendly relationships between the Japanese people and the American people. It was through such efforts as Dr. Niblo's, that the recreation clubs and folk dance clubs were established one after another, through Japan and helped enhance the people's morale and hopes for the future, at the time when Japan was still struggling from the ashes of the war."

Part II - Japan As The Occupied:
Chapter 7 - *ffiagoya and Kyoto* - Destruction and Preservation

What difference if they had either outlived the others or had died first, because they never lived at all. The family group, - with formal and lifeless decorum now fading like an ancient photo, grim and implacable, unforgiving, had taken security and all that living means to her, fall into ruins about her feet - had fought for honorable years for the soil and traditions of the land where she had been born. Nothing to face the future with but her bare hands. Men with valor and strength, but without pity or honor. Is it no wonder that heaven saw fit to let us lose?

William Faulkner,
Absalon, Absalom!

Nagoya: Destruction

A high price to pay for being *the* successful, industrial giant of Japan - 89% of the city area was destroyed in fire bombings, the last year of the war. Only Hamamatsu had seen more destruction - 93%, and much smaller than the bustling, one million population of Nagoya. Being centrally located, both on the main island of Honshu, and basically the whole archipelago of Japan. Nagoya, as later called, had historically been the cross-roads in its nineteen hundred year existence. Astuta Shrine was the first root in building Nagoya's growth, as second only in national, historical culture and Shintoism, to the

Great Shrine of Ise. The landscape took on added importance, when it became one of the main stops on the Tokaido Road, between Kyoto and Tokyo. This also established its basic growth, as well its need for various industries - transportation, metal forging, pottery, and clothing.

Ieyasu Tokugawa, who made the final consolidation of Japan from the numerous warring clans, was from the Nagoya vicinity. He chose it for the building of a castle for his son in 1610. With this important designation, Nagoya was quickly filled with, and thrived from, numerous Samurai, monks, merchants, and tradesmen. The port was greatly expanded to handle goods being shipped both north and south. By the late 1700s, proud to be the fourth largest city in Japan, after Kyoto, Tokyo - then called Edo - and Osaka.

Being surrounded by the large Nobi plain, crop production was never a problem for the burgeoning population, and a balanced wealth was established. Though quite ambitious, Nagoyans were not known to be aggressive like Osakans. They accepted they would never be the number one city, so a basis of conservatism was built-up, almost in defense. This tradition of wealth without national status, in an extremely caste or tacit, hierarchal-group society, then imprinted a slight insecurity on each future generation.

Real industrial growth came with the Meiji Restoration in mid-1800s. By the 1900s, factories for the production of textiles, ceramics, vehicles, steel and clocks were scattered throughout the city and suburbs. Nagoya's foundation had been laid, and its claim to fame for industrious, hard-workers and technicians was built. The lumber industry expanded, and the flowing rivers increased the importance of the port. Nagoya soon the number three city, as Kyoto changed to the cultural, rather than political center. Tokyo assumed its Capital-rank.

Even the Great Depression of the 1930s, did not

crush Nagoya, but simply changed it from consumer-oriented light industry, to the growing, powerful military production, and heavy duty manufacturing. Prior to the American oil embargo of 1941, many of the machines and their replacement parts had been British and American. Once they were no longer available, the engineers had to learn the *art of copying*, or duplicating what they did have. It became a forced-technology which they built into almost a science. Feeling dire-straits, they copied every piece of machinery or part they got their hands on, with no ethical-concern for patents or prior ownership.

The bustling, modern city was proud of its success, and spent its money well in facilities and infrastructure, which neither Osaka or Tokyo had done. The central water supply, sewer and drainage systems were installed throughout the city from 1914, 1923, and 1934, respectively. The citizens also enjoyed excellent trains, streetcars, a canal system and convenient, wide paved streets for the various traffic to flow easily. To celebrate their finally attaining a remarkable population of one million, a new contemporary designed Civic Assembly Hall and City Hall were built.

Following in 1937, from March 15 to May 31, Nagoya boldly made its entrance into the international arena, by sponsoring the Pan- Pacific Peace Exposition. More than twenty-nine countries participated, and almost five million visitors came to share the technology, and supposedly, the intentions of peace. Unfortunately, all this effort was soon overshadowed, and embarrassingly shown to be hypocritical, by the invasion, then later "Rape" of Nanking, China in December, of the same year.

As the largest industrial center for production of war materials
- motors, trucks, machinery, and chemicals were produced city-wide. But, the star and centerstage product was the famed Mitsubishi *Zero* fighter planes. Nagoya was the largest supplier, 60% of the national total - more than ten-thousand of them flew off the assembly lines. They

were the bane of the slower, less maneuverable American fighter planes. The hatred of these Zeros, and their imminent destruction, targeted Nagoya's fate for destruction. Nothing thrilled the American bombardiers more, than to be the ones who 'got to blow them to smithereens,' as they joyfully announced.

As with most Japanese, tenacity was part of their make-up, though the city by the end of the war had been brought to almost a standstill. Yet, within forty-five days of surrender, the City Assembly approved a massive Reconstruction Plan. Total optimism existed, surrounded by waste and devastation. All the more, after having lost almost half of their population to evacuation and death, they planned for a base which would serve a population of two million people. One of the central features of the blueprint was an outline for the construction of two - one hundred meter-wide 'park roads' and nine - fifty meter-wide 'main roads.' Streets were straightened and blocks were created and squared.

The obvious Western influence from the American Occupation was easily recognized. Soon, Nagoya became known for having sidewalks wider than the *streets* of old Kyoto. No other Japanese city took advantage of its destruction more or better, as they carefully planned for a modern future. Added to this, was a positive memory of their regretful past, as in all military manufacturing installations, which bombs and fires had so quickly erased, were turned into parks, instantly making Nagoya the 'greenest' metropolis in Japan.

Into this creative, determined construction commotion came the Occupation Troops in mid-October, 1945, - the largest American contingency outside of Tokyo. They should have been hated, but for a few exceptions, they were loved. Perhaps, no city was happier to see the war over than the burned-out Nagoya. Indeed, putting up with the Americans on the ground, was better than having them rain their death-down on them from above.

The tens of thousands of troops were stationed in

the large Tsurama Park with its cherry trees, ponds and gracious old ornamental fountains and statues. The glorious castle had been gutted, by 'mistaken' fire bombs. They were supposed to destroy the nearby Prefectural capital, the past May, and only the scarred, massive stone-ramparts of the castle were left standing. The American Village, residential domain for the Officers and Occupation staff, was located between Tsurama and the castle grounds, later called Shirkawa Park, in the zone called Sakae. For almost six years, the Occupation Troops totally reorganized and sometimes upset, the lives of the Nagoyans while installing, then enforcing the directives from SCAP in Tokyo.

Nagoyans had made their money and fame on manufacturing for the military. Now, it was back to work manufacturing for the people, who had done without everyday goods for almost ten years of war. This group consisted of Toyota Motor Cars, and their later 'upstart'-competitor, Sochiro Honda, as well the expansion of Noritake China into the ceramics. Later budding, electronics industry, Brother Sewing Machine Company, and of course, Mitsubishi, with its extensive machinery for various manufacturing entities. Many new companies, and old ones quickly built makeshift factories out of the remains, or whatever facilities they could beg, borrow or steal.

Everything was needed, as just about everything had been wiped out. The competition was keen, and truly survival of the fittest, for like everywhere else in Japan, food was the commodity to bargain for and with. Family heirlooms, treasured calligraphy scrolls, priceless art, lacquerware, and exquisite kimonos, were traded back and forth to the farmers, or the black market, with little thought of yesterday, or for tomorrow. Life was truly lived on a daily basis, as the new reality of what most could handle at the time.

Nagoya's other claim to fame, or to some

embarrassment, the cultural history, or at least recreational creation of *pachinko* - sort of a vertical, pinball machine. Certainly, there was no pachinko in ordered, controlled, serious-minded prewar Japan. The truly mindless-pachinko was much too puerile, frivolous and exceptionally pointless. Which was exactly what made it so popular after defeat, yet continued to make it popularly grow in modernized Japan. Interestingly, before any great reconstruction plans sprung from the ruined city, pachinko parlors appeared, as if by magic. They were inexpensive places of pleasure, or more honestly, escapism to oblivion from the poverty- stricken environment. The interiors may have been spartan and tawdry, but the noise alone of the clacking, falling metal balls could put anyone into a zombie-state. Therefore, not have to deal with the total lost of security of who they were, which came with the annihilation of the city, jobs and life in general.

In their group controlled-society, where no one must stand-out or speak-out, pachinko served the purpose of being the sole-recreation which could be played alone. One may go with a friend, but was not expected to leave if the other lost all his money, nor to wait around if the other was winning. It also required zero talent, education or mental input - literally anyone could play and did. With the insertion of a coin, a certain number of metal balls were released - usually twenty- five. Then they aimlessly fell, on their own with little physical assistance, such as 'body-English' in pinball, for the machines were not to be abused. There were no flashing lights, to add excitement to a high score being racked-up, for no competitive scoring per se.

One's only reward was more balls, which could be exchanged for cheap goods, and the those exchanged for money. This was not a socializing situation, as each person sat quietly, maybe smoking in front of their machine, elbow to elbow. The only supplied amenities were a toilet, wash basin, pay telephone and cashier's booth. There was no drinking or eating in the pachinko parlor, and the background music was loud and abrasive, like at a race track, or right after the war, military marches.

At first, the patrons may have been the jobless, and later the hopeless, forlorn-repatriated military, so rejected by those who had once cheered them, when they had faith in success. To some, the droning cacophony was like meditation chants or prayer wheels, which could take them away from their mundane existence, or battle with survival. A wordless communion could be built up between the man and the machine, to such an extent this respite could actually result in feeling refreshed. The lines formed at the doors long before opening, since the faithful must get to his 'own' or 'personal' machine, in which a connection, or rapport had been built.

Perhaps it had a positive side, in it was not destructive to the body like alcohol or drugs, though the addiction was the same, so any claims to mind damage could not be ignored. Of course, such escapism and addiction did not go unnoticed, and soon the pachinko came under the 'protection,' if not control, of the *Yakuza* - the Japanese mafia - in one way or another. (*Even in modern Japan, over fifty million people play regularly on over fifty thousand or so, pachinko parlors taking in over $200 billion a year, or over eight times what the auto industry earns. Thus, this escapism is still the nation's past time, if not obsession.*)

~~~~~~

A second life and reincarnation came to Nagoya with the unexpected Korean War. The old war machinery was dusted off, or re-oiled and put back into action, as it was cheaper and quicker to have the Japanese make the war materials, than have it made and shipped from the U.S. Also, many of the American manufacturers were roaring out domestic products and did not want to take the time or money, to re- tool their machinery for a short-term profit. To the prior starving Japanese, any profit was worth the effort, as labor was cheap and easily exploited. Because the immediate and willing cooperation, more bigger orders were fed to the Japanese industries, who never said 'No.' What they did not know how to make, they learned.

Technology was 'loaned' to them from the United States, and they gleaned every morsel, as food for their mind, and future money for the pocket. A little company, with family money and roots in Nagoya, began to bloom in Tokyo. Akio Morita took its profits in 1952 of SONY, and bought the rights from Western Electric, of something called a *transistor*. As history shows, he turned it into a miracle for Japan, and innovation for the world. Suddenly, as the Korean War ended and the Occupation left, there was no unemployment. And, eventually there were also no more hungry people. Life could be good, if one just worked diligently to make the country strong, and build it into a competitive economic power. Everyone was asked once again to give their all, but with a difference this time, it was for the company and personal affluence, not for a war or the Emperor.

Personal History: A Japanese male, experienced bombing and the Occupation of Nagoya.

I was born in 1937, in January, and in about six months, the Japan- China War started. So when I realized this, the war to me had always been, it was a constant state, as it were. I think I thought the war would never end, and it would always be with us, forever. The only thing I remember doing about that time, is the air raids by the American aircraft. Saipan fell in 1944, in July and after, the air raids to the main- land started, but not serious in that year, at least not in Nagoya area. In the next year, 1945, it became a real thing and very often, American aircraft, B-29s, were over Nagoya. But, until March of the year, we didn't think, at least I didn't think, seriously about it, of course, there were anti-air-raid drills very often. A very simple way really, people handed a bucket making a long line, and they really thought they could extinguish the fire, in that way.

I was living in rather a big house, which didn't belong to us, but to my uncle, who was a military officer, as they were living in Manchuria. We were staying in the big house and then it was burned out by the air-raid, March the 25, 1945. I was my second year in elementary school, and in the spring time, so we had no school (the school year starts in April). But on the next day, we were to have been sent to a place the country in Aichi-Ken (prefecture or state area) for group evacuation. School children over the third year living in Nagoya, I think we were all sent to the country for safe-keeping. So they had to part with their parents, and lived together with other school classmates. I was ready for going on the next day, I packed everything in my bag, and my mother told me various things about it.

I went to sleep that night, then awakened by my mother. She said, "Wake up, we have to go." I was very sleepy and said, "No, I don't want to get up. I'd like to stay here." But she said, "No, it's dangerous! All of us, we have to go. You must hurry up!" And I said, "No, I'd like to stay here, I don't want to wake up." But she said, "If you don't get up right now, you'll die!" And I said, "I don't mind dying, leave me alone!" They got angry at me, I suppose, but anyway, I got up and got dressed. We went out of the house, and there was an anti-air raid shelter or dugout in my yard. So, first we went into the dugout, kind of a hole dug in the ground, with a kind of a floor made from some wooden planks. It was floating, because of the rain water coming inside. So, I think I was on the floating floor, but other people might have been standing or crouching in the water. I think we stayed there for a while, but it was noisy outside and something made us uneasy or ominous on that night. We heard people running or walking outside, and somehow we get uneasy, so left the dugout and went out away from the house.

Already there were many people walking to and fro, and they were shouting and saying to each other, "You'd better run, run away to the school! … to the school!" They kept saying that, so we started to run, my mother and my older sister, my bother and my little sister, four years old. My mother took my hand and carried my sister on her back, and we were running, aimlessly, but somehow we heard people still saying, "To the school!" It must have been an emergency meeting spot, it was a girls' school and we managed to arrive there, and of course, it was in the night. We saw lots and lots of B-29s flying over, and the air-raids had already started. I don't know why those aircraft came over that part of Nagoya, maybe there were some factories producing weapons. But our place was in a residential area, so I think they didn't drop so many bombs, they rather dropped incendiary shells all over the district.

I realized it was unusually light, like the day time and somehow we knew they were flare bombs, which came down floating, and lights-up the whole part. Maybe you have seen some scenes like in the Vietnam War. Very light, you could see each other's face very clearly. Very unusual, and it may sound a bit strange, I thought very beautiful. I was so young and maybe still sleepy, but they looked like giant fireflies, very attractive, beautiful, almost dream-like. We stayed there a very long time - at the school grounds. There were many people and they were crouching on the ground, outside the building in the playground area. There must have been many, many dugouts there, but I think most people stayed out on the ground, crouching and looking at the sky.
There were lots and lots of aircraft flying over and of course, there were some anti-air raid guns which were shooting, but it's very rare to hit an aircraft in the sky. But just one aircraft was hit by the anti-air raid gun, and I remember the airplane, B-29, came down wrapped up in flames. It's like watching some melted metal, very red coming down and many people were watching it. I think some people clapped their hands, not so close to us. But after the war, I found a place where an American aircraft

crashed, and there was a big hole. I heard pilots on the aircraft all died. There was a sign on a pole and a line went: "A person who sacrifices his own life for a friend's, there is no deeper love ..." or something like that from the testament, it's the only thing I remember.

Anyway, we stayed there for a long time and towards the dawn, everything was finished. Some of us knew our houses had been burned out. In the morning, we went to where our house used to be, and all of the houses were burned. We saw the remains of our piano, the refrigerator and things like that, but nothing was left for us except some dishes or bowls, which we kept in the dugout. I don't think I felt fear about it, but I don't think I felt hatred toward Americans, or the people we were fighting. Maybe I was too young.

After that we stayed near the place, Imaike area, for a while living together with another family, in a very small house. Of course, we couldn't keep living there, so we decided to go to the countryside. We fortunately had a very, remote-relative living in the country, and we went there to live in a kind of an old, small factory, or workplace where there had been some machines. There were, let me see, a family of seven living in the two rooms.

My father worked for a big factory, producing aircraft or war airplanes, or things like that. He often went to Tokyo on business, so he wasn't with us on the night our house was burned out. The company he worked for originally produced clocks, or gas meters and things like that. But during the war-time, it became a military effort and made things for the aircraft (technical instruments), so it was a big business. He was in charge of a section which bought lots of materials from other companies, so I think he got kind of bribes from other companies, (this is still a common way of doing business) so we had many things sent to us. Beside that, I think he got a rather good salary, so I thought everything was going all right with us. We were rather better at that time, but when the war was over, we had to live a really poor life, but we thought it was a kind of punishment.

We had very little to eat, and I was always hungry. Even among our family members, we were very jealous of what each other was eating. I was thinking my bother has more than I. We were always hungry. We stayed in the country four and a half years. In those days, people were very narrow-minded, so people coming from the city were treated very coldly, at first. Afterwards, of course, we became good friends, but at first they looked at us very oddly. In those days, the people living in the country were farmers, and at least they had a lot to eat - rice, vegetables and things like that. But we were very poor and we couldn't get enough to eat, so I think they kind of looked down upon us. (Poor people are very disrespected in Japan, rather than empathized.) My father did join us there, and he kept going to his company, but it took a very long time on a crowded train.

Finally, we came back to Nagoya and we rented a small room, which had been used for an office of a little firm. So, not a usual house, but everyone was in the same situation. I remember when the war was over, and Japan accepted the Potsdam Declaration of the 14th of August. On the next day, the Emperor declared it on the radio. Still eight years old, so I didn't know anything about it, and during the summer vacation. But my brother, who was in middle school, had to go to school to listen to the broadcast. He came back in the afternoon and said the war was over. I didn't know what it meant, but he said we lost the war, and it's what I remember about the time.

Although we were all very poor, I think most people had some kind of hope. In the school, the teachers started talking about the peace coming back to Japan and about the future. Of course, most people were angry with the Japanese government, or military people at that time. I don't think they talked a lot about their hatred toward Americans or British people. Somehow, to be honest, I could never bring myself to hate American soldiers or Americans in general. When I was an elementary student, in the country, sometimes those people (Occupation Troops) came in a jeep. I don't know for what purpose, but of course, just to investigate what's happening in the school. Whether they are giving the wrong education to the children, or maybe also for a goodwill visit to the school. They came with some softballs and bats, so the children can enjoy playing softball.

One thing I remember about them is, they looked a bit different from what I expected them to be. My only image of foreigners or Westerns, came to be from some movies. At the time they were always mean, very cruel to Chinese people or Japanese people. Of course, they had very, long noses, blond hair, and tall. These were not so different when I saw them, but they were younger, and they were very clean and beautiful. I think I got a very good impression of them. When I came back to Nagoya and went to the center of Nagoya, Sakae, I saw many, many GIs. They were walking very happily, and didn't look sloppy, they always looked correct and proper, clean and beautiful. There was no wrinkles in their trousers, and they were very young and good looking. Of course, they looked very casual and very friendly. Many children went after them, and young girls and street girls as well.

Sometimes I passed by a place where those American officers were living, there was a section saved for them. There were many newly, built houses and also barracks for the soldiers. In front of some big building, there were some MPs stationed, and out of those buildings came those soldiers, officers. To be honest, the feeling towards them, when I saw them was just pure admiration. It lasted for a long time. After I grew a little older, I started to go to see movies in the town. We mostly saw American movies of the 1940s and 50s. In those movies, I saw Americans living happily, and compared with their life, ours was very poor. I thought America was an ideal country, a kind of utopia.

You must have heard of our kind of inferiority complex toward Americans, and I know there still is, but I can't blame those people who feel a kind of complex toward them in my generation. So for a long time, America was a country of my dream and I wanted to go to the Unites States some day. Although, I didn't realize it until the Vietnam War, I really liked Americans. I don't mean I hate them now, but I liked them more before that time, when they believed so in their cause, when they were confident. Of course, the Americans now must be better than those people at the time, but people in general are quite naive, it's true. But they were really confident of their way of life and they were confident about the war. My image of the Americans since the Vietnam War is different. I was kind of disillusioned or disappointed by it.

Now, I don't think of going to the United States so strongly, as when I was younger. When I was a student in high school, France pulled out from Vietnam, what was it - Dien Bien Phu, I don't remember what happened after, maybe Americans came right after … At first, I still believed in the Americans, or Western side of the world. I didn't like North Vietnam coming into the South, or things like that, as I don't believe in Communist. I thought Americans or South Vietnam would finally win, but it took a long time and the air-raids to the North. By and by we were informed Americans would never win the war. But at the time, I don't think I was very informed, rather after or toward the end. I gradually became disillusioned about the Americans, or about the American cause of war.

It was the 5th Air Force in Nagoya, and the first headquarters was in the Tsurama Park (city) building. Ordinary Japanese people were not allowed in the park at that time. We saw many signs of "Off Limits." Later it was given back, and we often went to the concerts then. There must have been another headquarters at Sakae, in an old building, bank or something. I think it was near the Tokai Bank at Sakae. Close to that place, there is now a park (Shirakawa), but then it used to be the residential area of the American officers, many barracks as well. When we passed by, we saw the families living there with a Japanese maid. We saw American children, how I envied them. They looked very comfortable in their life, and seemed to have everything.

I was quite surprised and impressed when I saw their automobiles, they were so different. They were so beautiful, they were so new, so big and everything was different from what we had. During the war time, we had very little gas, so we didn't have many cars running, and we couldn't afford it, too. Even our buses were run on wood (charcoal-burner engines) and we had tram cars, called trolley- buses, which ran on the electricity. So no railway tracks, they moved along on the pole. So when I saw those beautiful cars, I understood why we lost the war. We said, "Gosh, what people were we fighting!" I felt that way. So you can't blame me if I felt such admiration towards Americans and all the things they had.

I don't think I had any resentment or grudges toward Americans. Sometimes I wonder why, but that's how I felt at the time. People a little odder than I, might have felt some resentment toward them. One time I was talking to some people in this school (university where he teaches) and I heard one of the teachers, who was about five years older. I said something about it, and just abruptly he said he still felt resentment toward Americans. People of my generation were different, a little too young. After the war, we were taught at school how kind Americans were toward us, who lost the war, not like the Japanese soldiers in Asia.

I remember during the war, once my aunt came to us and said she had a dream the night before. In the dream, Japan had lost the war and Americans came to Japan for Occupation. She said in her dream all the Japanese people were their slaves and then taken to the United States. I think I had expected if we lose the war, that kind of thing might happen to us. But nothing happened, so we were taught how generous Americans were, which was true because we had very little to eat, and they gave a lot of things to us.

Even at the time we had school lunch, and we had milk, powdered milk, which came from the United States. We used to call it 'milk without fat,' it's a kind of waste I thought. It's not the ordinary milk with fat, but even it was enough for us, for we were very hungry. Of course, we knew about the atomic bombs at Hiroshima and Nagasaki, so people in that area might have felt in a different way. Here in Nagoya, I didn't see or hear people talking about their resentment. I remember a friend of mine, who is about ten years older, saying he might not mind fighting the war again with Russians, but not Americans. Because he said Russians at the last moment, the Non- Invasion Treaty or something, suddenly joined the war. I thought it was very interesting. I think it is another reason why most Japanese don't feel resentment toward Americans, for if Russia had come to Japan for the Occupation, it would have been very different.

There were some special trains for American military people. They were painted in a different color, mostly blue and they looked more beautiful, it's true. I was too young at the time to ride the trains with them, though. There was always a PX (where soldiers were stationed) and some people who fortunately got acquainted with American soldiers, got various things from the PX, and other people envied them. At the PX there was everything, chewing gum, chocolate, food, and what do you call it, like lunch box for soldiers, yes - K- rations. My parents had to go somewhere to buy rice and vegetables, mainly to the country. It took them a whole day to go on the crowded train with a rucksack on their shoulders, then they came back with a little food and it's how we survived. It was not only from our relatives, but those they didn't know.

I think they felt humiliated, because the people in the country were not so kind to the people who came to buy food. We had to sell many things to get a little money. My mother had to sell her kimonos, her record player, camera, and things which couldn't be gotten so easily. They had to exchange those things for food. I think there are still some people, who talk rather angrily about the attitude of the people in the country at the time, saying they were not generous, not so kind to us.

We later moved from the little office-building room to another place in Mizuko-ku (neighborhood area). There were some little houses built by the municipal office and we were living there. One of the neighbors, living there together were a young husband and wife, with her younger sister. She was about in her twenties and she was working for the PX. She fell in love with an American soldier, a Nisei from Hawaii and they started to live together. So the Nisei-man came very often to our neighborhood, a big car, which was a Buick, a beautiful car (laughs jovially). Of course, we were very curious, as we were across from them. So sometimes we were invited to their house, which was very small, but the man was very kind and they were living happily together.

One time on Christmas Eve, the man gave me a present, a pair of gloves, socks or something. Of course, since he was a Nisei, he looked like a Japanese, but still he was an American, so he had many things we didn't have. I wanted to talk to him in English, because he could speak very little in Japanese. After a while, they got married and went to Hawaii, but somehow some years later, the woman came back alone, she got a divorce. Both of them were very nice people. They said he was a kind of engineer, electric or something, so I think he was well paid.

When I was about twelve years old, and a student in the junior high school, some of my friends in the neighborhood went to church. I started to go to church, because I was interested in Christianity, because my brother and sister used to go to a Missionary school. They often talked about the Bible and many hymns, I liked singing hymns. Sometimes an American who belongs to the Army and is a Christian, came to us to talk. He kind of preached to us Japanese. So, even today when I see those Mormons (very common in Nagoya) they remind us of the others, very clean cut, with short hair. I was almost

Baptized, but then changed my mind.

Very common in those days, for many people to call foreigners, not just Occupation Army people, what we call *Shin Chugun*, which means 'occupation.' So Americans are Shin chugun, whether they are in the military, or not and even afterwards. Later, I got acquainted with Americans, mainly teachers, and when we went drinking together, some of my friends saw us and they said, "You are with Shin chugun." And, I said, "No, no, he's not a military man, he's a teacher." And they said, "It's the same thing." My friends were not being critical, but I think some people were. Once when I was talking to an American friend, we were teaching at the same company and there was a drunk man. He was looking at us, and he came up to us and he said, "Why are you talking friendly with that American?"

And, sometimes when I went drinking, some people tried to say something bad to us - "You're talking with an American and America was our enemy," or something like that. So when some people get drunk, some people might recall some bad feelings toward Americans or foreigners. That term - Shin Chugun, was used for at least fifteen years after the war, and even now, sometimes I might hear the words, especially from older people. You must have already known some people, or at least the government, avoided using the word - 'losing' the war, but saying just 'ending' the war, or the end of the war.

My mother didn't say anything bad about the Americans and my father didn't either, but what they said was they were very unlucky getting involved in the war. They didn't know much about a war, and they had been told a lie. Because my father was working for the big factory producing weapons, he said it was a kind of punishment, and no wonder we lost the war. My uncle, whose house we had stayed in, that got burned out by bombs, some years later he did finally come back from Manchuria, but he did have to go to Russia.

He was a rather high-rank officer, so was lucky they didn't find him guilty of some-thing, but they did treat him quite badly. I remember when I was a little child, because he was such a high-rank officer, one of his men came for him everyday with his horse. When he (the uncle) came back, there was no job for him, and he was rejected from everyone. Finally, he got a job working as a security guard for a department store, but only at midnight (so he would not be seen), then later he got ill and died.

When I went to junior high school I wanted to be good at English, because my interest in English, and Americans. I remember I sometimes would try talking to Americans on the street. When I became a teacher, I still wanted to go to the United State to study, but somehow I lost the chance. After I got acquainted with many British and Americans people in Nagoya, I always enjoyed talking to them. I think some people find it a bit strange, I'm so interested in Americans or in English. Rather it's shallow or not, I must admit I always like English and all things American.

Lots of information came to me from those movies I saw in the 1950s, like *From Here to Eternity, How Green was My Valley*, some Frank Sinatra, Jerry Lewis, Dean Martin, James Cagney movies, and all those things make up my image of America. When we saw the move *Gone With the Wind*, especially the war part, in which the South was defeated, the fire part, it reminded us of our air-raid. The part where Scarlett O'Hara says, "I'll never be hungry again," it's quite the same. I felt a bit nostalgic about the war, and my mother said the same thing. We knew the same feeling.

I was a student in the junior high school before I realized how rebuilt and changed everything was getting in Nagoya - the new, wide streets and such. We didn't move around very much, because of the poor transportation system was so overcrowded. Also, in those days children were suppose to stay around the house. Just after the war and for several years, it was a city of ruins with even children doing something for money. Among those ruins we found lots of little pieces of broken glass, and if we get a lot, we could sell it and get some money, even the melted iron or copper could be sold. So even the children of elementary class, after school, we went out to get those things in a bucket, so it was all recycled. The children are grown-up and knew how to survive.

The Occupation troops suddenly disappeared, maybe after the Peace Treaty (1951). I hadn't realized it until after they had gone, and I was a bit disappointed. One day I noticed there weren't any GIs walking in the street, and I wondered what happened to them. Really naive, maybe others had known or expected it, but I didn't know what had happened. During the Korean War there were even more Americans, but they were different.

One of my friends, who was four years older than I, said some of his friends were working for the air base in Komaki. Everyday what they did was to carry bodies of the American soldiers (flown in from Korea), and some of the arms and legs were separated, and their job was to get them back (to America). That was the only job in which you get paid a lot, and one thing they said was, most of the bodies were black people. I don't know if it was true or not. So it seemed to them, those people were on the farthest-front of the battle field. That's one thing I felt was wrong with war.

Although I said all those young GI soldiers looked very clean and beautiful, we were all aware many of them were walking together with Japanese women. They used to be called *pan-pan* girls. I wonder if they (GIs) used the word pan-pan girls or whores, but it was the word at the time. My parents never talked about them in front of us children, but in a sense I think they felt we were making a sacrifice of them (the prostitutes). We didn't use the word so openly, but those prostitutes, especially with Americans, the word pan-pan sounds like English, so one reason it was used, it had a special *flavor* of meaning. There was another word '*only*,' English word, a prostitute, but who belonged to just one American soldier, so did not take other guests, and who used to live at the air base. A few maybe, the 'only' girls, got married and went to the United States. Some of them lived happy together, and others came back to Japan after a short while.

After they (the Americans) were all gone, the city government tore down all the military housing and made a public park - (Shirakawa) and those Japanese buildings were given back to the original company or owner. Some of the big, private (Japanese) houses, occupied by the high officers, there were many stories about them. For example, an American officer started to live in such a big house and he didn't like the furniture, or the things, so he painted over all the walls of all the house. Well, it can't be helped, (he laughs uncomfortably) the culture is different (obviously, it ruined some traditional design). The Japanese probably would have done the same thing in Korea.

My remote relative, we had gone to live with right after the bombing, he was one of those big land owners in the district, so he lost a lot of land. Since I was a little child, I wasn't told a lot about it, but he must have complained about it a lot (the redistribution of land- program instigated by SCAP). Because he was a big land owner, he didn't do farming (he had tenants), he didn't have much experience of farming, so after he had to work for himself in his old age. It must have been very tough for him, as he started to cultivate the land left to him. Those poor peasants around him started to come to his house in a rather arrogant attitude, because now they are the same as him (his land was given to them). So even now, some of those old, big land owners talk about it, as if a very bad thing happened to them.

Suddenly, the tenants got a lot of land for nothing, and most of them didn't know what to do with it. Many people who received such a large (amount of) land, kept it and the price of the land rose-up very much, and they became very rich. Those people who had owned it remembered, as it used to be their land, for a very long time before the war. The affect of the war then, had a different meaning to each person, long after it was over. My mother still thinks her family is a declining family, because before the end of the war we were rather rich, but after we are very poor. My mother and father never recovered who they had been before the war, and they had thought they had saved enough money to keep them survived for their life, but it wasn't.

Many people who had works of art, or beautiful kimonos sold them to the military people. Nagoya changed very much, but those black markets were in the area behind the Nagoya station. It was said to be a rather dangerous place for ordinary people. A certain Yakuza presence was known around the area. There was an old man living in our neighborhood, and my mother warned me about him. She told me when the man got off the tram car, he didn't pay, and when the conductor asked him for the money, or the ticket, he got very angry and said, "Don't you know me?" (He was a Yakuza boss)

We don't know what all he was doing, but at the time when everyone was very poor, we are dressed in very poor clothes, he was wearing clean, white, new suit (laughs) and wearing sunglasses (still only gangsters were them). That's one thing I remember also, when I was young, I often went to the pachinko parlor and inside the pachinko place there were some Yakuzas. They changed (pachinko balls) for money to the person who won the game and they looked very different (from ordinary Japanese). Yes, I'm sure the Yakuzas had something to do with the black market at the time. I think they got some money from each shop or place (selling).

Unless you were working as translator or PX, or some such thing for the military, you could not go into the military areas. There were lots of signs, they said "Off Limits.' Sometimes the military rode the trams, but they were not separated, nor the buses, so they were very crowded in with us. The Japanese were only curious about them wanting to do that. The military children though, rode their own bus to the American school, so we only saw them riding on their buses.

Those military men moved mostly in their own cars or military buses or trucks. We often saw them in a place like Higashiyama Zoo, walking with their girlfriends, or pan-pan girls and they were some- thing special. Of course, there were many people in those days, because there were no subways, the people were walking outside. Especially around the Sakae area, we saw many American soldiers at the time. There were some people who earned some money from those Americans, shining their shoes or painting portraits, or maybe making some little things for them.

It is interesting, so much of what I remember is always related to something to eat - even if it is just chocolate or chewing gum or things like that - sugar. You must have heard how all the children would run after the military, calling for chewing gum or chocolate. I didn't have the chance to do it, but if I had, I'm sure my parents would have said, "Don't do that." But occasionally, my father came back with some food, or especially those lunches for soldiers (K-rations). Inside the box there were many things, like chocolates and candies or cheese, and we are very happy to eat them. We don't know how he got it, maybe in the office at his company. So, there were always some people who managed to get those things from Americans.

When I was a little child, I think people envied those people who could speak English, and some people who were working for the army as translators or interpreters. Of course, they envied those people, but they were also the object of hatred of ordinary Japanese, because they tended to act arrogantly toward the other Japanese. In those days, when some people wanted something to be done, I think very often they took advantage of those people, who had some relations with American military, or they might have used some money or bribes to get it done.

Personal Story: An American priest, who stayed in Japan.

I lived in Tokyo most of 1950 and through 1951. At that time, I was in language school, so I didn't have much to do with the American military. But definitely, as a *civilian*, we were not accepted very well by the military. Like if I wanted to go see a movie, at the military theaters, I had to have some young GI take me in. And, we weren't allowed anything like PX privileges, or anything extra being American. From what I saw in relationships between the Japanese and the military, I didn't see any real harassment, if you want to use that word, but maybe the years before it was different. I don't know.

If there was anything which disturbed me more about the Occupation, by the time I got here all the real veterans were gone. So, they had a bunch of these kids here, 17, 18, 19 years old, and they were running around, as if they owned the country, you know. It really disturbed me, and any of us who wasn't in the military, to see these kids going around, carrying their guns like they needed them, quite disturbing. Over all though, considering everything, it was a pretty good Occupation. Now, there were incidents, but they were isolated.

MacArthur was certainly a revered man over here. He was very well liked, he was kind of a little god, but *it was his* program. Compared how the Japanese military were, he did a good job, and the people respected him. For one thing, he was a father-figure, he kind of replaced the Emperor for a while, in their way of thinking. He was number one, and the Japanese people like a power symbol. Of course, you can't believe the difference in Japan today and Japan 45 years ago. There was very little food, the kind of food we ate - powered eggs, stuff sent from the States in Care packages. You couldn't buy a fresh banana, or anything fresh. We weren't allowed to go into the special restaurants for GIs, or Occupation people at all. So, even as Americans, we were also second-class citizens in the Occupation. Better treated than the Japanese, but not by much.

I was a Missionary then. The man in charge of our area, was head of the CARE program, in the Catholic Relief Association, I don't remember his exact name. But he was in a high position, so he knew General MacArthur, I wouldn't say as a good friend. But, he knew a lot of the higher-class military, the officer-types, because his job was distributing relief kits. I used to go with him, once in a while to some of their hotels, and I would say overall, the officers were pretty high- class, but they should have trained those kids to behave better. Which kind of follows what you'd expect, I think. I saw a lot more of the military in Tokyo, than I did when we went down to Kyoto. Because in Kyoto, I found a very different atmosphere. I found most of the military were very helpful and kind to the Japanese people.

For instance, there was one priest down there, he came right after the war and setup a relief service. The GIs used to load up Army trucks with food, bring it to him for distribution. This was done all by themselves, this was, of course illegal, but still, they used to bring him all kinds of things and he'd distribute it. So, on the individual level, there were some really wonderful military people who were working hard to help the Japanese. I didn't see any really bad incidents. I can remember one, it was on a train going from Kyoto to Otsu, and it was kind of crowded. Two of these young GIs got on it, and they walked up to two Japanese and actually grabbed hold of them and said, "Get out! I want to sit down." So, there were those unnecessary things. They weren't officers, they were just young, brash GIs.

You did have some incidents in the clubs and bars. There was one place there, called the "Million Dollar Mile," any place near any Army base, you's have one. (laugh) There you had all those low-class places for the most part, and they'd have fights and stuff. However, my general impression of the Occupation, it was a pretty benign. Particularly, if you'd compare it to what would have been the opposite situation. (laugh) We all heard how bad the Japanese military was in Korea. By the time I got here, it was pretty organized, though they really didn't have much they were needing to do, that I could see.

As I remember, Yoshida was Prime Minister. Of course, the previous leaders were all tried, or being tried as war criminals. It's one thing I objected to, and I still do very much. I think those war trials were not fair. Some were deserved, of course, some got what they deserved. But a lot of people were taken-in and convicted, who were not in charge at all, they were these little people. But, it is one of my peak complaints about the Occupation, the way the war crime trials were handled unfairly to many Japanese. They (GHQ) listened to whomever told them things, without checking any of it out.

I wasn't too familiar with Japan before I came, because we only knew six months before we got here, and all of our language study was here. I had no choice of where I was sent, and I probably wouldn't have chosen this, but now I'm very happy I did come here. I was very impressed then, at how hard the Japanese worked. Especially since they didn't have anything any more. We landed here on August 15, 1950, and the priest I was talking about, met us. Now, he had one of the few cars in Tokyo. It's five years after the war, and still very few cars, other than the military ones. Those Japanese cars were a lot of the, so-called charcoal-burning things. I could remember our house was on a kind of a slope, and when we'd get to the bottom of the hill, the driver would ask us to get out and push his car back-up the hill. (laugh) So we had a lot of interesting experiences in daily life.

Most of the older priests had previous Japanese experience, which made it easier on us. They had been here at least ten years before the war, and several had been interned during the war. Or those who left, came back shortly after the war. Several of them were familiar with Japan, so had worked with the U.S. government language schools or other stuff, training people coming to Japan, because they knew the language. There were ten or twelve of them who helped. The church had very little contact with the Occupation in Tokyo, overall. In Kyoto, it was different. Kyoto was smaller and farther away from the GHQ, and folks were a little closer. I never saw any real incidents where GIs were beating-up on people, or deliberately causing trouble there. Though I heard, right after the war when the military first came in, there were quite a few incidents.

After language school in Tokyo, I was sent to our center in Kyoto. I lived a little bit outside the city in a country place. My boss there was a former, Navy Chaplain, so he got permission to get a car. It was the only car in Sonobe, the village. We used it as a taxi, as a funeral car to take the body to the cemetery, or whatever it was needed for. Another thing, we had up there, was a small clinic. And, though a Japanese doctor ran the clinic, we got permission to get some medicine for it. A lot of military stuff was not available in Japan, at all. So, the farther you got away from Tokyo, the closer members of the Occupation were to the Japanese people. In Tokyo you had all those GHQ military officers and police, who had to OK something or not, and wanted to know exactly what you were doing. Some also wanted kickbacks, even if working with the church.

I had a few bad experiences. I bought a used Jeep from the military, they were going to get rid of. I was driving out to this country place and on the way to it, I had to go through a small village run by North Koreans. Even in Japan, the North Koreans and South Koreans were separated by choice. Anyway, as going through, about ten guys came up and stopped me. They started rocking the Jeep up and down, and I didn't know what was happening. They were saying something like, "GI go home! GI go home!" Gees, I didn't know what to do.

Because the Korean War was still going on, I guessed. So I said to them, "Look, you got me all wrong,

I'm not military. I'm from the church down in the village."
Luckily, some old guy came out and he recognized me. I
was really scared for a few minutes there. We were the
only foreigners between Kyoto and Sonobe. But, it's the
only incident I recall, I guess I could say I was actually
attacked.

We used to visit about ten villages, carrying food.
This doctor and I went together, so took care of the people
who were not accepted around Kyoto. Even with everyone
lacking so much, there was prejudice among them. The
clinic did a lot for these people though - food, clothes, and
whatever they could. They even had a place once a week,
anyone could come into, the military didn't handle this,
but they gave the supples and gave permission for its use.
They had a doctor and a nurse, and they would delouse
them. A terrible problem, so once a week, you'd have
twenty, thirty, forty people, out there waiting. So, from the
time I got there, the military was relatively helpful.

One time, I went with the doctor up to his
hometown, and we went to an *onsen* (hot springs).
Because he was a doctor, and had helped a lot of people
during the war, we were given tremendous service.
Actually, the years between 1951 and 1957, which was
when I went back to the States for the first time, they were
really interesting years. I think I could say I felt much more
productive particularly between 1952 and 1955.

Japan began to recover a little bit around 1955, as
after the work for the Korean War, all things began to
improve. But before, they didn't have much. So really the
U.S. government did a lot for them. I mainly worked in the
clinic with the doctor, since we always have a few months
of basic, medical training. Secondly, as a missionary, I had
to go around and say mass or something to visit the sick.
And then, I began to teach at a junior high school, which
had been set up by a Spanish mission many years before.

Of course, in the early years the travel was tough.
They had the trains divided into three classes, first, second

and third. First class, was only for military, and maybe five or six guys riding in this car, with the rest of it empty. The second class, would be people like me who could pay a little more money. Then third class, they just jammed them in. It was something which used to bother me a bit. The big, beautiful empty car, the military could ride in. There certainly were privileges given to them, as an occupied country. But the way it worked in those days.

I got to know one Japanese man, who had been in the diplomatic service, so he'd been around several countries. He had served as a middle-man between the GHQ and the Japanese government. He used to tell about several experiences, and he said most of the upper-level people were good, but some of the lower-level ones didn't really understand, or care what it was all about. The upper-level ones he knew, he thought had a pretty good plan for straightening things out. Though I felt they did make a few mistakes.

For instance, I think they had tried to revise the educational system too quickly. They should of had a little more time for thought, they might have come up with something different. I also think breaking up the Zaibatsu, though they had to do something. They were the back bone of industry, and had they let them continue, even in a weakened condition, they could have had some leaders run things. You know, Japan is a country which needs leaders, and if you take the heads off, then you got problems. I think one of the key problems, they made industry so weak (no leaders), it delayed the recovery.

Some of the people who had the toughest time, were the Japanese who repatriated to Japan from Korea, Manchuria, and places Japan had occupied. Over there, most of them were in rather high positions, and then they are back here, they didn't have anything. No work, there was very little work, but certainly not for them, and no place to live. So, they went from the top to the bottom, but the American government tried to help them.

I remember one lady, her husband had been maybe the head of the Manchurian railway, a really big job, and he died at the end of the war. She came back and had nothing. She was about sixty years old, I suppose. So she helped us as a language teacher, then we tried to help her, and through the military, she was able to go to the States. She had a daughter living over there, from before the war, she had stayed all through the war in the States. I'm not sure if she was in the American Internment camp or not. Anyway, this lady was allowed to go live with her daughter. There were several cases, where the military really made

exceptions, and tried to make life easier for some people caught in between. Families should not be blamed for what Japan did in the war. They sent a lot of the atomic-bomb-victims to the States for treatment, too. Most of this was experimental, of course, but some- thing was better than what they could get in Japan. I know they sent a large group of young women over, who were badly scarred. But, it's a discussion I don't want to get into. As terrible as the atom bombs were, I think some of it (city fire bombings) might have been worse. As I traveled up and down the main highway - just a dirt road or took a ferry every hundred yards or so, you'd find these gun emplacements, in these caves. The Japanese would have fought to the last man, *if told to*. Of course, they still would have been defeated, because they didn't have any ammunition or fuel. But still, they would've fought, and there would have been an awful lot of people killed, but not all in one place though. We can't believe the amount of respect they have for the Emperor. I think the greatest thing they ever did was not depose the Emperor.

I was in Tokyo when Truman replaced MacArthur. The streets were solidly lined from GHQ to the airport, so the people really thought highly of him. They never really knew how MacArthur disdained them. I never met him directly, but I was at several receptions he was at. He was an impressive person, though kept his people tightly around him, as if uncomfortable. He made a good physical impression, which many Japanese took to be the symbol of all Americans. Of course, Japanese always defer to authority, and he was *the* authority. They used to close the streets along his route from his house to the GHQ, so he didn't have to stop for any other traffic or *even see* the Japanese. (laugh) Their idea of solidarity, working together in their own way, is probably one of their strongest points Though things are changing a little bit now.

I think in my early years here, I think we as Americans, showed most of us could still mix with the people who survived in the economy. I used to sleep in their houses. There was one house I used to go to, way up in the mountains. At least an hour and half drive up. We would go up there to take medicine to take care of them, and brought food, as we'd stay over night. The house where we stayed, was one of those big family houses, they're gone now. Anyway, they always would give me this one special room to sleep in, beautiful nice Japanese room, as nice as a farm house could be. The only problem was, (laugh) outside my wall was the urinal, you know they had them outside back then, you could hear the family all night long using it. (Walls are singles layer with no insulation) Their openness about bodily-functions (sex included) always freaked most Americans out. Many of the restrooms, even in the exclusive (Tokyo) theaters were coed, and the GIs couldn't handle it. So, the Occupation tried to change it, because they felt it wasn't proper. So, the Japanese, not really understanding, put-up a sign for women on one door, and men on the other door, but the bathroom was still the same room. (laughs)

Another thing I can say, and I think I'd be pretty correct, then there were not too many problems with the GIs and the Japanese girls, except maybe in the clubs or bars. Of course, they had very strong rules about intermarriage, at first. In the beginning the GIs weren't allowed to marry, or if they went through a tremendous amount of red tape. As it loosened up, we found two things, the Japanese girls were either really high-class or rather low-class.

The high-class were the ones working on the bases, as secretaries or interpreters, well-educated and came from good families. And the others were in the clubs. The problem we ran into, because we were kind of acting as consultants, you get these high-class girls who spoke real good English, and wanted to get to the States and have the good life. And many times, she would pick-up an uneducated-type GI who could hardly spell his name. You could just see from the day they got there (U.S.), they were going to have problems.

When I went to school in Tokyo, in 1950-51, an old concrete building and probably didn't have more than three or four windows left in it, and just wide open. Of course, they didn't have many trains left either. You get on a train in the morning, and literally you're feet wouldn't reach the ground, you'd just be lifted right up by the crowds. Nowadays, Japanese people are quite a bit taller, but in those days, most Japanese heads came to about my chin. They used to wear something called a *Brillanteen* or some name, to grease their hair. There was one very popular brand with a sickening, sweet smell. I'd get on the train, and a guy's head is right under my nose, and I could not move no matter how I might try. (Laugh)

I don't think I had a real egg, until maybe 1953. We didn't have any ice cream, either. Wheat was very limited, also. What food you got, you had to be careful with, as there weren't many ice boxes, or refrigerators or anything. When I look back, I laugh now, but my first couple years over here, I thought every Japanese looked alike. It took me about two years to distinguish. My very first impression of Japan, we arrived on a ship into Yokohama, a typical GI ship, a freighter. We had military tanks filling the whole upper deck, they were going to Korea. In the hold, we had mail and beer. I noticed this ship next to us being unloaded. It looked filled with just a bunch of big ants. They (the Japanese men) were wearing just the *fudoshiki* (diaper- looking wrap), and they would go down into the hold, come back up carrying something, down a platform and back up. Just rows and rows of them, in and out, up and down. (laugh)

We had baggage, of course, and some pretty heavy, so we had it shipped up from Yokohama. I had a trunk, pretty good size, quite heavy, I couldn't lift it alone. They brought it into the house. The little, old Japanese woman working for us there, I said to her, "Would you ask this man, if I can help him carry it upstairs to my room?" She said something to him, he took a band of some kind out of his pocket, and tied it around his head. He then put the trunk on his back with the strap around it, and trotted it right upstairs. He must have been sixty years old, if he was a day.

The things I remember most, from my view point, I could see now, how people would feel prejudice and discrimination, like a black person then. We couldn't go into a GI restaurant, or theater or even buy an American newspaper, because we couldn't go into the hotel to buy one. They weren't sold on the street. There weren't many Japanese restaurants even open for us either. You could probably eat better at home, though. I think by my time, the military thought we were helping, not at the beginning, of course, they only wanted to control it, do it themselves. The living conditions at the beginning were so poor, they didn't want to be bothered taking care of us either. So, they eventually accepted our help, but we were still considered outsiders (to the military). In Tokyo, mainly. In Kyoto, as I said, it was totally different.

When I came back in 1958, I was sent back to Tokyo for about five years. And, I was then connected to the military. I was a civilian chaplain part-time, especially on weekends, or if one of the other chaplains was gone for some reason, until 1961. This time I had everything, the ID cards for the PX, however I wasn't living on base. I certainly saw how the other-half lived, much better than we did. I was assigned to the language school, but we weren't so busy sometimes. I still hear from some of the military I dealt with then, those still alive.

Then in 1962, I went back to Kyoto area. Not Kyoto itself, but to Mie Prefecture. I was there for a couple of years, then went to Kyoto to work for the mass communication center. It's where I met my (Japanese) wife. We were working together, first the radio programs, then later the TV programs. We put out two pamphlets a month, too. She was working as a translator. I was still with the church, then left it in 1968. This media project was more sponsored by one man, than the church, though at one time it was nationwide. It still exists, but on a smaller scale. It was an interesting experience. We used to interview famous people, so I got to know movie stars, writers, directors, all kinds of people. I look back on my life and I think how much (laugh) things have changed. I went out drinking with them.

One of my most memorable experiences was this very famous Japanese movie star. She acted sometimes as the narrator, so I got to know her quite well. So one time, she, her secretary, her driver and I went up to the mountains, and went mushroom hunting. She's a very nice lady. Some of the writers and performers were Catholic, in their own Japanese way. A lot of entertainers of the '60s, were of mixed- blood, from the Occupation. Easier for them to get into the entrainment world, than to get into industrial or business world.

Around the Kyoto area, since there weren't as many military, there weren't so many mixed-blood ones. But we did have a home for handicapped children (they are considered cursed and rejected by the Japanese) at an old folks' home, and a Catholic hospital. By the way, it was a very famous Bishop of ours who was quite instrumental in keeping Kyoto from being bombed. He had documented the cultural importance of the city to American government, it took a while to convince them, though.

We never had a problem of acceptance from her family. (Talking about his marriage) Her parents were dead, though I had actually met her mother back in 1954. I was sent to a small village on the other side of Kyoto to build a church. My wife's family was Catholic, so I got to know her family very well, before we met again with the media broadcasts. They were quite high-class, well educated, and interesting in their beliefs. Her family goes back over two hundred years, and respect for a name in Japan goes very deep, more than we Americans can understand.

I remember when I worked in Mie, the young man working with me was of the Tokugawa family. (The most famous Shogunate family, who consolidated, then closed Japan for 250 years.) His father was the first man to get a pilot's license, which would have been expected. Anyway, when I would go into someone's house with him, the people would put their heads right down on the floor. This was in 1964-65, so almost a hundred years since his family's overthrow, but they still respected the name.

I remember one time after we moved to Nagoya, I met this man who invited me to his club. He said he had been a Naval officer, and actually this was a Naval officers' club. I asked, "Are you sure they want to see me in there?" And he answered, "Sure, Sure." I went within, what a place. They had guys all dressed in Naval uniforms opening the doors, the waitresses were all wearing Naval outfits, and they had all these pictures of the ships around, a real patriotic place. I wasn't so sure they wanted me in there or not. But some of them came up and talked, and it turned out to be a very interesting evening, but I did have some concerns going in.

With one or two minor exceptions, I've never had any personal bad feelings or personal attacks against me. I have seen them against other Americans or foreigners. (Laugh) Of course, no one will sit down along side of you (as a gaijin-foreigner) on the subway, but it's part of their culture. I really feel if a person comes over here with the idea he's not going to be happy, he won't be happy. Or, if a person is here a few months and decides he's not happy, then he'll never be happy. You either have to take it as it is, or clear out now. If you don't like it, go home. Nobody's forcing you to stay here. Some kid points and says, "Gaijin, gaijin!" So what? It's not going to hurt you. I can't recall any incidence where a foreigner was attacked on the streets and robbed, or mugged or something. There is harassment, but nobody is going to shoot you. You certainly can't say that about some countries, and how they treat foreigners.

Personal History: Interview conducted and translated by Kazuyo Mizutani - Japanese man, born - raised in Nagoya.

I was 29 or 30 just before the war ended, and I worked for the Ministry of Posts in Nagoya (he later became Post Master General of Aichi Prefecture). I made an air-raid shelter beside the street in front of our house in Higashi Ward. The main purpose of the shelter was to store food. When we got several bombs, we got out of the shelter and ran away to a shrine at midnight. Everybody was in a panic, so we just ran to the shrine without thinking.

There was a storage for weapons near there, so people knew they had to avoid the place. Since I worked for the personnel division at the Ministry, I was the person in charge of the draft, so I wasn't drafted. I was very lucky. I was a kind of leader for the community, so I organized people in the neighborhood and taught them, as I was instructed how to use a spear for fighting (the bombs, yes, seriously). Then I got awarded from the government for doing so. I went all the way to Tokyo for this ceremony, in the middle of the war.

Important documents at the Post Ministry were taken to Takayama (a city far north in the mountains), so not to get burned from the fire bombs. Some savings-ledgers (Post Offices also handled savings accounts) got burned, so some people had to file their own savings amounts. Then, I had to investigate each one of them. One director at the post office in Shizuoka (a different prefecture near Mt. Fuji) bribed a local police director and judge. He embezzled money from that post office. I was asked to check his accounts and I found him out. After that, this guy threatened revenge on me.

I went to work everyday. Although it was in the war, most people want to work everyday. One day I saw my area on fire from work, and I went to check out my house. Luckily, my house was OK at the time, but then later at night it burned down from the fire bombs. The first floor of my house was a post office, I and my wife lived on the second floor. My father ran the little neighborhood post office, but didn't live there. We tried to take our stuff out of our room, but it didn't work out, the fire was too strong. Eventually we had to give up, and we lost everything in the fire. After all of our fire prevention, the neighborhood was burned down, because it was near the weapon storage place. The bombers were very good. Fortunately, few people died. Food storage was a big problem those days. The biggest problem was how to get food. It was all controlled and distributed by the government. Especially, we couldn't eat fish and meat, because it wasn't available.

One day I went to Mie Prefecture, (just southwest) for business and a local fishermen sold me two big yellowtails (tuna). I brought them back home, and shared them with many people. I hid sugar and kimonos in the shelter. We had no rice available, so I went to the countryside to exchange kimonos for rice, this was illegal, but we had to or starve. People depended on relatives living in the countryside a great deal. We didn't go to just one place, we went to many places to get some rice. One day, I and my father went to Nagano Prefecture (northeast, a long distance) on the night train to buy rice. My father had a friend there. We were very carful not to be found out by the police, that we were buying rice. This went on after the war, too, but then it was so very common.

I grew some vegetables on my land, and also grew some at work. As a matter of fact, people at work didn't work really. We did farming. After the war, GHQ occupied the Ministry of Posts building, so we had to move to a school next to it. We used the school as the office temporarily. One colleague brought a chicken from home. We cooked at work and shared with each other. Most of the nice (undamaged) and large buildings were taken over by GHQ. There was a rumor American soldiers were going to rape Japanese women, so they shaved their heads, or cut their hair very close-cropped, and hid in the mountains, but it wasn't true.

After the war, I built two apartments for GHQ officers. I got along with one officer's family. I showed them around Nagoya. This officer came to the office where I worked. We were good friends. When the officer left Japan, he gave me a TV, refrigerator, stove, etc. as they had no need to take them back to the U.S. He was very nice to me. My neighbor's children and my co-workers came to my home to watch the TV. Few people had a TV in those days. When my son was born, the food shortage wasn't so bad. My wife's brother was a doctor, so she wanted our son to be a doctor, too. Actually, he didn't want to be a doctor, he preferred to be a journalist and travel overseas. But he's a doctor. (He's a famous kidney-transplant surgeon in Japan, and also does surgeries in Hawaii. But, he still likes to travel overseas.)

KYOTO:

Preservation of a Nation's Cultural History

Heijo, or Nara, was actually the first capital of Yamato, old Japan, but it had a very short span from 710 to 784 AD. Everything was then moved to Heian or Kyoto, where it stayed until after 1600. It was then, Ieyasu Tokugawa surfaced as the victor from the great battle of Sekigahara. Ieyasu, as Shogun, or the real military power, finalized the uniting of the country, and moved the capital seat from Kamakura on the eastern coast, north to Edo, or what later became Tokyo. The Emperor stayed in Kyoto, as the traditional figurehead and religious symbol. The two capitals were linked by the old pine-lined, Tokaido Trail, or Highway, with its fifty-three stops or stations along the way. These developed into inns, trade-villages, then towns with growth.

The feudal lords, - the Daimyo - used to make their way, in elaborate processions to appear before Tokugawa, the Shogun on their knees,. He demanded they spend six months of the year in Edo, and leave part of their families there as hostages, when they returned home. The Daimyo were carried in palanquins, which gave the appearance of royalty, but must have been quite uncomfortable. Their retainers were on horseback, with their equipment in bullock-carts, and in bamboo baskets carried on foot, along stony roads and across unbridged-rivers.

They were colorfully-draped, with the banners of the Daimyo's family crest, and the cavalcades could be seen from a considerable distance. The enormously expensive trip was cleverly conceived by Tokugawa, as the Daimyos naturally competed in size and ostentation. Also, the smart way Tokugawa kept them under his control, as they did not have the extra time or money, to raise up their own armies to fight against him.

Japan's Golden Age, of almost eleven hundred years, were spent cultivating rituals, especially the Kata. It contained every feasible, and indeed, minute realm of life in the exquisitely flawless, albeit feudal, life-style. Nothing left untouched or ordinary, as all was turned into works of art, from everyday objects - combs, belt ties, etc. *Netsuke*, an excellent example, as they were individual miniature sculptures, whose real purpose was to keep the men's jacket cords tight. Yet, they became prestigious, showy ornaments for men.

There were 'pens,' specific to the *mode* of the letter, personal accessories to clothing, service appliances for eating, tea ceremony utensils, flower arranging design 'rules,' as well as every other conceivable spectrum of the arts - calligraphy, pottery, drama, music - on and on. The more elaborate and personally-distinctive, the better. Of specific note also, over two hundred of those years were spent hermetically sealed-off from the world. Tokugawa wanted no outside influence to disturb his family's reign. Only four ports were allowed open to receive any of the restricted goods, but no people.

With nothing but time and money, the Feudal Lords explored the essence and possible extents of beauty. Virtually every thing was made specifically for their Daimyo, so every moment the nobility had absolute, pure serenity for their personal pleasure. The basic theme behind almost every action followed the axiom: "Pleasure does not lie in the end itself, but the steps to that end." The castle court was an enclave, totally untouched by the warring clans and battles which ensued its peripheral. Truly time was not wasted, nor the efforts gone unrecognized. UNESCO has given World Heritage List standing to seventeen temples, shrines, and buildings around Japan.

With the forced opening in 1853, under the canon barrels of Admiral Perry, the next fifteen years or so, saw numerous bloody battles. The resumption to direct Imperial rule came in 1868, with the disintegration of the Tokugawa's iron-fisted rule. The Meiji restoration came into full swing, with Japan rushing to catch up and learn Western technology. The Meiji Emperor formally moved to newly-named Tokyo, and into the great Shogunate castle. Time and energy were now spent on politics, military and governing, rather than the leisure indulgence of culture and the arts.

Luckily Washington politicians, particularly Secretary of War Henry Stimson, had gone to Kyoto, and struck it off the bombing list, - many missionaries groups from years in Japan had also petitioned for its protection, - as "a shrine of Japanese art and culture." So, being aware of the classical, cultural heritage spared the city. Considering its size - over half a million people, the only city saved. Likewise, it did not have to put up with very many Occupation troops either. Most came on their own to ogle and awe over its magnificent buildings and numerous Buddhas. Truly, where the quintessence of the famed Orient was enshrined. With roughly thirteen hundred Buddhist temples and over four hundred Shinto shrines, one would not quickly run out of unusual things to see. It remains the Spiritual capital of Japan, so opposite of Tokyo. In this way, too, Japanese people could relive their glorious-past, just by returning to visit the eternal city. Perhaps with defeat, this was appreciated more by the natives than by the foreigners.

* * * * * *

Personal History: Japanese male raised in Kyoto. This written personal history was translated by Kazuyo Mizutani

When the war was about to end, I was thirteen years old and in the second year of junior high school. We had a hard time getting food. Also, at this time we had to work, three times a week, on orders from the military, tearing down houses to construct new roads. After the work, we were fed a kind of beans, which stank and tasted disgusting. Although, we had diarrhea from this food, we had nothing else to eat, so we had to eat it.

My family's business, a textile factory, closed down as no business, so then we had to move to a small house which had no land to farm, and no yard to keep chickens. Since we didn't get enough distribution (rationed) food, we made a kind of bread from dried mandarin peel, rice bran and corn. People who only ate distribution food died, so we had to make something else to eat, and not just wait for the rations. My mother exchanged her kimonos and chests of drawers for some vegetables from the farmers. Currency had no value, because of inflation. I never forgot seeing my mother begging for food for us. It was heart-breaking.

I began to keep rabbits under the floor, but I had to look for food for the rabbits from farm to farm. The hardest job for me was to kill a rabbit, my father just couldn't do it. I killed a rabbit once a month for food, cutting its throat. But one day, I failed to kill one right away, and the rabbit was running with its internal organs out. Finally, I caught it and killed it completely. It scared me so bad, I couldn't stop shaking for a long time.

This kind of life without food went on for two years. If you don't have this experience, you could never imagine how terrible it was. Starvation kept on going, day in day out. My family wasn't an exception, everybody in Japan, except for farmers, was suffering from starvation. We were taught and brain-washed, "We should protect this country," in school, and we all believed it. The war-training in school was to hold a fake bomb and jump under an oncoming (American) tank. After the war, I found out we had no bombs for doing that, so it was just an absurd training. But, I was very serious then, and believed I should die for this country.

After the war ended, the Occupation force came. I knew from newspapers the Americans would not kill men and rape women, so I had no fear toward the Americans. One day in October, 1945, a jeep passed by in front of my house. Mind-boggling, I thought it had an engine for an airplane. I'd never seen the like of it, as so fast, strong. In those days, we only had vehicles for fires and hearses in Japan. The Occupation force impressed us very much, at the first stage. The force came to our school to restore school facilities. They brought a bulldozer and power shovel. These machines could put the ground flat in two hours. We were all amazed about the power they had.

After 1944, Japan didn't have any large weapons and machines or fuel. America says the nuclear weapon was necessary to make Japan surrender right a way, but I don't think so. At the time, if Japanese saw thirty American cars running in a line, we would realize we didn't have a chance to win the war. We didn't have bullets to shoot Boeing B-29, which dropped the bombs, as we saw this situation, we knew we had no chance to win. Also, when we had a training to fight, we were so hungry, we would almost faint. We had no energy left to fight.

To high school students like me, the first impression of the American force was powerful and brilliant. As the Occupation went on, our lives were changing rapidly. The best thing was to get food. When we got cheese, my parents would not eat it because they thought it stank, but to me it had a great taste, then we got crackers and bread, too. A friend of mine bought cigarettes from an American soldier and sold them to support his family. Soon he started selling blankets and canned food, too. He didn't come to school everyday, then he had to leave school.

In front of my house there was a family, mother and daughter. After the black American soldier started coming to their home, later, I didn't see her anymore. They said she went to America with him, but nobody knew the truth. I saw many American soldiers coming to my neighborhood to see women. Kids begged them for chocolate and chewing gum all the time. We called the prostitutes for Americans, pan-pans, for spite. But they were saying they sacrificed themselves, so other Japanese women were not raped by American soldiers. They tried to justify themselves. These women had a miserable life during and after the war. They just wanted a more materially-abundant life, and gentleness from Americans. Hunger made them prostitutes.

Malnutrition led to death and also tuberculosis. I know some people died of it in my neighborhood. In my family, first of all my brother, who just returned from the war, got sick from tuberculosis then me, next my mother then may father. Fortunately, none of us died. Some women I saw were walking arm in arm with American soldiers everywhere. We called those women, who had an American boyfriend 'only,' which was a higher rank than pan-pan. When they became 'only,' we didn't see her any more, because I heard she could live on the base. I don't know for sure though.

In 1950, The Korean War started and American soldiers were coming and going constantly, then the prostitutes followed them. Most soldiers never came back to Japan, so many women were left alone. Also, some women went to America, which was a strange place to them. Obviously, Americans would have discrimination toward Japanese. To think of this, I believe some were full of fear, but still wanted to go to America. About the same time, there was a big problem about women and children of mixed-blood, who were left alone in Japan. Miki Sawada established an orphanage - "Elizabeth Saunders Home" in Kanagawa prefecture in 1948. She took care of thousands of orphans by 1970, this was a famous story in Japan.

I saw many signs, "Off Limits" all over the city. Since Kyoto didn't get bombed, there were a lot of mansions which survived. Those mansions had "Off Limits" signs, and so did entertainment facilities. These signs told us we were *the losers* from the war. Since elementary school, we were taught Japan was a "God" country - descended from the gods, and Japan the strongest, most honest country, to compare to any other country. But in August 15, 1945, this illusion was destroyed. Then, I started getting offensive to my country, politician and adults. I was really angry at my country, including the Emperor. By this time, I didn't have anger toward the Occupation force.

When I heard the rumors, which GHQ censored freedom of speech, and they hid troubles happening everyday, I started getting offensive to America. There was a rumor, a Japanese woman was raped by an American soldier, or a Japanese man was shot to death near the base. I don't know if this was true or not, but this image of America came to my mind. When the Korean War took place, I started getting angry at the Japanese government, *and* the Occupation force very strongly.

We've been suffering pain under a totalitarian country, and we just got away from the pressure of authority. But, I could't believe America really released us, or got us freedom. Of course, we didn't know North Korea invaded South Korea, so I couldn't justify military intervention of America into Korea. Even more, I believed America did it for their own benefit to sacrifice Korea. I took it as American's ego.

When a train, loaded full of weapons to Korea came, I lay on the railway to try to stop the train, and I quarreled with a policeman. I had an antipathy to Japan and America. Ironically, the Korean War put Japan back into a good working-shape economically. I realized Japan's development was based on Koreans, who were killed and injured. After the Korean War, Japanese started to trust America.

I burnt my diary when I was in high school. Since then, I never wrote a diary. I regret it, but this talking-writing reminds me of my past, and I would like to think my past over again. Using this opportunity, I would like to look back at half of my life.

Personal Story: A Japanese woman raised in wealth.

I was born and brought up in Kyoto. Kyoto and Nara didn't have any bombing or air-raids, but one pilot missed. (Laughs) Only one bomb dropped in Kyoto, but it was a mistake. A tremendous, wonderful thing this happened, the no bombing. Kyoto and Nara are very, very historical, cultural, religious cities, so it was decided, to be kind of important for all human races in the world.

So, when the war finished, I was eleven years old. I was still in primary school, so really scared when the air-raid happened. They bombed Osaka completely. Even at night, the whole sky was just red, because of the burning in Osaka. Even now I remember, and it's scary. So, the biggest problem was food. The Occupation Army gave a lot of canned food and corn flour to the Japanese government. One funny thing, was a lot of sugar came from America, (laugh) and the Japanese government decided to distribute it to the whole nation. So, we don't have any rice or bread or anything, just sugar! We're starving and all we got was sugar (laugh).

Anyway, food was the biggest problem We ate anything we could, but nothing was left, so really chaos. In Kyoto, because no bombing, the houses were all right. My mother had kimonos, so she took those to the countryside and asked the farmers to exchange them for rice. Everybody did it, but Japanese police, when they found out those people have rice, they put them in jail. The government wanted to control the rice, and we weren't allowed to have rice, to buy it personally from the farmers. It was all supposed to go to the soldiers. Fortunately, my mother wasn't arrested, but many people were arrested. I saw them taken by police, and then they had no rice. Women would wear a big coat with special pockets to hide the rice, it was very common.

A very, famous true story about one judge. He decided not to buy any illegal rice - not from the farmers or the black market, so he starved and died. It proved, if you wanted to live, you have to buy rice illegally or die. So, all other Japanese people who were living, lived on illegal food. (laugh) There was no other way. Only those American soldiers enjoyed life in Japan, because they got plenty of food. Many Japanese wanted to work on the Army base, and some American soldiers sold food to those people, canned food, any food. Then the Japanese took it back home, and sold it in the neighborhood. It's illegal too, but those people made money too, many made a fortune. Many people envied them, because they could get food at the Army base, and then also they could get money for their jobs, so they were really lucky. But, ordinary people didn't have food, money or job.

When you think of that time, it's really amazing we survived. And, also when you think about how quickly we built back up, because by the 1960s, it really was all built back. You know the Emperor Showa - Hirohito, always felt responsible for the war. But, he didn't do it, he didn't have any power over the military, they just used him as a symbol. Anyway, after the war, he traveled all over Japan and he encouraged the Japanese people to survive, to rebuild, and I think he really helped. Many people worked hard to rebuild the buildings, the roads for him, kind of a spiritual thing. Even though the Imperial Palace was bombed, he decided not to rebuild anything for himself, until the ordinary Japanese people had a place to live. Others, of course, insisted it be rebuilt sooner.

I know the Japanese kids learned very quickly to say to the Americans, "Give me chocolate, give me chewing gum!" You know we didn't have those things before. I was in Bali island last year for the first time, and the kids there, when they see us Japanese, they come and ask for money and things. It reminds me of those times, after the war and the situation in Japan. Some Japanese girls went with Americans to the States, but it didn't work out for many. And, some soldiers actually had other families in America. So, when these girls came back, they had no place to live. They weren't accepted back, of course, if they had children by the Americans, they were rejected, too.

I mean, families really ashamed, and many of these women became prostitutes in order to live, in order to eat and feed their children. We had a special term for the many levels of those women and girls. Some of them, just standing in the street, but some just for one man, we called those "Only." Because they had kind of an oral contract with one soldier. He rents an apartment and keeps her there, just to serve him.

I learned the word when I was very young. Kind of a mistress, I guess. So many girls, not a question which family she's from, some of them were from very high class families. But, if they had no money, no food, they had to work however they could to help the family. There's so many stories about them. So many boys, young kids became shoeshine-boys to shine the American soldiers' shoes, and they made money doing it to help their families. I read some papers, there was no television, but I heard on the radio too, about all the related jobs.

Actually, my mother had a very difficult time because my father died right before the end of the war. She had three of us children, I have a brother and a sister. She had a hard time to find food for us. Fortunately we all survived, but my mother sold things, … We were a very traditional kind of family, so we had many, very good Japanese swords and similar stuff, so my mother sold it. You know the famous hanging scrolls, and various kinds of art (many were priceless treasures), she sold or exchanged for rice. In the end, we didn't have anything left, not even any more kimonos, nothing. Fortunately, we survived,. We were lucky we were living in Kyoto, and we were rather well off, but other people really had a hard time.

In the countryside, our family was the landlord, so many tenants sent us rice, secretly. These peasant were OK, because they didn't tell the police, … well my father, my parents had been good to them in the past. Then the American Occupation Army decided to change the socioeconomic system. We were living in the city, but we had land in the countryside, and a big house there, too. For instance, our land, … the whole area from the train station to the mountains was our land (an enormous amount of property). You didn't walk on somebody else's land, even past the mountains, the area belonged to our family. So, we got enough, even during the war, because we had charcoal, rice, vegetables, everything came in by train, one whole car of the train was for our household, we were OK, we could survive.

But, of course, it was a kind of a class society then. And yes, some landlords were not so nice to their tenants, but my parents were very good and took care of theirs. But, the Occupation Army didn't think any of it should exist.

So, they decided to destroy the whole system, so we lost all of the land except for the one house in the city. There was no real compensation, just a piece of paper - one day we owned it then next, … we didn't. Many families like us lost every- thing, just like that - instantly.

They gave it to the peasants, our tenants free. So, now a lot of people are very, very rich, because the land is now kind of suburb of Kyoto city. But, it wasn't the tenants who are now rich. They didn't know about how to care for the land, so they sold it to the first person who offered them a little bit of money. So, none of them really benefited, but the people who had money then, they buy it. And, the Occupation, did nothing about it, and they knew what happened.

Those people, our former tenants, told us to come back to the countryside, because we could have some land with the other house, but we're not farmers. Generation after generation, we just owned the land and they farmed it. We didn't know how to do all the various kinds of work to take care of the land. My mother was a city girl, so especially she can't do anything with three children. So, we lost everything, and it was a real shock for my mother. I didn't understand much then, but now I think it was totally unfair to just treat all landlords the same. It wasn't even divided equally, the tenants got everything, and they had never had any real responsibility before. So, they didn't know what to do with it, so most of them lost it, too. Honestly, such a stupid waste.

When my father was sick, my mother went to the dress-making school to learn how to make dresses. Then, she started doing her business to support us after he died. It sounds funny, but right after the war, people needed something to wear. So, many women who still had kimonos, brought them to my mother to make them into Western-style dresses. My mother built a good business for herself and us. During the war time, people didn't care much about their clothes, but after the war, they wanted to wear better clothes. We had enough space, so she hired a couple of girls, because the business was in our house. Gradually, when other materials came out, she expanded more. Then not so many dressmakers, and my mother liked doing it, too. I think she did a good job and got a good reputation, because she always had good customers.

So, I started to help her when I was twelve, or thirteen years old. I remember some of those "Only-san" women started to come to my mother to have her make them dresses. They had gotten material from their American soldiers, I remember how nice it was. Then, some of the people accused my mother for making dresses for those girls, with the American soldiers. But, she had to live and she felt they had a right to live, also. Still, some of the neighbors really looked-down on my mother, because real easy to see which customers were those girls coming to our house. We didn't have much cosmetics or good clothes, as those girls always wore make-up and pretty clothes. Most of the customers were ordinary people, some from the neighborhood, and very typical-looking, not conspicuous. (laugh) But, my mother made sure we were raised to take care of the house to help her, and could not wear makeup, though we did get some nice clothes made from her.

At the same time, my mother helped many widows, who had lost their husbands in the war. She taught some of them too, how to make dresses for free, and then those women started to make dresses at home, too. There was lots of business, so she wasn't concerned about any competition. My father never fought in the war, because it was a class thing again. His class, with title and such, paid a certain amount of money to the government. Then they went into the Army or Navy, but just stayed in the camp and became officers. But, they didn't have to really go to war and fight, or anything dangerous. I know it's not fair, but it's how money and polities were.

I read it was the same in Britain, and some other countries where they have more of a class system. So, I have a picture of my father in his Army officer's costume, with his sword and all, even though he never actually went to war. See at the time, those people in his class had to pay tax, ordinary people didn't have to pay tax. One of things with owning land, my father's family paid a lot of tax, and his not having to go to war, one of the benefits.

Especially, since Japan had been having so many wars for almost forty years. It's kind of a delicate subject, so I never talk about it to other Japanese. They really don't like it, or understand it all, of course. Now, though, all Japanese have to pay taxes. (laugh) But, with the new constitution, we can't have any more war, so the government can spend the money on whatever.

We had some very nice American soldiers in Kyoto, and I was impressed with how polite they were. Whenever I got on the train, … I went to the junior high at a distant place, so I had to take a train. So many times they were standing, but if some of them were sitting and old people or women got on the train, they got up to offer them their seats. They were real gentlemen, we didn't see it before. Japanese men are privileged, and don't give up their seats for anyone. I don't remember those soldiers doing anything bad in Kyoto, but in other cities I heard about some tragic things happening. We just heard, because you know the newspaper was controlled by the GHQ, so they couldn't print anything bad about the soldiers. I heard MacArthur made the law, his special rule, they could only report the good things.

One thing I really remember, and a kind of cultural difference thing. One old lady, was picking some weeds in a field, you know Japanese eat a lot of things like weeds or mountain vegetables, so she was gradually coming closer to the Army base. There was a watchman - soldier, and he kept saying to her, "Go home, go home! Don't come here! Go Home!" But in Japan when you wave this way (demonstrates palm down, fingers slightly cupped), it means come here. So, he repeated "Go Home!" three times, but she doesn't understand, she thinks he's calling her, and finally he shot her, this old lady. She died, of course, and it became a court case.

But he was not guilty in the Army court, because it was a cultural difference, and he obeyed his rules. He said something three times, she kept coming, he shot her, so he's not guilty. So, Japanese people didn't like it. But since in the countryside, they kept it out of the city. Years later, after the Occupation, there were some books printed, and told about many incidents the GHQ had kept out of the newspapers. So, we didn't know what all they did to many Japanese.

Those mixed-blood kids, especially those born between Japanese and black soldiers, really had a hard time. First of all in Japan, nowadays it's a bit different, but then those mixed-blood didn't have any future. Maybe, I don't know in the back of the Japanese people's minds, it's enemies, kids or something. But there were some famous homes set-up for them to help, like Miki Sawada's Elizabeth Saunders Home. One time there was a special program on NHK- (Public broadcast station) about where are they now? If they were still in Japan or other countries. Some of the people don't want to talk about any of it anymore. But it's important, all people know about how things were. It seems since the diplomatic relations were set-up with America, every twenty years or so, some kind of problem develops - immigration, trade war, and economic conflict.

There were many articles in the newspaper, celebrating when the Occupation left. Though we still had the American military presence with the Security Treaty, even now. One of the biggest differences was before, whatever product are made, it had to say: "Made in Occupied Japan." But after, of course, it could just say "Made in Japan." A big thing for companies and for their business, but for the ordinary people, not much difference. Because so many of the bases stayed in Japan, the Self Defense Army was started. You know, the American government made them start it. The Japanese people were really upset, *they didn't want any army of any kind any more.*

My mother died rather young, I guess she worked too hard. She continued the business until all of us started to work, or finished our schooling. She got sick and cut-down on the work, but still continued to do some work until she died. I went to dressmaking school after I finished high school, and helped her. I went to college after my mother died and studied English.

I was really interested in the relationship between Japan and America, you know the history of it. Good for Japan, America had power, because it could then control Russia. If Russia had been a bigger force in Japan (during the Occupation), then Japan might have been destroyed, like in Eastern Europe. We had to have a special treaty with Russia after the war, and even to today most Japanese don't like Russia. It's a feeling we can't trust them, because they came in at the end of the war, and then took our islands (Kurile Islands).

At the university, I wasn't sure if I wanted to become a teacher or not, but I knew I didn't want to be a dressmaker. My mother was really good, but I'm kind of a clumsy person, so I didn't like doing it. I wanted to do some job using English, I could see it was a coming- thing. We had a long history of studying English, just before and during the war, we weren't allowed to study it. We didn't have very good books, but my father had studied it, and had some really good books, leather covered and all.

I was lucky to have them, and many people envied me for them. My father and his uncle used to speak English, even when in his nineties. My father went to university too, but then they studied a kind of British English. But right after the war, the government decided we should study American English. So, very lucky to have a conversation class with a Japanese teacher, a Nisei. I was real amazed with his accent and his pronunciation. I liked American movies, mother too, so while still in high school, my mother let me go to the YMCA (they had language classes) for English conversation courses.

I remember one time as a child, we were in the movies - besides Japanese, we had German and Italian ones - and the air-raid sirens started. The planes flew over Kyoto to get to Osaka sometimes. Once the sirens started, everything else stopped - the movies, the buses, everything, so people could go to the shelters. We had to walk home, we lived in the suburbs then, so I saw the bombers in the air heading for Osaka. We didn't have much to eat, but we would go to the movies to forget, since we really liked movies. So after the war, I really wanted to understand those American movies, the Japanese sub-titles weren't very good or enough for me. I wanted to go to English conversation class (laugh). I was very serious about my English study. After the university, I worked as a translator, and also I started to teach English conversation in an English language school in Kyoto.

It was where I met my future husband. He was the assistant manager at the time there. When I decided to marry him, no one in my family opposed me. I remember when I went to say good-bye to the next door neighbor, she said, "It's good you're marrying an American, America is number one country in the world, so it's good. I'm glad you're not marrying a Korean." (laugh)

It's really discrimination, I thought. But you know, Japanese people don't like Koreans, for a very long time. There might not have been many Japanese men to choose from then either, especially because of my character. They didn't want to marry me, because I was so independent (and too much education). Too independent for a Japanese man. (Also, she was older, most Japanese women marry by 25.) When I was still studying, I had several American friends, and some of them were boys, so some of them came to the house and we had supper together. Then my mother said, - she was a very interesting woman, not typical Japanese - if you do not want to marry, it's find. It's important you decide your own life, by yourself, it's OK, she said. And, if you want to marry a foreigner, it's OK, too. It's always only your decision, she said. So, she never forced me to get married.

We did though, have some discrimination from other Japanese people. I've had two kinds of experiences. One side of people treat me too nicely, not natural, very uncomfortable, because I have an American husband. The other side of people, they look down on me, treat me like dirt. I don't care, what they think, as they usually don't know me at all. Maybe in Tokyo, it's different or better, but in Nagoya, it's difficult for them to treat us naturally. So, I guess they either have an inferiority complex, or (laughing) superiority complex.

We got married in Nagoya in 1970. At the time, there was something like twenty-five Americans in Nagoya, so he was kind of conspicuous. (laugh) When we were in a restaurant, people at another table were really watching him ... and me, too. Really rude. I remember one time in the subway station, and we're standing together, then one old man comes and stands right in front of us and just stares, first at me, then at him. I want to say, "GET Lost!!" but of course, I couldn't say it. He was an old man. (laugh)

In Tokyo, no problem, and in Osaka, or even Kyoto or Kobe, they didn't do anything at all. But Nagoya, so conservative, and historically not so many foreigners, or welcoming. It is difficult to make friends here in Nagoya. Many of those we have, are originally from outside the city. The people running the bars and clubs aren't that way, because they want your business, and they don't care who their customers are.

But restaurants or coffee shops, small shops, not so good, not so comfortable. It's funny sometimes, you could see the waiters or waitresses discussing who was going to go to our table, because they didn't want to deal with us. (laugh) What would be really disturbing would be when the Japanese family lets the kids come right up to our table to watch us, just right here. The parents don't say anything. Only here, in Nagoya, no where else, really rude.

One time in Nagoya, I had a very uncomfortable

experience. We went to a bar, called some British name, we sat at the counter and one group of Japanese doctors came in. They sat at a table, started to drink and kept asking us to join them. My husband wanted to join them, but I knew what was going to happen, so I didn't want to go. Though the invitation had seemed just to him, he insisted I should go with him, I really didn't want to, but he wouldn't go alone. Finally, he felt he should go and respond to them. The next one hour they completely ignored me, and I was really uncomfortable, then got angry. They just wanted to have English-practice with him, but evenso, they could have said "Hello," to me at least, but nothing. I don't know if it was just because I was a woman, or because I was a Japanese woman, married to an American man. Awful, and I was so angry. I think my husband learned a lesson from it, as how Japanese men are toward Japanese women.

When we went to the States, we usually just visited his brothers and sisters, and they were always nice. But one time, really unusual, outside Los Angeles, it seemed a rather high class restaurant, and his sister and husband were with us. Those people at the next table kept looking at me, especially the woman kept staring at me. So, I thought maybe she doesn't like Orientals.

What was even more interesting was after they left, the next group who sat down, also stared at me. I didn't understand, maybe some kind of resentment or something. (1975, right after Vietnam collapsed.) I know it's confusing sometimes for most Westerners, because one time I was walking in Paris, and a woman spoke to me in French (commonly spoken in Vietnam). So, I guess it is confusing, as they don't know one Asian from another. I even had it happen one time in the resort area of Toba, (Japan) when we were together in a restaurant - a waiter spoke to me in French, and thought I was Vietnamese. What can I say, to most we all look alike. (laugh)

Part III: Living As A *Gaijin* in Japan ~ A Different Cultural Perspective Chapter 8 ~ The Missionaries: Their Bane and Benefit to Japan

In 1945, "… a sense of superior Christian virtue, a sense of global mission, a sense of responsibility and capability for bringing enlightenment to a dark and superstitious world, for overthrowing ancient and new tyrannies, and for making backward infidels into Christian men of enterprise, …" neatly sums up the awesome responsibilities Americans felt to be theirs, when setting out to evangelize the American way of life to the Japanese.

John Curtis Perry,
Beneath the Eagles Wings

Brief History on Japan's Two National Religions:

As stated prior, Japan's beginnings were taught and believed, to have come from the Shinto gods (8 million+ of them) according to Jimmu's traditional rule-dates of 660-585 BCE. So, actually older than Christianity. And most importantly, all Japanese were their descendants, until January 1, 1946, when Emperor Hirohito renounced his own *deity-ship*. Shintoism was considered an animistic religion, as spirits were believed to be within many things of nature, animate or inanimate. It also celebrates the whole process of fertility with the seasons, the equinox and solstice, so typical to many ancient religions, such as the Druids.

Totemist-ancestors were included among the *kami* or deities worshiped, and no line drawn between man and nature, reminiscent of early Greek mythology. (Also related to ancestral Native American beliefs) Shintoism also had no theology, per se, or even a concept of ethics, beyond an abhorrence of death, and the defilement of the body. Its main thrust, was then an emphasis on ritual purity, cleanliness.

Buddhism from India, originated around 500 BCE on the other hand. It came to Japan diluted via China, and further by way of Korea, in the early fifth century, or less than nine hundred years later. While Shintoism concentrated on one's ancestors like Confucianism, Buddhism comes closer to paralleling Christianity. It too, is concerned with the afterlife, and the salvation of the individual.

Buddhism played much the same role in Japan, as Christianity in northern Europe, as the vehicle for the transmission of a whole, higher culture. A greater part of subsequent aesthetic-expression in architecture, sculpture, and painting was associated with Buddhism. It permeated the whole intellectual, artistic, social and political life of Japan, from the ninth through the sixteenth centuries. In sad contrast, much was ruthlessly-destroyed by Japan's unifiers. It stood in the way of the creation of an Emperor-centered, Shintoist, new Meiji style government and political system.

Interesting Side Note:

Considering how frequently the Japanese military referenced the Samurai, they twisted it however they chose. In research, the Shinto beliefs connected the samurai to their people and land. In reality, Confucianism taught them to respect authority of the established social and political hierarchy of Japan. But actually, Zen Buddhism gave the samurai the morals, which allowed them to be effective warriors, *without* committing atrocities.

~ ~ ~ ~ ~ ~

After World War II, once religions were allowed open by the Occupation, Buddhism took on new intellectual and religious vigor, partly in response to the zealous, Christian missionary movement. They developed publishing ventures, schools, and indeed a progressive Buddhist missionary movement in East Asia and North America. Meanwhile, American Occupation, with its natural abhorrence to church-state entanglements, attacked "State Shintoism" with vigor, as a dangerous manifestation of xenophobia, patriotism, and military enforced Emperor-worship.

Certainly, there seems to have been an especially wide-gap between the historical brutalities of all Japanese armies, and the gentleness, orderliness of life in earlier, everyday traditional Japan. The soldiers had been taught the strictest of discipline, and suffered castigation. Often death was implemented for not following the simplest of indoctrinated regimens. They believed surrender was the ultimate personal disgrace. Thus, this attitude was passed on to their prisoners, with exceeding contempt when suicide was not committed by them. Every Japanese, military and civilian, had been taught to do it at their earliest opportunity.

Over and over they were told, "One must not embarrass, or disappoint the Emperor," of course, the Emperor never uttered these words or requests. But these country-boys, for a millennium under feudalism, having always done what they were told, without ethical bearings, continued to do so without question. Higher-ranking officers, also often came from a rural background, and had much disdain for the educated, cultured, wealthy Japanese, and treated these men cruelly. Shocked, Christian-Westerners rarely stopped to recall their own past, violent-transgressions of extermination of the American Indians, any African slaves and their descendants. As well, done by the Australians to the native Aborigines, New Zealanders to the Maoris, and numerous other people of color. For over 400 years, through colonial expansion, specifically done, practiced and encouraged by the British, who had created the 'white superiority' belief.

Specific Influence and Control by Shintoism - Prior and During the War:

When a highly, integrated-style added religious motives, plus patriotic incitements, to the actions of the defenders of the Military-State's power, the result was a campaign of terror. From mid-1930s on, it swept as holy-indignation through the the population - the wrath of the gods, no less. Shintoism in wartime Japan was the sanction, which made every little, police-functionary a servant of the gods. Around every political, and military decision, was a structure of patriotic and divine sanction. It gave the force of those decisions the power of heaven itself. Shintoism itself was a clever device to give Japanese militarism the ultimate protection against criticism, which no power on earth could penetrate. Added to it, as if the Emperor's prerogatives or requests insinuated, if not stated. Which were neither true nor known.

Thus, wartime Shintoism in Japan was a manufactured product, a creation of those master classes in Japanese society. They needed it for the sanctification of their takeover-purposes in Asia, and the world, so Shintoism brooked no rivals. Polished into a complete and orthodox system of beliefs. Its tenets were driven into the minds and hearts of two generations of Japanese, and sealed there, as a powerful inward- faith. Shintoism made service to the State the cardinal, ethical virtue, and was a close-cousin to the worst forms of Nazi State-worship.

With the first-flush of victory, the broadcasts were cocksure and flamboyant. The score proved beyond a shadow of a doubt, this was a 'holy-war,' and the eight million gods of the Empire were fighting Japan's battles. Hachiman, the god of war, had incarnated himself in Japan's fighting men, so they were invincible. The spirits of the Samurai were riding again, and reinforcing Japan's forces, wherever they lifted the sword - the Samurai's symbolic-soul.

From Confucianism, Shintoism adopted a system of ethics, built upon the principle of relationships. It especially stressed the virtues of filial-piety. The code of subjective-relationships - child to father, wife to husband, student to teacher, subject to Emperor, servant to master, and so forth, to be firmly rooted in Japanese society. It produced an orderliness in the culture, which was highly useful for the militarists to control, and manipulate. By declaring itself, not just a religion, but a *nationalistic* belief system, it put itself above and beyond other religious beliefs. Before one was a Christian or Buddhist, one was a Japanese, - therefore, a Shintoist.

The liberalism of Christian teaching was totally in contradiction of the Japanese authoritarian structure of society, and it began with the regimentation of its education. This resulted in Japanese youths being a highly-uniform state, they thought as one, and was totally homogeneous to a fault. To question the authority, any authority in the hierarchal pattern, or the content handied down, was a breach of etiquette, and a social offense for one to be ostracized. Again, much like the Nazi youth-teachings.

Eventually, and basically for ultimate survival, the Christians and their churches accommodated themselves to the social milieu. They became chameleon-like, sometimes indistinguishable from the harsh environment around them. Many Japanese Christian churches were criticized for sacrificing its message and evangelizing power. But for many, a simple decision, adapt or die, and most believed the it would not be forever. Those responsible for the welfare of the church, also felt it was better to stay on the job and compromise, than to go into hiding, or be put into prison. The policy of the government was to persecute Christians, in order to unify the people around Shintoism, and the war. In the courtroom, as trials proceeded, they were a parody of justice, a game of words which would have been ridiculous for intelligent men, if it had not been so deadly serious.

Worshipers were frightened by the police into believing the Christian churches were linked to a spy system. Many Christians were charged with being spies and quislings. In motion picture circles, films produced to inflame the martial spirit, often staged the spy scenes in a Christian Church, or in the home of a missionary. Some three hundred Protestant ministers - almost all Japanese - were arrested during the war, and ruthlessly grilled by the 'thought-control police.' One hundred and twenty spent months in captivity. Six died in prison, and many others weaken by malnutrition, were sent home just before dying, so as to reduce the negative criticism.

In the prisoner internment camps, there was a cross-section of the Western world, as to the nationality, cultural background, profession, occupation or religious belief. The camp life was a day-to-day experiment in cooperative-living, worked-out in the hard way. Every man's special training, his native talents, as well as his hobbies, were brought into play in meeting the exigencies, and cushioning the hardships, of the confined existence. Sharing was no longer an idealist's dream, but the daily practice of inter-camp relations and living. Truly, a life of all-inclusive give and take. This unwritten-rule applied to everything. There were no unused garments of any kind, - in any suitcase, in the camp building - if needed by someone else.

This was not what the military and police expected. Within their own ranks, the men had been trained to spy on each other, and report even the slightest infraction for their own personal advancement or benefit. Even for food and better treatment, rarely did any of these ministers or missionaries turn on one another. Then, as time brought familiarity between guard and prisoner, a respect developed. For many Japanese, even with all the propaganda, there was no hatred in their hearts toward enemy-aliens. Gestures of friendship, flashed across the towering-hate-barriers of war, despite the fact of the lives of the guards might have been in danger for doing so.

Still, the die-hards at the top, pushed to break the ministers or missionaries and their followers, who hung on to their Christianity. Eventually, Sunday was abolished as a holiday, so people were not free from work to go to church. Many Japanese pastors still free, were called from their churches to work in factories, or even serve with the armed forces overseas. There were also numerous instances of Shinto and Buddhist coercion of the families of deceased Christians, to bury them according to non-Christian rites, in order to bury them at all. Catholic cemeteries were desecrated by hoodlums, fired up patriotic- motives, broke the crosses on Christian graves in cemeteries. When the church appealed to the police for protection of their people's graves, the police countered by ordering the erection of crosses stopped all together. Every Christian grave was then marked with a simple plaque.

The *Kyodan* - government's Christian supervising board during the War, had bureaucrats prescribe every Sunday sermon topic, at the government's insistence. Then, finally the traditional forty-day Lenten period was cut down to one week. In 1943, they issued an order the day of Easter would be changed, because the Japanese lunar calendar was somehow 'different,' from every other lunar calendar in the world. The absurdity of this order, ran into so much objection on the part of the local churches, the Kyodan finally said, "Celebrate Easter when you please." Throughout the war, the church officials played down the fact Christmas was the birthday of Jesus. Instead, they played-up the fact, it was the anniversary of the death of the late, feeble-minded Emperor Taisho, father of Emperor Hirohito.

* * * * * *

The Japanese were non-rationalizing realists. They had lived so long under controlling feudal regimes, and suffered so much, they had learned not to quarrel with the inevitable. They had a genius for philosophic-adjustment to experiences and situation, over which they had no control. Again, the common, constantly-used phrase - Shikata- ga-nai - "It can't be helped!"

The phrase passed from lip to lip then, and even continuously, as to their life. Its philosophy pulled them out of many an awkward predicament, neutralized many a blow. It enabled them to forget the past, and keep facing the future, under any, and all circumstances. At the same time, to some it endowed them with a resilience of spirit which knows no defeat. To others, an acceptable rationalization for not even to attempt to do anything, or try to change circumstances or whatever may hold them back. Unfortunately, more of the latter than the former relied upon.

Short History of Christianity in Japan:

Fifteen hundred years after China had made contact with the West, Japan had her first recorded European visitors - and this was only by accident. Three Portuguese were ship-wrecked in 1543, on the Southern Japanese coast of Kyushu. They managed to save their firearms, which were examined with great interest by the Japanese. Since civil wars were still going on, the arquebus rifles were copied and manufactured in record time, but the saltpeter and gunpowder were soon needed along with more guns.

The new technology was significant in deciding the outcome in clashes among waring-clans, and would favorably influence a dramatic shift in the balance of powers. The Portuguese ships began to ply the waters between their colony Macao, in the southwest corner of China and the Southern Japanese island. They soon used their papal and royal connections, to link this trade to their missionary activities. Rome rarely hesitated to use marital-forces for the bottomline of converting heathens - which all other belief-systems were considered to their Catholicism.

Following closely behind in 1549, the famous Jesuit missionary, Saint Francis Xavier, came to spread the word, yet its ultimate affect did not make the same lasting-impression, as the weapons. At first, the Shogunate encouraged the Christianity in order to discourage the growing political ambitions of some Buddhist sects (The Japanese-version of Buddhism was also quite adapted to Japan's preferences). Also, the Feudal Lords befriended the Jesuit missionaries, because they had some knowledge of foreign military tactics, as well in contact with Portuguese merchants from whom weapons might be obtained.

Several of the Lords thought it would be more expedient for them, all of their retainers and serfs, to adopt Christianity to gain favoritism in the increasingly-competitive trading for arms. If a local Lord wanted the Portuguese to use a port city in his fife, whereby he would reap substantial profits, he had to permit the Jesuits the freedom to preach. They then naturally established small churches and permanent communities. Thus, a mutually-convenient and also exploitative-relationship developed initially.

So, the growth in numbers of nominal Christians was spectacular, and rose to over half a million by the end of the sixteenth century. The converting meant more to the many farmers and fishing communities, as they saw the transcendent message of loyalty to an omnipotent God, as a way to liberate themselves from centuries of oppression and submission. Soon, they began to view traditional Japanese Buddhists temples and Shinto shrines as having been in collusion with the Feudal Lords, who had so long kept them in abject poverty. As more Franciscan and Augustinian orders came from Spanish-Catholic Manila, the inspired, zealous preaching spilled over into violent action, as numerous temples and shrines throughout the prefectures of the southern area were put to the torch. Christianity soon became the 'people's' main religion.

With power and success, too quickly the Portuguese and Spanish missionaries, like the Buddhist priest before them, became haughty and began to mix in political affairs. They fell under the suspicion of being emissaries for foreign powers, which conspired to subjugate Japan, as done in other parts of Asia. So, the Shogunate Ieyasu Tokugawas was not about to let it happen. The Dutch and English brought Protestantism with them, while Tokugawa allowed the missions to function, and trade to grow, as it kept competition tight and prices low.

Then, due in part to the advice of Englishman, Will Adams, whose Protestant world-view saw the Catholics as "papist pirates," Ieyasu Tokugawa gradually became more hostile to the Portuguese and Spanish interests. He issued his own Christian expulsion-order in 1614, and after his death his son, Hidetada, promoted the suppression of the Christian faith all-through-out Japan in 1616. His heavy-hand fell, creating many stirring-scenes of martyrdom, as supposedly stamping-out Christianity. The government gradually-closed the country, to all foreigners from 1638 to 1853.

In Southern Japan, only the port of Nagasaki, then later limited to the man-made island of Dejima, was allowed to be the closely- guarded funnel for trade goods, and information from the outside world. A few secret societies, of tiny, faithful communities of Christians survived and over time they lost the real knowledge, yet kept the ritual tenets of their 'Japan-ized faith.' The government would make suspected Christians stomp on the picture of the Virgin Mary to prove their disbelief. To Protestants this was no problem, yet, many devout Catholics sacrificed-themselves, rather than desecrate the icon. A unique distinction to the Catholic Church, as it survived for more than two centuries in the hearts of thousands of uneducated, downtrodden-Japanese people.

Rebuilding of the temples and shrines began with more government pressure on public participation, supported by wealthy businessmen and community leaders. Many of the religious leaders had learned their lessons, as they made more benefits such as *matsuris*, - festivals - and the use of portal-shrines - *mikoshi* - for the people to carry through the streets. Then, the priests became more involved with their day to day community activities. So, only a matter of time, as three or four generations, to have almost all remembrances of Christianity erased.

~~~~~~

Seven shipwrecked-Japanese sailors were living at the Macao home of the gifted and widely traveled missionary, Karl Gutzlaff. He did, of course, treat them quite well, and eventually converted all, totally to Catholicism. So, in the summer of 1837, he and several others tried to return them to Japan - first to Edo and then to Kyushu - with the hopes also of opening Japan once again to Christianity. After the ship was visited by numerous Japanese, it was fired-upon in both places. Finally, the sailors chose to return to Macao, rather than take their chances at the hands of their own countrymen. Four of them afterwards, turned out to be of great help to the missionaries language-wise, as Genesis and the Gospels of Matthew and John were translated into Japanese. Still, until the forced-American opening of

Japan in 1853, with the subsequent arrival of more foreigners, was the whole subject of Christianity, and its challenges begun again.

The Catholics had their first church completed by January of 1862, in Yokohama. In February, 1865, they dedicated a church and monument to the Twenty-Six Martyrs of Nagasaki, but no Japanese visitors came. Yet, a month later, when a small group did approach and whisper their sacred convictions, the revelation of thousands of secret- Catholics was made. Hundreds were then persecuted and killed over the next eight years, while thousands of others dispersed to various prefectures. The government encouraged deep hostility toward any Christianity, through much of the nineteenth century. But it eventually realized the strength of Western feelings, as well their influence on government and trade. Finally, in 1873, it dropped its prohibition, and reluctantly began a policy of religious toleration.

Before then, those few brave souls, who ventured out as early as 1859 into Yokohama and Nagasaki, literally were taking their life into their hands, in the political turmoil. Since the full Meiji Emperor system had not come into total power, some Samurai loyal to the last Shogunate, as they walked the streets wheeling their swords, would indiscriminately kill any 'barbarian' foreigners. This happened frequently, including several British and American diplomates, as well as international seamen.

Of course, some political and religious emissaries never made it past the sea voyage, as shipwrecks were a common occurrence, with typhoons being deadly on land and sea. These new Catholic and Protestant missionaries would be existing on little more than blind-faith, for few knew anything of their future country, nothing of the language, and little of the negative-reception for those representing a 'heretical religion.' They were also kept separate in makeshift buildings from the other few foreigners, to keep their 'church' problems away from the business and government community. The Japanese government offered to give the missionaries guards for protection, but these were mostly spies reporting back every action or move made.

On the other hand, most missionaries viewed their prospective converts as pagans, heathens, and from the Protestant point of view, idolaters. There were many references to Japan's promiscuous sexual practices, 'shockingly' open, compared to conservative Western-mores for 'Protestant-Christian countries.' With time, those who did work closely with the Japanese would say, "let them come out of their darkness to the light, ... and forth they are fine, clever men" and although "there are abundant proofs of human depravity among them,... they have reached a much higher grade of industry, ingenuity and taste for the beautiful ..." It may be considered now a bit sanctimonious, pious, or possibly paternally-patronizing from a white- superiority position, but considering the times, a common belief most Christians were more civilized.

The Bible had been translated into Chinese by previous missionaries, and in 1861 was being translated into Japanese by Dr. James C. Hepburn and Rev. Samuel R. Brown, of the Dutch Reformed Mission in Yokohama. There was no point in preaching, or evangelizing without the language, though some enterprising missionaries did quite well with a kind of pidgin-sign-language. Dr. Hepburn, had for a short time run a medical clinic, with small banners covering all of the walls with quotations from the Bible in simple Japanese. Though it was quite busy, and he'd helped thousands who had never had treatment before, the government closed it after less than a year, without any real reason given.

Japanese leaders came increasingly to learn Great Britain and the United States had a far more dominant role in the Pacific waters, and in the world than Holland. Since their historical preference to always side with the biggest and strongest competition to learn from, action was taken.

The greatest opportunity came when the Japanese government decided to set up an English school, for certain of their diplomats, and the missionaries quickly took up the jobs. Naturally, one of the first books they began to teach was the Bible. Nagasaki was also busy with the Rev. G.H. Verbeck, of the same mission, setting up an English school. He eventually converted the young, warrior-class students. He later was called to Tokyo, as education advisor and helped in establishing South College, which eventually became the prestigious Tokyo University.

As the chaotic conditions of the Meiji Restoration were finalized with the last battles in Hakodate, and the civil disturbances settled, the Meiji Emperor was moved from Kyoto to Tokyo on September 8, 1868. With the government established, Shintoism was the official religion and replaced the Shogunate's State Buddhism. The government still kept strict surveillance on the Christian missionaries, and the Japanese, who went in and out of their Yokohama settlement. Still, the tenacity of these first evangelists could not be denied, as they held services in cramped quarters and taught the Bible through their English lessons. The converts were slow, but steady and more influenced by the belief in the missionaries' 'life-style of earnestness,' than their understanding of what they were being taught. Thus this "Christianity" had to be a good thing, if these people were willing to put up with so many hardships, to bring them the message in battered, broken and often inconceivable Japanese. Even some spies converted. Until the spring of 1872, only ten brave and devout Japanese had received baptism from Protestant missionaries, five in the North and five in the South. Several of these did end up in prison, and most were ostracized from their community, if their actions were revealed.

When missionaries came into the strange Japanese culture, they had to make their message attractive, with or without the language. Etiquette demanded they not be too outspoken in criticizing life around them. The result was they produced a church which never offended anything or anybody. Once the prohibition of Christianity was formally removed from all public notice boards in 1873, the missionaries truly hit the road with their evangelism far and wide. Much of this travel was actually on foot or horseback, as little other transportation existed outside of the city limits.

Some say, an American Baptist missionary named Johan Goble converted a baby carriage into a conveyance for his ailing wife. The Japanese promptly adopted the idea, jin-riki-sha - man-power-carriage. Of course, they then credited a Japanese with the invention. There was also the Japanese form of palanquin, which was cramped and jolted its passenger with every step on the uneven, rocky road. It beat walking, but not by much. But, a feudal-remnant considered to be used only by nobility, and did not convey the neighborly love which the missionaries so wanted to show to the Japanese. As well, dealing with the mountains, which span Japan from top to bottom, made traversing difficult, to say the least.

Still, one of the most famous evangelists was Rev. James Ballagh, who walked mostly and sometimes rode a horse. He covered almost every kilometer of the thousands, in the Northern half of Honshu, for about thirty of his over fifty years as a missionary in Japan. He would follow the old Tokaido Road along the Pacific coast, over the Fuji mountain range and then down to Ise, or from Nagoya, he would head either into the mountains of Nagano, or follow the Kiso River into Gifu. He carried a sleeping bag of sorts, an old black umbrella, and wore geta, or straw sandals. His reputation soon preceded him. And again, more his dedication to his belief and kindness to people, as he stopped to speak to each and everyone, which impressed the Japanese.

Actually, he never attained a real fluency in the language, but his fervent ardor with total devotion, made people listen to his street- corner sermons and spontaneous preaching. Stoning was not unusual at first, yet it just forced him to choose another corner, or another village. He went on his way spreading the Word, as if everyones' life depended upon it, for in his heart it did. Rev. Ballagh received a travel allowance, but this was saved up and contributed to those little community groups, which over time were ready to brave ostracism to build themselves a church.

There were the four international ports, which the missionaries could work from - Nagasaki, Yokohama, Kobe, and Hakodate in Hokkaido. Twenty-nine more missionaries poured in during the single year of 1873, only two less than the total thirty-one who had come in over the past fourteen years from 1859. The Japanese government now specifically asked for famous American educators, like William S. Clark, to set up a higher school of agriculture. Without first asking about any strong Christian influence or material to be used, he and others passed on the Bible to their new students. Many other 'English' teachers were credited with spreading Christianity from their direct use of it in teaching, or merely professing it with their dedicated life. It gave a significant backbone to what the pure, evangelist missionaries were doing, as the Japanese were reached from different angles.

The Catholic and Protestant policy was to turn as much of the preaching and teaching over to the Japanese, as soon as they were trained and able. In 1891, Pope Leo XII established the Japanese- Catholic hierarchy, while by then the faithful had swelled in Nagasaki to almost twenty-five thousand, and over three thousand in Tokyo. Most of the Catholic missionaries were from Europe and sponsored by the Paris Society. The Catholics founded the first of their eleven leper- asylums in 1887 at Koyama, twenty years before the government decided to do something for the thousands of lepers in Japan.

Later tuberculosis sanatoriums were added to this church- supported network, while the orphanages started in Yokohama in 1872. Then, an Old Peoples' Home at Amakusa in 1889, rounded out their extensive charity programs, as many Japanese took serious note. Neither their government, nor the two national religions had ever done these things for them, as it was considered an cultural embarrassment to even *admit* the need of such social health services. Many times also, the old Japanese superstitions regarding any disease or disability, was considered a punishment, or Karma placed on the family. Then, they alone had to accept and deal with it, since the least attention did bring the lost of face on them. This open approach to help, amazed them.

A historical fact, the first Japanese newspaper, the Kaikgai Shimbun, was founded buy the Catholic, Joseph (Hijozo Hamada) Heco. He had been a castaway in the Pacific, who was saved by an American sailing ship in 1850, and taken to the United States. Eventually, he was baptized, given the Christian-Western name, became a naturalized U.S. citizen, then served as an interpreter to Townsend Harris in Japan in 1867. Language was not the only problem the missionaries had in being accepted. For the Japanese had been compelled and indoctrinated for centuries to fear the diabolical- foreigner, with his ultimate plan to conquer and control them. Some territories were strongholds of Buddhism, especially if they had played an important role with the feudal Shogunate. And especially, if a history of oppressive persecution of Christians from the previous, short-open period of the early 1600s. Not unusual for the Japanese to hold power-memories for over two hundred years.

~~~~~~

The case of Aichi and Gifu Prefectures - the cities of Nagoya and Gifu

When the Tokugawa clan had regained control, three thousand Christian believers had been executed in 1640. Nagoya was also the home of Atsuta Shinto Shrine, one of the three most sacred in Japan, for it held some of the Treasures of the Imperial Family. Into this history, came the persevering and unfaltering Rev. Ballagh. After ten years of struggle, he had more followers and churches in the surrounding town of Seto or Gifu, than stubborn Nagoya would allow. To say the Japanese in this district were slow to change, was an ironic understatement. So, it was not without hesitation, he happily turned the 'hostile area' over to his future son-in-law, the Rev. Robert McAlpine in 1885. Although, he did give him a choice of Nagoya or Kochi, on the island of Shikoku. After a brief inspection and report from the local Japanese pastor, Rev. McAlpine went to Kochi. Since this was his first tenure as a missionary, perhaps he wanted some experience under his belt before tackling the tough, Nagoya audience.

By the summer of 1887, Rev. McAlpine returned to Nagoya, and soon had his new bride by his side. He had accomplished great things in Kochi, so had happily turned the growing churches over to the newly-trained Japanese pastors. His dedicated wife, having been raised in Japan surrounded by her father, Rev. Ballagh's evangelistic fervency, there was no telling what changes or furtherance they might bring, even to Nagoya.

One of their biggest opportunities came in the form of Mrs. Anne E. Randolph, an older missionary, who had been teaching at a girl's school in Hangchow, China since 1872. (She is briefly mentioned in a book by Pearl S. Buck.) She had visited Japan for several months in 1876 for health, and recuperated mentally as well physically, before sailing back to America. As difficult as Japan may have seemed, actually a piece of cake compared to China. Also, quite taken aback, and totally impressed how quickly Japan had progressed, not only industrial changes, but in its eagerness for education and Christian growth.

Upon her return to Japan, Mrs. Randolph consulted with the McAlpines, while they were visiting her in Kobe, and then joined them in Nagoya in August. Rev. McAlpine got her a job as an English teacher, as employment was required of foreigners by the government. Several other missionary-teachers soon joined them and they were able to have two houses in Nagoya next to each other for moral support. It really had not become any easier in Nagoya, there was still persecution from the politically-active Buddhist, and the soldiers from the nationalistic military bases. The church services and prayer meetings were constantly interrupted with the missionaries and congregation abused by foul language, spat upon and stoned. This time, with reinforcements of like minds, they stuck it out, feeling no place needed them more than Nagoya.

By the spring of 1889, Mrs. Randolph decided to take her own money and build a two-story building on the same property the McAlpines lived on, and opened a girls' school in September. Rare for any Japanese girls to be educated, and only three (one was later the grandmother of WW II veteran previous mentioned) applicants signed up for the boarding school, which had four teachers. Mrs. Randolph, a small, plump, dignified sixty-two year-old, had the brightest, big blue eyes and taught the girls knitting, English, and the Bible, the things she knew best. Though a strict teacher in class, she was a sweet- tempered mother and sister for the students, whom she called 'good girl' or 'my girl.' The American mission recognized education for women as a suitable method of work, and supported her efforts. She named the school Kin jo Gakuin

- Golden Castle School, and it became a success story like no other.

In October, 1891, triumph came for the missionaries out of tragedy and disaster. The Nobi plain, of which Nagoya was centered, was struck by an enormous earthquake, with hundreds of aftershocks which went on for a month. Nagoya had prided itself on the modernistic brick buildings, railroads, streetcars, iron bridges and lovely, graceful wooden houses. The fires wiped out more than the quake, though the streets were blocked by the fallen bricks and rubble with people lying dead underneath the debris. Riverbanks collapsed and sunk, as flooding added to the devastation, dying and wild chaos. Almost seven-hundred had died and another ten-thousand were injured. This had been the city with the strongest opposition to Christianity, and it was said, Aichi and Gifu also had the largest number of prostitutes in Japan. When the local newspapers called attention to the relief effort of the missionaries and other foreigners, aiding the injured and homeless, the superstitious-Japanese took it as an omen. Time to change.

Mrs. Anne Randolph retired from Japan in November, 1892, when Miss Ora Patterson was sent to take over her position, as principal of Kinjo. It had been just four years, yet this solid foundation was lasting, as courses offered were expanded and the Christian atmosphere became preferred for girls. She was followed by more than two hundred other missionaries teaching full time, including Rev. Robert McAlpine, his son Rev. James McAlpine with both of their wives. Kinjo's first real problem came in 1908, when rather than read the Imperial Rescript on Education for the Empress' birthday, they chose to read a poem which the Empress had written.

As the Rescript tied the educational system to a religious loyalty to the Emperor, with absolute obedience to the nation was considered sacred. The problem was their strong Protestant-stand against idolatry, and everyone was required to bow. The conflict arose with two Japanese teachers, who opposed the Christian-stand of the head teacher. So they reported the incident to the local newspaper. The owner of the newspaper was a devout Buddhist, and for three weeks the editorials severely criticized Kinjo. Community opposition became intent and many students withdrew. It took years before the rift was settled, the enrollments built back up, and the school was able to expand its facilities and classes.

By 1937 though, State Shinto with its demands of absolute obedience to the Emperor, became the controlling force of the Japanese people. The tablets issued by the great Shrine of the Imperial Family, should be placed upon an appropriate shelf in every home. For the time being, Kinjo school life was continuing uninterrupted. Demand for higher education for women was strong, and over one thousand young ladies were studying, since Kinjo was virtually the only school for women in the region with native American teachers teaching English. Since the fighting had expanded in China, by September students went to the army hospital, made utility kits for the fighting soldiers, and went to train stations to honor the ashes of those who had died in battle. Soon, representatives of the student body were taking gifts to men going into the military, and the first of the Japanese teachers were drafted in December.

Just as students were coming for Christmas worship, a group of patriotic-extremists stood by the gate and distributed leaflets. They again claimed the 25th was the anniversary of the death of Emperor Taisho, and the Christmas celebration of a foreign religion should not be held. Some students dropped the leaflets and, of course, some were stepped on. The angry men noisily forced their way into the campus, declaring it was disrespectful to trample on papers with the name of the Emperor on them. The military police were called, and though everything was eventually settled, pressure by anti-Christian, nationalistic groups were growing stronger.

The nationalism was increased by 1938, as the government insisted upon frequent visits to the shrines to pay homage to heroes of the past, and to pray for the souls of the men killed in the fighting, as well for victory on the battlefield. Once Kinjo succumbed, the Executive Committee of Foreign Missions began to question whether it should keep its support of the school. The next blow came with the forced traditional New Year's - January visit to Atsuta Shinto Shrine by the entire staff and student body. The Mission ordered the missionaries to withdraw from the school, and financial-emotional support was severed.

Many of the missionary teachers were divided in their feelings, as they could see the situation first hand. By acquiescing to the government, Kinjo was allowed to stay open to somewhat-function in its Christian-state. On the other hand, some of the Japanese teachers were quite nationalistic, and accused the missionaries of forbidding or influencing the students not to attend shrine ceremonies. Again, there were newspaper accusations, which created considerable agitation in the community, and not much could be done to quiet the dissension. Some people in the government, in spite of the fanaticism of the military regime itself, had learned sufficiently from the historical consequences of the previous persecutions to avoid a policy, which could only result in the recurrence of martyrdoms on a large scale. When government officials tried to force the Catholics to sever their ties with the pope in Rome, the ordinary members and laity insisted such separation was contrary to the essence of their faith. They preferred imprisonment or death, and martyrdom to obeying an order of this kind.

The government then backed down from insistence on this point. Eventually, by mid-1940, the missionaries had left. By the fiftieth anniversary of the Imperial

Rescript on Education, five Kinjo teachers received the highest awards. In early 1941, Kinjo had set up an exchange program with Manchuria, and five Chinese students for each grade level were accepted. Yet, food rationing enforced, as war was part of life.

The missionaries outside of Kinjo were experiencing much of the same thing, as Rev. James McAlpine, the third generation in the Nagoya-Aichi domain, and his wife were living in Gifu. They constantly felt the pressure of suspicious looks, with their activities severely restricted, and all of their interactions observed openly with a haughty attitude. For the general populace, it was another agitation and suppression of their ordinary freedom. A conversation with foreigners brought surveillance by the the special police, and even suspicion of being a spy. With the enforcement of the Religious Bodies Control Act in 1940, all Protestant denominations were merged into one organization under the Kyodan. They each had to secure official government permission to operate. Those religious groups not recognized were transferred, and became subject to police control of doctrine, teachings and meetings. Several churches in Aichi were not recognized, thus restricting their autonomy and freedom to preach.

Finally, all organizations and individuals having any connection with England or America were under suspicion as spies.

The harassment continued until the military ordered a purge of all missionaries from education leadership. For fear of their own life, the Japanese did not attend Christian sponsored functions. The McAlpines returned to the U.S. in December, 1940, and a year later there were only five missionaries in the central Japan area, and one on his way back to America, had to return. The three men were interned and the three ladies kept under house-arrest in

Kobe. Rev. McAlpine served as an instructor in the U.S. Navy language school, until July, 1946.

Meanwhile, demands on Kinjo students and teachers to work in factories two or three days a week increased steadily, from the beginning of 1941. There was only a limited time before studies and school activities became more rigid, with military titles for staff and subjects, along with the addition of athletic exercises, drills, and marching to classes in military formation. With full war by 1942, stronger emphasis at school was placed on discipline, fire prevention, use of gas masks, first aid and techniques for getting people into air- raid shelters. Inspectors from the National Ministry of Education kept close, and frequent checks on the activities of the school, because of its previous American support and Christian basis.

Next, students began to raise vegetables on the campus, and were sent to help farmers in their fields for weeks at a time. Others had to collect scrap materials, gather used tea leaves to feed the army horses, visit the wounded in hospitals, and make more utility kits for the fighting soldiers. The sacrifices increased as the war situation worsened, and by October 1943, the government requisitioned radiators, chandeliers, gallery rails, and any steel object from the school for military repurposing.

The following month all high school graduating classes were required to work full time at the military factories. Within six months, it was the next younger grade, and then all high school students had to do factory work, and struggle side-by-side with the older, stronger men and women. Schools and companies were asked to raise money for military aircraft, and Kinjo worked very had to collect enough to have an aircraft designated with their name by April, 1944. This project created accusations against the Kinjo president after the war, though at the time he felt it kept worse things from happening to them.

Many students and teachers lost their homes, as the heavy bombing of Nagoya began in early 1945, and some younger students moved out to the countryside. Absenteeism from factories increased, and military-overseers issued sever notices reprimanding the school for this supposed action. The president, staff and teachers were repeatedly questioned, scolded and accused by the military for being uncooperative and disloyal. Only about ninety students were still trying to come to what few classes were available, and those were dressed in farmer's trousers, with air-raid hoods.

The incendiary bombs took their toll on Kinjo, as all buildings were destroyed, with the only exception being the badly damaged Eikokan Chapel, and stone gate-house survived. The students managed to escape from their dormitories, so the only girls killed were three who had been working at a Mitsubishi factory, when it was bombed. The previously beautiful, hilly-campus was a field of ashes. Yet secretly, the students and staff continued daily worship services, with regular Bible classes, as the wind blew-through the broken glass of the sacred Chapel.

On September 1, 1945, fall classes started, two weeks after the blackout rules had been removed, with remarkably over one thousand students returning to school. All had not been lost, for sections of the red brick walls were still standing, and old stoves, or other heavy equipment not confiscated, had survived the bombings and fires. Alternate classes were held in the Chapel, as rain came in the useless roof, or blew through the glassless windows. There were no chairs or desks, so students sat crowded-closely together on the floor, in classes of seventy or more. Their own clothes were patched, darned, and in various stages of shabbiness. There were only about half-enough textbooks, and one girl in five had a copy of the New Testament or hymnbook, yet they read and sang together.

The Occupation troops moved in October 28th, and though people were fearful, expecting violence, Kinjo classes were not canceled. Slowly, activities became organized, if not normalized, for the aftermath of the war had put the currency in drastic devaluation. Daily functioning concentrated on getting enough money just for salaries, and a building fund was begun. As damaged as the Chapel was, it was one of the few remaining and available auditorium-style buildings - the Occupation officers had taken over all of the other government ones. Its rental by other groups, brought in sufficient funds to pay maintenance, repair, and restoration. All of 1946 was spent just reorganizing, building temporary classrooms and dorms, as it regained a semblance of a school, if not the glorious one it had been. Once the attention was drawn to the president being expelled, the U.S. Army Counter Intelligence Corps ordered an investigation, and twenty-six charges were filed against him. It took almost two years for him to clear himself, and resume his post. As whatever cooperation or support was given to the Imperial military, it had been done for the survival-sake, as his Christian consciousness was never abated.

~~~~~~

After the war, the competition from Communism was quite keen to Christianity. Usually, the city, educated and more middle class, or affluent became Christians, yet they were the most also attracted to the Japanese Communist Party. The farmers, and ordinary workers, needed to be attracted at a level they could understand, which was a sincere show of goodwill toward their welfare. The directive in December 1945, separating church and state, made it necessary for Shintoism to become self-supporting.

It had to undertake various kinds of business enterprises in order to meet its financial obligations. The Shinto Shrines did not try too long on their own, and soon turned to those who could profitably help them - the Yakuza. There were numerous reported cases of extortion of small shop owners, who were forced to give the little bit of money they had been able to save. The Occupation forces did little to abate this cruel and continuous practice, for they felt it was none of their business, saying it had *no relationship* to democracy. Of course, they were the ones who created the problem by the separation of church and state, but they would not acknowledge the point.

Under the religious freedom granted by the new constitution, the number of different religions jumped from the restricted forty-four, during the war, to 571. Superstition played a large role in the new organizations, or new sects and cults, which indicated the feelings of the people. Just a representative few were: The Way of Man, The Way of Light, The Goddess of Light, The World Messianic Religion, Companions of the Spirit, The Dancing Religion, The Smiling Religion, etc. These pseudo-religious cults, with their feverish quest for imponderable values, threw into sharp perspective the spiritual vacuum, in which multitudes of the Japanese were groping.

Once the Emperor had given his proclamation on January 1, 1946, denying his deity-ship, and the special superiority of the Japanese people, the explicit doctrine of more than a half century of spiritual foundation was demolished. To many, this was more physically and emotionally shattering than the military defeat and surrender. It left literally millions to reconstruct their beliefs and standards of value, a task which most Japanese were hard prepared for, by previous non-experience of personal choice. In their two-thousand, six-hundred year history, they, as a people, a singular group, "We Japanese" - had always been told what to think, and how to believe. Now, they were on their own, and spiritual confusion reigned along with the physical devastation.

With this loss of direction or mooring, large numbers began to turn to Christianity. Many felt it the main religion of their *conquerors*, so it must have worked for them! As they had been taught, 'Whoever is in power, you follow.' Churches, and church schools, were soon filled to overflowing with many who came as earnest seekers after faith. In general, however, the churches were not adequately prepared for the opportunities presented, particularly an influx of inexperienced inquirers. Pastors, and laymen alike, were as physically, and often perhaps as psychologically exhausted as their non-Christian neighbors, who zealously came to them for guidance. The Catholic expansion made a special appeal by the various committees, to the hierarchies of the U.S. and Australia for help with missionaries and priests, money and goods, and other countries were requested to give aid.

The Occupation Forces required all returning missionaries had to bring with them at least one year's supply of food, plus all of their household necessities, and also have guaranteed housing for themselves upon arrival. All of these requirements would be time-consuming to fulfill, expensive to the supporting American churches, and put definite burdens on the Japanese congregations. Likewise, the American Bible Society printed and shipped two and a half million copies of the New Testament by the end of 1947. The Japan Bible Society had been depleted, as many personal Bibles had been burned when confiscated. Paper was almost unattainable in Japan, and any printing facilities were at a premium.

~~~~~~

In January, 1947, Rev. McAlpine, along with several other Japan-born missionaries returned to the scorched earth to rebuild, and help make the plans for the new frontiers of their evangelism work. Then, many of the individual churches wanted to be separated out of the joint Protestant Kyodan, they had been forced into by the previous military regime. This caused some in-fighting, as well as chaos. By early 1948, a large number of both Catholic and Protestant missionaries came to Japan, as they were expelled out of China with the civil war. They brought their own financial support, and thus greatly strengthened the entire Japanese program. Not until March of 1948, the four previous missionaries returned to Kinjo, and re-established the clarified principles it was to follow.

One clear point made, there would never be any shrine obeisance, and no idolatry practiced of any sort. Then Kinjo came back under the auspices of the Presbyterian Mission, who promptly sent tens of thousands of dollars for the rebuilding and expansion of it, and many surrounding churches. By this time, Christians began with new earnestness to care for the orphans, the vagrants, the sick and others needing help. And, all those who could not share comparably, in the gradually emerging prosperity of the nation as a whole. Food and clothing by the ton began to pour into Japan, and many Japanese remarked the U.S. certainly was taking better care of them, than they probably would have done in the reverse situation.

~~~~~~

It should be noted Nagoya also had the prestigious Catholic University of Nanzan, which began in 1924, as a Normal Training School. It obtained university recognition in 1949. As co-ed, it had a full-time enrollment of about two thousand, and followed the high standard of Sophia - for men, and Sacred Heart - for women, (which the Empress attended) both in Tokyo. Sophia was the first Catholic university in Japan, and was chartered in 1928.

Another interesting historical fact was the development of the Russian Orthodox Church, specifically through the effort of the missionary known as Nicolai, first in Hakodate and then later in Tokyo. It had tremendous later growth from its tenuous beginnings in 1861, but unfortunately with the Russian Revolution, and the Communist rejection of support, it had but a small, modern following of less than thirty thousand. The magnificent edifice, of Byzantine design with the glorious cupola, became a main attraction in Tokyo in 1891. Destroyed during the Great Kanto Earthquake in 1923, rebuilt in 1930, then some bombing damage during the war. All Russians were interned, but after their release, a diplomatic battle between the clergy and Soviet government erupted, which took years to settle.

The East-West tension, and the Communistic invasion of nearby South Korea, radically changed the picture, as compared with the situation when Japan adopted its pacifist constitution. This change in the international climate, augmented by pressure on the part of the U.S., led Japan's government to interpret the ban on the maintenance of armed forces with a large degree of latitude. The re-established religious groups, led primarily by the much stronger Christians and Buddhists spoke out against any rearmament. Once the new Japanese Diet established a Self Defense Force to be trained, and equipped to protect her existence as a nation, the Christians and Buddhists joined forces to hold forums of protest.

The mood of the Japanese people, as a whole, had not changed. Their dire experience with the atomic bombs at Hiroshima and again at Nagasaki, were renewed with the Bikini hydrogen bomb tests. This had showered deadly atomic dust on Japanese fishermen, and across their fishing fields. The future possibilities hovered over them, like an unforgettable nightmare. Rice and fish constituted the two main staples of the Japanese diet. The atomic poisoning of one of the nation's fishing fields, therefore hurled a terrifying menace into every kitchen, and on to every table. The religious coalition stood alone against the governments - U.S. and Japanese.

~~~~~~

Personal History: Missionary life in Japan after the Korean War

Excerpts of letters sent back to America from a missionary family who went to Japan in 1957. The husband Merle was a music teacher, (actually a graduate of Juilliard School) the wife, Arlene was an English teacher and they had three sons Larry, 7, Charles 4 1/2, and Roy, 2 1/2. A fourth son, Glen, was born after they had lived in Japan almost 1 1/2 years. Most of the letters were written by Arlene, when otherwise the name will be Bold. The family was originally from West Virginia, though they had also taught in Florida and North Carolina. Full names of people will be avoided for privacy sake. The author's comments or explanations will be in parenthesis.

8/22/56: **Merle** Arlene has packed about 53 boxes without my hardly knowing it. Packing gets me down. Last week she came to the band office to help me, and I was one irritable mess for the simple reason I just could not bear to throw things away. Arlene - Things Larry throws away, Charles wants to keep. The boys and Merle all want to check every box I discard, to be sure there is nothing they want.

Christmas Letter - 1956: After considering it for several years, during the past year we decided to serve our Lord in a more definite way. Last July we met with the Board of World Missions of the Presbyterian Church. We applied, took physical examinations, and now we are on our way to Japan. The Board asked us to spend this winter in school, so we are at the Presbyterian School of Christian Education this winter. Next year we will all be in the same boat - only we will be learning Japanese instead of English. We will be in language school in Kobe, Japan, for two years. After that, we go to Nagoya where Merle will be developing an instrumental music program at Kinjo College. The "Golden Castle School" is the largest of our mission schools, and has an enrollment of about 4,800 girls ranging from junior high through senior college.

4/57: We are sailing August 15 from San Francisco on the SS California Bear (a freighter). There is lots of paper work involved. Yesterday, I spent all day making an inventory of the kids' clothes to see exactly what I still need to buy in sizes from 2 - 12. Last night Rachel, who teaches here and taught at Kinjo one year, … had us over for super. She met us at the door with Japanese greetings, wearing her indoor slippers, with Japanese music on the record in the background. We ate a real Japanese dinner, cooked at the table, with chopsticks. After dinner she showed us Kinjo slides.

NO DATE: The class on missionary preventive medicine is especially interesting. After August 15, we won't eat an unpeeled apple, unless it is scrubbed with soap, water, brushed or scalded in boiling water, or soaked in clorox water!!! Lettuce will be a thing of the past. (Japan used unprocessed, human-fertilizer at the time.)

8/57: San Francisco - We have worked on freight for three full days. We have 34 pieces of freight, besides the baggage in our cabin. Since it is a freighter, we watched them loading a number of cars yesterday. We kept the big boys awake, to see the tug boat take us through the Bay and the Golden Gate Bridge. We entered the Pacific about 10:30 pm. Will be on the ship ten days to Yokohama, two days there and then two more days to Kobe.

9/2/57: Merle - We arrived in Yokohama at 7:00 am, and went ashore with one of the engineers on the ships right, after we ate. He got two taxis for us (other missionary family on board), and took us to the home of one of his friends. A lovely Japanese home behind a high wooden fence and naturally, we removed our shoes at the door The wife showed us the house. They had a 'Western-style room' with radio and television. Their living room was the tatami room, with special woven (rice) straw mats on the floor. So soft, it felt good in stocking feet. The officer of the ship persuaded the daughter of the family to play the *samisen* - a three-stringed instrument picked with a little square paddle.

They served lemon soda and brought in pineapple (very hard to get). We left after taking some pictures. The officer said they would have served us all afternoon, had we stayed. We went to another home, took off shoes again, and there no time before she served pineapple. Both families were gracious hosts - having nine people barge in, didn't seem to fuss them a bit. In this home, I saw a Westinghouse refrigerator, a bed, and bunk-beds for their two girls. The first home had just bed mats (futons) which are put in closets during the day.

We ate supper at a nice restaurant - left our shoes at the door, and ate the meal sitting down on pillows around a low table. The three waitresses, in kimonos, had a hot plate with a rubber hose to a wall jet, and cooked our sukiyaki right at the table, as we ate. Delicious - and only $1 each.

We watched the Japanese longshoremen load and unload the ship. The Japanese barges were interesting, and told the family lives on them. They sleep, eat and have their babies right on the barge. I bet they unloaded over forty automobiles in Yokohama. I saw at least three Cadillacs.

Arlene and the boys saw an accident as we left, and I saw part of it. A drunk sailor was being carried along the pier with his drunk friend. The friend fell, throwing the carried-one on solid concrete. His head hit like a busted watermelon, and soon blood was running slowly from his head, out of his ears and later his mouth. An ambulance came and got him - still breathing when they put him in, but the captain said he bet he 'met his Maker,' before they got him to the hospital.

We arrived at Kobe, and several couples of the Japan Mission came to get us They came aboard the ship to help, and waited while the immigration officials looked at our passports, etc. After all official papers were signed, our baggage was carried off, and all of us got through customs without incident. You should see Kobe! Our first impressions were something terrific. Some buildings are actually more modern than anything I've seen in America.

9/5/57: Larry was to register at school the day after we got here … and yesterday morning he got on the school bus alone, and started off. We gave him the business card of the place where we are now, with phone numbers and address, both in English and Japanese - and told him how to call us, if he gets lost. I went to school to meet him yesterday afternoon, and Merle and I will go today and until he gets his bus stop well in mind. I was surely proud of him. He came home all smiles. Larry has grown so much in the last two or three months. They have all taken everything in stride, very well. Now, they get concerned if we don't take off our shoes properly.

Merle: I went over to our house this morning, to take Yoshida San - our maid, some yen to pay for two chests Arlene bought the other day. I had quite a time making myself understood. The best department store has seven floors plus a roof garden, and is about a block long - really fabulous. In the bargain basement, everything is 100 yen ($.30) and there is nearly a whole floor with nothing but fish, meat and groceries. Never saw so many different kinds of edible seaweed. I think it will take a long time - maybe a lifetime, before I go for a lot of Japanese food! We have to peel all fruit, and only buy fresh vegetables that have been grown in commercial fertilizer.

9/8/57: Merle - We are spending our first Sunday in Japan in Kobe, and I taught the adult Sunday School class at the Kobe Union Church. Need I say, I taught it in English! Arlene brought the boys home, since they have no place for them during church. There are about a hundred at church - no choir. Arlene and the other wives will attend the afternoon service at 3:00.

Yesterday, we worked nearly all day at our house sorting clothes from one barrel to another, for we have nothing to put clothes in yet. Our freight goes through customs tomorrow. Yoshida San has all the linen, the kitchen-ware etc. already put away. Two men have been putting up a solid board fence on the street side of the house. A safety to protect the boys from falling over the twelve-foot retaining wall, a drop to the street. The department stores were all open today - Sunday, for business - we aren't in a Christian country.

Our house is on the same block as the Catholic Church and school. What was in front, and at the side of the house, had been bombed out and never replaced. On the way up the steep hill to Larry's school, there are holes in the rocks, that were put in as air-raid shelters. Now some poor people are using them for places to live.

9/12/57: For the first time I'm a foreigner, who is fingerprinted and registered with an identification card to be carried. And, who is the one who looks different and gets stared at, as well who can't talk right, etc.

When we ask direction to some place, all we know when we get through is the direction to start off in. If we ask often enough, we make it. If we get lost, we can always get a cab and can usually make ourselves understood to get home. Japanese are fascinated to see and touch Roy's blonde hair.

The (street) noise is deafening. The person who gets the right- of-way, seems to be the one who toots his horn the loudest. Wish you could see the way traffic moves, down the middle of the road, along with all the bikes and jay-walkers. Japanese drive on the left side of the road, a real adjustment.

Yoshida-San, the maid, is just as cute as she can be and I'm crazy about her. She knows about as much English as I know Japanese, but it is amazing how much we get across to each other. She is good with the boys, and goes ahead and does things she sees has to be done. Here you cannot leave a house without someone in it, (because of danger of fire and robberies) so it is nice having someone living with us who is also Christian.

9/15/57: A man is making our beds from the packing crates. Our swing set takes-up about half of our yard, but the kids have enjoyed it. Larry worked with the carpenter most of yesterday, and came up last night at supper talking about Roy *Chan* and Charles *Chan* (terms of endearment for children).

Yoshida San … with her Japanese/English dictionary and my English/Japanese dictionary, took us about half an hour for me to tell her to use her recipe, instead of the one in the book. I call our friends and get them to explain over the telephone other things I can't say. Quite complicated, but it works. The biggest problem now is meals. I don't know what to buy, where to buy it and what is available. Yet, I have to plan menus and tell Yoshida San what to fix. Our 'super- market' is about the size of Daddy's study and we buy meat, raw vegetables and fruit elsewhere. Living takes longer here - preparing meals itself is a much longer process. Go to the store nearly every day for food. Yoshida San will spend half or 2/3 of her time in the kitchen, after we get settled. I have spent as much time buying groceries and planning, as I have getting settled so far. (Japan requires missionary families to have maid.)

My washer is due here Tuesday, probably another week in customs and another week getting installed. Have a lady coming once a week to iron. I'll probably do washing myself, as I can hang indoor lines in basement, which is the garage coming from the side of the hill. Fifteen steps lead up to the front door. The large picture window overlooks the bay and harbor. Ships are visible all the time. Real pretty and breezy, most of the time. Three blocks from bus, streetcars and about one mile from language school, a mile and a half to Larry's school.

9/18/57: I am waiting on my bath water to heat on the stove, and then I'm going to bed. Haven't got our hot water heater going, and don't have much furniture. It takes so long to shop - I can't ask for anything - just have to look until I find it. Language school started Tuesday - Walk about eight blocks and ride a bus about ten minutes. There are 47 students in the school - interesting and intensive. We only have two- dozen English words or so spoken in class. In fact, the teacher knows little English, so we find it almost impossible to ask questions.

Merle goes to Kinjo this weekend, but we will not go with him. He is to sing tenor over Japanese religious radio. He will see Kinjo while in Nagoya.

9/20/57: We have a nice kitchen, large dining room and front room, downstairs flush toilet, Japanese bath - in separate room from toilet, a study and a Japanese tatami room with mats on the floor and no furniture. Upstairs we have three bedrooms, one very large, other two small and bath. We have running hot (very rare) and cold water. Biggest problem is the small yard, fenced with gate. Bus and streetcar service is fine, lots of bicycles, motor scooters, not many American big cars, but lots of small Japanese cars. Many three-wheel-trucks and most vehicles are delivery trucks or taxi. Roads are narrow, drive down the middle, dodging walkers and bicyclers - who never bother to get out of the way.

Open ditches along streets with drainage water, plus trash. No paper sacks (for shopping), so everything is individually wrapped and tied - harder to manage packages. Most Japanese dishes run toward blue - occasionally you can find ones with green, gray or red. Hard to find any that even have another color mixed with the blue. A Japanese dinner table has a great mixture of dish patterns - the more different patterns, the prettier the table. I bought a tea pot, cups without handles, rice dishes, covered large bowls, 5" plates and pickles dishes.

Our Japanese bath has a drain in the floor, so people can wash before getting into the tub. The tub is deep, a square hole, going far below the floor. A gas heater is in it, which is lit from the outside. Water is shoulder deep, heated to steaming and kept hot by the heater - sit in it as long as you want (it is for soaking, not washing). Big things like groceries are delivered. I feel like a real plutocrat having a cook, etc. around all the time. Real awkward feeling, to sit down at the table and never have to get up, is strange.

Pitchers are terribly hard to find over here. Prices constantly amaze me. American things about double what they are at home. Many other things terribly cheap. I paid

$.65 for a loaf of bread and the quality varies a great deal. I give Yoshida San 1000 yen at a time, she uses it for groceries and other expenses, she keeps track of for me.

Larry had his first experience playing with neighborhood Japanese children this afternoon. Came in all excited and thought he had a big time. Said, "I didn't know what they said, but just went on and played anyway." I was walking the other day with my three, and passed three Japanese children about the same age. They all passed each other properly, but about three-feet later, all six children turned around and stared at one another for a few minutes, then went on.

Recently a 3 or 4 year old girl, who was helping her mother in a store, was quite fascinated with me. I bought something - she grabbed it and wrapped-it-up, typical, small-child fashion. The mother put a rubber band around it, as it was and gave it to me. When I left, I thanked and bowed to the mother, then turned to the child, thanked her and bowed very seriously. She beamed a smile from ear to ear. So cute watching her.

Japanese children are darling, and Japanese people make over children so much. They will give the children a seat on the bus, before giving me one. No one ever gives a seat to women here. Men rush out ahead of you from the elevator - even though you are standing in position to logically, or even almost by necessity go out first.

So many pretty Japanese girls. It is easy to see why service men married them. Pretty dark features and tiny, dainty figures. Many of the men are short enough for me to look over their heads. Haven't seen a 'fat' Japanese yet. Almost no young people in kimonos. Occasionally, a child or young person, but mostly old women, or at least middle age. Few men wear them, and every-day kimonos are mostly drab colors - only color proper for older people here. Gorgeous ones in the stores - probably used like we wear party clothes and formals. They are sewn by hand, taken apart to wash in one long piece, 12" x 12' approximately. Really fascinating, as they are stretched to dry between fence posts, on netting of some kind, with pencil-thin, bamboo pieces every two or three inches to hold it out, on the 12" side of the material.

10/10/57: Yoshida San is going to plan most of the meals from now on, which will make things so much easier. It is interesting to see her use chopsticks, rather than spoons in her cooking. There is always a pair of wooden getas at the back door if she is in the house, or in her room, her slippers are at the door to her room. She has tatami on her floor, so I never go in there without taking off my shoes.

Australian food sometimes is as cheap as Japanese food. Our corn flakes come from Britain, our oatmeal from Holland. Many American products are made for foreign consumption, and directions are in several languages. We use some canned milk and cheese - both very expensive, but mostly use the powdered milk we brought with us. Japanese milk is pasteurized, but cows not tuberculin-tested, so you take chances. Flowers here are beautiful, and everywhere. Japanese idea of beauty, is with one or three flowers - single beauty, rather than large clusters. We see flowers on buses - there is a built-in flower vase in front of the bus, with fresh flowers in it. You see real flower arrangements in the bath rooms or restrooms, seems so funny.

Recently when we were riding a cable car, Roy pointed to a sign and ask me to read it. I told him I couldn't, and he said he knew what it said, 'for little boys to hold on and not fall out of the car.' Roy corrected me this evening, when I asked Yoshida San in English for something for supper. Roy told me in Japanese.

Charles informed me tonight his room was a Japanese room, and no one was to come into it with their shoes on. Larry has learned to shop, and dearly loves to run up to get us somethings at the store. I don't know exactly how he makes out, but he enjoys it, and always comes home with what he went after. You buy bread either by the whole loaf, or they will cut it any size you desire. Larry informed me he knew the Japanese word for 'big card,' and he figured he could use the same word by bread. I told him to get some donuts, if he could make himself understood. You bet, he got them!!!

Sewers are usually not covered, and we frequently see men standing up, or little girls squatting over the sewer urinating. Japanese children on their mana's back are so cute, especially when sleeping.

10/15/57: There is plenty of ice cream - tastes like home-made American ice cream. Candy is about the same and about as varied. Much of it is wrapped in paper, with an inner-wrapper which looks like cellophane, but is rice paper. It breaks if you try to take it off - you are supposed to eat it. I can't go for it myself, so if possible I always wash it off at the sink, as it dissolves in water.

10/20/57: Merle - Mt. Rokko is certainly a nice park, but I was a bit shaky from the bus ride. No safety posts on those mountain roads, but the bus driver seemed to be used to driving quite rapidly, and as we swerved around, we could look down a 'fur' piece into the valleys.

We are going to use one of our packing barrels for kerosene, setting upright, knock a hole for the pipe line in the side of the house, opening into the false fireplace, where we will place our space heater. The barrel will be put at the front corner of the house, and a brick foundation put under the barrel, lifting it high enough for gravity-feed. **Arlene -** The cold weather brought out the pretty kimonos - oodles of bright blues, pinks, reds, etc., just like we always thought Japan ought to look. Hard in town today, amazing not to just stop and stare at all the pretty kimonos. The children in their pretty kimonos are cute - many of them just toddlers. Elementary school and preschool children wear long, cotton stockings. Their dresses are so short, you can see the garters up as high as they will go - much shorter than in the States.

We got a note from Larry's school saying Larry had to have a TB exam, and eyes checked for glaucoma - all students are required to have these by the end of the month.

It takes three or four hours to make the trip (to the Mission hospital), an hour each way, plus getting to the train stations, waiting for doctor etc. Both tests are routine here.

In Japan, you must tell the taxi driver the section of town and then direct him to your house - there are no house numbers in Japan. (The Post Office assigns number for their use only, but not usually consecutive, by date.) In coming home, Larry directed the driver tonight - telling him to turn right, then left, then where to stop - all in Japanese! Our entrance way is about eight-feet-square. The front half is tile, then a step, and then the wooden floor. We step in the tile part, remove shoes and wear slippers in the house. We are gradually going 'Eastern' on not wearing shoes in the house, and I suspect when we get rugs down, we will go completely without the shoes inside. Living on a dirt road, we track in so much dirt from the street.

With open sewers, as they have in Japan, along with flies, etc. you feel like the dirt is 'germier' than our dirt at home. Japanese who come, take their shoes off and we have several pairs of slippers for them. I got the little kids 'tabi' socks today, ... they fit like gloves, with a place for the big toe and snap up the back. Japanese people use them like socks, either with or without shoes. Should be warm.

Wish you could know Yoshida San. The more we have her around, the more we are enjoying her. The kids just love her to pieces, and the two little ones are so cute trying to talk Japanese to her.

Yesterday, and today is the big Harbor Festival here in Kobe. Last night they had 65 boats on parade in the harbor, with lanterns on them. We could see them from the house, and they had fireworks. The whole festival opens with a Shinto shrine ceremony. In Japan, the custom is for guests to walk into the entrance way of the home and call out. The other day someone walked in, called and I went to the (inside) door. There was a man, dressed-up with a dragon head in one hand, and a hood which was over his arm. When he held the head up, the hood fell over his body. He saw me, but started speaking Japanese, by the time Yoshida San came in. He held up the head and started under the hood, growling, hissing, and doing some kind of dance. About this time, another fellow came to the back door, and starts the same thing. After they had gone, she got her dictionary and pointed out two words to me - Shinto shrine and festival. They come once a year and want money.

10/25/57: Everyone carries everything in a *furoshiki* - a square piece of cloth with the four corners to tie-together. The smaller ones are about the size of head scarfs, but it is not unusual to see men and women alike carrying very large ones, with boxes maybe three or four foot square wrapped up in cloth. You almost never see anyone carrying a naked - unwrapped article, they are always tied in a furoshiki. I usually keep one in my purse, so now never go shopping without one, and also a cloth or plastic carrying bag over my arm. Japanese deliver groceries in wooden boxes. They do not want the boxes back, so we have a number of them downs stairs - almost no cardboard boxes.

10/27/57: Today we are going on a picnic at someone's home. We talked about going to a public park, but figured as foreigners, we would attract so much attention, it would be more fun in a private situation. You have no idea how much attention we (as a whole family of gaijin) attract, when we go to any public place.

A man comes by to buy our newspapers and tin cans, to recycle them. He picked up a bunch the other day, and gave us 25 yen - $.08 for them. Had a fire across the street yesterday. We had ringside view from our upstairs window. Maybe six fire trucks out, oodles of men - in Japan there are always two or three people doing what one would ordinarily do in the U.S.! We could see no flames, but there was lots of smoke. A real concern, since the houses here are so close together, and so many are all wood, so a fire is really dangerous.

There are so many people. Any time you wake up at night, you can hear the wooden getas, clicking against the road. That click is every place, all the time, you never get away from it. Larry was drawing a picture last night in his Sunday School book, about things God made. He said God made Japan, and he was going to draw a picture of Japan. I asked him how he was going to do it, and he said he'd just draw lots of buildings close together.

11/57: Mission Board Letter - We have been particularly impressed with the Japanese people. They have consistently been patient with us, and gracious in all their dealings with us, so helpful in every way. So many have taken time to draw maps, or escort us to where we want to go, when language was limited to one or two words. They laugh good naturally, at our efforts to use Japanese, and their sense of humor and vivaciousness bubble-over, even through the language barrier. How much the people would mean to the Kingdom of God, if they can be reached for Christ! Every Wednesday night, we attend the weekly prayer meeting of Presbyterian missionaries in the Kobe area. We always come home with two thoughts, vividly impressed on our mind. One is the large number of people, who are always going some place on Japanese streetcars and buses. The other is the small number of faithful missionaries, who are trying to reach these people for the Kingdom of God. Won't you join with us in prayer, that others can be sent to help in the work of God in Japan?

11/5/57 Merle - Our friends invited the whole family up to see Kinjo this weekend. I had choir duties at church here, on Sunday morning, so Sunday afternoon we left here at 2:15 pm, by the semi-express electric train and got to Nagoya at 6:00 pm. Our friends made tempura, and they have a house that is entirely Japanese - thin walls, many sliding (paper) doors, unpainted wood, concealed closets with sliding doors. They have a beautiful Japanese garden - big for Japan. Monday morning we awakened, after nearly freezing, despite all the blankets we had on. Of course, no heat in the house - too, expensive.

After breakfast, the Kinjo school car came by for us, a black 1953 Chevy - really kept shining, like-new. The college was an imposing site, with about eight, huge white buildings on top of the hill, with rows of dorms and faculty houses around the middle of the hill. A gravel road to the top, and on the way to the top we passed a Shinto shrine. Our first stop was in the conference room ... Arlene, the boys and I had tea. then, we visited the gym-auditorium, which would seat about 2,000, the two home-economics buildings, music rooms, the new cafeteria, student-center, and finally the library. The latter is the only permanent building, and it will have to be renovated somewhat. Everything else is considered temporary. They have a master plan - blue prints, etc., will be ready November 15.

We went back into town, to the junior and senior high schools. Again, we went into the room where the board of directors, etc. meet. This time it was plush and leather-covered chairs! Time out for tea - an important part of Japanese life! The highlight of the trip was a 28- minute movie, just finished on the life of Kinjo College -...with English narration ... It is going to the States, the end of the month and will be shown around for about three months. In the room, where we saw the movie - B & W, there was a large TV, large hi-fi speakers, dimmers, and other expensive equipment. Auditorium was large and had a concert-grand piano on the stage - most impressive to the students. The head of the English Department took us over a few blocks to the junior high, a third campus purchased a few years ago. Old buildings, built at the end of the war, used inferior materials and so looks pretty run-down.

Adjoining was a new dorm for thirty-four girls - built this year. This campus had a swimming pool, and an exceptionally, large playing field. We ended our tour by hearing a part of the orchestra - about 30 out of 50, gotten together on a last minute notice. They played quite well, for a junior high group. Looked like nice instruments - said that they had a budget of $1,000, so things look fairly-rosy - though it is a drop in the bucket for 5,000 students. We went upstairs to see the assembly room of the building, the alumnae built. Around the walls were the pictures of those missionaries, who had been responsible for starting the school back in 1869. I couldn't help but feel humble, to think I would be part of this wonderful Christian school, and wonder if I would be able to contribute anything worthwhile.

Lunch in the board room was a Japanese meal, with beautiful lacquered wooden bowls to eat from. The first course was roasted eel! About four pieces 2" long over a bowl of rice. In the other covered bowl was soup - clear with a small egg, and about five, small peas in the bottom of the bowl - a very pretty dish indeed.

11/6/57: Many of the U.S. programs are rebroadcast here. We have one English radio station, news every hour and our English paper is eight pages, but is mainly international news, editorials translated from Japanese, articles on correct-English, for those learning English. No recipes, magazine section, Sunday cartoons, or human interest articles. We don't see as many trees, as we do in the States, for everything is cultivated, or houses built on it. Kinjo is far prettier and better equipped than we had ever thought. The college is on a hill - the school owns much of the hill - it is really quite a campus.

Harvesting rice is interesting. Ox carts in the fields, a small wagon which men could pull, a thrashing machine which is not much larger than a washing machine on wheels and with handles, so people can move it from place to place, and apparently run by kerosene. Everything here is done by hand, and every inch of the field is cultivated -

no room for tractor wheels, etc. Irrigation ditches, run at intervals throughout. Many times we saw the thrashing done with a large sifter, being shaken in the field by some individual. In the middle of one field, we saw a shrine.

Wish you could see the nurses at the hospital. Japanese girls are flat-busted and short with thick pigtails, so very popular with working girls and bobby socks. When they come after you with a hypodermic needle, they look like they should be playing with dolls instead. I can't do much talking, and it is a funny feeling never to quite know for sure what they're wanting you to do.

Thanksgiving, 1957: In Japan some advertising is done with large, balloons-flying over the store, in Tokyo recently they flew such a balloon with a dog inside of it. When buying meat, it is placed on a thin piece of paper, then wrapped in a dried-out, and rather stiff bamboo leaf. It is then tied with a strip of bamboo leaf, about 6 inches wide and 18 inches long. Merle is in (language) school today - Japanese Thanksgiving was last week. Larry is off since the Canadian Academy has one Japanese, one American and one Canadian holiday each year.

The Union Church (they attend) has twelve nationalities represented. The minister was a retired worker in a prisoner of war camp in Siberia, and the treasurer of the Sunday school was one of the prisoners he knew there.

It's getting cold and the fire feels good. People tell us not to worry about heating, but put on more clothes, and we are beginning to see what they mean, as it is real cold upstairs. We didn't have much of a Thanksgiving dinner, as you have to order turkeys ahead of time, and I just didn't anticipate it far enough ahead of time to do anything special. We have started on our second barrel of fuel oil. We only heat the living room, dining room, kitchen, as the upstairs remains like an iceberg, except for the bathroom when we are taking baths, we heat it with an electric heater.

12/14/57: Christmas is in the air. Stores are about like at home, very crowded, full of gifts, highly decorated - except for the fact you can't read anything, you'd think you were in America. Although Christmas is not a holiday and there are very few Christians here, it is a Japanese custom to give year-end gifts, ... as they get an extra month's pay at this time of the year. (The New Year is a really big holiday, gifts are given by everyone.) One thing, particularly interesting is Christmas is usually spelled X'mas. Carols and other Christmas songs are being played continually downtown - a secular Christmas with Christianity left out. So, much in the papers about other religions. There are so many shrines-(Shinto) and temples-(Buddhist) all over. The biggest department store in town has a Shinto shrine on the roof. It is good for business. The local Messiah concert was beautiful with 175 in the chorus, from the three local Christian colleges here, and 40 in the orchestra. With only three foreigners on the stage, the other two with dark hair, Merle's blonde hair stuck-out like a sore thumb!

Merle - visiting Nagoya to help Kinjo with same concert. ... We took a ride on Nagoya's new subway - again the prettiest and nicest I've ever seen. Bright yellow cars, light glass walls, and a large city of stores underground by the station. Most amazing, and the ride was only four minutes long for 15 yen - that's all they have finished so far, but it is fast! The other night we saw them making *omochi,* special New Years pounded-rice cakes. They steam the rice, then pound it with huge mallets, make it look like dough, and then someone kneads it, and makes it out like biscuits, before it is cooked. Teams go around and pound it in different areas. We just accidentally ran into a team about eleven o'clock the other night. One fellow was on one side of the road, steaming rice on outdoor charcoal stove. Three men on the other side of the road, pounding it in a large wooden crock - mallets about the size of croquet mallets. Three men pounding in rhythm and on the fourth beat, the fourth man sprinkled the rice with water and moved it, so they would hit another place. After the rice was pounded, a lady made it into cakes in a store which opened on to the street.

1/10/58: We see a lot of strange English (Jap-lish) - in the biggest department store in Kobe, an English sign was hung upside down for weeks. Hope you can see the movie *Sayonara*, as it was filmed in Kobe and is much like what we see every day. We saw pretty kimonos frequently around New Years - they are expensive and most people do not wear them even then.

The biggest problem to Christianity is Shinto. There was recently a series of articles in the English papers about Shinto. These presented Shinto as the one religion which will draw the East and West together, and gave a poor account of Christianity, misquoting several Bible passages. Before New Years the government in Kobe sent orders that students should be taken to shrines at New Years. This puts Christians in the position of compromise and points to the high nationalism of pre-war days. Many went to shrines who have never gone before. To some Christians it is a real religious problem, to others they see it as culture, and no problem at all. The missionaries are concerned. The Japanese Ministerial Association immediately had a meeting, sent protests to the Japanese newspapers and also to the National Ministry of Education.

Dollars can legally be converted into yen easily, but only a limited amount of yen can be converted to dollars. If we left the country, regardless of our assets here, we could only convert a couple hundred dollars back into dollars.

The Japanese are born imitators, and many times products look like American products, even down to similar wrappings, but they are not the same. Many of them do not have the producers' name on them, which means inferior products cannot be traced. American 'look' likes, they don't know the language, so tourist 'bargains' are not always what they appear.

1/28/58: Yesterday I went to the Takarazuka Theater and saw the show there, it was wonderful. Much like Radio City Music Hall, dancing and a play. The first hour was Japanese dancing with kimonos, tall wigs, and white painted faces. The next was a two hour show - a typical play held in New Orleans, all in Japanese. After the play, there was about 45 minutes of chorus line dancing.

Girls' day festival dolls are in all the stores now, and are quite expensive, ranging from $8 to thousands a set. They are all ceremonial dolls and elaborately dressed, very pretty. I'm dying to buy a set, but probably won't. For boys' day, people fly fish-kites for each boy in the house. Both this and girls day were Shinto holidays before the war, but most of the religious significance has gone … They are filling in the bombed-out ruins below our house. I suspect they are going to make a playground or build another building for the Catholic school. Trucks all day long, coming and going. Japanese stores instead of having a printed menu, has regular-size dishes with wax food showing what they have to eat. For us it is convenient.

We heard an interesting war story last week from one of the Japanese members of Union Church. She, with a few others, held things together during WW II. The missionaries, of course, were gone and Americans were the enemy. Because one of the American trustees had failed to resign, the property was considered enemy property, since the property belongs to the trustees. However, only the building and grounds belonged to the trustees, with the equipment in it belonging to the people of the church … There was a group of English-speaking people here and also the German congregation. The German pastor spoke English, so he became the pastor also for the English people, and the government tried to disband the English congregation. The German pastor told them he was the pastor, and if he decided to preach some of his sermons in English, it was his business. For almost the entire war, services were held in English regularly. The church also helped the American and 'enemy' internees stationed here in Kobe.

The city officials here in Kobe, recently prepared a booklet which they sent down to all the school children, to tell them how to act in a Shinto shrine. When the Christian ministers protested, the booklet was withdrawn, but no public explanation has been made. The news- paper refused to get involved in it, and will not print the ministers' protest, or anything against Shinto. There is a move in the national government to take 'religious Shinto' classification from the three biggest shrines, and place them again under the government. This means the government would support the shrines. The pressures put on the Japanese people and especially the pastors are hard. This whole problem of ancestor-worship is tremendous. Even in one of the Christian publications now, there is advertised a family shelf with places to put the pictures of the departed ancestors. It is so hard to get away from something that is so much in the culture. This week for the first time, I have found an English account for tourists on how to worship at the shrines. Taxi drivers all have dangling dolls in their taxis. It seems they are for good luck. In ancient times, dolls were rubbed against the body on certain days, in the Shinto shrines, thinking these dolls took bad luck and illnesses from the body. They were then thrown into the river, later the dolls were kept as good luck symbols.

We see articles frequently in the newspaper about atom bomb victims who have committed suicide - have seen probably six or eight already this year (1958) They have more cancer and malformations of the bones, TB and general higher susceptibility to disease.

2/13/58: (Charles eye exam) Instead of the privacy of an examining room, like we have in America, it was more like a public clinic, with a large room … One of our biggest problems in raising kids here is, our foreign youngsters are so 'cute' every place they go. From the time we step out of our front door, we are stared at all the time. One gradually gets used to it, but it does keep you on your toes. In shopping, five clerks watch you when you try to buy something, and the whole streetcar full of people look up and stare at you, when you get on. This is especially true if you are talking English, or if you have children with you. Anyway, here was little Charles having his eyes examined, with fifty people staring at him.

On our way to the train station, we went past the big Buddhist temple, so we stopped the taxi and walked through the temple. A large cluster of buildings - along the outside were six little stands all selling the same things. At the temple, they were selling peanuts to feed the pigeons, which were so thick and so tame … Inside we just walked around the grounds. I didn't have enough nerve to go inside the temple, but we could see the rows of shoes on the outside, from people who had gone in. I probably would have gone in if I had been alone, but wasn't sure it was smart taking Charles. Had no idea what it might be. The whole thing was about two blocks square. The little stands on the outside sold postcards, Buddhist rosaries, big hats, incense and fancy scarves.

2/14/58: Merle - I saw a 1958 Edsel in Kobe, and a few weeks ago a 1937 Ford, which looked like it had just come off the showroom floor. Labor is cheaper here, and all the autos are well taken care of. You hardly ever see a car that doesn't have one or two, long feather dusters, along the back window ledge. Yesterday, I saw the man at the gas station dusting off his customer's car. That'll be the day when they dust off your car at home! Just had our 6th barrel of fuel oil delivered. **Arlene** - Got all three of the kids getas a couple weeks ago, and they are so thrilled. They are wooden shoes which have the strip through the two big toes, and are worn outside with cloth socks called tabi.

3/10/58: Took the kids to a Kabuki show, ... a stage play with all the parts taken by men. Slow, recited in a sing-song type of language, so we understood nothing. Kids were good for the first three hours, we left and missed the last hour and half. We were pretty tired of it - didn't enjoy it much. Merle took Larry ice skating Saturday afternoon, and he had five or six Japanese adults helping him - he knows how to skate, but they were showing hm some fancy steps, etc. The Japanese love children, so with their desire to use English, and not being afraid to try it on children, and with Larry's being unafraid to try Japanese, he has had a lot of interesting conversations, whenever he goes out.

We see men urinating any old place they want to. In most places, the toilets are for both men and women with no distinction. The women have little private rooms on one side, while the men line up in plain sight on the other using the urinal. We have so ingrained our boys, with the need of privacy they refuse to go, until there is no one else there, or unless they go over to a little room. We are strictly in a man's world here. The men will almost knock you over to get in and off a bus ahead of you.

The kids (Charles & Roy) dig our yard up pretty much, but since they are happy, we just let them do it. So, they play in the yard and get stared at by the Japanese children. You have no idea how this staring keeps up. I guess we'll get used to it, but we surely do get looked over all the time, when we are not in the house. As soon as we step out the front door, someone is watching - I'm not exaggerating. It is one of the problems and adjustments I never anticipated.

We got a cabin at Nojiri for the entire summer (an old foreigner's retreat area in north Nagano Prefecture, also used for their war internment.). The first summer, we have had to plan what to do with a vacation. We never had them. Another thing which impressed me, is the slowness of work in Japan - the few numbers of baptism, the numerical smallness of the church, the amount of help necessary to the national church. I knew before we came, numerically Japan was the slowest of all our mission fields, but I never realized how slow, and how hard the Christian work in Japan actually is. Numbers are in the tens and twenties, rather than in the hundreds and thousands. Of the many who hear, so few are willing to break with ancestor worship, and with family ties and traditions.

That's one reason why student work is one of the most rewarding, as most converts are young people. They are away from the families, and a little more independent. You have no idea how many crowds we draw every place we go. I'd like to know how many photo albums we are in. Roy is especially popular. If he sees someone taking a picture, he gets self-conscious. With his blonde hair and young innocence, he makes a good picture.

5/5/58: I always thought babies were alike the world over, but I was wrong - also mothers are different (Arlene is now pregnant). American babies weigh at birth about two pounds more, and are fatter and bigger boned than Japanese children. Their bottoms and chubby legs just don't fit into Japanese rubber britches!! And, the main reason we stopped using them for Roy at night. Just buying larger sizes doesn't always solve the problem, since Japanese mothers dress their children in skirts and pants inches shorter than we consider decent.

5/16/58: Merle - Larry asked me before his birthday party, "Please don't sing 'Happy Birthday,' or have cake, or open presents outside. For if we do, there will be a gang of Japanese children watching over the fence." He simply did not want to be the center of attraction.

Larry and Roy bought a stack of comics. We can buy American comics second-hand for about three cents each, new ones cost about fifty cents each. Saturday Evening Post here cost $1; can you imagine for a 15 cent magazine? Someone gave us about fifty, English-Army and Navy hymnbooks this morning, with a bookcase to put them in. The military chapels are closing, and all equipment has to be given to charitable groups.

We will need slippers for meetings in our homes. We must have a pair for each person who comes into our home, they are left here, but twenty guests means twenty pairs of slippers. Many Japanese shoes are wooden and cannot be worn inside, and their western shoes usually have metal cleats in the heel, to make them last longer. We had to get Larry some *zori* - sandals. I knew they would be cheap, the gym shoes he wears are less than a buck, I was shocked when they cost only 10 yen. They are thick, straw-soles with straps through the toes.

5/30/58: Now it is warm, so you can tell the difference in a Japanese complexion, as they tan quickly. The children are getting a dark suntan. Adults are very careful not to get a tan, if they can help it. The women use umbrellas in the sun, tie scarves up around their necks, and the men put extra sleeves over their arms.

In the public baths, people take off their shoes and put them in a shoe boxes at the door. They go on and take off their clothes and put them in a wooden locker. Then they sit down on little stools, and with a bucket of clean water - sometimes cold, wash and rinse themselves before they enter into a big, pool-like tub. They then sit in steaming water, as long as they want. Of course, there maybe dozens in the tub, too. They take a cold shower afterwards, if they want. The whole thing costs 15 yen. There is a women attendant at the door, or sometimes a man who sees in both the men's side and the women's side, to take-up money, sell soap, etc. Until the war, it was mixed bathing, but the American Army of Occupation put a stop to it. The Japanese consider our bathing unsanitary, since we wash and sit in the same dirty water. We consider theirs unsanitary, because it is public.

6/4/58: Tomorrow I'm going to Nagoya to look over the house. Army houses are being torn down and one is available to move to Kinjo campus for us for a good price, provided the house is OK. The Nagoya missionaries think it is a good deal, and want us to see the houses before they went farther with their plans.

Merle - This morning the family went together to walk to a neighborhood shopping center, we had not been to before. I wish you could see it - no amount of description would make you believe it! Imagine a one-way street - room for only one car, most of the time, and imagine a mile or more of nothing but small shops both sides of the street. What they have to sell is arranged on boxes, which extend out into the street. When they close, they have to bring their products into the shops, and put up either wooden or metal grill work for protection. I noticed more of the shopping areas - due to prosperity, I guess, are putting up steel awnings over the street, with plastic corrugated sheets. These can slide back to let fresh air in, or can be closed during the rain or excessive sunshine, so business can go on as usual. Some areas are like low-ceiling tunnels, with little shops selling everything. In this 'tunnel,' the shop keepers are singing or yelling, inviting you to buy from them. The noise, added to the pungent smells, creates an interesting trip. In general, or until my taste buds change, everything in the cookie and candy shops, look a lot better than most of it tastes!

6/11/58: Merle went to Nagoya last weekend to see the house and came back enthusiastic over it. Four bedrooms, lots of closets, etc. No maid's room, but it can be built-on in back. No place for trunks, but the common practice is to build a little outside shed, for that type of stuff. However, there is a real problem about the land, since the place they had in mind is probably too small.

The biggest inconvenience over here, is our physical size. Not being able to buy clothes or shoes is a problem. Probably the worst thing is never finding a comfortable seat. When we go to a concert, it takes about fifteen minutes before I look at my watch, to see how much longer before it is over. The seats just aren't for someone as tall as we are. Merle and I can hardly sit together on the bus, in a double seat. Folding chairs are virtually impossible. Ice cream parlors use regular stools or chairs, but the tables are low - like a child's table. Even the Japanese have to lean over. I always feel so awkward, and alway glad when I finish, usually bumping the table with my knees when I sit down.

Coming home from school one day last week, Merle saw the Police Band in the ball field down the road. The Police Band is a full- time, professional band and we have heard them play frequently. They play for boats-departing, for athletic functions, and for many of the occasions a high school band would play for at home. There are about thirty in the band, in full military-type uniforms, and really good. Orchestras seem to be more popular here than bands, and bands don't seem to go out for maneuvering, like in America.

Merle goes to Nagoya Friday and stays until Monday. Going to play Mozart's Requiem with Kinjo choir and the radio orchestra, with rehearsal Friday and concert Saturday. Sunday they are taping for the mission radio programs. He goes for this about once every six weeks, stays in the control room and acts more or less as the producer.

I hardly know what to do sometimes, during those hours when I need to be with the kids, yet not much to do except play with them. I get itching to cook especially, but everything in the kitchen is so low and it soon gets me down. My kitchen sink is two inches below the bottom edge of my maternity smocks! I see the girls at the school in their summer uniforms, with large brimmed white hats. The rain umbrellas are plain and dark, but the parasols are bight colors, so pretty, you almost never see a woman without one. The language school gave Merle a mimeographed list, containing all the kanji characters in the hymnbook, and their pronunciation and meaning. We will leave for Nojiri in about three weeks.

6/23/58: All of the older missionaries talk as if Nojiri is about next to heaven itself. And, from the stories we have heard, all of us new ones can't possibly see how it can be much. No running water, drinking water has to be boiled, no gas, but there is electricity, which is so weak you frequently can't read at night. But, plenty of activities - music night, stunt night, water shows, children's swimming lessons, climbing mountains, the lake, Vacation Bible School, mainly for missionaries.

I don't like chopsticks, and the kids can hardly manipulate them. However, I do manage to get a meal down, with the telltale marks on my dress, lots of scraps left on the plate, and cramps in my right hand. We always get chopsticks when eating out - one time they brought me a fork - sometimes bring the kids a spoon, and we use them in eating Japanese food here at home. I sometimes give up before the meal is over!

Merle - Went to a wedding of a teacher at the Canadian Academy this afternoon. Complete with a 3-tiered cake, bouquet,, throwing rice and the tin cans with shoes tied to the car. I wondered what the on-looking Japanese thought of throwing away good, rationed rice. Maybe they feel the rice and the shoes were just part of the odd superstitions of the Christians. As the car pulled away, one of the most surprised looks came from the rag-picker, who was searching the garbage box across the street - quite the contrast to the joyful celebration of the wedding. I am constantly amazed and amused at the kids, to hear how much Japanese customs and words come-up automatically in their conversations - in ours, too, for that matter. When Charles and Roy are 'selling things' now, it is always in yen.

7/17/58: (On the way to Lake Nojiri) Left Kobe Monday about noon, took a lunch with us, and rode four hours on an electric train - had seats all the way. Spent the night in Nagoya, got a train about 10:00 and rode until 4:30, also had seats. A coal train, and our only air was open windows. There were 52 tunnels, and the air really got foul in them. Even when we closed the windows, going through the tunnels, the smoke was bad inside. We really felt our lungs were seared by the time we got here. At most of the stations, vendors went by the train selling lunches, frozen tangerines, ice cream, Japanese tea, coffee, etc. It fascinated the kids. We had our lunch and our thermos, but got ice cream several times. We got to our station here, got a taxi on up to Lake Nojiri. We drove about three miles over bumpy roads, that no pregnant woman would dare ride on in America. My heart sank, as I saw us approaching the place, grown up with weeds on either side. Finally stopped in front of a house, set-up in the midst of weeds up to our waist, all around it. Our cabin is nice. All unfinished inside, about the size of a six car garage, with beautiful views overlooking the lake. There are about four feet of yard in back of the house, and the rest is nothing but steep hill. The boys love it - I don't really mind - so far at least. We have a hot plate in the kitten and two hibachi - charcoal burners on the porch.

There are 214 adults and 220 kids, plus maids here now. Not all English-speaking missionaries in many denominations. There is a Japanese worship for maids, and local Japanese people on Sunday afternoon. Thursday night there is Japanese Bible class, and recreation for the maids. Even up here, we can look out and see a Shinto shrine. Larry has become very conscious of who is, and who isn't a Christian. He is constantly asking me, the difference between Christian and non- Christin. It stares you in the face all the time.

Summer '58: Merle - If we take to Nojiri, and it looks like we will, we will probably end-up buying, or building a summer cottage here. We just got a card yesterday, saying the mission made the highest bid on a group of army-surplus houses, and have a house for us in Nagoya. They have to tear it down and move it within forty days. The area where it is, will then be used for a city park (Shirokawa). The houses are about eight years old, so should last a long time.

Walter said the way Japanese do things, the house wouldn't be ready much before we are ready to move in (Sept., 1959). They will build it on the junior high campus, and get a bulldozer to level off the land. The Japanese move grown trees around like flowers, so will plant trees when it is finished. We have just come back from being on the lake, where we had our first hymn-sing on the water this year … They put a pump organ on one of the boats, and anybody who has a sailboat or a row/motor boat, loads up with people to go to the middle of the lake. They also rent several boats from the village. About three hundred people were on the lake singing.

8/16/58: In the church, there was a special session meeting to solve the problem of what to do about shoes, as people come to Church: Where can we put them all, or should people start wearing shoes in church? Instead of ushers, people were putting shoes on shelves - the Japanese version of parking problems.

There is a good supply of small baby clothes available in the mission. Many churches send clothes, and don't allow for the time- element of transportation, so the small things get here too late. If it is a boy, I cannot use anything red or with a sailor motif - strictly girls- stuff here. Here adults stand and give children seats on the streetcar … I stand and let Roy have a seat - even though I could sit and hold him. That's Japan!

JUMP AHEAD IN TIME

5/13/59: Dolls little girls play with, are Western-style dolls, usually with blonde hair. There seems to be a real liking for blonde hair, and mannequins at the stores - even those modeling kimonos usually have blonde or red hair. Other dolls in Japan are objects of beauty, and are exhibited much like we would use a pretty vase or a bouquet of flowers. These are usually tall, thin, willowy, unrealistic dolls with some unrealistic bend of the body, and are on stands to be put under a glass case. They are beautiful - some of them. Some have weird faces - sometimes wearing historical masks, etc. They run anywhere from a quarter to hundreds of dollars.

Yokan is a candy made from gelatin and soy beans. It is quite a luxury here, but frankly we aren't wild about it. Bean past is usually black, and is in the middle of almost all buns and sweet rolls. One of the first Japanese sentences I learned, was how to ask if there was anything in the middle of a roll, I was buying. However, getting used to it, and eat lots more bean paste-rolls now than we did on arrival.

Merle - Exciting to see three to four thousand people gathering for a Christian meeting at the Osaka Crusade. The average Japanese church is between six and fifty in attendance. The Osaka Crusade was a big success, and for Japan almost unbelievable. Three hundred churches went together to put on the Crusade … Last night there was standing room only, with 3000 outside unable to get in. Nearly 8,000 people have gone forward, in response to the Gospel Call.

5/27/59: Movers were out today to check on things, and I am ready to start packing. They said I would have nothing to do, unless I wanted to put a few things in barrels. First time I haven't done it all. We will be leaving here on July 11, pack here during the day, movers will drive at night, and get to Nagoya by 9:00 the next morning. We will go on up to Nojiri soon, as the house isn't finished enough to live in it. Sembi - Rice crackers is much like peanuts or pop corn. You may not be wild about it, but after you take one piece, you can't resist one more.

Most diapers are made of kimono material - seconds, but about one and a half yards long, ends sewed together, so as to make a circle. They use two, one circle is folded under the crotch, another folded around the tummy and tied. They consider pins unsafe for babies. To dry, a bamboo pole is run through the sewed circle. Hung to dry, they are colorful.

7/18/59: **Merle** - Last Monday morning the movers came at 9:30 am… didn't leave until 9:30 pm. Arlene said they arrived at 8 am (in Nagoya) after having left Kobe about midnight. The floor varnish was sticky, but we hope it will be dry by the time we get back (from Nojiri), carpenters and painters came for last minute touch-ups, etc. Kinjo officials came by, and we spent an hour or so deciding what to do about a fence around the house. But our living room windows will not have any 'protection' from curious Kinjo girls ... the main point of the fence, venetian blinds will be nice.

With shrines and temples, wayside shrines, god-shelves in the stores, etc. Charles and Larry both are still quite conscious of the difference between Christian and non-Christian. Raising children in a bicultural, bilingual, biracial situation certainly gives them a different kind of duration.

8/28/59: The move to Nagoya has been the most hectic move we have ever made. They worked in the house some this summer, but there is still lots to be done. Yesterday, they painted three rooms, plus all the windows. The house was awfully dirty, the tatami room was full of building junk. None of the closets are ready to use - either they were done wrong, or not done yet. The floors are ruined, will have to be done over again. Something seems to be wrong with the paint, for they are still sticky. We are a fascination to the Kinjo girls - we're really living in a fish bowl. The staring will probably stop before long, but they come right-up looking into the windows now. This morning at breakfast, there were five or six watching us. Last night, when I was reading to Larry, three had their ears to the screen, listening to the foreign language.

9/20/59: Merle - I sat through three junior high classes today, and understood almost nothing except what I said. A company which cleans office buildings waxed the (house) floors professionally. The floors are not deluxe, since it was old wood and not #1 grade, but with stain, polish, lacquer and wax, they really look nice now. We have a yard man trying to get the yard in shape for grass and shrubs. Tomorrow I will be teaching four classes of 9th grade girls, who don't understand any English, so 'I will be on my own' - mistakes and all.

9/22/59: The boys enjoy the Kinjo girls. Larry plays with them as equals. Charles is a little self-conscious around them. Roy wraps them around is finger. Scarcely a day passes that one of the girls doesn't bring some trinket for one of the boys.

One of our Nisei missionaries broke a minor traffic regulation, and was stopped by the police. When he could't understand the police, the police thought he was being impudent, got mad, and took him into headquarters. The more the missionary tried to explain, the madder the police got. Finally, the missionary showed his alien registration, which gave all the information … Everyone cooled down and apologized, and let him off. I have never been stopped to show mine, but Merle was stopped once on the streetcar, and asked for his.

9/26/59: Last night the Isewan Typhoon hit Nagoya. The house really shook, roof was partially blown off and leaked like a sieve. We first started to protect the walls under the windows, then put pans to protect the floors. Finally got so much water in the attic, we took slacks off the celling, so the water could come down. The water came in gushes - we waded in inches of water all over the front part of the house.

Some of the houses around us are completely down, others pretty beat up. Today we have no water or electricity, and very little gas. The morning paper says, "Japan was walloped by the worst typhoon in a quarter of a century, counted about 2500 dead, or missing yesterday, with more than 900,000 homeless. The harbor of the industrial city of Nagoya, one of the hardest hit, was described as a 'sea of dead.' Seven ocean-going ships lay-grounded like beached- whales in the area … A deadly blow was given to the rice crops, ready for autumn harvest, as well the fruit and vegetable crops."

In town, huge trees were uprooted, concrete fences blown down, lots of houses collapsed. Helicopters and airplanes flown all day today and yesterday to bring in wounded, and transported emergency supplies. Kinjo will have no school for a week or more. Merle plans to help in relief work today. Red Cross, Church World Service, etc., have sent in plane loads of blankets, etc. Helicopters picking up and landing within view of our house, then seeing them load and land again later at the hospital. It is gruesome.

9/30/59: The newspaper said some 300 ships sunk. Kinjo College is 90% unusable, roofs of two new buildings completely destroyed. Lots of the worst-hit areas haven't been heard from yet. Afraid of dysentery epidemic, still boiling water, fighting-flies furiously. There are still 160,000 people on rooftops waiting to be rescued from the seawall collapsed. The problem in rescuing is mainly not having boats, as so many were washed away.

We have requested the mission hospital to send some doctors and nurses, if they can spare them. Unless rescue teams can work faster than they are now, the death toll will rise considerably. The houses may not stand up long, with the ocean waves. Seems the problem is the need for boats, equipment and trained people like doctors. Two doctors from the mission hospital came today and spending the night in Nagoya.

10/1/59: People are walking out of the water, boats cannot get clear to dry land, soaking wet in shorts, slips etc., half dazed, almost in a state of shock, too much so to be hungry. Various workers and medical people are waiting for them, giving medicine, treating wounds, spraying everything and everyone, coming out of the water with disinfectant. Pastors and churches are organizing a Christian Relief Center from which supplies can be sent. A work camp is being organized by Christian forces in one of the worst areas. It is a God- given opportunity for Christians in this area to show the love and concern of Christ for individuals, and to do something about it.

An American ship came to Nagoya to help with the rescue operations. They have been here in port since

Wednesday, using as best they can the facilities of the ship. The men on the ship donated

$3,000 for relief. They located a school in which some 500 children are being housed, their parents have as yet not been rescued or found. In nearby buildings, another thousand children are housed. We spent time trying to get a relief program into operations, all exasperatingly tied-up with useless red tape and confusion.

There are two (mission) doctors, two nurses, two drivers and a lab technician living in Nagoya now, and they are sharing our mission homes. We can expect two to four men in here for dinner almost any time after 6:00. As of now, I'm not sure how many are spending the night with us. Of course, they need gallons of boiled water, lunches, laundry, etc., so it keeps us jumping. The U.S. aircraft carrier in port gave a truckload of gauze to the Japanese officials, but it was in yards and not ready to use. Hundreds of Kinjo students are spending the afternoon cutting, folding, and preparing bandages from this gauze. Yesterday the radio station called, wanting to interview the staff on the medical team and to hear about what the missionaries were doing …

The aircraft carrier has been in the harbor for three or four days with both large and small rescue boats available. However, they have to have a navigator who know the seaways, a sailor who knows the boats and an interpreter. City officials for some reason haven't warmed up to missionary interpreters. They can't work without being asked by the city officials. Missionaries are doing all they can to speed up operations, get the several thousand sailors on the ship to work, etc.

10/9/59: The industrial damage is terrific, and many people are without jobs. Lumber companies in the area had millponds full of huge logs. These were bounced all over the place in the raging wind and water, literally pounding on buildings and houses, until they are crushed under the weight. Many people, who got out of their houses were killed by logs. Bodies are still being recovered everyday. Today a medical team from the Baptist hospital came … As far as anyone can find out no pastors or missionaries in the area suffered personal injury or death, within their families. We still don't know who or when people are coming in for meals, but things throughout the town seem to be taking some shape. Now the figure is over 5,000 killed.

The Empress-to-be is pregnant. She told the gods in the Shinto ceremony recently, putting on the traditional blessed-belt, which she will wear until delivery time.

Merle has visited, either alone or with a team of his organizing, some fifteen housing centers - he's now pretty independent with his Japanese. Mine surely has improved during the last three months. The medical work is going fine, too. Work teams of Christian students from mission schools all over Japan came in … Yesterday the whole operation got a big write-up in the English newspaper.

11/8/59: Today I went down to the school where the medical team has been working, and spent all morning making-up powdered milk and distributing it to the children. So much trash and debris all around, although people are busy cleaning up. Just carting the debris away is a terrific job. Acres even yet of trash, broken wood, just as the wind blew it. Japanese medical teams were ashamed, since our team gave- out vitamin pills, and they didn't, so now they are giving them out.

Government officials were so taken aback when the Christian workers went into areas with fresh vegetables, so they started to do it, too. Went out on the milk routine again this week, fixed over 100 lbs. of powdered milk - enough for 1600 children. The floors are not yet fixed, and still have only temporary tin-repairs on the roof. Merle left at 6 am to visit six refugee centers, it is 10 pm. and he is still not back.

End Note: These letters go on for several hundred more pages, and deal with the daily life of this missionary family in Nagoya, and how they handled situations great as the typhoon, or simple interaction between their four growing boys. It took several more years before 'shocks' did not affect them, such as a Japanese teenager committing suicide by immolation, because he had failed his college entrance exam, or the anti-American riots and demonstrations with "Stay Home Ike," over the 1960 Security Treaty Pack.

They also had to deal with the adjustments of reverse-cultural shock, when they returned every five years or so, for their one year furlough to the States. To this would be added, children whose Japanese was sometimes better than their English, or English heavily peppered with Japanese. They did get a cabin up in Nojiri, which became their retreat and haven, for not only its relaxed atmosphere, but also being a mutual foreign community, one place in Japan where they were not "gaijin on parade."

As noted at the beginning, Merle had been a graduate of the prestigious Juilliard School of Music, but unlike his famous classmates, he chose to teach junior high in a Christian school in Japan. He had great distinction at Kinjo, and as a musical educator, he developed an instrumental music program, trained the orchestra, directed concerts of The Messiah, and was responsible for starting the handbell and harp programs. The handbell program at Kinjo was the first in Japan, and served as a model for other schools. Merle assisted many schools in developing musical activities, community musical activity, assisting in the development of church music, participating in and presenting musical programs, and helping to organize the Japan Bandmasters Association and the Handbell Ringers of Japan. He was also the first foreigner to be honored, as an outstanding teacher in Central Japan by the Chunichi Newspaper Educational Award in 1979. Unfortunately, Merle died suddenly in August, 1980. Arlene stayed on at Kinjo teaching English until 1989, its one hundredth birthday, when she retired and returned to America the last time.

~~~~~~

The Japanese themselves have kind of settled into a balance of their 'use' of foreign religions in Japan. Other than those devout Christians - there are those who are quasi or Sunday Christians - of whom there are perhaps a million, most Japanese follow an eclectic combination. Many young people like to be married in a church, (particularly if they've chosen a 'love' marriage, instead of an arranged one) and the denomination usually does not really matter, they just like the atmosphere. Though many will also follow it with a Shinto wedding service, and most are traditionally buried Buddhist, as it requires the family to continue to honor them, at periodic set-intervals.

The Japanese no longer put Santa Claus on a cross, as they did the first Christmas under SCAP, but it is still a secular 'Xmas' for the majority. They may not know who St. Patrick was, but love the green, and may celebrate St. Valentine's day in two days rather than one - February 14th, for girls to give to boys, and March 1st, "White Day," for boys to give to girls, not as heavily practiced, of course.

Even Halloween has become quite popular, believing it to be the Christian version of Obon, their celebration of the return of the ancestor spirits. Japanese still think all Americans are 'Christian,' and they basically want to imitate anything American, so holidays are enthusiastically adapted, if not misconstrued. Many of the Western/ Christian holidays are also picked-up or practiced, because it is good business, another excuse to give a gift. Or simply, they look like fun things to play at, or celebrate in their own Japanese way.

Most of the trains still have good luck Shinto talisman-tokens encased in glass for travel safety, and half of the population goes to the Shrines or temples at New Years, their biggest family holiday. Yet, Japan is not tied to any true doctrine or belief, as it was before under the Emperor system or the Shogunates, and most doubt it will ever happen again. It has even had *Christian* Prime Ministers! Few in Japan take their religions seriously, however many they may follow, arduously, and what seems to work for them. Still, most will usually say, 'they are not religious.'

The golden missionary days of the 1800s and post-War are over, and few are sent any more for serious evangelism, except the Mormons and the Seventh Day Adventists. There are still a few Japanese 'nationalists' who ride around in their sound-trucks playing old national war songs, but they are laughed at by most, and an embarrassment to the rest. Today enough foreigners speak at least some Japanese, and only in the back country are they stared at, with a vigor which bothers the new gaijin, who have never been the object of staring or prejudice.

The colorful and raucous festivals of Buddhism and Shintoism are enjoyed greatly, without piety, by foreigners and natives alike. Especially the fertility ones, where giant, plastic penises are carried around and fondled. Sex is considered more a bodily function, than the romanticism or moral responsibility Westerners, especial the American Christians attach. Therefore, unwed mothers, or illegitimate children are rare, more a matter of choice. An open acceptance of abortion, rather than a child not being well-supported, or looked down upon by society. With all the modern affluence, since the 1980s/90s 'Bubble Economy Era,' the commonality of 'business-sex tours' to Seoul, Thailand, and the Philippines, AIDS was the final retribution, not Christianity, but Karma. Still, even with the current economy, the older Japanese men would prefer to buy Viagra, than a new silk tie.

PART III: Living As A *Gaijin* in Japan - A Different Cultural Perspective Chapter 9 - Education of the Masses - English and Otherwise

There is a certain kind of arrogance of trying to show that they are better than foreigners especially. This may most often be common from government clerks, office people, customs inspectors, etc. The typical little person who holds an important position in making some decision in the foreigner's life. You know, they have to resent the money, prestige or special treatment foreigners receive, just because they are foreigners. There are also those Japanese of relatively brief acquaintance, who expect more of a foreigner than they are really entitled to. Sometimes they think because they have a certain fluency in English, they have an instant friendship and privilege to make demands, which they become quite indignant when you refuse. The implied obligation in Japan is one which is not expected to be rejected and when a foreigner does, he is usually totally rejected thereafter.

Robert Christopher,
Japan As We Lived It

Japanese Education:

Foreigners have long presumed there was something mysterious about the Japanese, which made their character so extraordinarily different. In past days, some thought it was their diet, or even the way they ate, their "Zenish" spiritual beliefs and practices, or maybe their ability to perfect minute things. Yet today, as we have learned, emulated, and perhaps improved on each of these and others things, we know the difference is in their group-behavior. The more Japanese people one knows, the more their similarities are duplicated. To such an extent, now, they have become the most stereotyped people in the world.

It is no longer the 'Mysterious' Orient, with all Asian nations categorized together. For those who have studied Japanese, know they are all quite unique. Even with China's largesse, the numerous ethnic areas are intrinsically-individualized. It seems then, the *only large* population of people to be *so similar* in their actions and behavior is the Japanese. Actually, the answer is very simple and easy to explain: education. But, the trick here is, it is more the education *outside* the books, than inside them.

The formalized culture and systemized role-playing, which influences the deepest and most personal levels of the Japanese, are taught - to all, in exactly the same manner. At least the ones who want to fit into, not ostracized and be welcomed in 'the group,' and this means any group, which is important to them. This is not a magic wand, but as previously mentioned prior, the step-by-step process of 'ka' Japanese acculturation, systematically embedded from infancy to adulthood, or longer if necessary. It is also called shikata, kata - for short or '*the way* of doing things.' It is more than just the mechanical process of doing something, as it incorporates the hundreds of physical and spiritual laws of their cosmos.

Most importantly though, it teaches the way things are *supposed* to be done. Years ago, before a lot of gaijin came to Japan, or the Japanese traveled to other non-Asian countries, they actually believed the whole world was taught these same things. Ignorance of them was then, considered to be extremely stupid, and therefore *not to do them* a shock, as if 'how did they - others, exist without the ka?' - Japanese way. The Japanese Way of form with order, is a means of expressing and maintaining wa, 'harmony' in the society. Thus, the absence of shikata is *virtually unthinkable* to the Japanese, for it refers to an unreal world, without order or form. Much like they consider the United States, where people do what they want most of the time, somewhat within their laws.

Early in their history, the Japanese developed the belief 'form' had a reality of its own, and it often took precedence over *substance*. They also believed anything could be accomplished, if the right 'kata' was mentally and physically practiced long enough. Since most of Japan's numerous kata have been well established for centuries, the average Japanese neither thinks about them, nor questions them.

Over the generations, more than habits, the kata not only became institutionalized, they also became ritualized and sanctified. Doing things the *right way* was often more important than doing the *right things*. Eventually, the proper observance of kata was equated with morality - thus doing something the wrong way was a *sin* against society, which could be fatal. This linking the individual to society, meant if one did not follow the correct form, one was out-of-harmony with both his fellow man, and their perfect kata-world.

Cultural conditioning based on the kata system, made the Japanese extremely sensitive to *any* thought, manner, or action which did not conform perfectly to the appropriate kata. In formal, as well as most daily situations, every action was either right or wrong, natural or unnatural. There were no shades of gray to accommodate individualistic thought, preferences, or personal idiosyncrasies. Just as there was only one acceptable way to perform all the various actions of life in pre-industrial Japan, from using chopsticks to wrapping a package. Thus, there was *naturally* only one-right-way of thinking - the "Japanese" way. This is still shown most often, so unconsciously, by Japanese when they speak: "We Japanese ," as if each individual has the ability, knowledge, and permission to speak for the other one hundred fifty million Japanese.

The shikata, or cultural molds, responsible for making the Japanese formidable in peace and war, began as mechanical processes designed to perform specific actions, and create specific products. Among the earliest and most pervasive of the shikata were the way of wet-rice farming, the way of court etiquette, the way of writing kanji, the tea ceremony, the making of arts and crafts, the way of the Samurai, the use of layered-Japanese language honorifics and a strict daily etiquette based on a hierarchical system of seniority and sex.

The most foundational was the wet-rice farming, introduced into Japan from China some three thousand years ago. To be successful, - and unsuccessful meant starvation - it demanded a highly organized group system of cooperation and coordination. Any minor deviation angered not only one's family, friends, and neighbors, but the *gods* as well.

One could say, it was the basis of kata because it began the need for group behavior, self-sacrifice, and made harmony mandatory. Since non-conformity could spell death to all, any individual who did not conform was quickly ostracized to protect and sustain the group, which became vastly more important than the individual. It would be understandable the planting, cultivating, and harvesting would have to be done identically, so no problems helping each other. Yet, the singularity of form was then carried over to the cooking and eating of the rice, also.

Another exacting-example of kata was the kanji system of writing, also imported from China. It required years of concentrated effort to master, so had a fundamental effect on the psychological and physical development of all educated Japanese. It ingrained in them patience and diligence, enhanced manual dexterity well beyond the norm. It prepared them for a lifestyle in which a step-process and order were paramount. Learning how to draw the thousands of kanji characters, also imbued the Japanese with a highly developed sense of harmony, form, and style. This combination gave them a deep understanding and appreciation of aesthetics, making each of them an artist of no little skill. Another side benefit, they became experts at doing small, complicated things with their hands, which enhanced their sensitivity to balance and design. The kanji training also conditioned the Japanese to persevere in their goals, and thus became a mold which shaped them physically, emotionally, and intellectually, while homogenizing and binding them to their culture.

From the 12th century on, the Samurai warrior class began to develop their own set of kata, involving discipline, physical ability with weapons, as well their own spiritual training. Since Buddhism came into Japan in the next century, stylized from Korea, the Samurai adapted it as the basis of their lives, from their loyalty to the Shogun, to the mesmerizing affects of Zen concentration against pain. Because they were held in esteem of the highest class, many Japanese were inspired, wishing to possess or emulate their stylized manners, fearlessness of death, and shear sacrifice for a belief. Though they fell from the pedestal, and disintegrated with the Meiji Restoration, their spirits were resurrected, punched up, and used *falsely* as the fake term of 'Bushido,' to pump up the naive, invading Japanese soldiers.

Among the warrior-class Samurai, who followed a strong sect of Buddhism which forbade the love of women, it was frequently proclaimed love for a woman was an effeminate-feeling. The love of a man was more than mere sensual gratification or desperation, based on a lasting relationship of loyalty and devotion. Homosexuality was less of a taboo, as most gay men marry to have children, as the necessary facade of a home life for modern business.

Many women, therefore, accept a hidden-homosexual husband, because less chance of losing her own position, or of having her home broken-up by another woman. Japan is more accepting of having its arts practiced as much by men as women. The best and most famous of the male prostitutes were in the Kabuki. Yet, most Western men see Japanese men as either the cold, cruel war stereotype, or being quite effeminate, unending smiles of their polite repartee, displayed today.

The arts were kata-ized in Kabuki and Noh drama forms - the ultimate in method acting. Once the model and order of movements of Kabuki had been established by a master, the style he created became sanctified. Every movement, down to the blinking of the eyes, was minutely prescribed for all of his disciples. Virtually, no personal interpretations were allowed. The challenge for each performer was to follow the kata absolutely. Success was based not only on the artistic interpretation of the plot, but also on how precisely the player repeated the set precept. Noh, actually, became more stylized and kata-bound than Kabuki. It developed into a crystallized scheme so esoteric, only a limited number of dedicated aficionados were attracted to it. The essence of Noh is for the actor to merge his *whole personality* into the wooden face mask he wears. He is to physically and spiritually put himself into the mask, allowing himself to be taken over by the character represented by the mask.

This total sublimation of character and personality is put into an unchanging wooden mask, and making an art out of it. Thus, the mask becoming both the medium and the message, precisely the goal of all kata, and characteristic of Japanese culture in general. Kabuki and Noh are excellent examples of the power of kata in producing illusions, and giving reality to the unreal, both vital ingredients in Japanese culture. The death scene - in all classical Kabuki - reflected another kata of the culture. Suicide, what one might think of as the *ultimate* private last act, had become the kata-detailed ritual of hara- kiri. While suicides in Japan are still common, the only kata left to it tends to be one's age and sex: i.e. a grown man would not take pills - a woman's kata; hanging is preferred by teenagers; though jumping from buildings, cliffs, or bridges, etc., open to all, as an acceptable channel.

The people were taught not to protest, or go against traditional feudalistic hierarchy system of submission. So, rather than try to change laws or rules, they were encouraged to find ways to go around them. Protest meant death, not only to oneself, but one's family, so the safest means of protest against an unfair lord was suicide. This way everyone would know the lord had been unfair to the serf, which would make the lord *lose face*. In suicide, rather than being killed for protesting, the serf felt glorification, for he had succeeded in his protest. Granted, he was still dead, but his family was saved and his protest made. Today, in modern Japan, suicide is the ultimate-insult to a boss or family, who demanded too much. There is no law against suicide in Japan. For the modern worker who does not want to commit suicide, he still endangers his life by not protesting. Japan has the highest level of gastric ulcers, which is medically noted to result from repression of emotions.

The hallmark of Japan's kata-ized culture from earliest times, has been the promotion and maintenance of wa - harmony, balance, social accord. Personal behavior, as well as all relationships, private and public, were based on strictly controlled harmony-consensus in the proper inferior-superior context of Japanese society. One of the most important cultural factors which evolved, came from the need of the Japanese to maintain a facade of harmony-agreement in all things. So, the use of ambiguity in speech and nonverbal communication. Ambiguity to avoid commitments, disagreements, and responsibility, and to help maintain the appearance of harmony-concord, became a vital part of the Japanese Way.

Importantly, used to keep outsiders, competitors and enemies uncertain, a clear disadvantage. The fundamental effect on the nature and use of the Japanese language itself, was imperative. Honorifics - the highly-respectful, subservient language, could be called a linguistic form of groveling. The demands of non-confrontational wa, not only influenced the way the language was used, it also contributed to the appearance of new words and word-endings.

The language itself tends to make less of the individual, and more of society, as well the State. The numerous different levels between people are shown by the actual words, and amount of honorifics. But this usage comes to the adult-individual naturally, which indicates the extent to which gradations are taken for granted. It has been said, if two Japanese businessmen, who had never been introduced, were put into a room together, they would never speak, because neither would know which level of honorifics to use on the other. Standing in silence would be less loss of face, than using the wrong verbiage. Self introduction is considered rude, abrasive and unacceptable. A third party is *required* to recognize the position of each participant, then do the introducing, so the level of honorifics is understood between them.

There is no word for the English equivalent of "love" in Japanese. The closest they have are words which mean - duty, loyalty, honor, respect, and desire. One might say the personality is clipped like a hedge, as self-sacrifice is made an universal obligation, and patience means to "hold back emotions." The Japanese can and do, in fact, communicate clearly, candidly and bluntly to members of their own families, close friends and subordinates. But, they automatically go into an ambiguous-mode when confronted by anyone else. This ambiguity-enigma is usually helpful in maintaining surface, harmony- kinship, and keeping foreigners especially, outside their inner circle.

If the Japanese language is an impenetrable barrier keeping outsiders from looking in upon the Japanese people, it is also a barrier keeping them from looking out on the larger world. The restrictions of language do not magically work like a one-way mirrored glass, seeing out, but not seeing in. Knowledge of the language erases the translucent, or opaque protection. The price they pay for this privacy is high. It is emotionally demanding, and at least for those who have become partly de-Japanized, because of their foreign-living experiences, it is often frustrating as well. The younger generations are rebelling more and more on this, because of the extensive Western openness they see, hear and experience from their travels overseas. Social media alone has unbelievably also changed them.

Lifelong conditioning in this intricate, finely-meshed web of rules and forms, makes it second nature for the Japanese to expect every situation has its exact process and order. When they are confronted with a situation, which does not have its own kata, they are either incapable of action, or take action which is often the opposite of common sense - and sometimes violent. This inability to make a decision based on deductive/cognitive thinking is the significant difference between the Japanese Way, and the customs developed in most other societies.

Since the Japanese kata-ized their whole existence, practically nothing was left to chance or personal inclination, much less choice. The kata factor was applied to everything - down to the arrangement of food on a tray. Further, the Japanese goal was not just the minimum acceptable standard of behavior, action or work, but perfection.

While few Japanese achieved total perfection in their behavior or pursuits, a very large percentage of the population certainly achieved a level of competence in the culture. This then starkly distinguished them from other national groups. This, of course, gave them a number of real advantages in competing with the outside world.

Unfortunately, the over zealous, - no matter what field of endeavor - would then use the kata like a vicious circle of more and better, without end.

Hence, the unique situation of *karoshi* - death from overwork. Which may not be uncommon in any country, but when the number of deaths from overwork reached estimates of ten thousand a year from the mid 1980s on, as it was uncalled for, even in a third-world country. Especially, when these were white-collar, office workers, not laborers under slave-conditions.

Japanese naturally became so sensitive to the rightness, or correctness of any service or product, measured by absolute Japanese- standards, they knew almost instinctively when something did not measure up to these standards. This traditional, characteristic-reaction made them among the most discriminating people in the world, and often the quickest to pass judgement - using only their standards, of course. Their reputation for shoddy-products in the early Westernized years, was more the results of copying shoddy samples, and using the Western idea of quality. Once they were strong enough after the Korean War to learn, and set up real quality control (under different Westerners), the kata system was put into the workplace.

With the masses never seeing, much less experiencing, any other way of daily life, the Japanese became acutely sensitive to any deviation from their way of doing things. This factor contributed significantly to their developing, especially strong feelings of being unique in the world. Unfortunately, for the majority, particularly those born before 1950, these feelings persist today to influence their personal behavior toward non-Japanese. This affects their business relations with foreign companies, as well their government policy in international affairs.

It is also difficult for them to relate, or accept Japanese who have broken some of these kata-molds, usually from spending extensive time aboard. These *quasi-Japanese* are often treated, in varying degrees, as outcasts in their own society, making it difficult to work or continue with their lives in Japan. This perceived uniqueness is also used to justify discrimination against both foreign nationals and products. Which is supported and encouraged, at every level of the Japanese society, by the national trade policy. So, while the government often talks loudly, about *Internationalizing* the country, it thwarts any true support in bringing Japan into the world-family.

There is a fatalistic streak in the Japanese character, which many feel has been instilled from the frequent visitation to the land by disastrous upheavals of nature: typhoons, earthquakes, volcanoes, and subsequent flooding or fire from them. The Buddhistic-inheritance is another influence of this acceptance to whatever is to befall one in a lifetime - Karma. This influences their usual submissiveness under regimentation, and feelings of helplessness of what life has wrought for them. To this response, since they can fathom nothing else, is *Shikata-ganai.* As mentioned prior, feeling they have no control over what is happening to do them, or not being able to change their fate.

The philosophy of this has become such an integral part of Japanese thinking, with its deeply-rooted habits and customs, it is what makes the Japanese, Japanese. This means, all the things which foreigners find either delightful or deplorable, have emanated from this all-encompassing kata-conditioning. This is why when the foreigner tries his/her hand at one of the kata-ized traditions, like flower arranging or tea ceremony, they are hesitantly-welcomed and then patronized for participating. Yet, the Japanese believe, no foreigner could ever *really* succeed at their endeavor, most importantly the language, simply because they are not Japanese. This has been proven by the foreign-professional baseball players, for they never lasted long in the kata-ized Japanese version of the game.

Uniforms are one of the best visual expressions of the kata-ized Japan, as virtually every group has their real or inferred code of dress, be it actual uniform, or insinuated Navy blue suit of the 'Salarymen' - businessman. At a glance, people know what company one works for, or what school one attends. The rank is also clearly delineated, as to its color or style. The construction worker does not just wear jeans or overalls, but billowing pants called *shichibu*, which fit tight over his shins. The policeman would never be confused as merely a guard, and the taxi driver would not think of presenting himself without his white gloves, grey uniform, and hat.

Likewise, the housewife, takes pride in wearing her apron to the market, as the beret and string-tie, aloofly-distinguishes the artist from the bourgeois. The greeters, usually young women at front doors of the department stores, and the elevator girls are not only gloved, but wear jaunty hats, matching their suits and high heels. For one to participate in sports, a standardized dress form is required also, such as the mountain climbers outfit. Even if one has never been able to afford to play on a golf course, (minimum $300/game in Jaan) a real golfer would have the coordinated clothes, which he wears when attending the practice range. Most uniforms are uniformly changed with the seasons - October 1st and June 1st. It would be a loss of face to be seen in clothes out of season, or out of uniform.

There is a Japanized-way to arrange furniture and office desks, for learning how to drive, for treating guests, for buying and presenting gifts, for virtually everything in life which most Westerns would not think twice about - how it should or should not be done. Companies, organizations, universities, and marriage brokers, simply weed out candidates who do not fit the national-mold of what is expected for the prospective position. Many say Japan is not just a homogeneous society, it has also been *homogenized* to guarantee the sameness. Granted, it makes them easier for the government to control, educate, and manipulate for the supposed good of the country, for whatever reason they choose. It also leaves them open to outside, echoed derogatory stereotypes called: androids, robots, clones, and worse. Yet, what the kata did to them was only the first step. The Japanese educational system was the giant leap in conformity.

The Japanese Educational System:

SCAP changed the mandatory free education from six years to nine, made it more accessible for females, and encouraged the number of universities expanded, so they may receive more students, with less class division. They also tried to de-centralize the system out of Tokyo, but singular-control and power was so embedded, even the minor changes reverted back, once the Allies were gone. Other than the year-system division being slightly altered, the Allies were more concerned in what was being taught. So they spent their time eradicating the military drills and Emperor-worship indoctrination, rather than influencing a more Western approach to learning.

Today, Japan is a country of 'average people,' the largest middle class in the world - 90%. But it is also with few Nobel Prize winners, yet virtually every citizen is functionally-literate. Which only means they are capable of basic math, reading, and writing sufficiently to socialize, work together in a group, and to follow instructions. Since all eduction is rote and memorized from the teacher lectures - no interaction or questioning is allowed - one could question how much they learned beyond the testing of those things memorized for it.

Though some 'educators' tried to influence General MacArthur into outlawing kanji and having all Japanese adopt English, he decided to have the kanji simplified in the strokes needed to create each one, and the total number of them to be used reduced. Significantly, MacArthur chose the number 1945, for the number of kanji to be available for the language function. China has an estimated six thousand kanji and theirs is still more complicated, with many kanji having more than a dozen strokes for its creation.

Though MacArthur may have felt he was benefiting future generations, the educators simply gave more definitions to each kanji character, which meant no one's life was simplified. During the transition time and to keep the masses informed, the newspapers converted much of the news into hiragana - the phonetic syllabary of Japanese, or to be able to read it without kanji. Today's youth have come to depend on the hiragana, and few have more than a basic working knowledge of more than five hundred, or at most, a thousand kanji. Nearly forty percent of all books and magazines published in Japan today are comic books, and they are printed exclusively in hiragana. Adults males, openly read pornographic comic books in public, as commonly as children do.

The average Japanese student knows well who Washington or Edison or Ford was, and could probably write in Japanese a pretty good essay on each. Unfortunately, these essays would all be the same, if not identical. The Gettysburg Address is a standard used as a junior or senior high school speech to memorize for giving in front of the class, and Lincoln's portrait hangs in numerous libraries, schools, and other public buildings (because he was Emperor Hirohito's favorite American.). Yet, no student would be able to give his or her personal opinion as to how, what Lincoln did related to America, or the beliefs the speech purported. They may not even know he was assassinated, or why. Again, they could only repeat, rote facts, they had been taught in class, which *never* accepted/allowed giving a personal opinion. They rarely exist, and no teacher wants to take the time to hear it.

Literacy in Japan does not mean knowledge, it merely means the ability to read and write. It is a key to unlock knowledge and further inquiry, but in Japan it has not been used for this purpose. Many Asian countries with lower literacy, have a higher percentage of individual, or creative knowledge. Education in Japan is a set system, transmission of set information, mental regimentation, and the rote memorization of *officially selected* facts and ideas. The key word is 'officially,' since all Japanese public, and most private schools are strictly controlled by the Japanese Board of Education, which in turn is a truly, government department.

There is only one Board of Education, and it is the national one, called the Mumbusho. The local, prefectural, or regional districts have virtually no-say-so in the whole process, except a limited choice of texts in elective courses, all previously approved, edited, as well changed, by the dictates of Mumbusho. So, amazing as it might seem, all students from Hokkaido to Okinawa, all learn the same subject, on the same pages, on the same days.

Only a natural disaster would be an acceptable excuse for the slightest variation from the set schedule. This is the main reason why most teachers simply lecture the planned information to the students, never slowing down, or allowing questions to digress from the goal at hand. Some private schools purchase the required books, and then use their own choices. Dozens of gaijin with a Ph.D. have been known to 'sell' their names to publishers to list them as "editors" for English texts and dictionaries. Considering the constant mistakes, few, if any, have ever even looked at the books, much less checked them for any accuracy of grammar or usage.

To many outsiders then, it is assumed the Japanese children are incredibly smart, in they can learn it all the first time. Since Western observers are colored by their familiarity, of their own model of education, they erroneously conclude, if the teacher is teaching calculus, the textbooks are open to calculus, then the students are learning calculus. Not true, the Japanese teachers are just following the schedule. But this is how the observers wrote their reports, and the superiority of the Asian, particularly Japanese-brains came into being. What the observers did not know, did not ask, and definitely were not told, Japanese textbooks target high achievers, not average students. Also, upwards of ninety-five percent of the students do not understand what the teacher is talking about; and a passing score in the prerequisites is thirty-five percent. Therefore, most students are studying calculus or whatever, without having passed the prerequisites. What the students do not comprehend is basically their problem, and they must sit there not disturbing the others.

This may answer the question of why after six mandatory years of studying English, the average Japanese cannot speak more than a dozen words of it, and only a few introductory phrases. It is also why so many attend the *jukus* to learn subjects they need for exams.

Other misinformation, taken more from statistics than their detail, is Japanese students spend more time in school. Granted, they are attending, but not necessarily studying. The three hours of classes on Saturday morning, make up for the three non-academic hours during the week spent on home room activities, and *mandatory* club activities. In a typical school year, some sixty-five to seventy days' worth of afternoons are either free time or given over to nonacademic activities. Students are also required to attend school in uniform for one day in the middle of summer vacation, so teachers can take the roll and then send them home.

Three or four school days per year are devoted to cleaning the school, which students must help with. The school exams are given nationally three to six times a year on the required subjects, depending on the grade level. Much classroom time is spent preparing for these tests, which means memorizing the facts, and students have the afternoon off on the test days. One or two subjects are tested at a time, so as many as three days are lost with each periodic testing.

It is fairly well known, the Japanese must take entrance exams, not only for the university, but for the better junior and senior high schools. One's life-work status is strictly related to the schools they attended, as their job, even marriage is the direct results. The self-educated or self-made man is a rarity outside of the arts, and the late bloomer is even more of an oddity. So, passing the all-important entrance exams - whether junior or senior high, or university is the goal of every parent, if not the student. Life success and academic achievement are so closely related, the stress or failure attached is the common spring cause of student suicide.

Most middle class families undergo economic privations, so their children may receive the advantages of numerous avenues to their success - private kindergarten, jukus, and tutors. No matter how small the family living space, each child has his own desk to study for homework, which begins in first grade. The mother's role in the child's success is a given, and her reward of being taken care of in her old age is equal to it. She is expected to stay at home with her children all the time, so her husband attends parties or other social functions where it would not be appropriate to take the children.

Her social contact is limited to the neighborhood shops, school functions and other things specific to the children. Educational success was responsible for the initial birth control practices of city dwellers. As just too depleting, financially and emotionally, to educate well, more than two children. Of course, preference are still given to the males. Mothers constantly tell their daughters, "Nice face and gentle speech," and they are taught not to protest against any slights, just be submissive to marry well.

What is less known about public schools, is there are three different track levels of these schools, which in essence determines one's future from as early on as junior high. There are academic, vocational, and commercial schools, which have little relationship to one another. The academic, are the ones most often purported in the media, and *inferred* to represent all Japanese, prepare students for college, and their notorious exams. These students come from more prominent families, or at least those who have the money, since the parents still cannot depend on this school to guarantee their child to be accepted into the highest institutions.

Never forget, like all other *Government-supported* programs, *education is a Business.* So, extensive amounts of time and money are spent, again repeated, on sending them to the chosen *jukus*, - the infamous cram schools - where they learn what they need to know to pass the exams. It is not really a guess, but a guarantee, because the largest cram schools *make-up the ten-thousand-question-pool,* most universities pull from for their entrance exams. Simple, neat, and clean, the Japanese Way - if you can memorized the material, and have the money to pay for the answers, you win the prize. It is also a system where students do not consider sharing information, such as answers on homework cheating, *just sharing.*

Ultimately important, loss of face is the most humiliating thing which could ever happen to a Japanese, for it says he did something *the wrong way, he went against it, or failed his kata.* For most, those years of junior and senior high school are unbelievably grueling in studies, horrendous in stressful competition, and most dangerous to one's health. Almost all Western teenagers, especially Americans, are running around to school sports, games, clubs, dating, or *at worst* suffering through some mind-numbing part-time job.

Japanese teens meanwhile, are burning the midnight-oil every night, and contemplating suicide if they fail. They receive support from their parents in the form of *demands* to try harder and being told, "Six hours sleep, you fail; five hours sleep, you pass." The child's success or failure is always a direct reflection on the parents, especially the mother, since she has spent the most time raising them.

Students at the vocation high schools are mostly male, and the academic program is much less rigorous. The students expect to graduate and go on to work as skilled, or semiskilled apprentices. These schools also support more sport teams like baseball, soccer, etc., and their competitions are followed closely regionally and *nationally*, since they are not rigged, like *all* of the professional sports. Many boys will choose the school as much for the sports team, as for their connection to a particular industry or manufacturing training. It is also not unusual for the best sports players to remain seniors for more than one year to support the school.

Though they still have to master the basics, their later school years have them already working part-time for the corporations, so they walk right into their jobs the day they finish. As always, the government supports the efforts of business, by having paid for much of their on-the-job training. It also niftily eliminates the role of unions. The boys do what they are told, and paid what the company chooses. Of course, the company in turn becomes their mother - housing and feeding them, help them choose a wife when the time is *right,* and get a house in the company development, with a company mortgage.

Again, neat, simple, their whole life wrapped up and controlled for them in the perfect package. Not as pretty as the while-collar boys, but still no worries, no decisions, no problems - the Japanese Way. Though in reality, the so-called lifetime employment is insinuated, but never actually guaranteed, as many over-fifty-year-olds found out in the recent recession. Still, if one compares it to the large number of minorities in Western country ghettos, it may seem utopian

Students at the commercial schools are for the most part female, and similarly their future is set on graduation. They will work in an office for a few years, and then marry by the time they are twenty-five, usually it is an arranged marriage. They will have had their flings, but nothing which can be traced by the marriage- detectives, and if they have had an abortion, they will usually have the follow-up operation which replaces their hymen.

They have learned the vital and difficult skills of serving tea, bowing to customers, and not responding negatively to the usual sexual harassment from their fellow male workers - married or single. They will be paid a pittance of a salary, as they are expected to live at home or in a dormitory, so it is inferred they do not need money. They are the OLs, Office Ladies or Office Flowers - decorative-servants to the men, who work and do the thinking. It would be redundant to say it was a sexist society.

OLs are of particular importance to travel on business trips, with one's boss for the sole purpose of opening his doors, following behind him to show his importance, and any other catering to his needs, sexual or otherwise. They may also learn the operation of complicated business machines, like a photo copier, fax machine, and calculator. Possibly, they may be given the opportunity to do a little bookkeeping, but it depends on the size of the office. One would not want to tax their brains, as the slightest competition with the men would be considered offensive. In return, the "Office Flowers," in their identical uniforms, are applauded for their decorating the room without intruding into the men's function of doing the business.

The girls live at home with their parents until marriage, rarely pay any rent, or contribute to the household chores at all, except for the major cleaning for the New Year's holiday. Their money is spent taking lessons of all sorts to make them a more desirable (salable) wife, buying the latest fashion fads, or taking short trips on their limited vacations. The most important thing is they keep their reputation clean, or at least secret from the neighbors, who are always interviewed by the marriage-detectives. More recently, these girls have begun attending junior college, as the competition for the better companies, and future husbands working there is more competitive.

To relieve some of their stress, as they are fragile-flowers, junior and senior high schools have added on a junior college. This way, if the girl can pass the junior high school exam, she is set all the way through, and does not have to sweat any big decisions, or major testing preparation. Her time will be better spent on piano lessons - the classics, of course.

Recently, the growing number of women who have qualified and chosen the academic schools, have entered the Japanese business on an *almost* equal par as the men. It would be reminiscent of the U.S. in the late 70s or early 80s, where they had to be twice as good to be equal. Yet, the Japanese women are more driven, as they have no government providing or protecting them from discrimination in promotion or salary. As the number of international companies and departments of large corporations have increased, many of these women have found protection and fruition with their English fluency. Still, to do so, most have to give up marriage, or more likely mother- hood, as the sole job of mothering is female, and daycare centers, while increasing, are unacceptable to most mother-in-laws.

It is an interesting Japanese concept, the easier one's school life is made, the more expensive it should be. Those private schools, considered the easiest to get into, are also the most expensive. Of course, the final pay-off is the same - they graduate, and why not, they paid their money. The only thing a student can be failed for is lack of attendance, and even it can be made up by attending X-number of sessions in the library. Attendance, it should be noted, does not mean participation - written, oral, or awake. To say these schools have rigorous requirements would be laughable. If there are three hundred freshman slots available, and three hundred and four pass the entrance test, the bottom four are dropped. 'Passing' scores can be as low as five percent, and failing students are given pricey-repeated exams, if there are still slots open.

There is a charge for all entrance exams, with the university ones being at least a thousand dollars. The easier schools give their exams first, and then those who pass, must pay at least one (nonrefundable) semester's tuition immediately - minimum five thousand dollars. Parents do so, even when their children are taking several exams at higher level schools, to guarantee the child will have a school to attend. It is not unusual then, for parents to have paid the entrance exam fee, plus the semester fee for three or more schools. Like everything else in Japan, again, education is a business, and quite a lucrative one.

Unfortunately, this is not the darkest side of Japan's educational system. The enormous number of suicides do not all take place in the spring, when students fail their entrance exams. There are also the summer, fall, and winter suicides from bullying. The amount of bullying, particularly in junior high school, and the number of suicides has escalated to such an extent to make national news, and cause the unthinkable - a lawsuit. (It is considered *most impolite* to bring a lawsuit against anyone for anything, no matter how blatantly- negligent the incident. **Note:** There are 14,000 lawyers in ALL Japan, a number strictly controlled by the *government*, which has no intention of increasing it. Comparatively, Los Angeles has 100,000+ attorneys.)

The common adage, "The nail that sticks-up, gets pounded down," applies more strictly in schools, and usually with the teacher's enforcement. Although corporal punishment is against the law, it is commonly practiced, and again, rarely questioned. The mighty-Sensei
- teacher, may discipline any student for whatever purpose he chooses, and he does. It is not unusual for them to physically abuse a student, or allow other bullies in the classroom to do the same.

The student, if it is felt, in some way has failed to follow the kata, whichever one it may vaguely entail, thus must be punished. Making a mistake while at the blackboard is sufficient excuse, as well as being late for a class, or interrupting the class, even for an illness. Every year, students die as a result of beatings from teachers. Many more are killed in what are referred to as 'accidents.' Sexual abuse and rape are also now being reported more, but truly not all of them.

The bullying by the students is often directed at the smaller, quieter, or weaker child who may have a physical impairment, as they are considered *curses*, rather than a mere birth defect, or medical problem. It often starts by the older, bigger bullies demanding money, which the student always forks over. It is when the amounts become so exorbitant - as in thousands of dollars, and they fear they cannot steal it from their parents, so the student reverts to suicide. Sports and clubs have also become common grounds for bullying, and though there is supposed to be a teacher supervisor, they leave the premises, so as to not have to be involved. Many of these suicides, have been students previously taunted, or picked on by the teachers themselves.

The parents have little recourse, for the PTA supports the teachers unquestioningly, with the parent and student tagged as trouble-makers. Parents are simply told it is their fault for not raising the child properly. The action of the teacher and/or bully are thus considered the group's action. To toughen up the children, schools are without heat in the winter (central heating systems are rare in any buildings, except the newest office high-rises). Of course, the teacher's rooms are toasty warm with portable heaters. Boys in grade school are traditionally made to wear short pants all winter, for more endurance-training. Of course, colds and flu are rampant.

The children returning from overseas, especially from English schooling, quickly learn they will be the subject of bullying, sometimes lead by the teacher himself. They have to be careful in English class, where the teacher's spoken English is almost nonexistent, and the student has obtained an excellent command of idiomatic-English. They are expected to follow the teacher -

mistakes, poor pronunciation, and all. They hesitate speaking to the gaijin teacher, should the school have one part-time. The Confucian philosophy, which so strongly influences Japanese thinking, along with the kata, preaches great respect should be shown to teachers. This respect has turned into ultimate, unchecked power and has corrupted the mostly male teachers, just as surely as it has the politicians. Most students capitulate, and resign themselves to the system, doing whatever is necessary to get through it all. It is sad their teenage years are stolen from them, as they go through all the necessary movements with a blank, despondent veil on their young faces.

Enter the Gaijin Teachers:

Though the first gaijin teachers came on the heels of the opening of Japan with the Meiji Restoration, and were usually connected directly with the missionaries, their numbers grew in a steady pace following the Allied Occupation. Once Japan got it's semi-independence from the Allied military, following the Security Treaty of 1960, (The U.S. Military still maintains American personnel and their dependents on bases in Japan, and with the 7th Fleet.) exportation of Japanese products was the goal of the country. There were no longer white bits of toilet paper on the rice fields from the night soil - 'fertilizer,' and the vegetables did not have to be washed in iodine.

Japan was finally moving into the 20th century, even if it meant economic development took priority over individual freedom. Prime Minister Ikeda proclaimed the same year the challenge of "doubling income in ten years," which was considered the heart of the postwar economic 'miracle.' The government made the growth- oriented economic policies its prime initiative. The actual doubling was achieved in seven years. The foundation of immortalizing defeat, they used it as a trade crutch. Maybe winning for the Allieds was only a transient thing, being just a respite from losing in the long term. Japan has yet to trade fairly.

This economic miracle did not fall from the sky onto Japan, and did not just start in 1960. The Japanese knew they could learn much from their conquerors, for they had never been beaten before, ergo, the Americans must be smart. Clearly, the only country to come out of World War II, practically unscathed was the U.S., and to become the world leader. So, the idea to copy the leader, like the adopted son, or stepchild looking for praise from its mighty father.

If necessity was the mother of invention, then the war- survivors were the most creative, making something out of the throwaways of the wasteful Americans. Once the Korean War started, they were given the opportunity and technical help they needed to produce the military goods for their benefactors. The growth step over, they could turn their newly developed manufacturing talents to consumer goods, since Japan did not have to waste time or money on the Cold War military armaments. Being a basically military-less country, all their energy would have one goal and direction - products they could produce to sell overseas.

W. Edwards Deming had been given to the Japanese in the late 1940s by SCAP, via the Agriculture Department. A statistician, who believed the only way to improve business systems, was to use statistical tools, which chart the variations causing problems, and pinpoint where the difficulties lie. Unlike the American managers in his native land, the eager Japanese listened to his lectures on quality, and were so inspired when they used his techniques for total success, by 1951 they had created the Deming Prize. Everything he taught epitomized their 'holy' kata-system - way of life. He became the icon of Japanese quality-control management, as the competing manufacturers followed his assessments, leadership, and training. Even today, his is the only gaijin portrait hanging in the corporate headquarters of Toyota - it is also the largest.

Quickly, these business leaders learned the newest technologies were in English, and much could be lost, or slowed down by translations or interpretations into Japanese. If they were going to sell to the world, they would have to speak its language - English. The Japanese government might give its businesses protection - the Anti- Monopoly Law enacted by SCAP was amended three times: 1949, 1953, and 1977; or expansion by joining GATT in 1955, and OECD in 1964, (promising to each country it would open up its trade barriers, but didn't) yet, only those companies which could do business in English, succeeded easily internationally. With every big jump in the Japanese economy, the number of English teachers-schools increased.

Akio Morita - as mentioned previously with his transistor radio, recognized the difficulty of his company's Japanese name - Tokyo Tsushin Kogyo Kabushiki Kaisha, and when they shortened it to Totsuko, still few Americans could pronounce it. You cannot buy, what you cannot say. So in 1953, the name was changed to SONY, set up like an acronym, but more like a nickname for the Latin word *sonus* - meaning sound, which was what they sold. Once their pocket-size transistor radio was invented in 1955, Morita decided to use an American advertising agency to market it. By 1970, SONY was the first Japanese company listed on the New York Stock Exchange. He knew the importance of speaking in the language of the market, something it took decades for most American companies to accept.

SCAP had set the yen exchange rate to the U.S. dollar at 360, and the government had refused to change it until 1971, when President Nixon threatened trade embargoes, because of the severe trade and payments imbalances. Still, only revalued to 308, and the first drop below 200 did not come until mid-1978. This not only began to move Japanese products out of the 'cheap' price range, it made it much more lucrative for foreigners to work in Japan. Prior, their yen only had real buying value in Japan, or other poorer Asian countries.

With business and trade first and foremost in Japan, a more aggressive stance was taken, as China opened in 1972. Apartheid was then ignored by Japan, making it South Africa's largest trading partner in 1987. Since they had never stopped trading with North Korea or Vietnam, Prime Minister Miyazawa later referred to it as, "A foreign policy lacking in moral values."

Japan shot into its famous "bubble-growth economy" by 1985, taking Corporate America by storm. Most U.S. companies were ill- prepared for the dire competition, and turned on each other to seek blame. Managers accused the lazy workers, while the unions pointed their fingers at ivory-tower managers, and the public suffered the *lemon*-consequences of having more cars recalled in 1977 than were even produced. During the Reagan-Bush Administrations, with excessive tax benefits, *forty percent* of the manufacturers moved out of the U.S.. Japan then became the world's banker until 1991, holding *one-third* of the U.S.'s debt, which gave it tremendous leverage over Washington and trade. In 1988, ten of the largest banks world-wide were Japanese, and there were no U.S. banks in the top twenty-five. While the U.S. was bogged down in recession and unemployment, Japan lead with twenty-five of the thirty-four vital technologies.

To those who could escape the Western world's recession, only a Bachelor's Degree from a university or four year college, was all one needed to make good money in Japan, doing what came naturally - speaking English. The hundreds of Japanese-owned English teaching companies, with thousands of schools scattered from one end of the country to the other, were waiting with open arms for the Eigo Sensei - English teacher. Learning English had gone beyond the six mandatory years at school, or the corporate need to have English knowledge to sell overseas. English was now *trendy*, the magical word which also made it a big business. How big? At its peak in 1989-90, learning English racked up $50 billion dollars a year! (English schools and text book sales combined.) That kind of money attracted two-legged sharks, seeking fresh blood.

Japan had replaced the U.S. as the most affluent nation, and with West Germany busy re-uniting with East, they were hardly a competitor. Japan was buying up Australia and North America like they were merely pieces or places of a Monopoly game. Even when they knew they were being swindled or cheated, they paid the inflated price rather than question, and lose face. Ten million Japanese began to travel every year overseas. Though they usually had short vacations of five to ten days at most, they would cover several countries in Europe, or cities in the States or Australia.

Most traveled in groups, on a tightly-escorted itinerary, covering every age or purpose including honeymooners. Shopping was the most important aspect, since they could buy duty-free the designer products they craved. *Omiage* - souvenirs - for friends, relatives, and co-workers were *required* of all who traveled. These group traveler- shopping-freaks soon became the butt of countless jokes, while being taken advantage of by the shopkeepers. Since most Caucasians cannot tell the difference between Asian races, the Japanese were thought to be the only rich ones. Other negative characteristics of rudeness and arrogance were attributed to Japanese men, when many Korean, Taiwanese, and Hong Kong Chinese were traveling, too.

They rarely needed to speak the foreign language, but just in case they got a chance-opportunity, they wanted the knowledge. Studying English became the most popular *hobby,* ahead of the other fads of driving/golf for men or shopping for women. Gaijin who could not get jobs in their own countries, kowtowed to flippant young people, who were more into the snob-appeal of attending expensive language schools, or taking private lessons. The gaijin joked at getting paid twenty, fifty, or even a hundred dollars an hour to talk to a student, who most likely understood perhaps thirty percent of the English. No real conversations, as an amusing recreational game, and a highly lucrative one, as few gaijin had qualified teaching credentials. Some of the young Japanese women in their early twenties, had nothing better to do with their money, and they loved the allure of a fairy tale romance with a gaijin man. Sex appeal was blatantly advertised to attract both sexes, with young blondes insinuating the party atmosphere most language schools had developed. Lessons were given in limousines, with the opposite sex, or on yachts, or holiday trips with gaijin escorts. The actual English success of many of these schools was not the issue, and the government had no standards set to monitor them. Besides, they were in *the business of entertainment,* not education, only the guise to make it acceptable to spend thousands of dollars - paid in advance, and classes often dropped after a few visits, like a difficult diet or exercise program. There were rip-off artists on both sides - Japanese and gaijin. Bosses who did not pay on a regular basis, or the promised pay, and teachers who did not have real degrees, or showed up drunk. Some of the gaijin-dregs used the students, especially the female ones, like they were a private harem. Likewise, the Japanese-dregs tricked female gaijin teachers into more personal kinds of leisure, or outright prostitution. Often not a pretty picture in person, or blabbed on TV talk shows, as the money attracted more riffraff, while the bubble's growth increased almost monthly the money being paid. Everyone seemed to be racing to get as much as they could before it all burst, which rudely happened in mid-1991.

The universities and colleges were not far behind the tacky English schools, yet putting on a facade of respectability by hiring only those gaijin with a Masters or Ph.D. The market was soon glutted with highly educated people, who had been unable to get employment in their own countries - as England, Australia and Canada had suffered recessions along with the States. With so many qualified gaijin to choose from, the most insignificant junior colleges were arrogantly being selective in who they would reward the 'baby-sitting' job to. It would be impossible to calculate how much talent, education, and experience was wasted on the ninety percent of the students who could have cared less, who stood before them spouting English.

Around the edges, after 1991, Japan went from being the fashion-centered-name-brand-designer-wear market (more Louis Vuitton bags were sold in Japan than all other countries put together) to having visible homeless on the streets. These were not the few alcoholics, who had lurked in corners and under stairways, hiding from the public. There were *thousands* living in the subway by night, and the parks during the day. With no actual welfare system to care for them, and no government to support them from being fired, most were over-fifty males with only menial skills.

Still, their lives had the Japanese kata-form, as each had his own domain of a cardboard box, with a newspaper floor, for which they removed their shoes before entering. With the usual exorbitant cost of advertising in Japan, and perhaps some charity in mind, many small and a few large companies took to hiring these men to be their advertisements. Like the *Chindonya* - traditional vaudeville-type advertisers of the past, these men walked around in costume playing instruments: drums, bells, etc., under a bright colored umbrella, as they chanted a song espousing the product or company.

Usually easy to get rid of the unemployed gaijin English teachers, as the language schools began closing and going bankrupt, as quickly as they had sprouted. The work visa was needed to stay in Japan, and it required a contract. Those who had become addicted to the easy money and cash payments from private students, took jobs as bartenders, cooks, or waitresses just to remain in the country. Many gaijin men married their Japanese students, as easier than getting a working contract. Then they had the 'golden spouse' visa, which meant they could work part-time for any English school. It became a mutual-admiration, as the school did not have the obligation of sponsorship.

Also, the part-time teachers were cheaper since they did not require a monthly, *guaranteed* salary for the immigration department. It had not taken long for most of the single gaijin men to learn they were put on a higher pedestal than Japanese men. The Japanese women were attracted to even the worst of the gaijin, who paid attention to them. Most Japanese men had no socialization skills, from all their years in a juku. Their escapism-party, of a free-gaijin life-style of drinking and carousing could also be continued, as the Japanese wife *never* questioned the activities of her husband.

As the recession continued and deepened, most of the universities and junior colleges began to replace the gaijin teachers with Japanese ones, who were cheaper. Since the contracts could be limited to a certain number of years, and then either only one renewal, those gaijin with Japanese wives no longer had any precedence over other gaijin. Few universities had given tenure to any gaijin, so just like the corporations had turned on their loyal, long term employees, the gaijin professors began to see the writing on the blackboard.

Those who had been in Japan for ten years or more, would soon be facing a loss of employment. They may have created not only a niche for themselves, but their lifestyle would not be easy to replace anywhere else. Those over forty, knew finding new employment, especially in their own countries, which they had let slip by so long ago, would be facing some rather stark realities. Many had put all of their eggs in the Japan-basket, which no longer was interested in catering to them.

The only other gaijin-problems the government ended up with in the recession, were the illegals - mostly Middle Eastern men from Iran, Pakistan, and other countries who had come as the lowest-level laborers. They now congregated in the parks, train and subway stations selling drugs and fake telephone-cards. Since supported by the Yakuza, the police did little to stop them, and few Japanese women were interested in marrying them, as they were Muslim. Life was not a party for them, as few spoke much English or Japanese. There were some ugly stories about Japanese women who did marry them, and disappeared after visiting the husband's homeland.

~~~~~~

Personal Story: British woman who met and married her Japanese husband in Germany, and then raised their biracial-children bi- culturally in Japan.

The reason why I went to Germany, was because I was running away from a life I didn't like (in England). Also, I was very interested in Rudolf Steiner's education (founder of Anthroposophy), so I applied to the Steiner School in Stuttgart, and I was accepted. Then I had the problem of where was I going to stay in Germany. I was looking through a magazine and read two students, had just come back from a working holiday at a youth hostel in Stuttgart, where I was going to attend school, and they had a very nice time. So, I decided I would apply to the headquarters to see if there was a position open for me to work in the youth hostel in Stuttgart, and they said there was, so off I went to Germany.

1967, and I was twenty-two at the time. I went off much to the distress of my parents, and an aunt who was calling me a traitor to my country, because I was going off to Germany, the enemy. That was an aunt who couldn't forgive anything. Anyway, off I went and started a new life without anybody asking me what time I was coming home. You know that kind of freedom bit, and I could wear what I wanted to, there was no coordination there. So, it was lovely to be by myself.

Then I was very happy, I went to school. I wasn't very interested in the religious side of Steiner's education, but as far as the children's education was concerned, I was very interested in it. Very, very different, very much to the way I would have liked to have been educated. Then after a year, this lonely Japanese (music student) came into the youth hostel looking for a friend, and somebody he could talk to in Japanese, because his German was practically zero and his English was also zero. So, I met my husband.

We didn't start off a relationship first of all, because I had a friend who's French and we weren't getting married, but we had some kind of promise we'd kind of stay friends. Anyway, my husband did make some friends, as he was a regular visitor to the youth hostel. When he found out I liked opera very much, he invited me to listen to him play in "Madam Butterfly" and "La Boheme" and other operas I went to see, and I thoroughly enjoyed it. I thought, "Wow," though we have a language problem, because we really couldn't communicate, there was something I felt very relaxed around him. He accepted me as I was, I didn't have to put on any airs and graces of being anyone different, and I really enjoyed it. I decided maybe I'd like to get to know him better, and he decided he'd maybe like to get to know me better, so we became friends. Then I broke off my relationship with my French-friend, so no encompasses.

Then my husband, of course, had to go to the University in Hamburg, the music university. Well, what shall we do - he would be in Hamburg and I would be in Stuttgart, so I decided to apply to the Steiner School in Hamburg. Again, I was accepted and went to the Steiner School, but only for a few weeks. It was so different to the school in Stuttgart, and I really didn't like it. The teachers were more strict, and kind of didn't treat the students as human beings, very different than the Steiner way. I didn't know, if it was I had a very hard time of adjusting to Hamburg at the beginning, because it was so different to Stuttgart. But then again, Hamburg was similar to London, so I don't know, it took me a time to adjust to certain things. So then, we found a flat and we lived together for a few months, then we decided we would get married. We got married in May, 1969, much to the opposition to my parents, but I didn't care about that. A very small wedding, without my parents, etc., but we had a lot of his friends there. My sister came over, she was the only one who kind of supported me, so it was very nice.

I thought if people always think about us, ... not so much that my husband was Japanese, but rather Japan is so far away, and if there would be any problems, I wouldn't have anybody to talk to. Just, they thought things out for themselves, there was no way we could be happy, and I'd be making a fool of myself, and making a big mistake by going into an international marriage. Happy to say, I've proven them wrong, and even to the delight of today.

I'm so happy about it all, because I'd never admit I'd made a mistake. Things were very difficult in the beginning, especially when I came to Japan. Of course, not knowing the language was very difficult, and the cooking was far more difficult than the language. I wasn't used to cooking in *shoyu* (soy sauce) and sugar and milling, things like that. We were in Hamburg for about two years, so we had gotten to know each other away from Japan.

But he didn't tell me much about Japan, he just told me he was from Kobe, a wonderful city and about Kyoto, too. But as far as everyday life, or anything no, he didn't tell me much. And unfortunately, I didn't know much about Japan. I knew about India, China, and other Asian countries, but not about Japan. We were not taught about Japan in school. I was quite surprised, I didn't know Britain didn't like Japan, because of things in the war, losing the Colonies, and all.

The first culture shock I had in Japan, after coming from Germany, was seeing the washing hanging everywhere, as in Hong Kong. Quite a surprise, because in Germany no one is *allowed* to hang their washing out, because it's going to mar the view of the neighborhood. It's just not a thing which was done. So, coming from a country strict in something, into one where you hang-out whenever the sun shines, is quite a difference. I thought it looked rather untidy. When I arrived at Yokohama, and saw this huge apartment building in front of me, with all of the mattresses (futons) hanging out windows, and lots of lines of washing hanging everywhere, quite a shock. Then, after Yokohama, we had to go to Osaka, but we didn't have anywhere to stay. So, my husband's friend allowed us to stay at his house for three months.

Gosh, wasn't that a shock. I was very surprised at the low ceilings in the Japanese houses, and also the rooms were very small. They're also rather untidy, (laugh) not just his house. I always thought the Japanese were hard workers, and they are hard workers, but only for one thing - work. I find they do their job, ... like even my husband's a musician, he's very good with music, but he can't do anything else. For example, put a nail in a wall or do anything else basic. It's just they're not use to doing things different from what they've been trained to do. They're not a kind of do-it-yourself country, so this rather surprised me. I mean, coming from countries where, of course, do things for yourself. A real shock for me to find out they feel, 'I do my one thing, but I don't do anything else.'

After being there two weeks, I was invited to work in a Japanese cake shop, me with no language whatsoever (laugh), and I thought, "Why not! What a challenge!" So, there was I, after being two weeks here in Japan, working in a cake shop, now wasn't that confusing. I had just about managed to learn how to count - 1-2-3-4-5; ichi, ni, san, shi, go; and now people started confusing me with *itsutu, sanko, sanmai*, (Japanese counting is based on the shape/size of the object) and all different ways of counting things. Wow, it was very, very confusing, but it was a very good experience, and I did it for months. But then, we moved to another of my husband's friend's house, who was a professor at Osaka University. We moved into his house, but only for a week, because he wanted me to do some translation from German into English.

Unfortunately, at the time, though I would have loved to have helped out, I realized I was going to have a baby, my first child, and I had this terrible morning sickness. There was just absolutely no way I felt like doing anything, and it was a job which had to be done immediately. So, I had to say no, I can't. My husband, in the meantime, had been flat-hunting and he'd found a flat, a very small one near Itami airport, and we moved there for a few months.

We couldn't live with his family, because they didn't have anywhere of their own. My husband came from a ... his grandfather was a very, well-known physician in Japan. Actually, he was the physician to the Meiji Emperor. But owing to circumstances, he died when he was about fifty-six. Then my husband's father was the second son, ... the first son was killed in the war, ... who had been kind of spoiled, and had absolutely no idea of how to handle all the money. So, he (her father-in-law) squandered it all on women and geishas and alcohol. Then he became an alcoholic and, of course, being an alcoholic he had debts and debts meant, they had to be paid, and all the houses had to be sold. So, when my husband was in grade school his last year, they had to sell their house in Kobe, to pay their father's debt, and moved into a very small one-room apartment. So, five people were living in one room. From then on, they just didn't have the money or income to have an actual apartment. They did have connections, though.

Even though I didn't know it, when I first met them the day after I arrived in Japan. My husband said he came from a very poor family, and he said they had really only one room. I didn't realize it, because the mother was so embarrassed about this, she asked her friend if she could use her flat for the time I was there. Quite nice, more spacious with furniture to sit on, and I thought it was theirs, but I learned much later it wasn't, it was her friend's. If I would have gone to where they were living then, it would've been just a one room, and absolutely no where to sit down. I think she had to cook outside in the hall, where she had this little table. (This was the 1970s, even now Japan has no minimum requirements for living quarters, or welfare system for poor families.)

So, she had quite a really tough time, and no job which paid daily, because she needed the money daily to buy her food. So, she got paid as soon as she finished her work, and she could go to the shops and buy food for dinner. So, my mother-in-law had quite a difficult time. Of course, their father being an alcoholic, was hospitalized for quite a few years. I think he'd been in three or four times, but they felt absolutely nothing they could do about it.

We were in this little room of ours, and of course, there's no bathroom, so it's my first experience to go to a public bath. Now, wasn't that interesting. Yet nice, because I could talk to the women, well I could gesture (laugh) and they taught me quite a few things. God, people really were kind there. They went out of their way to stay longer and help me, to show me how to use the bath and things.

And of course, I had to go shopping by myself. I found everybody in the market, which was close to the house, everybody was so kind. And maybe, I caught on pretty well with picking up Japanese, but by the time my daughter was a year and half, I was fed up with living the life we were living there, and I decided maybe I'd go back to England. A very big decision, because I knew deep down inside my husband was not at fault, receiving such a low salary from the orchestra. His salary was about, after deductions, about ¥33,000 (about $91) and the rent for the next apartment which we moved into, had one room, a bathroom and a kitchen, was ¥17,000. So, when I went shopping, I was always adding up in my head before I got to the checkout how much I had spent.

Really, I had a budget of not even a thousand yen a day. Sometimes only ¥500 a day. I did have a few private students (for teaching English), but having a baby, they could only come in the evenings, when she was usually sleeping, but then she'd wake up and feeding time, so it took time out of the lesson time, and they didn't have time to hang around and wait for things, so it was somewhat impossible to have private lessons.

I had this decision to make, and maybe I thought, I needed to go back to London, so I did. I thought maybe I would never return to Japan again. As I said, it had nothing to do with my husband, just living so poor, I just couldn't stand it anymore. Not saying I came from such a rich family, but my family was then quite comfortably-off. It was nice to go home and feel carpets under the feet, and sit on chairs and have comfortable things. But, I did realize material things were not everything, and I realized then human beings we love are more important. I wanted to come back to Japan and be with my husband. So, after being four months in London, - I had to stay because, I didn't realize at the time I left, I was carrying my second child, my son. So I had to stay the four months because of the possibility of a miscarriage with the flight.

Still, even though the time was in London, no one knew the real reason why I came home. No one knew what my life was like in Japan. I just said I came home because I felt I needed a break and I wanted my parents to see my daughter. They accepted it, because it was one of the reasons, but not the real reason. But I realized it's no good running away from anything, so I came back. I flew there because my husband sold an instrument, and he said I could use the money to come back to London, but I only had a one-way ticket. So now, the problem was, how am I going to come back again. I had to ask my parents for the money to come back to Japan. They said, "Well, why didn't you buy a return ticket?" So, I had to say my money didn't stretch far enough for a return ticket, so I came on a one-way ticket. I just told them, getting settled wasn't easy with a new baby and all.

When I came back, I came back to another house, and it was a house which my husband was renting from his friend, who's sister had just moved into their new house they built. Now, this house was so old, when you wanted to go to the toilet, this meant you went from one room going through an open corridor, and if raining, you had to use an umbrella. (laugh) We told the landlord about the roof leaking, but of course, he didn't do anything about it. Although, I tried to keep the house clean, there were mice in the house, and there was also something like a weasel in the house, which came in occasionally from the attic. I was really worried about my daughter, because if I left any milk around her mouth, ... I had heard cases then, the mice came up and were licking the child's mouth, if any stale milk around it's mouth. I thought, "Gosh, what have I come back to?"

It wasn't for very long though, because my husband had decided to give up working with Osaka Philharmonic, he realized in Japan you can't get on as a musician. Everybody, even in the music world, everybody has to be in a group, and you stay in a group, which my husband could not accept. So, he was deciding maybe we should go back to Europe, and gosh, wasn't I happy. But, it didn't last long, as when he when into Osaka to help out with the NHK (the national TV), and there he met this conductor, who was then a guest conductor with the Nagoya Philharmonic. He said, "Why not come to Nagoya? Nagoya is at the moment semi-pro players, but from now it's going to become a full professional orchestra. Why not come to Nagoya? There you'll have a chance..." And things sounded good, so my husband said, "Well, I might give it a try." So, he went off to Nagoya, and so for four months, he was living in Nagoya, and I was living in Osaka. I came a few times to his concerts, by Shinkansen - Bullet or fast speed train, and he said he had decided 'no,' we wouldn't go back to Europe, he would become a member of the new Nagoya Philharmonic Orchestra.

He was the first member to have a salary. Until then, the musicians, because there was no money in orchestras, they were only paid when the orchestra had money. Which meant once every two months, or three months, or it depends on what the money situation was like. My husband said he couldn't do it, because he had a wife and a child, and another child was on the way. So, they said well, OK, the city was going to put more money into the orchestra, because they wanted it to become a professional orchestra.

So, he was guaranteed a monthly salary of ¥68,000 a month, so then we moved into Nagoya, and I came to Kozoji, a new town, and we lived in Kozoji for two years. Then my husband was offered a job with the Nagoya Music University, and he accepted, but it was so far from Kozoji, he asked if he could move closer to the university. The rent was relatively cheap, like ¥17,000 a month for a three DK (Dining-Kitchen), which I thought was quite good, and new, so no one had lived in it before.

I enjoyed living in the new town, because there were many people from different parts of Japan, and I learned so much from them, about culture and things, especially language. But I had to think of my husband, he was the one who was the bread winner, how could I say 'no.' I didn't want to move from Kozoji, 'you're just going to have to make this long journey every day.' Very tiring for him, having the university and the orchestra. So, we moved into a place very much into the country, and again very different kind of people, very kind, but not so much into the culture, but closer to the university. From then onwards, like any other teacher at the university, we had students every night. At the time, my daughter was four, just entering kindergarten, and my son was two. When we moved, my daughter got into the kindergarten of the university, and she could go there for a minimum amount of money each month. Which was quite good for us, and we didn't have to expend the extra-ordinary amount of money at the beginning of the month.

Then my mother-in-law wrote to say, they were very lonely in Osaka, and they wanted to move near by, so they did. My sister-in-law worked for a year in Nagoya, then decided she really didn't like Nagoya, it was so different. Then she decided she'd like to go abroad. She's a very talented artist, and applied to a London university art department, was accepted, and off she went. This left the mother-in- law by herself, and the kind of thing, you know, she's kind of lonely by herself, OK. So, I went off one day to look for a larger house, found one and she moved in with us. And, she's been with us ever since, about seventeen years she's been living with us. There have been problems, many problems, but it's a thing mostly, if you think about it, it's about human relationships, you know.

I have to think she does have her own mind, and she does have the things she wants to do. I shouldn't - I can't really say to her well, … "I want you to do this, this, and this." When you think about it, she hadn't lead her life this far, to be told what to do again, by somebody. So, in one way, after her husband died, which was twenty-one years ago, I think the first time she had a few years of freedom. I think she rather liked it, and I realized as you get older, she was entitled to her freedom. I hope when I get older, I hope my children aren't going to depend on me to baby-sit or anything, because I feel I will say 'no', occasionally 'yes', but I'm not there to be a baby-sitter.

My husband is obviously not a typical Japanese, because he's not group-oriented, and perhaps it's one reason our marriage has worked out. He doesn't feel I, too, have to do exactly as the Japanese women do. So, I think it's he feels people have their own lives to lead, and he doesn't have a string around my neck, which keeps pulling me back to be here for him. He knows how his father really ruined their life, and his mother as a typical Japanese wife, never could say anything to stop him. The reasons I want to go back here, is because I want to be with him. We have so little time together, both working, when I feel he is coming home early, I feel I want to go home early just to be with him.

Even now, he's like an odd-fish in the orchestra, when they go anywhere to play and they decide to get rooms. Then they'll play shoji, or whatever, my husband is always the odd man out, he doesn't want to do it. He wants to be by himself, there's these books, he loves reading, and he goes off by himself to read. Or, if they're by a river, he takes his fishing tackle and goes fishing all by himself, or if he's in a hotel which has a pool, he has his early morning swim. But he is rather a loner, he doesn't like to be in these groups.

He is Japanese, in he doesn't express a lot of feelings and emotions for people. But for music, everything in his life is music. He puts everything he has into his music. It's taken so much from him over the years, when he retires, he doesn't want to play another note. It's now a problem for him, because he can retire at fifty-five, which is another eight years. He can retire, and what is he going to do? His life, everything from junior high school days has been music. He moves the earth, even going to Europe he had to, ... he's very proud, but he had to go and beg his uncle to lend him the money to study in Europe. You know, for my husband to ask for money, for help, it must be pretty serious, because he's not that kind of person.

I realize this, and I can't give him any problems, or anything, because he has to devote himself to his music. Which, in one way, people say it's very selfish. It may seem very selfish, but ... I myself, love music, his music, and I can understand my husband. If he doesn't have his quiet mind, or if he's really buckled down with so many problems of the house, then he won't be able to play. He'll be very, very upset, if couldn't give his best to his fans, and to the audience. I accept it. I don't feel as though I've wasted twenty-five years, or I've always given to him, and he hasn't given so much to me, or hasn't given so much, as a family man. Though maybe in our culture, I mean in Europe, it would've have been so different, probably. We would've shared together and done the chores together, when you're working. No, I don't have that.

But on the other hand, it's my life, and I've accepted it and I'm not begrudging at all. I just love music. In one way, I can't play music, but I would do anything I can to support music. I feel I'm doing my piece by working, by giving any financial, ... if I stopped work (She's an English teacher at a junior college.), I'd give financial problems to the family, which we could do without. So, I've continued working.

Now, the children going to Japanese schools was a problem, very much ... My daughter is maybe in a way like me. I think, OK, if you'd like to do something, let's do it, and if someone else says, 'Well, I don't want to do it,' then OK, then make the decision of which way you're going. Trying to be happy to please all, she didn't have so many difficulties in Japanese school, she was accepted. Now, my son, because he doesn't look Japanese at all, and in himself, he is very much like his father, he doesn't like to work in groups. He likes to work individually, and of course, as you know, it is just not accepted here in Japan. In school when they had to do certain things in groups, or the teacher wanted them as a class to do something, he was always saying, "Why should I do it?" - "I don't want to do it." And, it got him into a lot of trouble.

He wasn't accepted always, even from kindergarten. He was practically lynched by some small children, because they thought he was a foreigner, and not a Japanese. Such a horrid, traumatic time, he refused to go to kindergarten. He won't talk about it, it's a part of his life, it's a closed book. He's never spoken about it, even unto this day, as to why he refused to go to kindergarten. Something happened at the time in his life, it really frightened him, and he didn't want to talk about it, he wanted to forget it.

So strongly felt, he wouldn't go to kindergarten. He got up very early one morning and cut-up his uniform into

small pieces. He sat in the telephone room and he just, ...
I mean, marvelous the way he did it, I mean it looked just
like a jigsaw puzzle, in such small pieces. (laugh) Some
hate for his using the scissors, as if he thought, "That's it!"
For if he left it large pieces, I'd say, "It's OK. I can sew this
together." But, no, even for a boy of four years old, he felt
he'd have to cut it up into smaller pieces, like jigsaw
pieces. So it would be so ruined, there would be no way he
could go to kindergarten.

Then we thought, well, we said, "You'll have to stay
at home by yourself," he said, "I don't mind at all." So, I
thought about trying the nursery school. A girl he knew
who lived next door went, and she seemed quite happy to
go there. He said, "Well, I'll give it a try," and he gave it a
try, and he loved it. So for one year he was very happy, he
went to nursery school. His face, the color came back, and
his eyes became bright again. He came back again to being
a very, very happy boy. I was doing part-time work then.

It's quite interesting how my job came about. I had
a phone call one morning, from (a very large) juku. They
asked me if I'd like to go and teach my special program
children's class. They had heard about my studying in
Germany, at the Steiner School with children. So, I
thought to myself, well, I don't know. Then my mother-in-
law, who was living with us, I spoke to her and she said,
"Why not?" And I thought, OK, so I tried it out for twice
a week, teaching on Mondays and Wednesdays. Then
there were more students, so they asked me if I'd work four
days a week. I thought it's not too bad, my son and
daughter's in school, and my mother-in-law is in the house
all the time. She could go to pick my son up, as it was only
a five minute walk, anyway, so then I decided to go part-
time, at four days a week. So, at their Chikusa branch, I've
always been at Chikusa, and it's been what, eighteen years
ago.

So, it's how I came to work for the college, I started
teaching children, and I taught children for maybe ten
years in the children's department. Then, also teaching

German in the Junior College department. I had a little bit of a disagreement with the teacher, the person who was in charge of the children's department at the time, so I decided to quit the children's department. I was only going to the school once a week, teaching German, but then they asked me to teach in the Junior College. I said I would, but they asked me to go full time, and I thought about it, then said 'yes.' That was eight years ago. I had been at school almost every day anyway. I didn't get home until almost nine, because the children classes were in the afternoon and evening.

By then we'd moved into Chikusa, near Heiwa Park, so much more convenient for me to get to school, because we were in Nagoya city. The children liked it more in Nagoya, my son was accepted more in the schools. But again he had a problem, but it wasn't with the students, but with a teacher. Again, he had this, maybe about eight months, where he wasn't sleeping. There was something again, he didn't want to talk about, but he was becoming sick. So, I took him to my friend who was a doctor and she spoke to him. What it was, a teacher was *threatening* him because he didn't want to conform to doing things in groups, he wanted to think by himself. He actually told the teacher, "My mother has taught me that I have, ... she's always told me I have a brain, and I have to use it. I have to think for myself, and it's what I want to do, so I'm not going to do what you tell me to do." And, of course, it got him into trouble.

In his fifth and sixth year of elementary school was again, a very traumatic time for him. I tried to talk to the teacher, but he said it's like everything else, "Don't be silly." He said my son had a language problem, which is a very easy way for them to get out of it. A 'language problem'? He's Japanese, he's only been brought up in Japan, his first language is Japanese, how can he have a language problem? Yes, I do admit I have a language problem, but not my children.

Of course, my husband never could get involved with any of this. He again, as I mentioned, ... deep down I think he was very concerned, but a very crucial time for him, where he was just climbing up the ladder. He was getting to where he wanted to be, a top player and he was again, as I said, it might seem selfish, but it was a dream he had. Remember his life has been like living behind other people's shadows, because he was so poor, and all the friends around him were still from rich families in Kobe, so he's always had to stay like second best, ... in clothes and even in cups and saucers, they were given to them, because they weren't needed by his friends' families, and those little things. So, they've always had to accept from other people, and there's a streak in him, probably like a streak in his brother, they will go to the top, and they will get to the top by their own achievements, and nothing is going to stop them from getting there.

His brother had exactly the same kind of goal in the political world, and he's where he wants to be. But his brother is a little bit more family-orientated than my husband. As age has gone on, my husband now is taking more interest in the family. A very lonely life for me, as what I said, all the decisions and the fighting with the schools, had to be done by me, (laugh) with this language problem it was difficult. But, I was very determined to stand by my children. Also, to see if they were wrong, then they had to be taught, 'You are wrong,' but if they weren't, then I wanted to tell the teachers they were wrong, and please accept my children as *different*. They've been brought up very differently, they have to think for themselves, they do have a brain, and they want to use it, so let them. Stop trying to push them into some kind of group where they don't want to belong, but of course, as you know, it's impossible here, you have to go into groups, otherwise things don't move.

Then we came to Kani city, where we are now, and it was when my daughter was in junior high school second year, second semester - big mistake, very big mistake. The education school was so different from in Chikusa, where the teachers were really professional teachers, if you know what I mean. The junior high school in Kani city, of course, they had their teacher's license, but their way of teaching was so different. She just couldn't understand what the teachers were saying, they didn't make sense and they seemed to think, "Oh, well, we just have to get through the day, and that's it." So different, from the schools she was at here in Nagoya. She really didn't like junior high school, and she went on to high school, and well she liked high school, the teachers were very good.

Of course, she's a very fast runner, so she had to join the club, even though she didn't want to, she was kind of coerced into joining the track and field, and she said, "I'll do it for a year." But, because she was the only girl in the track and field club, just one, well ... (laugh), The teacher said, "Just for one more year, you'll be doing it for the school, can you imagine how the school will feel proud of you racing around the track." Anyway, they gave her the propaganda, and the boys in her club were very supportive to her, they helped her a lot, so she agreed.

But when it got to the third year, I went up to the school and I asked them, "Excuse me, but she would really like to carry on with her education now, because she would really like to go into a university. I want her to stop being a member of the track and field, ..." And the teacher would not agree. I went to the principal, and he said "Well, you know we don't like to interfere with the clubs, because we, ... it's the club teacher who makes all these decisions, and we like to think the teacher knows what's best for the students." And they would not give her a release from the track and field club, so she had to run for the whole year. It's a club!

Even when I wanted to take her to London, when she was in the first year of high school, I had to write a letter, pleading to the teacher to release her from club for the summer, so she could go to England, and the reply was, "No, she cannot!" That's it! I tore up the letter, made the arrangements, and took her. No more am I going to go through the right channels, no. She enjoyed the club, because she enjoyed the support from the boys, but the obligation to be an influence on the younger girls was too much, and all but two of them dropped out. She says looking back, she had some very good and some very bad experiences.

Now, my son, never belonged to a club, and he wanted to, they didn't have any in the junior high school. He wanted to belong to the brass band club, he got this trumpet. But the teacher was really not interested in the clubs, so he went with his instrument one day, and the teacher said, "Why don't you go home." and he said, "I've come for the brass band club." "No, it's too hot, and I don't want to do it." So, that was the reaction from the school.

Anyway, he had lots of problems in junior high school, again. Not with any of the other students, but with the teachers. In the second year, I think, it must have been again the most terrible time in his life, and I'm surprised he never committed suicide. The things he had to put up with, and even I got so angry, because every other day the teacher telephoned me up, for one thing or another. I got to the point where I dreaded the telephone ringing - "God, is it him again!"

The problem was he said, my son was not ... he had duty of cleaning the lockers and the corridors in the school, and he said he wasn't 'doing it properly.' Then he'd say, "I think I caught your son cheating today in mathematics." I said, "You did? Really?" and he said, "Yes, it seemed funny his friend and him had the same answers and the same mistakes." "Oh, Really? Well, maybe I should talk to him about it." He said, "Yes, you should. It shows a very bad sign in a student." And I said, "Excuse me, you picking on him for things he's known of?" And he said, "Of course, I don't pick on students."

Then again, he called up and I had to go to school because my son had smashed a locker with a broom. I asked my son if he did it, and he said, "Yes, Mum, I did, but I'm so frustrated. I don't know what to do with this teacher." So we went and talked to the teacher, and the teacher was so stupid, I went to the principal again. I said, "Excuse me, if nothing happened with this thing, I would take my child out of this school." And he said, "If you do, I shall make sure your son will never get into any more junior high schools in this area." I said, "Really?" So I went back and I told my husband, and my son said, "Mummie, don't worry, this teacher is going to leave at the end of this year. Then he won't be my third year teacher. I'll be OK." I said, "Are you sure?" And he said, "Yes, don't worry, now I've gotten the frustration out, I can carry on for the next few months." Needless to say, I had to pay for a new locker at school. In the third year, it was OK, the teacher wasn't there any more, but of course, by then my son had lost interest in school.

He went to high school, but it wasn't a very academic high school, because he hadn't studied very well in junior high school. He wanted to quit in the first year of high school, because he just wasn't getting any where, he wasn't doing the things he wanted to do. The teacher came to the home and spoke to my husband. He said to our son, of course you can, if you want to, you don't have to go to high school, but what are you going to do?

He said he wanted to play music, he wanted to play the electric guitar. My husband said, "If I were you, play the guitar as a hobby, but don't make it your life, I've made music my life," he said and, "I don't know how I'm going to carry on sometimes." My husband has said he wanted to stop many times, but the obligations to the orchestra, to the fans, and of course, to the family. He said, "Being a musician is a very hard life, you give up everything. Don't do what I did." So, the first time I realized exactly what my husband had been going through.

So, our son continued to the end of high school. But even now, my daughter seems to fit in OK here, but my son still has problems. Last Tuesday, my daughter's boyfriend crashed his car near the house, he wasn't hurt or anything, but the car's a write-off. But the tow-away truck brought it to the house, and he saw my son, and he said, "Come on back," and he's talking to him in Japanese, and the chap turns on him and says, "Can you write in Japanese?" (laugh) So, he's always got this thing of not being accepted as a Japanese. So, I think life for him is pretty difficult here. He's had opportunities in England, but turned them down, because he felt it would be running away from the problem here. He said, he'll go when he's ready.

I thought, after high school, it would be good for him to leave the country for about a year, to sort himself out, but he didn't. He did leave home, he moved into Nagoya, and he got himself into such a mess, because of getting into debt. He couldn't really pay the rent, and those things. He came home. And, I still think he's not absolutely, ... he's free, he's doing what he wants to do, but I still feel he could be doing something different. I still feel he needs to go abroad, at least for a year, like our daughter did. So he can see how other people are living, and try to sort himself out. But he said he doesn't need it, he's OK. He said he will go abroad, but he'll go when he feels he's ready, not before.

But then, if I remember, it's why I went to Germany, because my family always felt this or that, was what I should to do, and what they set me up for me to do, and I did them, because I didn't want to hurt their feelings. But on the other hand, I couldn't stand it any more. I left home, because I wanted to do what I wanted to do, and I thought I'd not want to go back. I would hate it to happen, if my son would do something because Mum said it, and the feeling he wouldn't want to come back. So, I think if he wants to do it because he wants it, then he'll feel he can always come back, anytime. He doesn't have much money saved, but maybe in two or three years, he'll be ready. He could come anywhere on holiday with me, if I paid, but I don't want to do it. He's had help enough, he's really got to start standing on his own feet.

He's doing very well with his business, but my daughter's doing better. Again, I think it's the personality. He's very proud, and I don't think he means to project it so, but sometimes they just stand in awe of him. She's easy-go-lucky, and gets on with everybody, but he doesn't. He gets on with most people, but not as much as she does. (The children both have English names, with a Japanese middle name, which they tried to register, but it was not allowed by the Japanese government, so her husband chose the English names over the Japanese ones.)

The only really big argument I had with my mother-in-law was the way I was bringing the children up was wrong. She felt they should be brought up differently. But, on the other hand, you know you hear about Grandmothers reading books to grandchildren, doing something, or the other, but I've never known my mother-in-law to read a book to my children. I've never known her to take them anywhere, she's never done it. So the thing is, my mother-in-law's life revolves around the television.

I think she may have felt I was being too free with them, and I was leaving them to make too many decisions by themselves. But I'm talking about, when they're already nine and ten years old, so to me, you have a brain, use it. It's how I'd been brought up to do, so I felt I don't want my children to stand there and say, "Now, OK, which would you like a scone, or would like the ice cream?" and they say, "Either is OK." I hate that, make a decision. (Typical Japanese is to not to make a choice when offered.)

Problems I had when I first came to Japan, I didn't have in Germany was, I felt I was a maid. In Germany, ... my husband hasn't changed much, and I'm pretty lucky because other women who married, like in their own countries, or foreign countries, and then came to Japan, their husbands have done a complete change, like Jekyll and Hyde. Just absolutely refusing to do whatever. But my husband hadn't done much in Germany, (laugh) so he really didn't change. But this kind of like saying - 'newspaper' - 'coffee' - 'cigarettes' without a please or thank you. I said, "Wait a minute here, I'm not a maid, get them yourself."

So, I did go through a period where I was saying, "I'm not a maid, I'm not a maid, I'm not a maid." Then it's like everything else, you give up. He was tired, and I wasn't doing anything, as I was just home. I had all the time in the world to clean the house and do what I wanted to do. So, I thought, OK. I started giving him his coffee, cigarettes, and newspaper on the tray without being asked. Then things went better, but now I get a 'thank you,' so I thought after all these years, it pays in the long run. I'm getting a 'thank you,' because he wanted to, not learned like a parrot. Our son is also not a parrot, too. My husband is fairly independent at home, I should say, because I do work and don't get home till late.

It's not just my husband, of course, this is the Japanese society. Men are on their little pedestals here, they've been put up there, and like it up there, and the way they expect to be treated. It's very difficult, especially living with my mother-in-law. There's many things I wanted to do and wanted to say, but of course, I couldn't. Probably if I'd started out doing for my husband, which we've never really argued, as I've said, because I've swallowed so much, I've given in. It would be worse, (laugh) because it would be two against one. My mother-in- law, of course, would have gone to her son's side, and sided with him. No, I've learned, I've seen, and this happens in every single house I've been in. So, it's just I have to realize I've married into a man of this culture, and I have to give in. So, I've been doing things like, I've never done before in my life, like waiting on somebody hand and foot. At the beginning very, very difficult, of course, things with my mother-in-law. I haven't agreed with everything, but instead of having an argument, I've ... "OK, let's do it your way," but ... apart from where it interfered with my children. No way! I've always stuck to my guns, and I'll not change anything now. There were certain things I wouldn't change, I don't care how much trouble I get into. If I weigh the pros and cons of certain things, and I think, "Oh, wow, it's no big deal," as you say, then I give in. "OK, let's do it your way." Then it makes her happy, my husband's happy because I'm doing what's his mother wants to do, ... (laugh) I don't like doing it, but then it's nothing worth causing an argument, if it's something very trivial, really. It would have been very different, of course, if she hadn't moved in with us.

My (Japanese) sister-in-law is married to an Englishman over there now, when she was having her first child, she invited her mother over for, like a few months or a year, if she could, so she could help. She was working in a bank, so she thought after she had her daughter, after the required two months, then she's go back to working in the bank, and her mother could take care of her daughter, and everything would be fine. So she went off to England, I even went with her and came back. Everyone was so happy here in our house.

Maybe rather nasty to say, but we all felt so free, you know there's only my husband and the children. We were doing exactly what we wanted, and it was so nice. More work for me, because I had to come home and cook. But not always, if my husband was home before me, he cooked and I came home for dinner. My daughter, when she was home from school first, would put the bath on. We all worked together and really nice.

Then a week later, after I came back (from England), a telephone call from my mother-in-law. "I'm coming back the day after tomorrow," and everybody said, "Oh, no! Why?" She couldn't fit into the British way of life, *and* she didn't want to. So she came back, and everybody went down in the dumps. (laugh) Such a short time, but I said to her, at least you know what it's like living in a foreign country, now you know how difficult it is.

But it would have been different, if she would've *had* to stay. She's never gotten along with her other daughter-in-law, so she's never wanted to live with them.

The other daughter-in-law is very, very strict - No television after eight-thirty, because it interferes with the children's studies; there's no smoking in the house; there's washing the dishes a certain way; washing the clothes in a certain way; everything in a certain way - her way. She said she couldn't live there.

I believe in everybody living their life, in a their own way. I mean, even I do, ... because I do like being at home with the family. I wasn't at home with my own family very much, because my actual father was always away from home, then there was the divorce, and then my mother remarried. Then my brother left home, because he couldn't get on with my step-father, my sister and I were there, but we were so different, not only the six maybe seven years difference, but even then .. we were so different. We didn't get on until I was about seventeen and she much older, married the first time, we actually greeted each other as friends. (laugh) Sometimes, I think, yes, I wish people would help more, maybe just around the house. I realize they've never done it, and they've never been used to doing it. It doesn't look as if they're going to start doing it now. (laugh)

It's not only my problem, my friend who's also married to a Japanese, she has exactly the same situation, apart from her mother-in-law lives separately, but close by. So when she goes to her mother-in- law's house, she goes, "GOD" and she can't wait to get out again. It's just so cluttered, she wants to get back to her own house. When her mother-in-law comes, it's again different, she sleeps all the time, so there's no conversation going on. It's not just in my house, other women are having the same problem. Apart from now, the younger generation, with these international marriages, like people in their twenties, are marrying foreigners, even foreign women, maybe it's different for them.

When I first came I joined the club, Foreign Wives of Japanese, and I hated it. When I went, they were always griping about husbands, or gossiping about other people. I didn't go there to gossip, or run my husband down in front of everybody. I wanted to go there because of culture, and to do things together, etc. I found out, at the time anyway, a little, gossip-circle. They were so unhappy, most of the women who were here, then I think of the women I knew, only one is still here. All the others are divorced, they've gone back to their own countries. They couldn't cope with being here in Japan. So the Foreign Wives thing, it wasn't 'what do you think I should do?' It wasn't anything like a concerted effort, just a gripe party. "Yes, I have the same problem ..." etc., etc. I didn't want to listen to it.

There was another British woman, I might have mentioned to you, she lives in Hamamatsu. It's how we met, my name on the list had British, she telephoned me and she said, "I don't know about you, but I can't stand these meetings." She had no gripes, her husband's different from mine, he always helped around the house, and he's such a lovely man. I always used to joke and say, "Let's change, shall we?" (laugh) and she'd say, "Well, no, I'd rather not." (laugh) So, she never again went to the Foreign Wives' Club either. I don't know what it's like now, I'm talking years ago - nineteen years ago, gripes, or pack your bags and leave, sort of thing.

I didn't really have any personal rejection from the Japanese close around me, they always went out of their way to help me. They kind of teach me how to cook, or how to say something in Japanese, or how to make something. I never felt any rejection at all from those. The only foreign women I knew at the beginning was the missionary, so I didn't really get mixed in with foreign people, until I started teaching. The missionary woman was very nice, she'd been in Japan maybe thirty years, so she didn't ask me any of those stupid questions, as to why I married a Japanese. The only real rejection I ever came across was from my own family, especially one Aunt, who went up in arms when I went to Germany. When she heard from my mother I was marrying a Japanese, even worse because of the war. She could remember the atrocities done during the war. As I said to my mother, if everybody in the world was like my Aunt, there'd be no peace in this world. It has to start somewhere, and I've always kind of believed it, there's always reasons for war, and reasons for arguments, and sometimes it can't be helped, but more often it can be helped.

As I said, more than often, it's something trivial it can't make much difference rather you do it, or you don't. Then again, if it is a big difference, and it's going against the grain in what you really, really believe in, then there's no way I'm going to budge. I still have certain things I feel are very important, very, very important. You learn what's worthwhile to argue about. The same with my mother-in-law, we are two women, who are very different, and two women in the same house is very difficult. Also, for my mother-in-law to live with me, I mean, I'm very particular about cleaning things, and she's not, so she feels if 'I make something for it, I'm going to dirty something,' I'm sure she thinks, 'Oh my God, what am I going to do ...,' she's burnt the saucepans for things so many times now, she forgotten about it and says, 'I'm really sorry, I'm terribly sorry,' but what can you do about it, an accident. I'm sure she's under a strain, living with me, too.

So I've got to also say, the song Phil Collins has, "Both Sides of the Story" everybody's life has got 'both sides of the story.' Why she's like she is, and when you hear about what she's been through, and how she had all those years of not only groveling to her husband, "Yes, Yes, Yes," she had absolutely no respect, and then because he wasn't working, she had to go out from early morning till very late at night. She hasn't seen her children all day, have they eaten, she didn't know, she had to work. You know, she had such ... I think she deserves her freedom. I don't want to be more strict with her, I mean I don't have the authority to be strict, you know what I mean? She's a human being who wants to live how many more years, I have no idea, but she's entitled to live her own way.

There are certain things, if she does go in and does this, I think it is private and I will say, "Don't open my son's letters!" She's up to opening them if they look like bills, then she'll say he got another bill, and I'll say, "How do you know? I don't open his letters, you shouldn't open them, they are addressed to him." Now, she doesn't, because she's been told, but it's another thing if she's burning the saucepans, or trying to catch the house on fire ... (laugh) She knows what's she done, so I don't have to make things worse by saying something, and make it difficult for her. As I said, I'm getting older, and what am I going to be like when I'm seventy-five, maybe I'll forget the saucepans. So I'm thinking what a stupid thing, anybody could do it. (laugh) It all boils down to getting along with people.

As for my future, as to where I will be living, - students ask me sometimes, I don't know. I don't like living where I'm living now, I really do not like Kani City. I feel the ideas of the city are back in the Meiji period, I really don't like it. I'd move to Osaka or Kobe, tomorrow, but my husband can't, so it's impossible. I'd even move back into Nagoya, if he came in and said we're moving in ten minutes, I'd go. But if he said we're moving into another part of Kani City, I'd say, "No WAY!!" I'd stay where I am, though I don't like where I am.

The people, it's not their fault, but they are very narrow minded and don't budge much. It's very difficult to get a conversation apart from, 'How's the weather?' and such. Nobody seems to be looking into the future. I don't have the time for them, but even if I did, I don't think we'd have very much in common. No, I certainly don't want to live the rest of my life where we are now. I'd rather go back Osaka way, anywhere in Kansai is OK with me. I like their way of thinking much better down that way.

If my husband popped-off before me, what would I do? Stay here? Go back to England? What is there to go back to in England? I mean the only things I like about England are the old Tudor houses, the greenery, the trees.

Would I get on with the people there? I don't know, I don't seem to get on very well, when I'm there in the summer. I want to hurry on, and get back to Japan. It always seems life there is a bit boring. I really can't say, it's a very difficult thing to decide. Will my children stay here? I have no idea. I have a feeling maybe my daughter will, and my son won't, I don't know why.

He knows not to get into trouble, besides he's twenty-two soon, so he's going to start doing more things for himself. My daughter's now living in Nagoya, and I see her about once a week. I think she's going to settle down with her boyfriend of the past six years. I really hoped they'd break off, and she's meet other people. She says she has, and she's looked around ... Her boyfriend is very much like my husband, very demanding in a way. But then again, his father's like that and his mother waits on him, "Yes, yes, yes, " so it's what he's seen, so it rubs off on everybody.

She knows this, but then again, those things she doesn't agree on, or if she really wants her own opinion, she doesn't want to budge an inch, she doesn't. So then they have their arguments, and she comes home and she won't give in. Then he rings up and says something which works, because then they're back together again. (laugh) He must then apologize, or at least say he doesn't agree, but accepts you have your right.

The problem is, what will my husband do when he retires? He can't really leave Japan, because he can't do anything but music. He says he won't do it after he retires, and once he says something, he sticks to it, so he can't really live in another country without some livelihood. Like I said, he can't even stick a nail in the wall, or weed out the garden, so what's he going to do. I can't see him staying away from music, he says it now, but it's all he can do. I just don't think he can stay away from it. I have suggested we could have a youth hostel, he loves cooking. We both enjoy talking to young people, we both get on well with young people. It's quite easy to do it, even here in Japan. I can't see my husband living in another country now, no. He's just independent, but he's still Japanese, so he could only live in Japan.

I can't even get him on a week trip outside of the country, he just won't do it. I've mentioned maybe next year we could take the Siberian Express, and go over by boat, then by train across Russia into Europe. He's kind of nodded at it, but a nod doesn't mean it's gone all the way to 100%, but he's kind of shown a slight interest in doing something like that. Summer is the only time we have long holidays together. We could fly somewhere, but it doesn't appeal to him at all, as he doesn't like to fly, but he doesn't want to admit it. He wanted to go by boat or by train, I don't care, I'd do it. So, if he really doesn't want to be involved in the music at all, then the only other thing I could think of was the youth hostel. Anywhere would be OK, Nagano Prefecture or down in Hyogo Prefecture, it doesn't really matter. I mean I don't want to be so far away, to be able to get up, and go somewhere. I wouldn't want like a day's trip just to get to the airport, or something.

I want to stay in contact, but again if you talk about friends, I don't really have any friends, foreign friends in a way, because you're all half gone. I mean for most of you this is just a stop over, and then you leave, so the only foreign friends I have are the teachers at school. Even my old friend married to a Japanese, she's only ten minutes away by car, but we're both busy. So, there really aren't any long-time foreign friends, the one we both know has problems, so I don't like to get too involved. I have friends all dotted out here, there, and everywhere, but almost all of my foreign friends pass through, come and they're gone. I'd really like to see some of them again, in their different countries, and what they're doing. Even at school, I talk to everybody, but friends, ... When I have lunch, it's just passing time.

I don't like the way some of the foreigners use their Japanese friends. I can't even think of doing things like some do, and they talk about it very openly. It's infuriating.

It sometimes gets me down when their running the Japanese down, right, left, and center. I happen to be in the group, and it does get on my nerves. Sometimes, of course, this is kind of being like 'not do-it-yourself-people' and 'only being able to do one thing,' and 'sometimes they're very clever,' but sometimes 'they haven't much common sense,' I mean there are lots of people like that, and I do agree with it. But people who have only been here a year, or maybe six months, and they start giving comments, or assuming everything, it's how it's done in Japan. They haven't thought about it, ... I mean I'm looking over the past twenty-five years, I'm thinking how Japan was then, how it's becoming ... it's certainly changed a lot.

I don't like the way it's going now, but then again, it's going through, ... Remember they didn't have any identity, they lost the war, and they lost everything. Then they started copying, mostly the Americans, because the Americans were here and they kind of made Japan more, ... gave them more freedom, right? They decided any religion would go, the education system would be like this now, and the Emperor was just a symbol, nothing more, and things. Of course, they've lost everything. They don't even have the Samurai spirit any more, it brought them together, but not any more, they're just lost. They're taking things from America, lots of things from America, and it's going through their sieve. They've taken things from Europe, and they're sieving it all the way. It's going to be another fifty years before they are going to have a natural character again, of their own.

My mother-in-law has talked, not often, about the war, how it was in Kobe, about the bombs. If you had the money, you could buy whatever you wanted in the black market, how she couldn't buy anything then, because everything was kind of frozen, she couldn't get the money. How she used to make the children's clothes from her own clothes, my husband was very often seen wearing trousers which came from her kimono material. (laugh) Food wise, it was very, very difficult, fortunately though, in Kyoto, where she came from, her brother had kind of a big vegetable patch. Whenever she went to Kyoto, she'd come back laden with the vegetables. She had to be very careful, so they weren't stolen, so she couldn't dare fall asleep on the train. She might wake up, and then find her cabbages, or whatever had been stolen by people on the train. Because they themselves were starving. They were rationed with food and things.

I think some of the problems here are the same as everywhere, the young people don't seem to have respect for anybody else, do they? (laugh) Though I don't always like things when I go back to London, the young people do still stand up for you on the train, I mean now especially since I'm getting older. (laugh) Where as here, of course, here the young take care of themselves first. It's just the way of the world, things are changing. I feel Japan has changed a lot, but then I've not kept myself open to how other countries, including my own country has changed so much. I find one of the nice little things I loved about Japan, were the little children used to sit on the trains and put their little shoes so neatly in front of them. I don't see it so much any more. I think it's like everywhere else, twenty-five years ago neighbors were standing at the doorsteps chatting to each other, in the summer especially. You don't see it anymore, our neighbors when they close the door, you're in your house, in there period. But then again, it might be the same at home, I don't know. I can't really say much there. I find the Japanese language has deteriorated over the past twenty-five years. It's not quite so polite as it used to be, but then again ...

I came to Japan in 1969, and then I didn't feel so much of the affect of Vietnam here as I did in Germany. I was surprised at how many Americans there were, those who didn't want to go to Vietnam, and they had the money to be over there in Germany. In Stuttgart, especially in the youth hostel, there were so many Americans. Young American men who were just hanging out, because they couldn't go home, or they would have been drafted or taken to court, or something for avoiding the draft. So, I felt it a lot, because they were just on drugs, it was such a pity, these young people. They had the money and the time, but they were so lonely. I think to overcome their loneliness, they were all on drugs.

When I came here, I was into the Japanese society straight away, I didn't mix with any foreigners. But in Tokyo, there were lots of demonstrations. Here there were more demonstrations against America, but not for Vietnam or anything, but for the returning of Okinawa to Japan. (It was returned in 1972.) Also, it was the building of the Narita airport, and there was a lot more demonstrations against America, for the Security Treaty, military bases and things. I didn't feel Vietnam directly here at all. Of course, I didn't have the money even for bus fare, when we first came, so there was no way for me to mix with any foreigners. I remember when we were in Kobe, and I talked to the British Consulate. He told me there was a British Club and I could join, but the fee was more than my husband's monthly salary. I just stayed in this one square mile, I walked around in everyday, and oblivious to what was going on even two miles away. I was just trying to eke-out every day of living, just buying the essentials. I couldn't give myself the joy of jumping on a bus and going into Kobe. (laugh)

Probably, I'd do it all over again. Because the things I say of why I married my husband, they're still all there. His individuality, honesty, hard working, and the feeling he wants to give pleasure to others through his music. I respect those things. I'd probably even put up with his mother. (laugh) I mean it's been very, very hard, and at times I've felt such frustration, like going in to buy an ice cream for myself, or whatever in those days, at the beginning. But I always thought to myself, don't worry, winter always turns into spring, and it's the things I'd live by. These hard times can't go on forever, somethings got to happen some day. Now, look at me, it's unbelievable I've got my own house, if you looked at me twenty-five years ago. Gosh, it's absolutely unbelievable, fifteen years ago we would have moved into our own house. It looked as though everything was there for other people, but not for me, kind of thing.

Everybody had money, in the music world they're either the girls come from very rich families, or the men who've come from very rich families. Music has been their hobby, and they've made it into their professions, kind of thing, supported by a family with money. It's only my little husband who came up the hard way, there's a few more in the orchestra, but they're not so dedicated, as my husband. They're more toward's their family, it's why their music is bad.

I mean I feel they should not be ... he should have the sack, because his trumpet is, it's terrible. I could do better than him. He's a wonderful man, he's so kind and he's absolutely family orientated, but as a musician ... GOD! He should have left it as a hobby. He doesn't give it enough time. My husband spends right from six o'clock in the morning blowing his horn, literally blowing his horn. It's just practice, practice, practice, so you just have to stay up and talk. Even when he's driving his car, we're going on a day trip, and he's sitting there blowing through his mouth piece, all the while driving, because he has to.

So, I'd probably do it all over again. It all must have been for a purpose, or it wouldn't have happened. In my last life, (laugh) I probably had it too easy. So, this one needed a little bit of struggling. I was probably a princess or something in my last life, perhaps I said 'no' to the Romanov family, maybe that's what it was! (laugh)

I rather liked the circle of friends we had when my husband was teaching at the university. Since many of the other professors and musicians had been abroad, so we could talk about those places. Very interesting, and sometimes we'd have some foreign musicians come, and they'd stay at my house. I wasn't missing foreigners as friends, because I had so many Japanese friends. If anything, I was kind of missing then, in a way my sister, because she was so terribly ill, and I felt I had to go back to see her. You know I kind of missed, ... I mean I now had my own family, but I realized all those years we were not close, and when we became close, I'd left the country so soon after.

We just didn't have the time to be friends, sisters in a way. When we did become friends through writing or the telephone, too late. I rather missed it, and rather sad. The same with my brother, he left home at sixteen, because he could not get along with the step- father. We never really lived together much as a family. So, I saw him just occasionally, then when I did go home and he was there, I saw him just for a few hours. Then, when I didn't see him for a long time, it was the time when he was so ill.

So, it's how my life's been. So there must have been something in my past lives, I've been meant to go through, so many struggles in this life. Of course, I do feel to take the easy way, would have been boring. It's why I feel nothing is impossible, I think we've done it. We've had to climb so many mountains, and we've been down so many times, we just had to get up, and stand on our own two feet again. Until the next time, when are we going to go down again? But it's life, it's challenging. Can I stand up again?

I got into Buddhism when I was in Germany, my husband then was into it himself, for a year anyway. He said there's this, in English, this magazine explained what he was trying to tell me. Because he felt I was into Steiner philosophy, I might be interested in it. No harm in reading anything, since I wasn't believing in anything. I read the magazine, and thought, "Ah, these were the answers the priest couldn't answer me, all those years I asked questions in church." So I came to Japan, and kept reading the magazines. Even my mother-in-law said you should do it. I said, "I'll do things when I want to, and won't do them before hand, you'll have to wait."

Anyway, it took me six years to decide to join in 1973. Then, my husband said if I joined, he would leave me, he didn't like the idea of my joining this religion, even though he introduced me to it. He was more on the Communist side then, which he felt was much better. I said, "This is my life, and I decide things like this for myself. It's an important thing where you're not going to tell me what to do, and I'm going to join." "OK, you join, and I'm going to leave you." "Fine, it's up to you, I'm going to try, and if I don't like it, but I want to try."

Anyway, I'm kind of thinking, what kind of mother am I, I'm so wishy-washy. Wanting something one minute, then not finishing it off, and I thought this is no good as a life, no it's wrong. So I joined, and waited for my husband to pack up his bags and leave me, but he didn't. He just accepted it, 'she's done it after all, I'll be damned!' I didn't force him to do anything, and I went to my meetings, he didn't mind and he's even driven me to a few places far away. He just doesn't want to be involved himself, but he has nothing against my doing anything.

I must say I'm very happy, and it's help me to understand about people more. I think it's kind of made me realize people do have their own ideas. I have to understand the backgrounds of their own life, to understand why they are like this way now. Everyone doesn't think the same as me, there are different people because of the experiences they've had. It kind of woke me up to things, I think. And of course, life before, life now, and life in the future. I've always believed in reincarnation, though not taught it.

I don't look at it as a religion, but more so as a philosophy of life, it's life. It's teaching me how to live, and how to live with other people, to respect the way they are living. If there is any disagreement, let's look at the disagreements with a three hundred and sixty degree point of view, and not one of a hundred-eighty, or even ninety. So, it's kind of gotten me to look around more at other opinions. People say, 'you don't get angry,' and I do get angry. But there's some things, I do get angry about, and some things aren't worth getting angry about. You learn.

PART III: Living As A *Gaijin* in Japan ~ A Different Cultural Perspective

"The urban populace has not been cut off from the farms as in most Western cities. It is second and third sons who go to the city, or surplus daughters who are sent off to be maids or courtesans. Whole villages have not been uprooted, as in nineteenth century England. This is not, of course, to say that everyone has a farm to go home to in hard times, but sanctions of a very ancient order do nonetheless seem to operate to keep the city under control, or at least its poorer districts."

"The Japanese learned many new habits from the Occupation Forces, but never new habits of thinking."

"Culture is like water, it seeks it's lowest level of commonality."

Edward Seidensticker -
This Country, Japan

Epilogue and Personal Experience:

I learned my first Japanese cultural lesson the day I landed at Narita, mid-February, 1988. The flight was over an hour late, due to really bad turbulence, so I missed my flight connection to Nagoya. Luckily, I had the phone number of the company-contact in Tokyo, a Brit who gave me instructions of how to take the bus to the train station in Tokyo, where he would meet me. Of course, I had to get change for the phone to call him, which within itself was mind-boggling, as the phones were complicated, and everyone used phone-cards, even back then.

But, the 'Pièce de résistance' was my large luggage had not made it to Narita, a screw-up in Los Angeles with changing planes. Since delayed, and contacting the company-man, by the time I got to the luggage-carousel, everyone had gone, so no luggage to be seen. I finally found someone, who spoke very little English, but managed to communicate regarding my missing suitcase. I had hoped they'd been overly-helpful and simply put it away, which she checked, but 'No.' She then began to gather assistants, until there were about six of them, and at last, one I deducted, must have been a supervisor.

Finally, I was given a form to fill-out, and I marked a photo- sheet picking the closest suitcase to my own. I did have the Nagoya office information of where I was going to be working, so simply had them send it there, once it arrived. I figured I would not be in Tokyo more than the next day, so no need to give their address. This whole problem took about thirty minutes, as each new person added to the group had to be bowed to, and my story explained again and again.

It was as if, no gaijin had *ever* lost luggage before. Though quite fascinating, obviously I was quite tired from the eight-plus-hour flight. And, the company-man was expecting me to get on the bus, shortly after talking to him. We did finally meet up, but he became quite concerned about me having gotten lost, which is no joke in Tokyo's millions of people. I had no cell phone, and virtually no way to contact him, other than at home. Without any additional fanfare, my suitcase arrived two days later in Nagoya. Thank goodness, I had put a change of clothes in my carry-on bag.

Language can teach you much about any culture, which it defines. It can usually refer you to the region by dialect, sometimes even the ethnicity of them, and the educational level of the individual or group within, from the language usage. Many people hoping to overcome some negative aspect of their heritage, or regional area, will work to refine their pronunciation, enunciation, figures of speech, or vocabulary use. On the other hand, a local accent or pidgin, quickly distinguishes those of whom would be considered 'outsiders.' And thus, not privy to any camaraderie, or personal association within the group. On the other hand, rather quickly, being blonde, a fully- endowed female, categorized more than I would have preferred.

It is only, when you *live within* another unfamiliar cultural group - whether within your country or not - you can come to under- stand, and hopefully accept those people, for who they truly are. Living within another culture does not mean *visiting* them, no matter how many times you may visit, you are still an outsider. Once you have *lived with* them - not in a compound with other 'foreigners' - but on a day-to-day basis for a number of years, can you say you know a particular group. Then more so, in your specific neighborhood if, you participated in their local, cultural experiences. Thus, my lessons-learned from living in Japan, new things daily, until the day I left.

When we speak of 'culture,' we also mean many different things which define a group - their style of clothes, housing, favorite foods, festivals, religious practices, common expressions, etc. Anyone who has traveled their own country, much more than a foreign one, knows 'regional style' is something most people take pride in practicing and displaying. Originally from the Chicago suburbs, I lived in five other, very different States, ethnically-based, regional places as an adult, and traveled overseas to dozens of countries. Many of these experiences are permanently etched in my memory, from both the negative and positive experiences I had.

One cultural past-time, which is quite international, is the film industry. And, Japan is not alone in their love of the movies, especially American movies. But, they do watch them with the sound turned- down, since they are reading the Kanji-characters listed below, and don't want the distraction of the English talk. Having gone to several movies in Japan with my friend Kazuyo, not easy to hear the English, which we both preferred. You would hear the characters talking and talking, yet the Kanji would be only a few characters, so we both knew they rarely got translated well.

Still, having been a film-buff since about nine years old, I stayed up late on Saturday nights with my father to watch the 'Movie of the Week,' long before Turner Classic Movies came into being. Surprisingly, my local Japanese video store did have both American films, and many classic Japanese with English sub-titles. Even before George Lucas was so greatly influenced by Japanese master Akira Kurosawa - Lucas happily admits lifting large chunks of Kurosawa's *Hidden Fortress,* 1958 for *Star Wars* - and Obi-Wan Kenobi's robes look-like something Toshio Mifune might wear in one of Kurosawa's samurai-epics. And, of course, *Magnificent*

Seven is almost a duplicate of *Seven Samurai,* 1954. Kurosawa himself admits, he borrowed from Shakespeare several times.

Yet, it was Kurosawa's earliest films right after the war, which impressed me so, as they showed the reality of a country coming back after devastation. When I saw his masterpiece, *Stray Dog*, filmed in 1947, it used a very-young, Toshio Mifune as a rookie, Tokyo-cop expecting to be fired for his mistakes. It held plenty of suspense-elements, with moral-complexities, so even I knew, built from the classic film-noir. Yet, he did not need a seedy-film set, as the city was so, by itself. It truly showed the real-view of day-to-day, post-war Japan. Once I got through all of Kurosawa's films, I moved on to other Japanese directors with English sub-titles, and shared my great finds with some of my gaijin friends, who were into good films.

So, I created and found my own happy-entertainment, living for over seven years in Nagoya. Many people, both Japanese and gaijin, who knew the regional areas of Japan, were quite surprised how I liked it. Nagoya has a reputation for being closed to *any* outsiders, Japanese or otherwise. Yet, I never felt it overly so. Some of it may have been because of my Midwestern, Middle-class background of Chicago, where people worked-hard and kind of kept to themselves, at least when I was growing up. I even became involved in the local, gaijin and Japanese-English teachers' community theater, doing musicals, comedies and dramas in English. My years in Japan affected me more than any other place I lived, simply being so totally foreign, even as I lived there. I still feel it a positive experience, though I have often called it a 'love/disdain relationship.' I loved the people, but disdained the society/government which extensively controlled them.

Following is a collection of notes about the Japanese culture, as I learned it. Information is knowledge which can be used for understanding, and can bring us all closer. Acceptance *does not* mean agreement, but simply acknowledging how others have chosen to express themselves. Accepting someone also means you are open to loving them, with a consideration, caring, and concern for another human being. Yes, Japan is rather superstitious and animistic in their beliefs, which was never a clash for my Spirituality beliefs.

Customs and Cultural Holidays Throughout the Year - Unfortunately, many of these are not popularly practiced by the younger generation.

January

Beginning a New Year, (biggest holiday) doors are decorated with Kadomatsu and people have made the year's first trip to a shrine or temple to pray for good luck in Hatsumode. Adults join children in the tradition of takoage - flying kites, on the first day of the year. The conscientious have started the New Year with a clean slate, having thrown out all the refuse from the previous year and devoted them- selves to their New Year's resolutions. When people see their family, friends, colleagues, for the first time in the New Year, they greet them with "Akemashite omedeto gozaimasu" - "Happy New Year!"

If you have followed the Japanese practice of putting up matsukazari - pine or shimenawa - straw rope decorations at your home for New Years, don't simply throw them away now the year has started. Wait until January 15th to take them to a shrine. There you'll see people gathered around a burning fire. This is Sagicho - also called Dondo or Dondon-yaki - the burning of the decorations, as the final ceremonial activity to celebrate the New Year. The gods who came to greet the New Year, return to heaven riding the burning smoke.

Since this fire is considered sacred, it is believed being exposed to the smoke can promote long life. Eating mochi - rice cakes or - dumplings toasted by the fire, or taking home some ash from the fire to sprinkle in the genkan - home entry way, also thought to protect one from illness. Even if you didn't put up any decorations, it might be interesting to go and view the ceremony. Osu Kannon is one of the more famous places in the Nagoya area, where this tradition is held.

Ichi-fuji, Ni-taka, San-nasubi - These symbols - one-Mt. Fuji, two-hawk, and three-eggplant, are considered good omens in order of potency if seen in hatsuyume - the first dream of the New Year, which foretells of good things to come. Other portents also include the ogi - folding fan in fourth place, with tobacco in fifth.

February:

Oni wa soto, Fuku wa uchi! - "Out with devils, in with good fortune." February 3rd is Setsubun - and in the traditional calendar represents the parting of seasons, the eve of the beginning of Spring. On this day, there is a ceremony to expel misfortune from the home. The above phrase is called, as beans are thrown from the doors and windows of the home. After the beans are thrown, the doors and windows are quickly shut to keep the good fortune from escaping. It is also a custom to eat a number of beans, the same as your age for good health. At large temples and shrines, people of the unlucky ages - 25, 42, and 60 for men; 19, 33, and 60 for women, also perform a bean throwing ceremony to exorcise ill fortune. In Nagoya, popular places to see this are Osu, Kasadera, Arako and Jimokuji Kannon.

February 8th is Harikuyo no Hi. In a traditional practice to petition the gods for proficiency in sewing skills, bent and broken sewing needles are stuck into pieces of tofu - bean curd, konnyaku or mochi rice cakes on this date. Although not as important in the modern home, people involved in the garment industry, fashion industry and sewing-students, maintain this quaint practice. In Nagoya, the Wakamiya Hanchiman-sha holds a small festival devoted to this ceremony every year.

March:
March 3rd is the Hina Matsuri - The Doll's Festival. On this day, also known as Momo no Sekku, Hina Dolls are displayed to celebrate the growth of young girls. The elaborateness of the display can be a thing of pride to families with daughters. These dolls usually represent the traditional Imperial Couple and their court displayed in ranks with the couple on top, above three court ladies, which are above a band of five musicians performing, and so on. If you look closely at these displays, you will see the middle court lady, in second rank, is a little different than the other two. Most noticeable, she has no eyebrows and her teeth are black. These show the woman represented is married. This practice in ancient Japan was for women who married, to shave their eyebrows and stain their teeth black. This made it easy to tell a married one from an unmarried one, and you can also see it in the dolls. There are other examples of these traditional practices in the representations of the Udaijin - minister of the right and Sadaijin - minister of the left, and in the dolls who carry shoes.

Another tradition, seldom practiced anymore, has children patted with dolls of paper. Any misfortune the child might encounter is transferred to the doll. The dolls, along with the misfortunes, are then put in a river to float away. The custom of Nagashi-bina, floating the dolls on the river is still practiced, and is especially famous in Tottori Prefecture. More locally, it can be seen on the Nagara and other rivers.

April:

The falling petals of Sakura - Cherry Blossoms on the sidewalks and streets can kindle feelings of nostalgia in Japan. Families, co-workers and other casual groups gather in the parks to picnic under the Cherry Blossom trees, eating, drinking and singing with each other, at the designated peak of the blossoms. They may also wander around as they drink, joining other groups, being very convivial with each other, so rather out of character for most Japanese. From my first Sakura, to my last just before I left, always my most favorite celebration. Nagoya Castle park the best place to celebrate.

The constant-comparison of the true soldier, following the Samurai death, likened it to the brief, beautiful life of the Cherry Blossom. It's almost indemnified upon many, to the point this was much more glorious than life could ever be - cluster, bloom, be glorified, fall and die. There was something about myths, the Japanese not only liked believing, but liked trying to live. To some, they were obviously more important than life.

April is the beginning of the school year, and for first graders, it is the start of a new life. Although public elementary schools generally do not require uniforms, it is easy to recognize students on their way to and from school by their 'randoseru' - from the Dutch *ransel* - book bags on their backs. Uniform in size and color - black for boys and red for girls - the young students will carry their homework back and forth between school and their homes in these bags for six years, until they enter middle school, then start carrying satchels by hand. Although many first graders have already had several years of nursery school, kindergarten, and various other classes, their entry into elementary school is a big event for the family.

May:

It is a time of transition. Spring is coming to a close,

the days are noticeably longer, and the sun is warmer. Summer is just around the corner. May 5th is Tango no Sekku - also observed as Kodomo no Hi - Children's Day, a day traditionally dedicated to boys and the last day of Golden Week holiday. As this day approaches, you will see Koinobori - carp streamers flying from poles outside the homes of families with boys. These streamers portray carp swimming against the current, and represent a prayer for health and well-being for the children. The traditional, sweetened-rice cake treats of chimaki and kashiwamochi can be found at stores at this time. Flower shops and supermarkets, etc. also sell shobu - irises. These of suitable length will be bundled with yomogi - mugwort leaves, and put into the bath when the water is being heated for Shobuyu - bath. The yomogi leaves help bring out the iris fragrance in the water. This tradition protects the child from illness throughout the year. For the same purpose, the iris leaves can be circled around, or tapped against the child's head.

June:

Ajisai - Bright Color on Grey Days. June is usually when tsuyu- the rainy season - begins. Literally "Tsuyu" means plum rain, because it occurs when the plums are ripening on the trees. The Japanese language has an onomatopoeic assortment of words which describe the different kinds of rain - Zaa-zaa, Shito-shito, and Potsu-potsu. During the month, there is little sun and much rain. One bright spot, however, it is also the time of the ajisai - hydrangea bloom. The beautiful blossoms help bring some cheer to these gloomy days. If you have some free time on one of those rare days when the sky is clear, Tsuruma Park in Nagoya and Hodaji Temple in Gamagori, and Rekishi Koen Park in Inazawa are good places in the area to see ajisai.

One scene of summer in Japan is Natsu Matsuri - Summer Festivals - both big and small. Many neighborhoods have small events, often starting in the early evening, as the sun goes down. If you see people in light cotton yukata - cooling themselves with brightly colored paper fans and walking with family or friends - follow them to discover a festival with little yomise - stalls selling yaki tomomorokoshi - broiled sweet corn, kakigori - shaved ice with fruit syrup, and watagashi - cotton candy. There also might be displays of mikoshi - hand-carried wooden shrines, festival floats - often lit with lanterns in the evening, Bon dancing, carnival games for the children, and a lot of people having fun, trying to forget the heat.

A Summer Poem - the onset of summer is heralded silently by the emergence of hotaru - fireflies. The larvae mature and arise from clear waters to live as adults, for only a week or so. The firefly, unlike the noisy semi - cicada, lights up its heart in a silent courtship. This has given rise to expressions, such as Koi ni mi wo kogasu - 'the heart burns with love' and Moeru yo na koi - 'a burning love.' The subject of many poems, people of long-ago felt the light of the hotaru was a symbol of a serene love.

Today, there are few places where you can still see hotaru. Many years ago, around this time of year, you would see children in yukata, carry fans and singing "Ho - ho - hotaru koi. Kotchi no mizu wa amai zo." They would catch the fireflies by whacking them with their fans, and then put them in baskets hung from the eaves, or inside mosquito nets, to enjoy their light.

July:

Summer is a season of more festivals, firework displays and bon odori - dancing, with children dressed in summer yukatas and small, roadside stalls selling nickknacks and things to eat, as they have for centuries. It takes people back to a Japan, as it once was. Tanabata Matsuri - On the seventh night of the seventh month, according to the old lunar calendar, many people gather to celebrate Kengyu - Altair and Orihime - Vega crossing the Milky Way together. This event, known as the Star Festival, or the Weaver's Festival, arose in ancient China and came to Japan during the Nara Period (710-794 AD). Tanzaku - strips of brightly colored paper, hang from bamboo branches, and offerings are made to pray for accomplishment in the arts, quite characterized this enchanting tradition.

The 'sport' of Sumo, has its origins in Shinto religious-rites to foretell the coming harvest of the five basic grains, and of course, pray for a good harvest. As you would expect, each individual movement the rikishi - sumo wrestler makes, as he enters the ring has symbolic meaning. The rinsing of the mouth with chikaramizu, and wiping the mouth with chikaragami, then the scattering of salt is to ward-off evil influence. Since ancient times, the water, paper and salt used have been thought to be spiritually purified.

The crouching and clapping gestures with the hands rubbed together, comes from a time long ago, when the bouts were held on an open field, and grass was used for purification instead of water. The spreading of the hands reveals no weapons, representing a fair contest. Raising the legs, to bring them down hard onto the ground, is called shiko wo fumu, and tramples evil spirits, while doing the preparatory exercises. With the continued popularity of Sumo, it is difficult to get tickets to see the bouts. But if you have a chance to get close sometime, you may find more fascination and enjoyment in the ceremony of the event than you expected. I certainly did. Although, Sumo is only performed for two weeks in July in Nagoya.

August:

O-Bon: The hot, sultry period from August 13 - 16 is the Traditional Festival of the Dead, or the Lantern Festival - where respect is shown to ancestors and the deceased. During this period, many people in Japan return to their home-towns to pay respects to the spirits of their ancestors. Who, in the Buddhist belief, also visit their former home on the 13th. To facilitate their journey, a fire is lit in front of the home. Three times during O-Bon, the spirits are offered meals or vegetables and fruits.

You will also see displays of eggplants and cucumbers arranged in the forms of horses and oxen with chopstick legs. The horses represent rides for the ancestors on their return to the spirit- world, and the oxen carry their baggage. The return journey is on the 16th of the month, when another fire is lit and the spirits who came on the 13th follow the smoke back to the spirit world. Also seen, absolutely everywhere in parks, temples, cemeteries, and shrines are the colorful origami cranes, the traditional symbol of peace and 'happy-quiet' in death. Remember, the origami are all made by hand and there are thousands of them.

Traditionally, offerings are packaged in straw in the form of boats, sometimes with a lit candle and set afloat on rivers or in the sea. But recently, it has been more common to burn the offerings at temples. Visits are made to graves, and priests are called to read sutras. The custom, more formally called Urabon-e, originated in summer during the festivals of the nomads of Central Asia - Persia and Turkey- and in the Buddhist ceremonies in India, to pray for peace of the souls of the deceased. It came to Japan in 7th century AD, by way of China, then Korea, and evolved into what it is today, after adopting various indigenous customs.

Bon-dancing and summer festivals are traditionally held during this period, so shops, companies, factories, etc. will often take their summer (O-bon) vacations at this time. With so many people returning to their home towns and others going on vacations, highways, railways and airports are especially crowded with travelers, particularly around the 13th and 16th. As usual, gift buying for those who are visited, creates additional crowds. So, traveling or shopping around the middle of the month may take longer than usual, though shops may not even be open during their usual hours.

My first year, I visited Hiroshima at this time, not aware of the sanctity of it all. The experience on its own was overwhelming enough, but to see literally millions of the origami cranes added to the memorial. It is indelible on my brain, and I'll never forget any of it.

September:

The harvest moon is as famous in Japan, as it is in other countries. Moon viewing is one social activity known to have been practiced all the way back to the Jomon Era (prior to 200 BC). It once held an *almost* religious significance, as people offered potatoes and beans to the moon in thanks for a bountiful harvest. Today, the tradition can be seen in the display of *satoimo* taro, and dumplings made of rice, then put on a plate with stalks of *susuki* grass.

In earlier times - when there were no TV's or radios - we can imagine families became closer, as they gathered together to watch the moon. There are probably many, who as children were told you could see a rabbit making rice-cakes in the light and shadows of the moon's face. The Japanese fairy tale of Kaguya-hime - Princess Kaguya was also probably inspired by the light of the moon. Although it has been more than 50 years, since man first walked on the Earth's closest, celestial-neighbor, the moon still holds much mystery and beauty.

Probably, the most noted time in September in Japan, is the night of the 15th day of the 8th month in the *old* lunar calendar - 'Jugoya.' It is the night of 'Chushu no meigetsu,' the harvest moon. In the clear, autumn skies, the full moon is especially beautiful, and carries special significance. It is the origin of fairy tails and songs in Japan. In the modern calendar, September 15th is Keiro no Hi - Respect of the Aged Day, a national holiday.

October:

The month of October in Japan has also been called *Kannazuki*, which literally means 'month without gods,' when written in Chinese characters. This comes from the Shinto belief, the *yaoyorozu* - many, many gods of the 8+ million, in this land gather at the Izumo Taisha Shrine in October, leaving the rest of the shrines around Japan temporarily bereft of their patron deities. By the way, in Izumo no Kuni - now the eastern part of Shimane Prefecture, this month has been referred to as Kamiarizuki - the month of gods.

It is said, there were some gods which remained to protect their domain, and Ebisu-sama is one of them. Around the 20th of the month, you will find places to make offerings to Ebisu-sama in a ceremony known as Ebisu-kou. As this deity is also known as the god of wealth, you will find some shops, such as boutiques, holding discount sales at this time, to 'please' the gods.

Koyo - the incredible red leaves of the Japanese momiji - maple, in autumn is so loved, it could almost be the national symbol - if not already taken by another country. The mountains surrounding the Owari plain are covered with the trees, and are especially beautiful in late October and November. Whether still on the trees, or fallen on paths and the stone stairways of ancient temples, the leaves represent the season, as well the beauty of the countryside.

November:

Nov. 15 is Shichi-go-san: the day when children of ages of seven, five and three (hence the name - 7, 5, 3) are dressed in their finest traditional clothing and taken to a shrine to pray for their well- being. On weekends and holidays, during the first half of November, you will often see these children dressed in beautiful kimonos, proudly together with their family, on their way to a shrine. In the Nagoya area, Atsuta Shrine is a good place to witness this charming spectacle.

In the old Japanese calendar, the twelve signs of the zodiac were identified by different animals. Names for the year are well known - if you remember the New Year's cards you may have received. These signs, however, are not limited to years, but are also used for hours and for days. Tori no ichi, is a festival which originated at the Ootori Shrine in Tokyo, on the day of the tori in November - changing dates. On this day there is an ennichi - fair, with stalls selling a variety of goods. One of the most popular items at the fair is a small kumade - rake, which has the meaning of Fuku wo Kakikomu or Fuku wo Tori komu. These are bought by trades people, as a symbol to draw-in or literally, 'rake-in' prosperity.

In practice, the kumade are priced very high, and through usual haggling, the price is reduced to often less than a third of the original. The bargaining is concluded with three rounds of the tebyoshi - clapping ceremony. Shops which hope to prosper, buy bigger kumade each year. Although just a superstition, the state of the economy might make practice of buying jumade even more popular. The Shrine encourages the belief of 'Paying for one's prosperity.'

December:

The warming rays of the sun are weakening and nights are getting longer. December 22nd, the Winter Solstice, everyone eats Japanese-pumpkin, or red-bean, rice porridge and takes yuzuyu - hot- citron baths to keep warm. It is also believed to keep them healthy. If you glance at houses, while walking your neighborhood streets in late December, you may see the windows being cleaned by industrious, family members. Within the house, everyone will be busy with oosooji- the year-end cleaning, to start the New Year afresh. Toward the end of the month, you will also see the traditional New Year decorations of kadomatsu, kagamimochi and shimenawa.

With the celebration of the beginning of the New Year, the Japanese greet the gods to wish for good fortune for the next 12 months. The decorations you see are for these deities. The kadomatsu -pine and bamboo - are placed before the door to welcome the gods. The kagaminmochi - rice cakes, are to serve the gods who come to the home. The shimenawa - braided straw rope, is set on or above the door. Although, it symbolizes a barrier to entry and exit, to demarcate a sacred area, for New Years, it marks a place for the gods to reside.

Funeral Customs:

Funeral Services in Japan: Religious practices in Japan include several non-exclusive beliefs, such as the indigenous Shinto and animism, and the imported Buddhism. Although it is possible to find Christian churches here, and various new religions have also been imported, their followers are still few with any funeral practices. In most cases, weddings in Japan are held with a Shinto ceremony and funerals are Buddhist. Although there are various sects in Buddhism with different practices, most funeral ceremonies entail the same.

Tsuya - Wake: On the eve of the funeral, relatives and friends are gathered to pay condolences to the bereaved family. Before the popularization of Buddhism, this practice would have been considered the actual funeral. In some regional variations, a banquet with food and drink would be held. The more modern wake has been simplified. Cash gifts in special envelopes for the bereaved family are delivered at this time, or the next day at the funeral. If you are unable to attend the actual funeral, a brief appearance at the tsuya is acceptable.

Soshiki - Funeral - Sogi and Kokubetsu-shiki: In the main part of the funeral, priests read sutras to pray for the happiness of the departed soul. The ceremony is comprised of the Sogi funeral for close relatives of the deceased, and the Kokubetsu-shiki farewell service for colleagues, acquaintances, etc. Participants in the farewell service will follow the directions of a guide to greet the bereaved family, light some incense before a photograph of the departed, and then offer a prayer with both hands together before leaving. It is not uncommon for participants to receive a courtesy gift as they leave. Proper dress for a funeral here is black wear for women and a black suit with white shirt and black tie for men. Any clothing with color is taboo.

Kaso - Cremation and Maiso - Burial: Cremation is the most common for the deceased in Japan. After the funeral, the casket is taken by hearse to a crematory for cremation. The remains will be placed in a jar and then interred in a cemetery. In some places, burial without cremation may not be allowed, or may be prohibitively expensive. A 'Bone-picking' ceremony may be held for the closest friends and relatives, where chopsticks are used to remove a bone from the ashes, as a keepsake of the individual.

Cultural Notes:

From the outside, or as a visitor, quite easy to see the attitude of the Japanese men toward their women. Here man is the absolute ruler, and hardly a moment a day goes by without him imposing his will over the weaker sex. It's also clearly evident among children, for even at play, boys will not be equal with girls, but will drive them away from whatever spot the boys chose for their activities.

Yet, as one lives in Japan, you learn the women have the last laugh, you might say, for they control the purse-strings, and the mighty-man is given an allowance for his spending money. Whenever they go out to eat, she is the one who pays for the bill, after closely checking it for any errors, while noting how much he had to drink.

He makes few decisions regarding the home, as his concerns lie with his job, which he rarely discusses with her. His salary and bonuses are *directly-deposited* into the *family* account, but she may have several *hidden* savings accounts. As mentioned prior, Japan Post Offices offer savings accounts. Not unusual for people to open bogus accounts even under their pet's name, though the tax office has cut down on these.

The wife always guards to save-face for her husband in public, but in the privacy of their home, she rules-the-roost, and rarely gives him peace for any negative actions he may have done. Notedly, if a Japanese woman chooses to not control her husband, either she has her mother-in-law in-house, or a lot of money is at stake. If she chooses to ignore, or not speak-up regarding an addiction her husband has, it would be to *not lose face* or simply to play victim - "What can I do?"

In the past, the women might not only have done all the domestic chores, but did so while waiting on their husband's every beck-and-call. The strength shown even by the smallest, frailest and oldest of women, made one wonder how she could do it, except for the fact of *precedence*. Education and travel abroad changed much of the tradition. She now has at least a part-time job, once the children are older, or sooner if day care is available. Though poorly-paid, it does get her out of the house to earn her own money, to do with as she totally and openly pleases. Nowadays, this usually includes more education and travel abroad with *other females*.

Even today, many marriages are still arranged, as romance is only in the movies, or what one experiences *before* marriage, and preferably with a foreigner. Because of acceptance of this, both the men and women do not have the need for guilt regarding adultery. A common occurrence, and what makes the 'Love Hotel' - they rent out by the hour, and deliver liquor or snacks to the *visitors* - business continues to thrive, even in tight neighborhoods, with covert exits.

Once a man or woman, reaches a certain financial level of success, having a mistress or boyfriend is *trendy,* to the point of a status symbol. Yet, participation must be done with the greatest decorum. Sort of like having plastic surgery, but never flaunting it, as being obvious. One must never cause a loss of face for one's partner, though they may also be having their own affair. If found out and it becomes gossip, protocol would require a negative reaction, even divorce, still rare, but increasing.

Many analogies are constantly written, about the Japanese rushing into the twenty-first century with their technologies, while still being tied down to their chopsticks, incense-burning rituals and exchanging their shoes in the bathroom for rubber slippers. Yet a woman, or especially a couple in formal Japanese attire of kimonos for a wedding, never ceased to stop me in my tracks and to momentarily admire the traditional scene. Also, there was always something curious about the late-night, noodle-stand on the subway corner exit, lit by bare bulbs and run by a portable generator. Or more so, the nostalgic, old man melodically chanting a sales-pitch, about his roasted sweet potatoes, from his push cart, on a cold, winter's night, walking the neighborhood sidewalks. I can still recall, the night time sing-song of the neighborhood, temple-purveyor of good dreams, as he drove through the alleyways.

And, I'll never forget the first time I heard getas, the Japanese wooden clogs, clacking-up the stone steps. I watched as the young woman walked across the court yard to the shrine, where she bowed- deeply three times, clapping her hands in-between bows. But most of all, I remember the little-old, nursery man, who would sit cross-legged on a wooden box, precisely-trimming and caring for his bonsai plants. His face and actions belonged in a classical painting, or book on traditional hobbies.

Unfortunately, it was only weeks after, I had not seen him, the nursery was torn down, and another ubiquitous, convenient store was built in its place. He must have died, and his son chose to not continue working the nursery. In its own minute-way, just as sad as when they tore down the Frank Lloyd Wright Imperial Palace Hotel in Tokyo. It was too old and costly to modernize, as well the land too valuable. Tradition, and real culture are sometimes wasted on the young, and long-lost by the time they are old enough to realize its value.

Personal Cultural Experience - Leaving Japan

On my last, and fifth trip to Australia, visiting some friends in Brisbane for Christmas 1994, at an outdoor holiday market. A *sort of* parade for some fundraiser came by. We all sat on a bench to watch the typical-Aussie, mash-up of men and women, baby strollers, in all sorts of summer attire, some with the designated T-Shirts, and a couple of banners, announcing their purpose. I loved the Aussies, and visiting them, as they exemplified the furthest-opposite from the Japanese. They did their own thing, even more so than most Americans, especially in this parade. I then mentioned to the couple, whose daughter worked for me at the college, exactly how precisely-different the parade would have been in Japan. Absolutely everyone, would be wearing identical clothing, and totally serious about what they were doing, as 'fun' would not have been accepted for such a public, though volunteer, demonstration.

Shockingly, I got tears in my eyes, as it all hit me. I'd often said, many long-term gaijin needed to know when it was time to leave, before they would not be able to fit back into their own country. I knew several who stayed too long, and were totally lost at home, with most of them returning to Japan. One obvious thing, we gaijin had joked about, having seen it so many times, the 'bowing' in a public phone booth on the street. The Japanese obviously was speaking to someone of a higher rank. As if, the person on the other end of the phone, would 'see' them bow, with each response. My one shocked friend said, "Wow! If I ever do that, kidnap me and put me on a plane immediately. That's being just too-immersed in the Japanese culture." So, my stark recognition of the comparison/contrast of the Aussies to the Japanese, told me I had become too acculturated to the Japanese- way of doing things, and it was time for me to leave.

I wanted to see one more Sakura - Cherry Blossom time, as nothing in the world compared to it, as fun and beautiful. March was the end of the school/work year, with a new corporate year and classes starting in April. So, a good time time as contracts were finished, and enough time for them to find a replacement for me. I had many Sayonara-sales for my furniture, etc., as I packed up my numerous boxes being shipped to where I would be staying in San Francisco. I'd been there many times and wanted a very international, yet especially Asian city to adjust back to, with my counter-culture shock. I also had many Sayonara-parties held for me, and learned quickly to tell people, I certainly did NOT want any large, Japanese dolls in glass cases!

Unfortunately, January 17, 1995, a magnitude 7.2 earthquake struck Kobe, Japan. It resulted in more than 6,000 deaths and over 30,000 injuries. Only about one hundred miles from Nagoya, we felt it and many of the strong after shocks, too. Though I had been through at least a half dozen strong earthquakes in my seven years, it was a bit scary, yet knowing as well, going to the earthquake-prone San Francisco. It had a similar one in 1989, I'd seen the aftermath of, on a stop-over there in the summer after it.

There were many ugly stories regarding the devastation in Kobe, and too many how the stupid bureaucratic-hierarchy had made it worse, when no one would make a decision without someone in charge. This included the simple act of turning the gas valves off, to not feed the fires. More than ironic and sad to me, as always some thing I taught my business management trainees, who were heading overseas to act, then apologize later. The Western-realist, gaijin-way of dealing with a very moribund-cultural.

The earthquake also destroyed several of the elevated-bridges for the iconic-Shinkansen - Japan's pride. Since the Yakuza controlled most of the construction contracts, the bridge destruction revealed many shoddy-shortcuts had been taken, which made the bridges weaker. The English newspapers had honestly reported much of the badly-handled situations, of the massive earthquake, which surprised many of us. The government NHK-TV news had not, of course.

I had two good, long-time, gaijin and Japanese friends take me to the airport, not really thinking about how many of my Japanese friends had asked me, when I was leaving. So, it was quite a surprise when we arrived at the airport, there were already a dozen of them there, with another eight showing-up soon, and apologizing for being late, as if expected. So, even up to the last day in Japan, I learned a great, cultural lesson about the strength of Japanese friendships.

I had been told by many of my adult-students, who had become friends, how I had changed their lives. And, several of my neighbors, whose children I had taught English to, in my little, home-classes, who wanted to thank me one more time. Years later, the youngest daughter of my landlord, was attending school in Washington, and contacted me to say 'thank you' again, as her 'good' English had made the big difference in her being accepted to the university.

Any trainer and teacher wants to know they made a difference in their students' lives, and many of mine wanted to make sure I knew how much I had done for them. I still tell funny and sad stories about Japan, either as an example or just conversation. Most importantly, as I said at the beginning, my seven years in Japan were the most pivotal in my career, and continue to influence me in who I am today.

Of Particular Note and Perhaps Interest -
Additional
Reference Material:

Svoboda, Terese. *Black Glasses Like Clark Kent - A GI's Secret from Postwar Japan.* St. Paul, Mn: Graywolf Press, 2008 *ISBN 978-1-55597-490-9*

Also: Kaplan, Alice. *The Interpreter.* New York: Free Press/Simon and Schuster, 2005.

Her uncle was an MP at the Tokyo prison for only the convicted American servicemen from the Pacific in 1946. Accurate records were either not kept, or destroyed accidentally, or on purpose to not reflect the number or race - mostly black - of the prisoners, especially those who were executed. Rarely did any of the records found report their race.

Eventually the Tokyo prison held about 600 prisoners, half of them in there for the death sentence - rape or murder. ". . . it was patently absurd that 8.5% of the armed forces could be responsible for committing 79% of all capital crimes." Alice Kaplan, *The Interpreter,* a book about the difference in sentencing for white and black soldiers accused of the same crime in the European theater of WW II. It almost always depended on the commanding officer, no matter if in Europe or the Pacific. Only blacks were hung for rape by MacArthur in New Guinea. Common knowledge he was racist, and while rape was a common unrecorded occurrence in Japan, averaging anywhere from 50 to 300 a day in the Tokyo-area the first years, rarely were the white soldiers brought in or accused. Groups or gang rapes occurred outside of Tokyo where military bases or installation existed.

Using the 'colored boys' as examples of

punishment showed the Japanese the court system and 'civility' of a Democracy - MacArthur's prime intent in the Occupation, but it perpetuated the Japanese-acquired-prejudice against blacks. MacArthur, of course, had the final say of all executions in Japan - only Truman could overrule him, if he was ever asked to do so, and the only record was of a white man. So, MacArthur's prejudice obviously extended to the Japanese, in that *twice the number* were executed than was done to the Germans, though more Germans had been involved in the war, and for a much longer period of time.

In fact, the Jews in searching down German war-criminals brought more to trial from 1960-on, than was done by the Allied Court proceedings. Of course, they had a more personal interest in demanding or tracking documents regarding incarcerations and executions, there was no organized group to do it for the Japanese.

MacArthur was well known for his iron-clad control of all types or levels of national and international media - in the name of establishing Democracy. Little, if any of the negative happenings in Japan ever got recorded, or officially documented. Any American reporters who violated this had their passports rejected and were sent home. Again, known to most was MacArthur's later plan to run for President, and he wanted a perfect record of his successful, peacefully controlled-command of Japan.

Most prominent, the repeated fallacy the Japanese were docile, never committing any acts of rebellion to the Occupation. While they may not have been extensively destructive, under the influence of the Communist Party, considerable Military property was destroyed and a dozen or so personnel were killed. But, the total-media-control lesson, the Japanese hierarchy picked-up on readily, and have been rewriting their own history, as well text books ever since.

Though one can say there is no real justification for rape or murder, in the case of many servicemen, there were several contributing factors. The cheap, local moonshine had a considerable percentage of *formaldehyde* in it, which easily made most imbibers crazy, definitely lacking any moral control. Also, the total chaos of death and destruction everywhere, especially the first year or so, was sickeningly depressing. Then, consider how young most were, and being in a totally foreign land, with an unknown culture can cause psychological trauma.

At the same time, little justice was offered or available to those incarcerated. If they didn't have an officer of some rank on their side, there was little due process, as much less formal proceedings. Much more about getting 'rid of' the embarrassment, their actions had caused. Basically, something known, which MacArthur did not want known. To say 'justice' in all of its infallibility, took matters into its own hands was obvious.

Since any condoned-belief system comes from the top down, it was not unusual - though again rarely recorded. Again, to have had acts of violence against the Japanese, while not common among all, they were frequent, but only recorded by the Japanese. In Tokyo particularly, hundreds of vehicle *'accidents'* monthly at the beginning, taught the Japanese to stay off the streets, as *only* the Americans had vehicles. Interestingly, MacArthur made the Japanese government pay its citizens for being killed by the Americans, as if it was their fault for being on the streets of their own city.

Servicemen looting, especially of any Geisha locations, or whore houses, were common, as they had the most collectible goods, but could not speak out or fight back. Of course, the most commonly known abuse was of the black market, where the Servicemen had financial access to so many goods, which the Japanese did not. Thousands of dollars were proudly made by thousands of Americans goods from illegal sales. There were also many hidden properties and land purchased, when SACP took all the land from the prior wealthy.

Acknowledged, these acts were minor compared to what the Japanese military, or colonial settlers did to its occupied lands. Still, SACP and continuously MacArthur, purported everything they did was for the instilling of Democracy into the Japanese. Eventually, DC did catch up, and the most effective act for Democracy, was Truman removing MacArthur.

References by Chapter Japan as the Occupiers and the Occupied

Personal Histories: These are edited only for some grammatical content, repetitive words, or the order slightly changed for continuity, when the speaker remembered something s/he wanted to add. Any comment or clarification of my own, has been put in parenthesis, such as when I have asked a question and s/he responded. I felt each person's terminology, or use of words in themselves, would make a statement about the person and their feelings. Sometimes this is Japanese/English, but I feel the meaning is understood enough, though perhaps awkward. Please remember *understatement is an indelible*, basic characteristic of Japanese, particularly when speaking about themselves, or other Japanese. Emotions are Always withheld.

Chapter 1 Most of the historical information is from two sources: Reischauer, Edwin O. *The Japanese Today - Change & Continuity*.
Tokyo: Charles E. Tuttle Co., 1988.

Schodt, Frederik L. *America & the 4 Japans - Friend, Foe, Model, Mirror*. Berkeley: Stone Bridge Press, 1994.

Details on the 'Comfort Women' was gleaned from two articles: Japan Times - *"Wartime Brothels Seemed 'Natural;'* May 15, 1993. Sydney Morning Herald - *"Cold Comfort for Japan's War Women;"* July 23, 1994.

Additional history on Korea and prostitution in Japan from: Price, Willard. *Key to Japan.* New York: The John Day Co., 1946

Chapter 2 Most of the historical information is from two sources:

Reischauer, Edwin O. *The Japanese Today - Change & Continuity.*

Price, Willard. *Key to Japan.* (Also Bushido and A Hundred-Year War*)*
Chang, Jung. *Wild Swan.* London: Flamingo/HarperCollins; 1991.

Soviet invasion information:
Images of War - The Real Story of World War II - A Marshall Cavendish Collection in Association with the Imperial War Museum; #50; 1969: London.

Chapter 3 Most of the historical information is from two sources: Reischauer, Edwin O. *The Japanese Today - Change & Continuity.*

Price, Willard.. *Key to Japan.* (Especially inspiring independence to the Southeast Asian Countries)

Southeast Asia Independence Information:

Images of War - The Real Story of World War II - A Marshall Cavendish Collection in Association with the Imperial War Museum; #8, #51 & #52; 1969: London.

Britain leaving Australia - The Courier-Mail Monitor - *"Was Keating Right? - Did Britain Leave Australia to the Mercy of the Invading Japanese?"*; Peter Charlton, Associate Editor. February 29, 1992: Brisbane, Australia.

Chapter 4   Most of the information on the Nisei is from: Hosokawa, Bill. *Nisei, The Quiet Americans*. New York: William Morrow & Co., Inc. 1969.

Information on the interpreters:
Passin, Herbert. *Encounter with Japan*. Tokyo: Kodansha International, Ltd.,   1982.

Chapter 5   Excerpts from the following books were used:
Emerson, John K. and Harrison M. Holland. *The Eagle and the Rising Sun*. New York: Addison-Wesley Publishing Company, Inc., 1988.

Perry, John Curtis. *Breath the Eagle's Wings - Americans in Occupied Japan*. New York: Dodd, Mead & Company, 1980.

Toland, John. *Occupation*. New York: Doubleday., 1987.

Wildes, Harry E. *Typhoon in Tokyo, The Occupation & Its Aftermath*. New York: The MacMillian Co., 1954.

Chapter 6   The information on BCOF was contributed by an Australian Intelligence Force member serving for 18 months in Japan and was a Special Correspondent to an Australian newspaper. Detail is taken from these articles published in 1946 and 1947.

Excerpts from books and other printed material used as indicated. Alperovitz, Gar. *"Considering the A-bomb beyond the Smithsonian flap,"* Special to *The Washington Post*, printed in the *Daily Yomiuri*, November 15, 1994. He is also the author of "Atomic Diplomacy: Hiroshima and Potsdam."

Cook, Haruko Taya and Theodore F. Cook. *Japan At War - An Oral History*. New York: W.W. Norton & Co., 1992. Personal accounts of Japanese trying to repatriate and being POWs.

Lane R Earns and Brian Burke-Gaffney, editors. *Crossroads - A Journal of Nagasaki History and Culture*. Number 2 Summer 1994. "'Dancing People are Happy People' : Square Dancing and Democracy in Occupied Japan," pp. 91 - 102.

Krisher, Bernard. *Japan As We Lived It*. Tokyo: Yohan Publications, Inc., 1989. The interview with Arfin Bey.

Faulkner, William. *Absalom, Absalom!* . New York: Random House, Inc. 1936. His account of the personal and moral destruction from the Civil War is perhaps the only thing Americans can relate to, as it was the only war fought totally on American soil, with only Americans.

Nagai, Takashi. *The Bells of Nagasaki*. Tokyo: Kodansha International, 1992. His personal experiences with the bomb and his later creation and devotion to the

Peace Movement are monumental. This book was banned by MacArthur.

City of Nagasaki - Nagasaki International Culture Hall - contributed the detailed information on the Prisoner of War Camp No. 14, Urakami Branch in Nagasaki.

Passin, Herbert. *Encounter with Japan.* Tokyo: Kodansha International., Ltd. 1982. Being an anthropologist and interpreter, made him an excellent observer and reporter.

Chapter 7
Kunii, Irene M. *"Mad About Pachinko"*: *Time* International Edition, December 5, 1994.

Richie, Donald. *A Lateral View.* Berkeley: Stone Bridge Press, 1992. His detailed description of Pachinko is priceless.

Simpson, Colin. *The Country Upstairs.* Sydney: Angus & Robertson, 1966. A fresh approach for visitors to Kyoto.

The City of Nagoya, Office of the Mayor - International Relations Division: *Nagoya; Sketch of a City,* Edited by Joseph W. Sheperd. Detailed history of Nagoya.
Chapter 8 Most of the historical information from these sources: Axling, William. *Japan At Midcentury - The Leaves from Life.*
Philadelphia: American Baptist Publication Society, 1955.

Baker, Richard Terrill. *Darkness of the Son.* New

453

York: Abingdon- Cokesbury Press, 1947.

Drummond, Richard H. *A History of Christianity in Japan*. Grand Rapids, Michigan: W. B. Eerdmans Publishing Co., 1971.

Lane R Earns and Brian Burke-Gaffney, editors. *Crossroads - A Journal of Nagasaki History and Culture*. Number 2 Summer 1994. "Historical Momentums at Nagasaki's Suwa Shrine," John Nelson.

Kelly, Arlene Woods. *Kinjo Gakuin, 1889 - 1989 - Educational Institution for Women*. Nagoya, Japan; Kinjo Gakuin. 1989.

Kerr, William C. *Japan Begins Again*. New York: Friendship Press, 1949.

Mizugaki, Kiyoshi. *One Hundred Years of Evangelism in Japan*. Columbus, Georgia. Quill Publications English Edition, 1966.
Translated by J.A. McAlpine.

Reischauer, *The Japanese Today - Change & Continuity*.

Sasa, Sho. *Mrs. A.E. Randolph*. Nagoya, Japan: Kinjo Gakuin, 1994. Spae, Joseph J. *Catholicism in Japan*. Tokyo: ISR Press, 1963.
Young, John M.L. *The Two Empires of Japan*. Tokyo: Bible Times Press, 1958.

Chapter 9 Bits and pieces gleaned from numerous newspaper and magazine articles, as well as my personal observations of seven years teaching in Japan.

Bibliography

Axling, William. *Japan At Midcentury - The Leaves from Life.*
Philadelphia: American Baptist Publication Society, 1955.

Baker, Richard Terrill. *Darkness of the Son.* New York: Abingdon- Cokesbury Press, 1947.

Chang, Jung. *Wild Swan.* London: Flamingo/HarperCollins; 1991.

Cook, Haruko Taya and Theodore F. Cook. *Japan At War - An Oral History.* New York: W.W. Norton & Co., 1992.

Drummond, Richard H. *A History of Christianity in Japan.* Grand Rapids, Michigan: W. B. Eerdmans Publishing Co., 1971.

Lane R Earns and Brian Burke-Gaffney, editors. *Crossroads - A Journal of Nagasaki History and Culture.* Number 2 Summer 1994.

Emerson, John K. and Harrison M. Holland. *The Eagle and the Rising Sun.* New York: Addison-Wesley Publishing Company, Inc., 1988.

Faulkner, William. *Absalom, Absalom!* . New York: Random House, Inc. 1936.

Hemphill, Elizabeth A. *The Least of These: Miki Sawada & Her Children.* Tokyo: John Weatherill, Inc.

1980.

Hosokawa, Bill. *Nisei, The Quiet Americans*. New York: William Morrow & Co., Inc. 1969.

Kelly, Arlene Woods. *Kinjo Gakuin, 1889 - 1989 - Educational Institution for Women*. Nagoya, Japan; Kinjo Gakuin. 1989.

Kerr, William C. *Japan Begins Again*. New York: Friendship Press, 1949.

Krisher, Bernard. *Japan As We Lived It* . Tokyo: Yohan Publications, Inc., 1989.

Mizugaki, Kiyoshi. *One Hundred Years of Evangelism in Japan*. Columbus, Georgia. Quill Publications English Edition, 1966.
Translated by J.A. McAlpine.

Morris, J. Malcolm. *The Wise Bamboo*. Tokyo: Charles E. Tuttle Co., 1953.

Nagai, Takashi. *The Bells of Nagasaki*. Tokyo: Kodansha International, 1992.

Passin, Herbert. *Encounter with Japan*. Tokyo: Kodansha International., Ltd. 1982.

Perry, John Curtis. *Breath the Eagle's Wings - Americans in Occupied Japan*. New York: Dodd, Mead & Company, 1980.

Price, Willard. *Key to Japan*. New York: The John Day Co., 1946

Reischauer, Edwin O. *The Japanese Today - Change & Continuity*. Tokyo: Charles E. Tuttle Co., 1988.

Richie, Donald. *A Lateral View*. Berkeley: Stone Bridge Press, 1992. Sasa, Sho. *Mrs. A.E. Randolph*. Nagoya, Japan: Kinjo Gakuin, 1994.

Schodt, Frederik L. *America & the 4 Japans - Friend, Foe, Model, Mirror*. Berkeley: Stone Bridge Press, 1994.

Seidenticker, Edward *This Country, Japan*. Tokyo: Kodansha International, Ltd. 1979/1984.

Simpson, Colin. *The Country Upstairs*. Sydney: Angus & Robertson, 1966.

Spae, Joseph J. *Catholicism in Japan*. Tokyo: ISR Press, 1963. Starhawk. *The 5th Sacred Thing*. New York: Bantam Books, 1993. Toland, John. *Occupation*. New York: Doubleday., 1987.

Twain, Mark. *Letters From The Earth, Uncovered Writings;* Edited by Bernard DeVoto. New York: HarperCollins Publishers, 1962.

Robert E. Ward & Frank Joseph Schulman eds. with Maasahi Nishihara & Mary Tobin Espey. *The Allied Occupation of Japan, 1945 - 1952; An Annotated Bibliography of Western Language Materials*. Washington, D.C.: American Library Association, 1974.

Wildes, Harry E. *Typhoon in Tokyo, The Occupation & Its Aftermath*. New York: The MacMillian Co., 1954.

Young, John M.L. *The Two Empires of Japan*. Tokyo: Bible Times Press, 1958.

Suggested Reading List - Not Just on the Occupation

Collins, Clive. *Sachiko's Wedding*. London: Penguin books, Ltd. 1991.
Excellent description of a modern Japanese girl's life and life-style.

Lee, Lillian. *Farewell My Concubine*. New York: William Morrow and Company, Inc. 1993. Translated by Andrea Lingenfelter.
Interesting contrasting story, and has their view of the Japanese Occupation.

Oe, Kenzaburo. *The Silent Cry*. Tokyo: Kodansha International, 1967. Translated by John Bester, 1974 English Edition. Difficult, but fascinating story of Japan during the 1960s transition. *Oe is also a Nobel Prize winner,* and quite outspoken regarding Japan's excessive-restrictive culture, and of course, it crippling-controlling government.

Acknowledgements

Of course, none of this could have been done without the volunteering of so many Japanese and Americans, who so willingly shared their stories with me. As well, I want to think all those long-time gaijin, who guided and directed me with suggestions and introductions, to many people and places. Most importantly and key, was Kazuyo Mizutani, best friend as well working assistant, in translating many of the recordings.

Author's Biography

Originally from Chicago, Alice Parker has degrees in psychology, marketing, and English ESL-bilingual–bicultural studies in graduate school. A Dale Carnegie Trainer for 3 years, leading classes, she's traveled to 36 countries and 40 states – lived in 6, and wrote for an international business-travel magazine, and others.

A corporate business trainer in Japan for 7 years, then 8 years in San Francisco as HR Mgmt. to 1000 employees. As a Life Coach, she used her published Self-Help book, *Move Past Your Past - A Process for Freeing Your Life,* to do numerous workshops, TV-radio interviews. She's passionate about her poems and empowering published memoir *Choices, Changes & Friends - 1970s After Divorce,* being made into a streaming-TV series. Four friends got their divorces together in the crazy 1970s, with great satirical humor they dealt with it all and grew into independent women.

In the Dallas area since 2013, member of Poetry Society of Texas, winning 1st in State several times, and past Chapter President 3 years. Alice is also a proud member of the weekly, international poetry group, Corroboree. For over 10 years she has taught memoir writing classes, and did editing to help her students publish.

Her most recently published book is on Australia, *A Trip To Oz - A Memoir of Self-discovery thru Australian Adventures.* And, ready to publish is her novel on Croatia *Change of View - A Romantic Adventure.* Her other finished biographical book regarding the American Occupation of Japan: *Occupied Hearts - Love the Long Way Around, is* 3 related love stories, 3 wars and 3 continents, from Occupied Germany to Viet Nam.

www.ingramcontent.com/pod-product-compliance
Lightning Source LLC
Chambersburg PA
CBHW070858120626
46546CB00001B/42